International Commercial Arbitration in Saudi Arabia

International Commercial Arbitration in Saudi Arabia

by

Dr. Ahmed A. Altawyan, LL.M.

COUNCIL on INTERNATIONAL LAW and POLITICS

Indianapolis, 2018

Published by Council on International Law and Politics
55 East 70th Street
Indianapolis, IN 46220, USA
http://www.cilpnet.org

Publications Coordinator: Frank Emmert

Editorial Assistants: Heather Leigh Grimstad, Cheryl Tawil

Cover Design: Salma Taman

Cover Art: ©Salma Taman

Font Myriad Pro

Printed in the United States by CreateSpace

12 11 10 9 8 7 6 5 4 3 2 1

ISBN: 978-0-9858156-9-1

Table of Contents

Chapter 3: Arbitration in Saudi Arabia Under the New Arbitration Law in Comparison to International Arbitration Rules

Chapter 4: Arbitral Awards Between Saudi Law and International Rules

About the Author

Dr. Ahmed A. Altawyan specializes in Commercial Arbitration, International Business Law, Islamic Finance, and Saudi law. He was nominated to work in the judiciary by the Supreme Judicial Council of the Kingdom of Saudi Arabia in 2011.

Currently, he serves as Assistant Professor of Law, Honorary Fellow of the International Islamic Centre for Reconciliation and Arbitration in Dubai, and Member of the Appeals Committee, formed by Royal Order to adjudicate violations and tax disputes.

He has been invited to various national and international conferences to present and publish papers on a wide range of legal topics. His academic credentials include an SJD (PhD) in Commercial Arbitration from Indiana University's Robert H. McKinney School of Law (Indianapolis, Indiana, USA); a Master's Degree in Comparative and International Law (LL.M.) from Southern Methodist University's Dedman School of Law (Dallas, Texas, USA); a Master's Degree with honors in Legal Policy and Saudi Law from the High Judicial Institute (Riyadh, Saudi Arabia); and a Bachelor's Degree with first class honors in Islamic Sharia from Al-Imam Mohammad Ibn Saud Islamic University (Riyadh, Saudi Arabia).

Acknowledgements

My deep and abiding gratitude is first and foremost to the most benevolent Allah, whose grace has brought me this far in life.

I am also extremely grateful to my family for their support during my journey through this extended study.

I wish to convey my heartfelt thanks to Prof. Dr. Frank Emmert, LL.M., FCIArb, the John S. Grimes Professor of Law and Director of the Center for International and Comparative Law at the Robert H. McKinney School of Law of Indiana University in Indianapolis, for being a constant source of support for my research. His patience, motivation, enthusiasm, and deep knowledge were incredibly helpful.

I also wish to express my thanks to Professor Max Huffman, the Director of the Corporate and Commercial Law Graduate Certificate Program at the McKinney School; Mr. James Reiman, Esq., FCIArb, a prominent international arbitrator; and Datuk Professor Sundra Rajoo, the Director of the Kuala Lumpur Regional Centre for Arbitration, for their encouragement, insightful comments, and pertinent questions that helped shape my research.

Last, but not the least, I wish to thank my family again, in particular my parents, and my wife and daughter, for their patience and endurance while I worked on my book.

Ahmed Altawyan

Preface

Dr. Altawyan is a wonderful example of the fruits of the Saudi Arabian Cultural Mission scholarship program. Educated in Saudi Arabia and the United States, fluent in Sharia law, Saudi law, the U.S. legal system, as well as international business and trade law, and equally eloquent in Arabic and English, Dr. Altawyan presents this book as the first comprehensive study of the new Saudi Arbitration Law of 2012.

In Chapter 1, Dr. Altawyan provides a thorough introduction to the legal system of Saudi Arabia and the way that mediation and arbitration have not only been part of Islamic law since the days of Prophet Muhammad (PBUH) but are very much encouraged, even favored, by Sharia over more confrontational methods of dispute settlement, including litigation. This part provides essential background information for Western readers but also reminds those who are familiar with Islamic law of the important benefits of mediation and arbitration.

Since arbitration in front of privately selected experts and tribunals can not provide all of its benefit without occasional recourse to the courts, for example if documents and other evidence are not made available voluntarily to the arbitrator(s), or for the enforcement of a final award, Dr. Altawyan proceeds with an analysis of the strengths and weaknesses of the Saudi judiciary in his second Chapter. The findings are very interesting and important for his recommendations for further improvements to arbitration law in Saudi Arabia in Chapter 6.

Chapter 3 is dedicated to a careful comparison of the new Saudi Arbitration Law of 2012 with important international codifications of arbitration law, in particular the UNCITRAL Model Law, the Arbitration Rules of the International Chamber of Commerce (ICC), the Arbitration Rules of the London Court of International Arbitration (LCIA), and the Rules on the Taking of Evidence of the International Bar Association (IBA). Dr. Altawyan shows how the reforms undertaken in Saudi Arabia have broadly harmonized its law with international standards but he also shows where this is not the case and why.

In Chapter 4, Dr. Altawyan specifically analyzes awards under the Saudi rules compared to various international rules.

Taken together, Chapters 3 and 4 walk the reader step-by-step through an international arbitration conducted under the new Saudi rules to show how they are applied in practice. These parts will be particularly interesting for Western lawyers and arbitrators who may become participants in such proceedings but it is also literally a textbook for Saudi lawyers eager to learn about and become qualified in arbitration law.

Going beyond the procedural context, Chapter 5 discusses what happens if international commercial contracts and arbitration agreements are subjected to Saudi law, rather than U.S. or English or some international law, like the United Nations Convention on Contracts for the International Sale of Goods (CISG). In particular for readers who are not very familiar with Islamic law, this analysis is invaluable and will save many business parties and transactions from misunderstandings and frustrations, or even failure. This Chapter alone is well worth the purchase of this book and essential reading for anyone considering or doing business in and with Saudi Arabia!

Finally, in Chapter 6, Dr. Altawyan brings all of his research results together in a series of recommendations, all of them based on scientific findings and presented in clear and persuasive terms. Written from the perspective of a true patriot who cares deeply about his country and its development and continuing success in legal and economic terms, this Chapter is addressed to the Saudi legislature. However, judges, arbitrators, and even partisan attorneys, will equally benefit from the analysis, which puts them into a better position for making their various contributions to the system of mediation and arbitration in Saudi Arabia and other parts of the Islamic World.

As an added benefit, the book contains expansive annexes with English language versions of the Saudi Arbitration Law of 2012 and the Execution Law to the Arbitration Law of Saudi Arabia. These texts are not easily available elsewhere. Together with the preceding analysis, they turn the book into a compendium of Saudi arbitration law every practitioner in the region will want to keep close at hand.

Frank Emmert

Introduction

The Kingdom of Saudi Arabia is a major Muslim and Arabic state in Western Asia that constitutes the largest part of the Arabian Peninsula. It is the birthplace of the Islamic religion and has two holy mosques, one in Mecca city and the other in Medina city. King Abd al-Aziz bin Saud founded the Kingdom in 1932. It has a land area of approximately 2,250,000 km^2 and overlooks both the Red Sea in the West and the Arabic Gulf in the East.[1]

On 5 September 2015, the Kingdom of Saudi Arabia announced that it would examine its entire trade and investment system to facilitate the business of international investors. It would also provide necessary incentives, including direct business access to the Saudi market.[2] Moreover, on 25 April 2016, the Kingdom announced its Vision 2030, which presents its plans for the next 15 years. One of the goals of Vision 2030 is to attract the best investments globally from major international companies.[3] As the Kingdom is a member of the Group of Twenty (G-20) and a major producer of crude oil in the modern world, the Kingdom of Saudi Arabia is an attractive environment for profitable foreign investments in different business areas, such as energy, banking, industry, and, more recently, the retail sector.[4]

As foreign investors prefer arbitration as the method to settle disputes between merchants, the Kingdom has initiated and still has to make additional changes to its legal system to meet the expectations of international investors and other businesses. The commercial arbitration process is more attractive for foreign investors because of its privacy, party control of the process, and the international recognition and enforcement of its awards.[5] Much more than litigation, arbitration offers the opportunity to settle differences between disputing parties by using a method that is responsive to business needs, as well as binding and enforceable in general.[6] Accordingly, in 1994, Saudi Arabia signed the 1958 UN

---

1 For more information, see WAYNE H BOWEN, THE HISTORY OF SAUDI ARABIA 1-13 (ABC-CLIO. 2014). See also COUNTRY PROFILE: SAUDI ARABIA at the Library of Congress, available at: https://www.loc.gov/rr/frd/cs/profiles/Saudi_Arabia.pdf.

2 See the Minister of Commerce and Investment website at http://mci.gov.sa/Media-Center/News/Pages/05-09-15-01.aspx.

3 Such goals are available at the Saudi Vision website: http://vision2030.gov.sa/en.

4 See David J Karl, *Islamic Law in Saudi Arabia: What Foreign Attorneys Should Know*, 25 GEO. WASH. J. INT'L L. & ECON., 131-133 (1991).

5 See AMERICAN ARBITRATION ASSOCIATION, AAA HANDBOOK ON INTERNATIONAL ARBITRATION AND ADR 27 (Juris Publishing, Inc. 2010).

6 See id.

Convention on the Recognition and Enforcement of Arbitral Awards, otherwise known as the "New York Convention," which became the legal framework for arbitration proceedings as a mode of resolving disputes within the Kingdom.[7] On 16 April 2012, Saudi Arabia issued a new arbitration law, which was inspired by the UNCITRAL Model Law. This new law offers greater independence in the arbitral process, provides arbitral tribunals with enhanced procedural powers, and also makes clearer provisions for the enforcement of arbitration agreements and awards in the Kingdom.[8]

Although Saudi Arabia has tried to reform its arbitration regime further, there are significant challenges that have to be overcome to make Saudi arbitration law attractive for the international community. These include the roots and role of religion in the legal environment and also the lack of support from the Saudi courts during the arbitration process. For instance, in the past, Saudi Arabia has been described as hostile toward the recognition of arbitration agreements and the enforcement of foreign awards. Indeed, many international awards were rejected by Saudi courts for different reasons, which will be explained extensively throughout the chapters of this study.[9] In addition to enforcement matters, there are some international arbitration cases where an international arbitral tribunal denied that Saudi law as applicable law in a contract is adequate and sophisticated enough to govern complex commercial disputes. As a consequence of such decisions, merchants tend to avoid Saudi law and subject their contracts to foreign or international trade rules instead.[10] Therefore, the study will shed more light on how an Islamic country like Saudi Arabia can improve its commercial law and specifically its arbitration laws within the confines of Islamic principles and roots so that they are more in line with globally accepted principles of arbitration. In the following chapters, a number of different challenges will be addressed and various suggestions will be provided for the further development of the legal environment in the Kingdom.

A. Scope and Limitations of the Study

The study will consider the challenges that must be overcome to reinforce Saudi commercial arbitration law in the international community and the possible

---

7 See the New York Convention website available at: http://www.newyorkconvention.org/countries.

8 See R. Mithani, *Saudi Arabia: The Emerging Arbitration Landscape*, CORPORATE DISPUTE MAGAZINE 2-5(2014).

9 See also Abdulrahman Mamdoh Saleem, *A Critical Study on How the Saudi Arbitration Code Could Be Improved and on Overcoming the Issues of Enforcing Foreign Awards in the Country as a Signatory State to the New York Convention*, available at SSRN 2315728, 9 (2012).

10 See, for example, Arbitration Between the State of Saudi Arabia and the Arabian American Oil Co, 27 I.L.R. 117, (1963).

solutions. Hence, the study will present an overview of the history of commercial arbitration in the Middle East and the roles of religion and culture in the legal system of the Kingdom of Saudi Arabia. Moreover, the study will present an extensive discussion of the significance of the new arbitration and enforcement laws in the arbitral proceedings and for arbitral awards, and of the technical rules that govern processes as set forth by the new arbitration law. The study will also provide an analytical comparison with important international commercial arbitration rules, such as the International Chamber of Commerce (ICC) Rules of Arbitration, the Arbitration Rules of the International Centre for Dispute Resolution (ICDR), and the London Court of International Arbitration (LCIA) Arbitration Rules.

Moreover, the study analyses the Saudi court system and its role in the arbitration process and the recognition and enforcement of arbitration awards. Furthermore, the study will show to foreign investors the possible challenges that may be encountered by choosing Saudi law as applicable law in international arbitration contracts and other possible options.

B. Research Problem and Research Questions

On the basis of the pertinent international literature, analysis of the primary sources of Saudi law, analysis of international arbitration rules, and interviews with legal experts in the Kingdom and in various international arbitration centers, this study seeks to answer the following questions:

- What are the characteristics of the new arbitration law in the Kingdom of Saudi Arabia?
- What are the differences between the new arbitration law and international arbitration rules?
- What are the challenges to reliable enforcement of arbitral awards in Saudi Arabia?
- What is the impact of such challenges on the appreciation and use of Saudi law in the international community?
- What is the role of religion in the legal system of Saudi Arabia, and what is its impact on the arbitration process, arbitral recognition, and enforcement?
- What are the challenges of choosing Saudi law as applicable law in the international arbitration contract and what are the possible solutions?
- What are practical solutions to reinforce Saudi arbitration law in the global community?

C. Significance of the Study

This study aims at developing an optimal scenario that can help Saudi Arabia to adapt its legal system to the international community. For instance, Saudi Arabia has been opening up to trade and is welcoming foreign investment widely in the Kingdom. Therefore, the legal system must be improved to enable seamless transactions with international public and private entities. The results of this study will demonstrate how a Muslim country like Saudi Arabia can improve and reinforce its legislation to make it more compatible with the expectations of international investors and traders while at the same time avoiding a conflict with its religious roots and principles, which it has been following for centuries. As such, the research results will deliver the following benefits:

1) Advance the state of law and business research in the academic community by comparing existing Saudi rules with international rules which may reveal interesting points of conflict or agreement that can open up the doors for further studies.

2) Prepare a comprehensive and practice oriented document for foreign investors and companies regarding the arbitration process in the Kingdom and how Islamic Sharia is applied in the Saudi courts.

3) Define a model that can help legal researchers and policymakers in Saudi Arabia (or other Islamic countries) to transform existing laws and adapt the legal system in a way that will not conflict with Islamic roots and principles and that, at the same time, will comply with international norms.

D. Non-Legal Aspects of the Study

The study will also investigate non-legal aspects of the society and the government and administration in the Kingdom of Saudi Arabia to gain more understanding of the traditional form of Islamic Sharia as applied in the Kingdom and its impact on the development of the legal environment. The interpretation of Islamic Sharia differs between Islamic countries depending on different aspects, such as culture. The differences appear in such varied fields as human rights, compatibility with democracy, and freedom of speech. Hence, the application of Islamic Sharia is affected by local cultures that led to different schools of thought in Islam. For instance, Egypt, Saudi Arabia, Iran, and Turkey are all Muslim countries, but there are significant differences between their societies and their legal systems. In the context of these differences, this study will investigate the history of arbitration in the Middle East, and the background of the Saudi judiciary and Islamic Sharia as applied in the Saudi courts. The study will also discuss sources of Islamic Sharia that may impact the legal system of Saudi Arabia.

E. Roadmap

In addition to this introduction, the research consists of six chapters, each of which has a separate theme. These themes are related and support the central theory of the entire study:

Chapter 1 explores the legal and commercial background of arbitration in Saudi Arabia. It consists of two main sections. The first section presents an overview of the legal system of the Kingdom and its primary sources. Hence, it will shed light on Islamic Sharia, and the legislative system and how it works within the Saudi system of government. The second section is about the history of arbitration in the Middle East, its roots in pre-Islamic times, and its development from the revelation of the Quran to the modern arbitration legislation in the Kingdom. Furthermore, this chapter will provide an overview of the differences between the old Saudi arbitration law and the new one enacted in 2012, and the significance of the new law.

Chapter 2 analyzes the legal system and the strengths and weaknesses of the Saudi judiciary and how they affect commercial arbitration, including compliance with international conventions ratified by the Kingdom, in particular the 1958 New York Convention. The chapter provides a history and background of the Saudi judicial system and its structure since the establishment of the Kingdom. The qualification and independence of the Saudi courts will also be shown. Finally, the chapter will discuss Islamic Sharia as it is applied in the Saudi courts, as well as Ijtihad as a vital tool with which to extract the rules in Islamic jurisprudence, how it works, and its impact on the enforcement of arbitral awards.

Chapter 3 presents the 2012 revision of the Saudi arbitration law and compares it to a number of international arbitration laws. It focuses on the significance of the new arbitration law with regard to contracts, the peculiarities of the arbitral proceedings, and the technical rules that govern processes as set forth in the new arbitration law compared with the UNICTRAL Model Law and other international rules, such as ICC Arbitration Rules and ICDR Arbitration Rules. Furthermore, the chapter will discuss some disadvantages and challenges that remain in the arbitration process and possible alternatives that may be useful to improve the arbitration process.

Chapter 4 looks specifically at the new Saudi Enforcement Law of 2012 issued by royal decree No M/53 and the accession by Saudi Arabia to the New York Convention in 1994, along with the new Saudi arbitration law issued by royal decree No M/34 and their impacts on the arbitral awards in the Kingdom, specifically when it comes to rendering, challenging, and enforcing an arbitration award. These points will be evaluated by comparing the Saudi rules with the modern norms in international commercial arbitration practice. The chapter explains why Saudi Arabia has been described as hostile toward recognizing arbitration agreements and enforcing foreign awards and why many international awards were rejected. Further, the study in this chapter shows the importance of reforming the arbitration award process and enforcement regime in the Kingdom of Saudi Arabia, describes the challenges that are presented in the current laws, and discusses possible solutions.

Chapter 5 focuses on the challenges that may be encountered when choosing Saudi law as the applicable law in an international arbitration contract. First, the differences between secular law and Islamic Sharia as applied in the Kingdom will be presented, in particular their characteristics in regard to litigation, some legal doctrines, such Riba and Gharar, as well as some specifics of contract and tort law. In addition, this chapter will explain extensively the challenges that may arise in interpreting and applying a contract that involves Saudi law in international arbitration tribunals and in Western courts. Last but not least, the chapter offers recommendations for foreign investors who have to or are thinking about choosing Saudi law as the applicable law in their contracts.

Finally, Chapter 6 contains a number of suggestions and solutions to be considered for the development of Saudi arbitration laws to make them more compatible with the needs and expectations of international traders and investors without sacrificing the Islamic roots and principles underlying the Saudi legal system.

Chapter 1

The Legal and Commercial Background of Arbitration in Saudi Arabia

It will be easier to understand how an Islamic country like Saudi Arabia can improve its commercial arbitration laws to be in line with globally accepted principles of arbitration after an overview of the legal system in Saudi Arabia and its sources including the history and background of arbitration laws in the Kingdom. In particular for international attorneys who do not possess detailed knowledge of Islamic business law and legal systems in the Middle East, it is imperative to gain some understanding how the laws are entwined with and confined by regional customs and traditions and, in particular, the Islamic religious rules and principles.

Hence, the first chapter of the study consists of two main sections. The first section provides an overview of the legal system of the Kingdom and its primary sources. It sheds some light on Islamic Sharia as the Constitution of the Kingdom and Saudi legislation that is always subordinate to Sharia and how this works within the Saudi system of law and governance. The second section is about the history of arbitration in the Middle East, its roots in pre-Islam and its development thereafter, all the way to the modern arbitration legislation in the Kingdom. Furthermore, this chapter will provide a comparative study between the old Saudi arbitration law and the new one to show the significance of the new law.

A. Sources of Law in Saudi Arabia

Before King Fahd bin Abdul-Aziz (1982 - 2005)[11] promulgated Saudi Arabia's basic law,[12] Saudi Arabia did not have a written constitution.[13] The Basic Law of Saudi Arabia, which is equivalent to the constitution of other countries, has several articles that clearly outline the primary sources of law for the Kingdom. According to Article 1, "The Kingdom of Saudi Arabia is a sovereign Arabic Islamic State. Its religion is Islam. Its constitution is Almighty God's Book, The Holy Quran, and the Sunnah (Tradition) of the Prophet (PBUH). Arabic is the language of the Kingdom.

11 King Fahd was the fifth king of Saudi Arabia and reigned from 1982 to 2005. The Kingdom of Saudi Arabia saw fundamental changes in the legal system during his reign. See Harvey Sicherman, *King Fahd's Saudi Arabia*, 55 ORBIS (2011).

12 The word "law", when translated into the Arabic language, is called "kanoon". However, in Saudi Arabia, it is called "nizam", because the ruler wants to distinguish Saudi laws that do not conflict with Islamic law from non-Islamic laws in other countries. See Maren Hanson, *The Influence of French Law on the Legal Development of Saudi Arabia*, ARAB LAW QUARTERLY, 289 (1987).

13 Rashed Aba-Namay, *The Recent Constitutional Reforms in Saudi Arabia*, 42 INTERNATIONAL AND COMPARATIVE LAW QUARTERLY, 295 (1993).

The City of Riyadh is the capital."[14] Article 7 states that the "Government in the Kingdom of Saudi Arabia derives its authority from the Book of God and the Sunnah of the Prophet (PBUH), which are the ultimate sources of reference for this Law and the other laws of the State."[15] Article 48 stipulates that "The Courts shall apply rules of Islamic Sharia in cases that are brought before them, according to the Holy Quran and the Sunnah, and according to laws that are decreed by the ruler in agreement with the Holy Quran and the Sunnah."[16] As can be seen from these articles, Saudi Arabia's Basic Law (constitution) states that Islamic Sharia is the primary source of laws in the Kingdom. At the same time, all laws must be of Islamic Sharia or from rules that do not conflict with Islamic Sharia. Accordingly, this chapter will discuss the primary sources of law and the legislative system.

1. Islamic Sharia

Islamic Sharia is the part of the Islamic religion that deals with legal aspects, such as criminal and civil issues.[17] Next to common law and continental European or civil law, Sharia is one of the three major global legal systems.[18] Its relevance has been extended in recent years beyond the traditional Muslim countries, as can be demonstrated, for example, by the expansion of Islamic finance throughout Islamic and non-Islamic countries and the establishment of an Islamic stock exchange in London that abides by Islamic finance rules.[19]

The most significant aspect of Islamic Sharia is that it contains five core *Maqasid* (purposes) that are derived from the primary sources of Sharia, and all Sharia rules must be in line with these objectives. According to Imam Al Shatibi,[20] "People

---

14 The Basic Law of Government (1992). Available at the Shura Council website http://www.shura.gov.sa/wps/wcm/connect/ShuraEn/internet/Laws+and+Regulations/The+Basic+Law+Of+Government/.

15 *Id.*

16 *Id.*

17 Islam deals with all aspects of life, including faith, politics, economics, and personal matters, such as sexual intercourse, personal hygiene, etc. However, since this study concerns only the legal field, the reader may find the other aspects of Islam in other studies. See HOSSEIN ESMAEILI ANN BLACK, NADIRSYAH HOSEN, MODERN PRESPECTIVES ON ISLAMIC LAW 4-9 (Edward Elgar Publishing Limited. 2013). See also RAJ BHALA, UNDERSTANDING ISLAMIC LAW 76-90 (LexisNexis. 2011).

18 ANN BLACK, Modern Prespectives on Islamic Law 1. 2013.

19 *PM Unveils Plans for New Islamic Index on London Stock Exchange* (29 October 2013). Available at https://www.gov.uk/government/news/pm-to-unveil-plans-for-new-islamic-index-on-london-stock-exchange.

20 Imam Abu Ishaq al-Shatibi (d.1388 CE) is an Islamic legal scholar best known for his knowledge of the legitimate purposes of Islamic law. See JASSER AUDA, MAQASID AL-SHARIAH AS PHILOSOPHY OF ISLAMIC LAW 20-21 (The International Institute of Islamic Thought. 2008).

[Muslim scholars] have agreed that Islamic Sharia has developed to maintain the five necessities, namely: religion, life, family, money, and mind. And the total of the Quran and the Sunnah refers to them in different places."[21] For example, the principle of the protection of property is stated several times in the sources of Islamic Sharia, one of which is in this verse:

يا أيها الذين آمنوا لا تأكلوا أموالكم بينكم بالباطل إلا أن تكون تجارة عن تراض منكم

> You who have believed, do not consume one another's wealth unjustly but only [in lawful] business by mutual consent.[22]

As a result, Muslim jurists must consider these *Maqasid* even if there is a conflict with the primary sources of Islamic Sharia. If there are exceptional circumstances that lead to the inability to achieve the purpose of the text of the primary sources of Islamic Sharia, the stated *Maqasid* should be prevail. For example, Umar al-Khattab,[23] at the time of his dominion over the Islamic State, did not apply the Islamic punishment for theft, which is to cut the hand of the thief, during the famine in Madinah city. He thought that enforcement of the punishment prescribed in the primary sources of Islam during a time when people are in need of supplies that are essential for their survival goes against the *intent* of divine law, which he considered more fundamental.[24]

Most Islamic scholars agree that there is a pyramid of sources in Islamic Sharia, with the Quran at the apex and then the Sunnah.[25] Other sources, such as analogical reasoning (Qiyas) and consensus of opinion (Ijmā), are tools that help scholars to understand and derive rulings from the primary sources. However, Muslim scholars do not agree about the appropriate weight to be given to these other sources.[26]

---

21 IBRAHIM BIN MOSA BIN MUHAMMAD AL-SHATIBI, AL-MUWAFAQAT 31 § 1 (Dar Ibn Affan. 1997).

22 Al Quran 29:4.

23 Umar ibn Al-Khattāb (583 CE - 644 CE) was the second Successor in the first Muslim State and one of the most powerful and influential persons in Islamic history as a leader and an Islamic jurist. He also established the Islamic calendar using the year of the migration of the Prophet Muhammad from Mecca to Medina as starting point. See BHALA, Understanding Islamic Law 122-123. 2011.

24 See AUDA, Maqasid Al-Shariah as Philosophy of Islamic Law 10. 2008.

25 See ANN BLACK, Modern Prespectives on Islamic Law 10-12. 2013. See also NOEL JAMES COULSON, A HISTORY OF ISLAMIC LAW 9-20 (AldineTransaction. 2011); FRANK E VOGEL, ISLAMIC LAW AND THE LEGAL SYSTEM OF SAUDÍ: STUDIES OF SAUDI ARABIA 3-4 (Brill. 2000).

26 BHALA, Understanding Islamic Law 313-321. 2011.

a. *The Quran*

The *Quran* is the book that was revealed by *Allah* (God) to the Prophet Muhammad through the angel Gabriel (Jibril) over a period of 23 years.[27] The holy book contains 114 *Surahs* (chapters), and each *Surah* consists of several *Ayat* (verses).[28] The *Quran* has not changed over the past 1,400 years,[29] and, as God states in the *Quran*, he personally guards this book and protects it from change:

إِنَّا نَحْنُ نَزَّلْنَا الذِّكْرَ وَإِنَّا لَهُ لَحَافِظُون

> It is we who sent down the Quran, and indeed, we will be its guardian.[30]

However, while Muslims do not argue about the divine origin of the *Quran*,[31] interpretations differ about some of its texts, as will be shown later in this chapter.

Muslim jurists not only believe that the *Quran* is a divine source but also that it contains complete guidance for all aspects of life, as *Allah* (God) states in the *Quran*:

وَمَا مِنْ دَابَّةٍ فِي الْأَرْضِ وَلَا طَائِرٍ يَطِيرُ بِجَنَاحَيْهِ إِلَّا أُمَمٌ أَمْثَالُكُمْ مَا فَرَّطْنَا فِي الْكِتَابِ مِنْ شَيْءٍ
ثُمَّ إِلَى رَبِّهِمْ يُحْشَرُونَ

> And there is no creature on [or within] the earth or bird that flies with its wings except [that they are] communities like you. We have not neglected in the Register a thing. Then unto their Lord, they will be gathered.[32]

As a result, many Muslims believe the *Quran* through the ages is the only source that Muslims need and that it contains a perfect and comprehensive model for life.

---

27 See ANN BLACK, Modern Prespectives on Islamic Law 6-9. 2013. See also BHALA, Understanding Islamic Law 292-293. 2011.

28 See ANN BLACK, Modern Prespectives on Islamic Law 11. 2013.

29 Id. at.7.

30 Al Quran 15:9.

31 See MOHAMMED BIN AHMED ABU ZAHRA, ZAHRAT AL TAFSEER 881 VOL. 2 (Dar Al fikr.). See also VOGEL, Islamic Law and the Legal System of Saudí: Studies of Saudi Arabia 4. 2000.

32 Al Quran 6:38.

Moreover, there are several categories of the contents of the *Quran*. The first involves God and the nature of the spirit. Other categories include the law and commandments, historical accounts, wisdom, and the prophecies.[33] Thus, the law is only one of several elements in this source. In total, between 200 to 500 of 6600 verses address legal matters.[34] This legal study will shed light primarily on the legal prescriptions of the *Quran*.

b. The Sunnah of the Prophet (PBUH)

The *Sunnah* of Prophet Mohammed is the second source of Islamic *Sharia*. It includes all of the traditions and practices of the Prophet Muhammad (PBUH), including teachings, deeds, and sayings.[35] The majority of Muslim jurists believe that the *Sunnah* of the Prophet is the essential source for clarification of the many rules in the *Quran* that do not have specific Quranic rules that outline how to practice them.[36] Muslims also believe that by looking at Muhammad's life they can discover what they should do and what they should avoid.[37] Since, as noted above, the most important source of Islamic Sharia is the *Quran*, this study will show how the first source sees the *Sunnah* of the Prophet:

وَمَا يَنْطِقُ عَنِ الْهَوَى

Nor does he (Mohammed) speak of [his own] inclination.[38]

33 Abu ZAHRA, Zahrat Al Tafseer 23.

34 See FEISAL ABDUL RAUF, MOVING THE MOUNTAIN: A NEW VISION OF ISLAM IN AMERICA 51 (Free Press. 2012). See also Hanson, ARAB LAW QUARTERLY, 273 (1987).

35 See COULSON, A History of Islamic Law 21-35. 2011. See also BHALA, Understanding Islamic Law 302-303. 2011.

36 See BHALA, Understanding Islamic Law 302-303. 2011.

37 See BRIAN KETTELL, INTRODUCTION TO ISLAMIC BANKING AND FINANCE 18-19 (John Wiley & Sons. 2011). See also BHALA, Understanding Islamic Law 302-303. 2011.

38 Al Quran 53:3.

إِنْ هُوَ إِلَّا وَحْيٌ يُوحَى

It is not, but a revelation revealed.[39]

بِالْبَيِّنَاتِ وَالزُّبُرِ وَأَنْزَلْنَا إِلَيْكَ الذِّكْرَ لِتُبَيِّنَ لِلنَّاسِ مَا نُزِّلَ إِلَيْهِمْ وَلَعَلَّهُمْ يَتَفَكَّرُونَ

[We sent them] with clear proofs and written ordinances. And we revealed to you the message that you may make clear to the people what was sent down to them and to which they might give thought.[40]

It is clear according to these *Ayats* (verses) that the *Sunnah* was, along with the divine revelation, directly taught by God.[41] However, unlike the *Quran*, the *Sunnah* of the Prophet did not receive a promise from *Allah* (God) to be safe and guarded. Hence, two major questions arise about the *Sunnah* regarding authenticity and the relationship between the *Sunnah* and the *Quran*, which will be extensively explained in the next part.

- The Question of Authenticity

During his life, the Prophet Muhammad prevented his companions from writing down his *Sunnah*,[42] so they would not confuse his sayings with the *Quran*.[43] However, he also asked the *Sahaba* (his companions) to publicize his sayings orally for as long as he was alive so that he could assuage any doubts.[44] Thus, much of the confusion over his *Sunnah* did not arise until after Prophet

---

39 Al Quran 53:4.

40 Al Quran 16:44.

41 See JALAL ALDEEN AL-SUYUTI, MUFTAH AL JANNAH FEE EHTEJAJ BE AL SUNNAH 5-77 (Islamic University. 1989).

42 There is an expanded debate between Muslim scholars about why the Prophet Muhammad asked his followers to stop writing his sayings and whether this command was in force for his whole his life or for only part of his life. However, this section focuses on the collection and compilation of the Sunnah after the death of the Prophet and the effects of the Sunnah as the other primary source in Islamic Sharia. See MUSTAFA SIBAI, THE SUNNAH AND ITS POSITION IN THE ISLAMIC LEGISLATION 153-166 (Islamic office, Damascus. 1982).

43 See KETTELL, Introduction to Islamic Banking and Finance 18-20. 2011. See also SIBAI, The Sunnah and its Position in the Islamic Legislation 153-166. 1982.

44 KETTELL, Introduction to Islamic Banking and Finance 18-20. 2011.

Mohammed passed away.[45] However, the question of authenticity arose almost as soon as the science of the *Sunnah* was established.[46]

After the Prophet's death,[47] Muslim jurists began to develop the methods by which the Prophet's heritage could be reviewed to determine which teachings were correctly attributed to the Prophet Muhammad and which were not. To this end, that the Muslim scholars analyzed the text of the *Hadith* (what the Prophet supposedly did or said), the routes through which the *Hadith* was transmitted, and the individual narrators involved in the transmission. On these bases, various *Sunnah* classifications evolved.[48] On this basis, the science of the *Sunnah* began to classify the *Sunnah* into different types to distinguish the reliable *Sunnah* from the weak narratives. For instance, one of the famous *Sunnah* is *Al Mutawatir*, which is indubitable because it is very widely known and backed by numerous references.[49]

Because this is a human process, mistakes can and have been made. For example, a famous Muslim scholar from the *Sunnah* majority in the contemporary world, Imam al-Albani,[50] at some point in time changed his evaluation of some *Hadiths* of the *Sunnah*.[51] However, in general, Muslim scholars have been able to evaluate scientifically most of the *Sunnah* of the Prophet as the primary source of Islamic *Sharia*.[52]

- The Relationship Between the *Quran* and the *Sunnah*

To understand Islamic *Sharia*, it is necessary to understand the primary sources from which it stems. As presented earlier, Muslims believe that the *Quran* and the *Sunnah* are divine. There are, however, differences. Mustafa Sibai states that "the

45 BHALA, Understanding Islamic Law 306-307. 2011.

46 Id.

47 Even those who argue that the Sunnah was written in the era of the Prophet do not deny that the Sunnah was classified and combined later, after the Prophet's death. See SIBAI, The Sunnah and its Position in the Islamic Legislation 160. 1982.

48 BHALA, Understanding Islamic Law 306-312. 2011.

49 There are many types of subdivisions for the Sunnah that depend on the power of the chain of transmission. See ABDULLAHI YUSUF JUDIA, TAHRIR ALOOM ALHADITH 65-113 (AlRayan. 2003).

50 Muhammad al-Albani (1914 - October 2, 1999) was an Islamic scholar, who specialized in the fields of the Sunnah and the jurisprudence of Islamic Sharia. His biography is available at the official King Faisal International Prize website at: http://kfip.org/sheikh- mohammad-nasir-ad-din-al-albani/.

51 See AUDAH BIN HASSAN AUDAH, 500 HADITHS MEMMA TRAGAA AANHA AL ALBANI (Dar Alnafais. 2003).

52 BHALA, Understanding Islamic Law 306-312. 2011.

Sunnah of the Prophet is a primary source of Islamic Sharia, and its function is to give more details as to what is concisely mentioned in the Quran, especially when there are legal rulings. Many rules, as well as other acts such as worship, appear briefly in the Quran. The Sunnah of the Prophet then explains and elaborates on such items and presents more details and, in some cases, interpretations."[53]

One example is *Zakat*[54] in the Islamic religion. The *Quran* says:

إِنَّمَا الصَّدَقَاتُ لِلْفُقَرَاءِ وَالْمَسَاكِينِ وَالْعَامِلِينَ عَلَيْهَا وَالْمُؤَلَّفَةِ قُلُوبُهُمْ وَفِي الرِّقَابِ وَالْغَارِمِينَ وَفِي
سَبِيلِ اللَّهِ وَابْنِ السَّبِيلِ ۖ فَرِيضَةً مِّنَ اللَّهِ ۗ وَاللَّهُ عَلِيمٌ حَكِيمٌ

> Zakah expenditures are only for the poor and for the needy and for those employed to collect [zakah] and for bringing hearts together [for Islam] and for freeing captives [or slaves] and for those in debt and for the cause of Allah and for the [stranded] traveler – an obligation [imposed] by Allah. And Allah is Knowing and Wise.[55]

While the *Quran* orders Muslims to give some of their money to certain classes of people, it does not provide specific guidelines on which types of wealth are taxable under the *Zakat*, nor does it specify the percentages to be given. The *Quran* states:

وَأَطِيعُوا اللَّهَ وَأَطِيعُوا الرَّسُولَ فَإِن تَوَلَّيْتُمْ فَإِنَّمَا عَلَىٰ رَسُولِنَا الْبَلَاغُ الْمُبِينُ

> Obey Allah and obey the Messenger, but if you turn away – then upon Our Messenger is only [the duty of] clear notification.[56]

According to this *Ayah* (verse), Muslims must turn to the Prophet Muhammad's explanation of the *Zakat*. On several occasions, the Prophet described the types

53 SIBAI, The Sunnah and its Position in the Islamic Legislation 377. 1982.

54 Zakat is the one of the five pillars of the Islamic religion, and it is the amount of money that must be paid to charity by an individual. This Islamic pillar depends on the amount of money and the type of assets that the person possesses. See ABDULLAH IBN QUDAMAH, AL MUGHNI 427 VOL. 10 (Cairo Library. 1968). Zakat is mandatory in Saudi Arabia, and there is a competent authority to collect it, the Department of Zakat and Income. Its website is available at https://dzit.gov.sa/.

55 Al Quran 9:60.

56 Al Quran 64:12.

of wealth that are taxable and specifies percentages to be given.[57] In one of these sayings, the Prophet states:

فيما سقت السماء والعيون والبعل العشر وفيما سقي بالنضح نصف العشر

> On land that is watered by rain or springs or any natural means there is (zakat to pay of) a tenth. On irrigated land, there is (zakat of) a twentieth (to pay).[58]

This shows that it is difficult to understand *Allah's* (God's) orders and instructions without following the *Sunnah* of the Prophet and its explanations. As a result, Muslim scholars developed a very scientific and sophisticated methodology to determine which narratives are authentic. If inconsistencies or conflicts exist between the *Quran* and the *Sunnah*, the *Quranic* view must be favored.[59]

c. *Islamic Sharia in Thought and Practice*

As noted earlier, Islamic *Sharia* deals with different aspects of life, including politics, economics, banking, and social issues. It has achieved goodness and integration of humanity by its sacred sources as shown earlier in this chapter. However, the question remains how, in practice, Islamic jurists set the rules that are called Islamic *Sharia*, not least because the world around us is changing ever faster. To answer this profound question, the study considers several major points about the primary sources of Islamic *Sharia*.

- Interpretation of Primary Sources of Islamic *Sharia*

Muslim jurists and scholars believe that the primary sources of Islamic *Sharia* are derived from a divine source and that these sources have a complete plan for all human activities. However, there are different historical views among Muslim jurists regarding the interpretation of the text of the primary sources and their requirements and even regarding how the rules apply when circumstances have changed. This disagreement has produced an Islamic *Fiqh* (jurisprudence) that

---

57 Many sayings of the Prophet explain the Zakat in all of its aspects. See MOHAMMED ISMAIL AL-BUKHARI, SAHIH AL-BUKHARI 104-132 No. 1395- 1512 (Dar Tawq Al najah.).

58 Id. at, 126 No. 1483.

59 See Abu ZAHRA, Zahrat Al Tafseer 24.

consists of several schools[60] with different opinions and philosophies, which then lead to differences in practice.[61]

One of the main causes for different interpretations of the texts of the primary sources in Islamic *Sharia* is the differences between Muslim jurists in using the secondary sources. From the beginning, Muslim scholars developed various secondary sources as juristic principles or doctrines to follow when the primary sources do not provide a clear direction[62] on a given question or issue.[63] These secondary sources are *Ijmā* (Consensus), *Qiyas* (deductive analogy),[64] *Istihsan* (juristic discretion to choose the good outcome),[65] *al-Maslahah al-Mursalah* (public interest),[66] *Urf* (custom),[67] *Istishab* (continuity),[68] *Shar'u Man Qablana* (pre-Islamic rules),[69] and *Fatwa Sahabi* (decisions or opinions of Islamic leaders who came after the Prophet).[70] One of the principal sources in *Sharia* is *Qiyas* (deductive analogy), which has led to different results in our contemporary world as will be shown later. However, before discussing this source, this study will first look at how Muslim jurists use secondary sources to extract rules from the primary sources.

---

60 BHALA, Understanding Islamic Law 387-407. 2011.

61 Id.

62 There is long standing controversy between the Islamic schools about most secondary sources and their authenticity. See AbdulWahab KHELAF, eulim 'usul alfaqqih 45-95 (dar al dawah.).

63 Id. at 313-46.

64 See BHALA, Understanding Islamic Law 319-320. 2011.

65 Some scholars in Islamic Sharia may use this source to express their preference for an exemption in a particular matter from a particular judgement for a specific reason by personal interpretation of Ijtihad. See KHELAF, eulim 'usul alfaqqih. 80.

66 Al-Maslahah al-Mursalah means any type of public interest if there is no relevant legislation in the Quran and the Sunnah, but there is a public benefit in taking advantage of them, such as prisons and bridges. See id. at. 84-88.

67 Urf is an Arabic term that refers to the custom of a given society. Most Islamic scholars consider the Urf in the society as a legitimate rule when it does not conflict with the primary sources of Islamic Sharia. See id. at. 89-90.

68 This source means that a situation that existed previously is presumed to be continuing at present until the contrary is proven. See id. at. 91-93.

69 This source means the body of divine rules that were legislated to the people before the Prophet Muhammad through revelation to their prophets. Muslim scholars have long discussed this source. See id. at. 93-94.

70 Fatwa al-sahabi, or as some scholars called it (qawl al-sahabi), means an opinion that one of the Prophet Muhammad's followers said or a considered opinion or a judicial decision if there is no applicable rule in the Quran or the Sunnah. See id at 94-95.

Chart 1: The Sources of Islamic Sharia

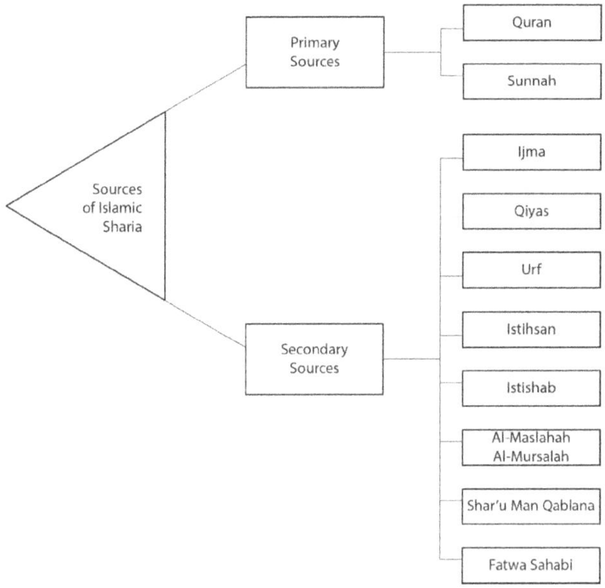

- *Ijtihad*

Obtaining the rules from the primary sources by using the secondary sources is the duty of the scholars or jurists in the Islamic schools.[71] The process of thought that may result in the discovery of such rules is called *Ijtihad*.[72] The practice of *Ijtihad* extends, in particular, to emerging issues, and is always based on one or more of the secondary sources. In the history of Islamic *Sharia*, a *Mujahid* is a Muslim scholar who has a high level of knowledge and meets certain additional requirements to deal with the *Quran* and *Sunnah* and who has a broad understanding of legal theory and precedent. This makes him qualified to practice *Ijtihad* in Islamic *Sharia*, i.e. to come up with new interpretations of the sources to address new questions and issues that may arise as the world around us evolves.[73] On the one hand, *al-Ijtihad* shows that Islamic *Sharia* is sufficiently vital

71 This Arabic term refers in Islamic Sharia to the decision-making process through personal effort. It is disputed who has the qualifications and thus the right to engage in Ijtihad. Only a few people during Islamic history have been universally accepted as Mujtahid. See AL-SHATIBI, Al-Muwafaqat 253-282. 1997.

72 Id.

73 BHALA, Understanding Islamic Law 334-335. 2011.

and flexible to apply to contemporary societies. On the other hand, the question who will and who will not be recognized as a *Mujahid* can lead to a preference for conservative interpretations and a stifling of evolutive interpretations. Nevertheless, since *Ijtihad* has always been practiced by many scholars, it has always been pluralistic and the results depend, at least in part, on the understanding and preferences of different scholars, which are likely to be affected by several factors, such as culture, era, and the environment.[74]

The most famous example in Islamic history is Al-Imam al Shafi'i.[75] He has two schools: one called old *Madhab* (old school) and another called the new *Madhab* (new school). The old *Madhab* is a collection of legal opinions of Imam al-Shafi'I while he was in Iraq. They are narrated by his famous student in Iraq, Imam Ahmad bin Hanbal,[76] the founder of a different Islamic school. The new *Madhab* refers to the revised legal opinions that Al-Shafi'i himself dictated after he migrated to Egypt.[77] This example shows how a jurist's decisions and views of the texts can be affected by several factors.

The difference in interpretation in Islamic *Sharia* shows the enormous room for discussions among scholars when a rule for a previously unknown issue is needed. In this context, a major factor for the interpretation of *Sharia* is whether one should consider one or more of the secondary sources to be primary sources or equal to primary sources.

- To consider one or more of the secondary sources as primary sources

The diversity of interpretations of the Islamic schools provides ample room for Islamic countries to create suitable laws to fit their circumstances without having to follow specific rules except for some legislation when there is a consensus among Muslim scholars, such as the *Hudud*[78] and *Qisas*[79] punishments prescribed

---

74 See MICHAEL MUMISA, ISLAMIC LAW THEORY & INTERPRETATION 153-157 (amana publicationa. 2002).

75 A Muslim scholar, who lived from 767 - 820 CE and founded one of the four famous schools in Islamic Sharia. See BHALA, Understanding Islamic Law 400-401. 2011.

76 Ahmed bin Muhammad bin Hanbal (780-855 CE) is a scholar in Islamic Sharia and the founder of the Hanbali School of Islamic jurisprudence, another of the four famous schools in Islamic Sharia. See id. at.403-406.

77 Some books collected the new and old Shafi opinions. See LAMEEN ALNAJI, OLD AND NEW IN SHAFI'I JURISPRUDENCE 107-118 (Dar Ibn Affan. 2007).

78 Hudud refers to punishments fixed in the primary sources of Islamic Sharia (the Quran and the Sunnah) for crimes considered to be against the rights of God, such as the penalty for theft. See ANN BLACK, Modern Prespectives on Islamic Law 221-227. 2013.

79 Qisas means a type of punishment that is equivalent and proportionate to the crime that has been committed, such as the death penalty for the crime of murder. Id. at. 220-221.

in criminal law. In addition to giving ample room to people to create their own regulations, they can use their own experiences and those of previous generations. To stop jurists and rules from coming up with ever more restrictions on the freedom of their subjects, *Sharia* prevents people from prohibiting what is not prohibited in God's text. The *Quran* states:

يَا أَيُّهَا الَّذِينَ آمَنُوا لَا تُحَرِّمُوا طَيِّبَاتِ مَا أَحَلَّ اللَّهُ لَكُمْ وَلَا تَعْتَدُوا ۚ إِنَّ اللَّهَ لَا يُحِبُّ الْمُعْتَدِينَ

> O you who have believed, do not prohibit whatever good things Allah has made lawful for you, and do not transgress. Surely Allah does not love the transgressors.[80]

A similar rule is found in the *Sunnah*:

> حَدَّثَنَا عَبْدُ اللَّهِ بْنُ الرُّومِيِّ الْيَمَامِيُّ، وَعَبَّاسُ بْنُ عَبْدِ الْعَظِيمِ الْعَنْبَرِيُّ، وَأَحْمَدُ بْنُ، جَعْفَرٍ الْمَعْقِرِيُّ قَالُوا حَدَّثَنَا النَّضْرُ بْنُ مُحَمَّدٍ، حَدَّثَنَا عِكْرِمَةُ، - وَهُوَ ابْنُ عَمَّارٍ - حَدَّثَنَا أَبُو النَّجَاشِيِّ، حَدَّثَنِي رَافِعُ بْنُ خَدِيجٍ، قَالَ قَدِمَ نَبِيُّ اللَّهِ صلى الله عليه وسلم الْمَدِينَةَ وَهُمْ يَأْبُرُونَ النَّخْلَ يَقُولُونَ يُلَقِّحُونَ النَّخْلَ فَقَالَ " مَا تَصْنَعُونَ " . قَالُوا كُنَّا نَصْنَعُهُ قَالَ " لَعَلَّكُمْ لَوْ لَمْ تَفْعَلُوا كَانَ خَيْرًا " . فَتَرَكُوهُ فَنَفَضَتْ أَوْ فَنَقَصَتْ - قَالَ - فَذَكَرُوا ذَلِكَ لَهُ فَقَالَ " إِنَّمَا أَنَا بَشَرٌ إِذَا أَمَرْتُكُمْ بِشَىْءٍ مِنْ دِينِكُمْ فَخُذُوا بِهِ وَإِذَا أَمَرْتُكُمْ بِشَىْءٍ مِنْ رَأْىٍ فَإِنَّمَا أَنَا بَشَرٌ " . قَالَ عِكْرِمَةُ أَوْ نَحْوَ هَذَا . قَالَ الْمَعْقِرِيُّ فَنَفَضَتْ . وَلَمْ يَشُكَّ

> Rafi' b. Khadij reported that Allah's Messenger came to Medina, and the people had been grafting the trees. He said:
>
> What are you doing? They said: We are grafting them, whereupon he said: It may perhaps be good for you if you do not do that, so they abandoned this practice and the date-palms began to yield less fruit. They mentioned it to the Holy Prophet, whereupon he said: I am a human being, so when I command you about a thing pertaining to religion, do accept it, and when I command you about a thing out of my personal opinion, keep in mind that I am a human being.[81]

As a result, legislation as divine law is restricted to the texts of the *Quran* or the *Sunnah*. This leaves ample room for people to organize their lives commensurate with their circumstances. However, in practice, some Muslim jurists have tried to fill this silent area of Islamic *Sharia* by expanding the use the secondary sources, such as *Qiyas*, to regulate other aspects of life in a way that is supposed to be

80 Al Quran 5:87.

81 MUSLIM BIN HAJAJ, SAHIH MUSLIM 1835 No. 2361 (Dar Ihyaa Altrath Al arabi.).

universally binding.[82] Jurists in different legal systems use *Qiyas* to extract rules from the text of *Sharia* that may not be there.[83] Moreover, because this process is undertaken by humans, it may contain contradictions,[84] even though the human-made rules claim to be based on divine sources of Islamic *Sharia*. For instance, many consider interest in contemporary transactions to be the same as usury, which is prohibited in Islamic *Sharia*.[85] In some cases, this leads to the practice of using *Hiyal* (tricks)[86] to circumvent rules and make something legal according to this expansive understanding of Islamic Sharia. According to Raj Bahala:

> What hiyal devices have been used to make payment of interest possible, without violating the Quran? One hila is for a debtor to give real property to the lender as security for the debt. The creditor is allowed to use this real property. The amount of use, ... the value of the portion used, is the interest.[87]

This example shows how some Muslim scholars deal with transaction in ways that are distinct from and potentially incompatible with the spirit of Islamic *Sharia* to suit practical purposes. However, this does not result from divine law but from human analysis (*Qiyas* as an example). First, divine *Sharia* is expanded and

---

82 Abū Muhammad 'Alī Ibn Ahmad Ibn Sa'īd Ibn Hazm, Al-ihkam Fi Ushul Al-ahkam 53-79 VOL. 7 (dar al afaq al jadidah.). See also AA Miftah, Refusal on Qiyas and Implications for Development Contemporary Islamic Law (Study on the Ibn Hazm Critics to Qiyas), 8 International Journal of Innovation and Applied Studies (2014).

83 See James R Murray, Role of Analogy in Legal Reasoning, The, 29 Ucla L. Rev. (1981).

84 Miftah, International Journal of Innovation and Applied Studies, 1549-1550 (2014).

85 Contemporary banking transactions in their current form did not exist at the time of the Revelation of the primary sources of Islamic Sharia. People were used to borrowing money from private moneylenders and returning double or more than the actual amount. Thus, the Quran said:

> O you who have believed, do not consume usury, doubled and multiplied, but fear Allah that you may be successful (the Quran 3:130).

Therefore, many Muslim scholars believe that there are similarities between interest in the banks and Riba (usury) in the Quran, and they have concluded via Qiyas that Riba covers not just exorbitant interest (usury) but all interest. Other scholars, however, believe that there is a difference between usury and interest, because interest is fixed by market operations to increase or decrease liquidity in case of inflation or deflation, while Riba is an exploitative practice leading to unjust growth as mentioned in the Quran. The study here wants to assure that interest is prohibited only on the basis of Qiyas, which is not a divine source. See also ANN BLACK, Modern Perspectives on Islamic Law 181-185. 2013.

86 Hiyal means "legalistic trickery" in Islamic jurisprudence. The tricks were developed early in the Islamic jurisprudence, and the main objective of Hiyal is the legalistic avoidance of cases considered excessively strict, such as the evasion of the prohibition of interest in modern transactions. See BHALA, Understanding Islamic Law 704-708. 2011.

87 Id. at. 706.

human-made rules are made into part of the divine legislation,[88] although other Muslims jurists declined to include a prohibition of all interest as a part of the sacred *Sharia*.[89] Then, more human-made constructs are required to circumvent the expanded rules. This example shows that interest – as distinguished from usury – violates the rules of some Muslim jurists as a result of their understanding of the text but does not violate the *Quran* or the *Sunnah* as explained above. Hence, the differences between the divine *Sharia* and human opinions about the sacred sources are central to understanding and applying Islamic *Sharia* in real life.[90] We must overcome obstacles against modernity by rethinking how some rules were put into place by jurists rather than by God, and allowing for independence and modernity in the Muslim countries, rather than sanctifying human work into divine law, which it is not and which would make everyone captive in the modern world to human-made rules developed by different cultures and in different eras.[91]

- To Consider Islamic Sharia as Law

Although the Kingdom of Saudi Arabia considers Islamic *Sharia* to be law, Islamic *Sharia* has a particular nature that differs from the law, which creates challenges in the Kingdom in several instances, as will be shown through the chapters of the study. As discussed earlier, there are many explanations, contradictory man-made rules, and vigorous scholarly debates that have produced various schools of jurisprudence, which are called *Fiqh*. It is also clear that, in the practice of principles of *Sharia*, there are differences between what is practiced in different Muslim countries, for example Saudi Arabia on the one side, and Egypt or Malaysia on the other.[92] All explanations of Islamic *Sharia* try to ensure that all laws comply with

---

88 The study does not argue about the judgments that jurists consider to be debatable, but the judgments that are attributed to a sacred source and therefore supposedly not debatable, although they are decided by people.

89 See ROBERT GLEAVE, ISLAM AND LITERALISM 150-172 (Edinburgh University Press Ltd. 2012). See also Miftah, INTERNATIONAL JOURNAL OF INNOVATION AND APPLIED STUDIES, 1545-1553 (2014).

90 In modern time, Islamic transactions do not provide real solutions to the financial transactions as an example according to the spirit Islamic Sharia and its purposes. One of the major reasons upon which they depended in contending that the jurisprudence in the Middle Ages was a sacred law is that it was in a different era. For example, many scholars seek the Islamization of financial transactions to comply with the jurisprudence of the former Muslim jurists, rather than taking advantage of the large area of the jurisprudence of Islamic Sharia to create new financial products according to roots of the Sharia and its intentions. See MUMISA, Islamic Law Theory & Interpretation 115-118. 2002. See also ANN BLACK, Modern Perspectives on Islamic Law 185-190. 2013.

91 Id.

92 See ANN BLACK, Modern Perspectives on Islamic Law 62-79. 2013.

the purposes and principles of the primary sources of Islam, but the differences in these explanations inevitably leads to different rules and dynamic jurisprudence. By referring to "Sharia" for the law or the constitution, a kind of uncertainty and ambiguity has been created in Saudi Arabia[93] since different scholars, let alone scholars in different countries, have their own interpretation what is and what is not *Sharia*. One of the possible solutions would be a codification of the particular rules of the primary sources of Islamic *Sharia*, in which the Muslim scholars determine the regulations that are closest to the spirit of Islamic *Sharia* according to its principles and roots. The desirability and feasibility of such a codification will be discussed extensively in chapter 2 of this study.[94]

2. Legislation

As noted earlier, Islamic *Sharia*, which is derived from understanding the *Quran* and the *Sunnah*, is the first source of Saudi Arabia's legal system, and all Saudi laws must comply with its roots and purposes, including the constitution.[95] The basic law shows that the primary sources of Islamic *Sharia* are the *Quran* and the *Sunnah*.[96] Other sources, such as *Ijma* and *Qiyas*, are secondary sources.[97] This division is significant to distinguish the divine law from human analysis, ensuring that the divine law remains sacred but also limited to the *Quran* and the *Sunna*, rather than including restrictions derived via *Qiyas*, as in the example noted earlier.[98]

There are some specific rules in the *Quran* and the *Sunnah* for some issues, such as the punishment of the crime of theft[99] or highway robbery.[100] Since they are clear in the *Sharia*, they should be and will be part of Saudi law according to the

---

93 For an example, see Shamil Bank of Bahrain EC v. Beximco Pharmaceuticals Ltd, 2004 19., k, [2004] EWCA (Civ) 19, [55], 1 W.L.R. at 1800. In this case, it was part of the court's reasoning that there are areas of considerable controversy and, therefore, difficulty with applying Islamic Sharia to matters of finance and banking. As a result, it concluded that it is improbable that the disputing parties were truly asking the Court to get into issues of Islamic religion and orthodoxy even though the Court agreed that there might be a general consensus in Islamic Sharia upon some of the principles relevant to the presented case.

94 Saudi Arabia adopted the Hanbali School as the Kingdom's official school of Islamic jurisprudence. See Karl, GEO. WASH. J. INT'L L. & ECON., 141 (1991). Also see Hanson, ARAB LAW QUARTERLY, 274 (1987).

95 The Basic Law of Government. 1992. Art: 7.

96 Id.

97 Hanson, ARAB LAW QUARTERLY, 274 (1987).

98 Karl, GEO. WASH. J. INT'L L. & ECON., 141 (1991).

99 See BHALA, Understanding Islamic Law 1240-1247. 2011.

100 Scholars have written at length about this crime and its punishment See id. at. 47-52.

basic law of Saudi Arabia, modernity or not.[101] However, the primary sources of Islamic *Sharia* are silent with regard to many other fields. Traffic issues are one such example. Thus, the ruler in Saudi Arabia has ample room to regulate these areas.[102] Muslim jurists during different eras of Islamic history have tried to fill this void and come up with rules for traffic and many other aspects of life by using one or several of the secondary sources of Islamic *Sharia*, for example *al-Maslahah al-Mursalah.*[103] Like all rules based on secondary sources and methods, these are not part of the divine law, although they seek to achieve its purposes, such as public benefit for the people.[104] As a result, the Saudi legal system relies on *al-Maslahah al-Mursalah* as one basis for rule making. However, this method is exercised only where there is no specific text in Islamic *Sharia* that regulates a given issue and it does not produce divine rules that become immutable.[105]

Because there is considerable room in which the Islamic ruler can craft the appropriate law, and for historical reasons,[106] the Kingdom is substantially influenced by the French legal system.[107] For instance, the distinction between public and private law in French law is similar to the separation of issues in which the state is a party, and other matters in private law, as will be shown later. As a historic fact, the majority of codes in Saudi Arabia were inspired by the French legal system via Egypt, which has been the conduit for the reception of French

101 The basic law stipulates that the Quran and the Sunnah are the primary sources, which means that all of the explicit rules in these sources will be a part of Saudi law. See Hanson, ARAB LAW QUARTERLY, 274 (1987).

102 See MUMISA, Islamic Law Theory & Interpretation 165-179. 2002.

103 See Hanson, ARAB LAW QUARTERLY, 289 (1987).

104 Maslahah mursalah (public interest) is a concept in Islamic Sharia that permits rules and laws to be established depending on the public welfare and interest in the many areas not covered by Islamic Sharia. On the other hand, Qiyas (analogy) applies a rule in the Quran or the Sunnah to a new case not mentioned in these sources, by virtue of the fact that the new case shares the same cause for which the original ruling was applied. Qiyas is often considered to produce an extension of sacred law, i.e. many believe rules based on Qiyas become part of the primary sources of Islamic Sharia. For example, the prohibition of banking interest is a ban based on Qiyas. The prohibition of Riba (usury), as is mentioned in the Quran, is extended to all interest because of the similarity between exorbitant and other interest. Furthermore, this prohibition is attributed to sacred sources and thus beyond debate. By contrast, maslahah mursalah is left to the people to achieve what they see as best for them, such as traffic regulations and the construction of schools and other life issues. Rules based on maslahah mursalah are not considered part of the sacred sources. See BHALA, Understanding Islamic Law 319-320. 2011. See also Hanson, ARAB LAW QUARTERLY, 289 (1987).

105 See Hanson, ARAB LAW QUARTERLY, 289 (1987).

106 See id. at. 275-278.

107 Id., at 288.

laws into the Islamic culture, including Saudi Arabia.[108] For example, the law regarding Saudi companies, which was promulgated on 21 July 1965, was copied from the Egyptian code, which in turn was taken directly from French law.[109]

Hence, what is Saudi Arabia's legislative form? What authorities have legislative power? Article 67 of the Basic Law provides: "The Regulatory Authority shall be concerned with the making of legislation and regulations which will safeguard all interests and remove evil from the state's affairs, according to Sharia. Its powers shall be exercised according to provisions of this Law and the Law of the Council of Ministers and the Law of the Shura Council."[110] Hence, according to the provisions of the Basic Law, the Law of the Council of Ministers and the Law of the Shura Council, there are four major authorities that impact the legislation in Saudi Arabia, namely the King,[111] the Council of Ministers,[112] the Shura Council,[113] and the Advisory Authorities[114] (religious authority).

a. The King

The King of Saudi Arabia has ultimate authority over all state bodies to the extent permitted by Islamic *Sharia*.[115] Article 55 of the Basic Law provides: "The King shall rule the nation according to the Sharia. He shall also supervise the implementation of the Sharia, the general policy of the State and the defense and protection of the country."[116] Article 56 provides: "The King is the Prime Minister..."[117] According to these articles and other articles of the Basic Law, the King, as the Head of State, and the Council of Ministers, the principal legislative authority, have the power to regulate internal affairs by enacting or amending any laws by Royal Order. They also have the authority to accept or reject proposals from either of the two legislative bodies.[118] In foreign legal affairs, international treaties,

108 Id. Also see ABDULRAHMAN YAHYA BAAMIR, SHARI'A LAW IN COMMERCIAL AND BANKING ARBITRATION: LAW AND PRACTICE IN SAUDI ARABIA 6-7 (Ashgate Publishing, Ltd. 2013).

109 Hanson, ARAB LAW QUARTERLY, 290 (1987).

110 The Basic Law of Government. 1992.

111 See id. at. Art. 55, 56, 70.

112 See The Council of Ministers Law (1993). Art. 20, 21, 22.

113 See The Shura Council Law (1992). Art. 17, 18.

114 See The Basic Law of Government. 1992. Art. 45.

115 Id. at Art. 44. see Karl, GEO. WASH. J. INT'L L. & ECON., 141-142 (1991). See also, George Sayen, Arbitration, Conciliation, and the Islamic Legal Tradition in Saudi Arabia, 24 U. PA. J. INT'L ECON. L., 907 (2003).

116 The Basic Law of Government. 1992. Art. 55.

117 Id. at. Art. 56.

118 The Council of Ministers Law, Art. 20. 1993. See also, The Shura Council Law, Arts. 17, 18. 1992.

agreements, regulations, and concessions are approved or modified by Royal Decrees after being reviewed by the legislative authorities as will be discussed later.[119] Hence, the King plays a significant role in the legal life of the Kingdom of Saudi Arabia.

b. The Council of Ministers

In addition to its executive function, the Council of Ministers has a legislative function.[120] The members of the Council of Ministers are appointed, relieved of their posts, and their resignations are accepted, by royal decree.[121] In general, the terms of the members of the Council of Ministers are limited to four years.[122] The Council shares the legislative authority with the King and the Shura Council.[123] There are two legislative functions. The first is that each minister has the right to submit and propose a bill or regulation related to the matters of his ministry.[124] The Council of Ministers will study drafts of laws and regulations and vote on them article by article, and then vote on the whole according to its internal rules.[125] The Council also studies issues related to and amends treaties, international agreements, and concessions before they are issued by Royal Decree.[126] The King must approve the decisions of the Council of Ministers, including those related to the approval of legislative proposals and amendments, before they are considered law.[127] Lastly, all decrees must be published in the Official Gazette, and they take effect from the date of publication unless another date is stated.[128]

c. The Shura Council

The Shura Council consists of the head and one hundred and fifty members, all of whom are chosen by the King from among scholars, experts and specialists. At least 20 percent of the members are women. The members' rights and duties and all of their affairs are determined by royal decree.[129] The duration of a term on the Shura Council is four years, beginning on the date specified in the Royal Order for

119 The Council of Ministers Law, Art. 20. 1993. See also, The Shura Council Law, Art. 18. 1992.
120 The Council of Ministers Law, Arts. 20, 21, 22. 1993.
121 Id. at. Art. 8.
122 Id. at. Art. 9.
123 The Shura Council Law, Art.17. 1992.
124 The Council of Ministers Law, Art. 22. 1993.
125 Id. at. Art. 21.
126 Id. at. Art. 20.
127 Id. at. Art. 22.
128 Id. at. Art. 23.
129 The Shura Council Law, Art. 3. 1992.

the appointment of a new member or the composition of a new Council. A new Council or member is normally appointed at least two months before the end of the term of his predecessor. If the term of office of a Council or member expires before the formation of the new Council, the previous board will continue until the new Council is formed.[130]

The Shura Council has two primary functions: advisory and legislative.[131] The first function is to provide opinions regarding public policy, if so requested by the King. These include general plans for economic development, social development, the interpretation of state laws, and the review of annual reports submitted by ministries and other public authorities. The Shuran Council also gives its views on international rules, treaties, agreements, charters and concessions.[132] The second function is to propose bills for new laws or amendments to current laws, and to study them within the Council.[133] It shares this responsibility with the Council of Ministers.[134] Opinions from the Shura Council are sent for review to the King, who decides which rules will be referred to the Council of Ministers.[135] There are two options for the King to send a proposal to the Council of Ministers. The first is when both Councils agree, in which event the new law or regulation will be issued after the King grants his approval.[136] As a result, the legislative proposal or amendment becomes law after getting approval by the two Councils and the King.[137] However, the second option arises if the views of the Councils vary, in which event the issue is returned to the Shura Council, which reviews and delivers whatever decision it deems appropriate.[138] The new resolution is then sent to the King again, who makes the final decision.[139]

---

130 Id. at. Art. 13.

131 Id. at. Art. 15, 17.

132 Id. at. Art. 15.

133 Id. at. Art. 23.

134 Id. at. Art. 17.

135 Id.

136 Id.

137 Id.

138 Id.

139 Id.

Chart 2: Steps to Issue Laws in the Kingdom of Saudi Arabia

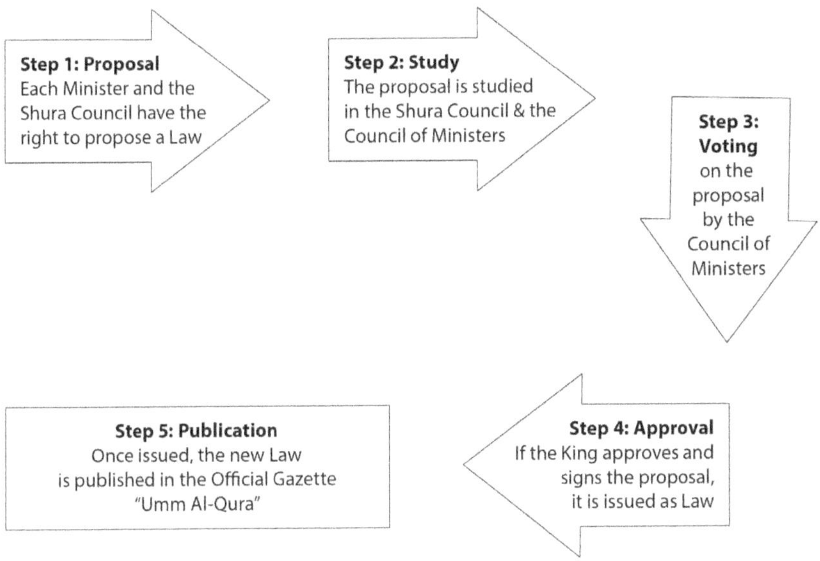

d. The Advisory Authority (the Religious Council)

This authority is an official body created by the King in 1971 to provide religious opinions on issues submitted to it by the King.[140] It consists of a board that contains senior scholars in Islamic *Sharia*, who are appointed by the King.[141] The Basic Law mentions the Board as a source for religious legal opinions in Saudi Arabia.[142] Although it is not a legislative authority, the Religious Board has an impact on the legislative process responsible for enacting statutory laws.[143] In many cases, its participation has been essential in winning public support for enacted statutory laws.[144]

140 STENSLIE, Stig. Regime Stability in Saudi Arabia: The Challenge of Succession. Vol. 40. Routledge 45-46, 2012.

141 Id.

142 The Basic Law of Government art. 45. 1992. Also, see STENSLIE, Regime Stability in Saudi Arabia: the Challenge of Succession 45-46. 2012.

143 See STENSLIE, Regime Stability in Saudi Arabia: The Challenge of Succession 45-46. 2012. See also, Karl, GEO. WASH. J. INT'L L. & ECON., 143 (1991). See also Sayen, U. PA. J. INT'L ECON. L., 907 (2003).

144 Id.; see also, see ANN BLACK, Modern Prespectives on Islamic Law 93-94. 2013.

An example would be Royal Order No. A/44,[145] which stipulates that women should be represented in Al Shura Council by at least 20% of the members of the Council.[146] This amendment obtained major support from the religious Council in Saudi Arabia.[147]

While the legislative authorities seek to enact legislation that meets the interests of the state and people, the process of legislation in Saudi Arabia must never conflict with the primary sources of Islamic Sharia or the law that is higher than a proposed law.[148]

The Kingdom is an excellent model of a Muslim country that is open to taking advantage of contemporary regimes while adhering to the principles of Islamic Law.[149] To this end, Saudi law often refers to Islamic *Sharia* as its Constitution or part of its Basic Law.[150] However, this creates uncertainty and unpredictability because *Sharia* is not codified but collected and interpreted by different schools with different jurisprudential heritages. One of the conclusions of this study is that it would be better to codify Islamic *Sharia*, according to the understanding of the most senior Muslim jurists in Saudi Arabia, before referring to "Islamic Sharia" as a legal reference.

---

145 The Shura Council Law, Art. 3. 1992.

146 Since there is an extremely conservative view in Saudi Arabia about women's issues, the King must support the rule by religious opinions to establish new rules in women's areas, because the legitimacy of the rule in Muslim eyes depends on Muslim scholars' vision. See Eleanor Abdella Doumato, Education in Saudi Arabia: Gender, Jobs, and the Price of Religion, in WOMEN AND GLOBALIZATION IN THE ARAB MIDDLE EAST, 239-242 (2003). See also Amani Hamdan, Women and Education in Saudi Arabia: Challenges and Achievements, 6 INTERNATIONAL EDUCATION JOURNAL (2005).

147 See Al-riyadh newspaper issue 16291, Scholars and elders: Women engage in "Shura" model reflects the right to consultation and practical application of Islam., AL-RIYADH NEWSPAPER, January 30. 2013. See also Al-riyadh Newspaper, Women Entering the Saudi Shura Council for the First Time in History, http://www.alarabiya.net/(2013). Available at http://www.alarabiya.net/articles/2013/01/11/259877.html.

148 The Basic Law of Government, Art. 67. 1992.

149 Hanson, ARAB LAW QUARTERLY, 271 (1987).

150 See The Basic Law of Government, Arts. 55, 67. 1992.

B. Overview of Commercial Arbitration

1. The Concept of Arbitration

Arbitration is one of the techniques of alternative dispute resolution (ADR).[151] ADR typically includes mediation,[152] conciliation,[153] neutral evaluation,[154] expert determination,[155] mini-trials[156] and last-offer arbitration,[157] as methods to settle

---

151 See Nsisong Anthony Udoh & Kudirat Bimbo Sanni, Supplanting the Venom of Litigation with Alternative Dispute Resolution: the Role of Counsellors and Guidance Professionals, BRITISH JOURNAL OF GUIDANCE & COUNSELLING, 4 (2014).

152 Mediation is one form of ADR. It is an informal and confidential way for disputing parties to resolve disputes with the help of a neutral third party, who is trained to help conflicted parties to work out their solutions to problems without deciding who is right or wrong or issuing a decision. See MARGARET L MOSES, The Principles and Practice of International Commercial Arbitration 14 (Cambridge University Press. 2012). See also JOHN W. HEAD, Global Business Law 584 (Carolina Academic Press Third Edition ed. 2012).

153 Conciliation is one of the non-binding methods of ADR, in which the disputed parties use a third party to try to resolve the dispute. The difference between conciliation and arbitration is in the process. The conciliator cannot issue a binding award, and he usually has no authority to take evidence or call witnesses. Some laws do not distinguish between conciliation and mediation, and some differentiate between them based on the amount of involvement of a third party. In mediation, the third party is more facilitative; in conciliation, the third party is more directive. See: MOSES, The Principles and Practice of International Commercial Arbitration 15. 2012. Also see HEAD, Global Business Law 584. 2012.

154 Neutral evaluation is the method in which the disputed parties present the case voluntarily to a neutral third party as they would in arbitration. The third party renders a non-binding opinion based on the evidence and arguments and what he expects a judge would render. The essential goal of a neutral evaluation is to make the parties focus on the strength and weaknesses of the case early to help them to be more realistic about their claims and to avoid unnecessary expenses for settlement the case. See MOSES, The Principles and Practice of International Commercial Arbitration 15. 2012.

155 In this method, the conflicted parties agree to appoint an expert in a particular field to adjudicate. This process can be useful, in particular, in technical disputes, and the expert's decision is frequently binding, or the parties can use this method under rules that permit a non-binding opinion. See id. at.15-16.

156 A non-binding mini-trial is one of the alternative methods of resolving a legal dispute as opposed to a formal court trial. In this method, the disputing parties present brief summaries of their respective cases to a panel of officials, who represent each side plus a neutral decision maker. After hearing the presentations, the panel convenes and tries to settle the matter. A mini-trial has some advantages that make the disputing parties prefer it, such as swift resolution, reduced cost, privacy, and less adversity. See HEAD, Global Business Law 584. 2012. See also, MOSES, The Principles and Practice of International Commercial Arbitration 16. 2012.

157 Last-offer arbitration (baseball arbitration) refers to arbitration in which both disputing parties are required to submit their final offer to an arbitrator, who must select one of these offers relying upon the arbitrator's discretion. This method gives the parties an incentive to make a reasonable offer and is intended to counter arbitrators' tendency to

disputes outside of the courts with the help of a neutral third party.[158] Arbitration is very often used in the field of commercial disputes, especially in the context of international business transactions.[159] For reasons to be discussed later, many countries restrict the use of arbitration in consumer case, labor disputes, and other cases between unequal parties. However, other countries, such as the United States, allow arbitration even in areas like consumer and employment law.[160] International investors prefer arbitration over litigation in most cases, because they are concerned that a state court might not be entirely neutral in a dispute involving that same state. By contrast, in arbitration, the investor and the state resolve their dispute by choosing an impartial adjudicator and both parties have equal say in determining the appropriate law and the process[161] that is used to resolve the dispute, which will still result in a final and binding award in most cases.[162]

Moreover, there are some benefits of arbitration that make many investors and businessmen and -women prefer it over the judicial system. The first benefit is that arbitration provides an opportunity to choose an arbitrator who specializes in the particular issue involved in the dispute rather than a judge, who probably does not have specialized competence regarding the merits of the case.[163] In addition, arbitration is often faster with limited rights of review and appeal in most legal systems.[164] The proceedings and awards in arbitration are in many cases not public but confidential.[165] Arbitration is also otherwise more flexible for businesses compared with litigation in courts.[166] For example, the language of arbitration can be chosen in arbitral proceedings,[167] whereas in the courts, in

---

make compromise decisions halfway between the parties' demands. See JOHN S MURRAY, et al., ARBITRATION 240-243 (Foundation Press. 1996). Also see MOSES, The Principles and Practice of International Commercial Arbitration 16. 2012.

158 See: KATHERINE VAN WEZEL STONE, ARBITRATION LAW 1 (Foundation Pr. 2003).

159 See: MOSES, The Principles and Practice of International Commercial Arbitration 1. 2012. Also see STONE, Arbitration Law 1. 2003.

160 See: MURRAY, et al., Arbitration 35-47. 1996. Also see STONE, Arbitration Law 160-176. 2003.

161 See MOSES, The Principles and Practice of International Commercial Arbitration 1. 2012.

162 See STONE, Arbitration Law 1. 2003. Also see MOSES, The Principles and Practice of International Commercial Arbitration 1. 2012.

163 MURRAY, et al., Arbitration 3. 1996.

164 See id. at, 4. See also HEAD, Global Business Law 585. 2012.

165 See MOSES, The Principles and Practice of International Commercial Arbitration 3-4. 2012.

166 See id. at.1. Also, see HEAD, Global Business Law 585. 2012.

167 See MOSES, The Principles and Practice of International Commercial Arbitration 169. 2012.

most cases, the official language of the state will automatically be used.[168] Finally, the most important aspect of arbitration is the enforcement of the awards: in general, it is easier to enforce arbitral awards in other nations compared to court decisions because of the provisions of the New York Convention 1958,[169] which the study will explain below.

On the other hand, there are some disadvantages to using arbitration as a method of resolving a dispute. First, the limited discovery available to the parties in arbitration may make it difficult for a claimant to meet its burden of proof, such as accessing documents under the control of the opposing party.[170] Second, the right to appeal is limited in arbitration and does not include errors of law or fact, which makes overturning an award because of an erroneous interpretation of laws or facts difficult to obtain.[171] Moreover, arbitrators do not have the power, generally, to enforce interlocutory measures or to impose penalties against a party if the party does not comply with procedural orders of the tribunal. This may require parties to seek court assistance for such procedural matters and is likely to delay the arbitral proceedings.[172] Less common problems relate to opportunities in some legal systems to enforce arbitral awards, which may be more limited and not the same as opportunities to enforce court judgments. Arbitral awards may have fewer enforcement options compared with judgments.[173] Furthermore, countries differ in the identification of arbitrable and non-arbitrable issues. For instance, antitrust subjects were not arbitrable in the United States until the 1980s.[174]

In general, regardless of the differences in views between the legal systems in some aspects of the arbitration, it remains the preferred method of resolving disputes, especially in the investment environment, as will be seen later in this study.

---

168 See Myres S McDougal, et al., Freedom from Discrimination in Choice of Language and International Human Rights, 1 S. ILL. ULJ (1976);id. at. 156.

169 See HEAD, Global Business Law 588. 2012. Also see MOSES, The Principles and Practice of International Commercial Arbitration 211-212. 2012.

170 See MOSES, The Principles and Practice of International Commercial Arbitration 4. 2012.

171 See Id. at.5.

172 See id. at 4.

173 See August Reinisch, The Proliferation of International Dispute Settlement Mechanisms: the Threat of Fragmentation Vs. the Promise of a More Effective System? Some Reflections from the Perspective of Investment Arbitration 111-114 (na. 2008). Also, see American Arbitration Association, AAA/ICDR Handbook on International Arbitration and ADR 4 (JurisNet, LLC. 2006).

174 See Mitsubishi Motors Corp. v. Soler Chrysler-Plymouth, Inc, 473 U.S. 614 (1985).

2. The History of Arbitration in the Arabic Middle East

The Islamic religion has left significant impacts on Arab communities in several aspects of their lives. Consequently, when the study talks about the history of arbitration in Arab areas, it is necessary to touch on two important eras, pre-Islamic and after the advent of Islam, to view most of the changes and developments in those communities.

a. *Pre-Islamic*

Methods of alternative dispute resolution have a long history in Arab communities before the birth of the Islamic religion. As their countries were populated by tribes, who claimed descent from a common ancestor, the resolution of disputes within the framework of the tribe was often favored in tribal culture as it was a portion of the ethos of the community.[175] People did not have an organized form of justice, but they obtained the protection of interests through the tribe.[176] The authority of the tribe was respected by its members on the basis of a body of unwritten rules, which grew in number and content over the years.[177]

Chieftains, soothsayers, and healers had a substantial impact on resolving disputes by different methods within the tribe or between conflicting tribes concerning all kinds of issues, including crimes.[178] During this era, the mutual agreement between the conflicting parties to resolve a dispute amicably was called *Sulh* (mediation).[179] Typically, resort to *Sulh* was not mandatory but depended on the choice of the parties, who very often trusted tribal justice and its proceedings, because they were simple and straightforward in examining any arguments and evidence presented.[180] The mediators tried to resolve the disputes by steering parties toward a point of compromise, usually to prevent either party from retaliating or escalating a dispute into interpersonal or intergroup conflicts.[181]

---

175 See HOSSEIN ESMAEILI ANN BLACK, NADIRSYAH HOSEN, MODERN PERSPECTIVES ON ISLAMIC LAW 156 (Edward Elgar Publishing Limited. 2013). See also Md Shahadat Hossain, *Arbitration in Islamic Law for the Treatment of Civil and Criminal Cases: an Analytical Overview*, 1 JOURNAL OF PHILOSOPHY, CULTURE AND RELIGION, 1 (2013).

176 Id.

177 Id.

178 Aseel Al-Ramahi, *Sulh: a Crucial Part of Islamic Arbitration*, 4 (2008).

179 See ANN BLACK, Modern Perspectives on Islamic Law 156. 2013. See also Al-Ramahi, 3-6 (2008).

180 Al-Ramahi, 3-6 (2008).

181 Id. at.4.

During this era, arbitration was another method used to resolve disputes. The major point in the procedure of choosing the arbitrator was that he had particular personal qualities and a great reputation, such as belonging to a family known for their competence in resolving disputes or for his unusual intellectual powers.[182] By contrast to the proposal of a mediator, the decision of an arbitrator was final, but it was still not an enforceable judgment.[183] The decision was a statement of who was right on a disputed point.[184] The enforcement of arbitral awards in that era depended entirely on the arbitrator's social status in the community or the tribe.[185]

One of the famous examples of arbitration in pre-Islam in Arabic communities involved a drastic disagreement between the chieftains of tribes in Makkah City.[186] The dispute concerned who would have the honor of placing the holy Black Stone back in its place after they removed it temporarily from its position to facilitate rebuilding work after a major fire had partly destroyed the structure of the Kaaba.[187] They decided to choose the next arbitrator who passed through the gate, who happened to be Muhammad before he became a prophet. He was known as an honest and trustworthy man. Hence, he asked the chieftains of the tribes to bring him a cloth upon which he placed the Black Stone. He asked each of the chieftains to hold a corner of the cloth, and they then carried the Black Stone together to its original position.[188] Thus, the serious dispute between them was resolved by a compromise found via the method of arbitration.

Different types of methods for resolving disputes during the pre-Islamic era were subsequently incorporated into and approved by the Islamic religion. However, Islam rejected some elements of these methods that conflicted with its roots or its rules according to its primary sources, as will be shown below.

---

182 ANN BLACK, Modern Perspectives on Islamic Law 156. 2013. Also see Arthur J Gemmell, *Commercial Arbitration in the Islamic Middle East*, 5 SANTA CLARA J. INT'L L., 173 (2007).

183 Al-Ramahi, 5 (2008). Also see Gemmell, SANTA CLARA J. INT'L L., 173 (2007).

184 Id.

185 Al-Ramahi, 5 (2008).

186 Mecca is Islam's holiest city in a desert valley in the western portion of the Kingdom of Saudi Arabia. See http://www.encyclopedia.com/topic/Mecca.aspx.

187 The Kaaba is a cuboid building at the center of a sacred mosque in Mecca City in the Kingdom of Saudi Arabia. Muslims face the Kaaba when performing prayer from any point in the world. See http://www.olemiss.edu/orgs/muslims/Al-Kaabah.html.

188 See Al-Ramahi, 6 (2008).

b. *Arbitration in Islamic Sharia*

Understanding the historical and religious aspects of dispute settlement in the Arab Middle East is an essential key to understanding commercial arbitration laws in this area of the world, because the Islamic religion prevails in different aspects of Muslim life in a country like Saudi Arabia.

From its founding days, Islamic *Sharia* recognized and even encouraged using the pre-Islamic ways to settle disputes in its different sources, albeit with some adjustments to comply with its roots and purposes.[189] The sources of Islamic *Sharia* encourage people to solve their disputes by peaceful and consensual ways known and settled in the Arabian context, in particular by using *Sulh* (reconciliation).[190] For example, one of the pertinent passages in the Quran states:

> وَإِن طَائِفَتَانِ مِنَ الْمُؤْمِنِينَ اقْتَتَلُوا فَأَصْلِحُوا بَيْنَهُمَا ۖ فَإِن بَغَتْ إِحْدَاهُمَا عَلَى الْأُخْرَىٰ فَقَاتِلُوا الَّتِي تَبْغِي حَتَّىٰ تَفِيءَ إِلَىٰ أَمْرِ اللَّهِ ۚ فَإِن فَاءَتْ فَأَصْلِحُوا بَيْنَهُمَا بِالْعَدْلِ وَأَقْسِطُوا ۖ إِنَّ اللَّهَ يُحِبُّ الْمُقْسِطِينَ

And if two factions among the believers should fight, then make settlement between the two. However, if one of them oppresses the other, then fight against the one that oppresses until it returns to the ordinance of Allah. Moreover, if it returns, then make settlement between them in justice and act justly. Indeed, Allah loves those who act justly.[191]

Another alternative method of dispute settlement is arbitration, which was approved and even encouraged in several texts of Islamic Sharia. For instance, in one of these texts that talks about a disagreement between spouses, the Quran states:

> وَإِنْ خِفْتُمْ شِقَاقَ بَيْنِهِمَا فَابْعَثُوا حَكَمًا مِّنْ أَهْلِهِ وَحَكَمًا مِّنْ أَهْلِهَا إِن يُرِيدَا إِصْلَاحًا يُوَفِّقِ اللَّهُ بَيْنَهُمَا ۗ إِنَّ اللَّهَ كَانَ عَلِيمًا خَبِيرًا
>
> And if you fear dissension between the two, send an arbitrator from his people and an arbitrator from her people. If they both desire recon-

189 See Ann Black, Modern Perspectives on Islamic Law 156. 2013. Also see Hossain, Journal of Philosophy, Culture and Religion, 1 (2013).

190 Al-Ramahi, 10 (2008).

191 Al Quran 49:9.

> ciliation, Allah will cause it between them. Indeed, Allah is ever Knowing and Acquainted [with all things].[192]

This *Aya* (verse) confirms that arbitration was a method of resolving disputes between married couples by two arbitrators, one from each side, trying to avoid the divorce that may occur. Also, several events in the Prophet Mohammad's life show that he accepted the settlement of disputes by arbitration. In another famous story, the Prophet agreed with Jewish people to submit to a mutually agreeable third party to resolve a dispute between himself and the Banu Qurayza (a Jewish tribe).[193]

Thus, alternative dispute resolution, including arbitration, was an essential part of the pre-Islamic and Islamic systems of dispute settlement. They were used in Arab Middle East history, and they have continued to be considered worthy elements of the spirit of the Islamic system of justice.

There is another method of resolving disputes in Islamic *Sharia* called Med-Arb. Med-Arb is an acronym of both mediation and arbitration, which has been recognized and prescribed in the *Quran* and has been practiced in Islamic history. The goal of this method is to reach an amicable resolution of the dispute before the issuance of a binding decision.[194] The *Quran* states: "If you fear a breach between them – the man and his wife – appoint two arbitrators, one from his family and the other from her's; if they both wish for peace, Allah (God) will cause their reconciliation..."[195] The next part of this text provides that, if the parties wish for reconciliation rather than an arbitral award during the proceedings, then Allah will show them the way of reconciliation.[196] Thus, it has always been encouraged and emphasized in Islamic *Sharia* that the arbitrator must explore the possibility to move toward reconciliation before beginning arbitral proceedings. This method of resolving disputes is being recognized as a universal principle in the modern world.[197]

However, the important issue when talking about arbitration in Islamic *Sharia* is whether the implementation of arbitration is binding on the disputing parties like

---

192 Al Quran 4:35.

193 MUSLIM IBN AL-HAJJAJ, SAHIH MUSLIM 1388 No. 1768 (Dar Ihya al-Turath al-Arabi.). There are many stories in the Prophet's life that show that arbitration was accepted. See Gemmell, SANTA CLARA J. INT'L L., 174 (2007).

194 See Hossain, JOURNAL OF PHILOSOPHY, CULTURE AND RELIGION, 4-5 (2013).

195 Quran 4:35.

196 See Hossain, JOURNAL OF PHILOSOPHY, CULTURE AND RELIGION, 5 (2013).

197 Id.

it is the case in most modern arbitration laws. This study found that there is a debate between Muslim jurists in this regard. Some Muslim jurists hold that an arbitrator has the same duties and powers as a judge, but other Muslim scholars see the arbitrator as an agent or conciliator.[198] Hence, one Islamic view is that arbitration does not have any binding nature. Consequently, it is not binding or final on the disputing parties; it is instead a form of conciliation unless the disputed parties accept its decision.[199] One of the passages of the *Quran* that supports this view is the one quoted above, namely that, in arbitration between conflicted couples, if they both wish for peace, Allah will cause their reconciliation.[200] As a result, those who hold this opinion have concluded that the *Quran* links the result of arbitration to a consensus between the parties before and after the procedure.

Another opinion is that arbitration in Islamic Sharia is similar to modern arbitration when it comes to the binding effect of arbitral awards.[201] This opinion depends on different texts of the primary sources of Islamic Sharia. One of these texts is the Quranic verse:

> إنَّ اللهَ يأمُرُكُمْ أن تؤدُّواْ الأمانات إلى أهْلِهَا وإذا حكمْتم بيْنَ النّاسِ أن تحْكُمُواْ بالْعَدْلِ إنَّ اللهَ نِعمَّا
> يَعظُكُم بِهِ إنَّ اللهَ كانَ سَمِيعاً بَصِيراً
>
> Indeed, Allah commands you to render trusts to whom they are due, and when you judge between people to judge with justice. Excellent is that which Allah instructs you. Indeed, Allah is ever Hearing and Seeing.[202]

Whoever supports this view believes that the Quran does not differentiate between judge and arbitrator in the requirement that they act with justice, hence both judgment and award are also equally binding. In other words, ordering the decision-maker to ensure justice in this verse and in the sayings of the Prophet regarding arbitration between disputing parties shows that both judgment and arbitral award are equally binding on the parties, because they must not ignore a just decision. Further, this opinion sees that arbitral awards are binding in the

198 See Al-Ramahi, 15 (2008). See also ANN BLACK, Modern Perspectives on Islamic Law 161-164. 2013.

199 ABDULLAH IBN QUDAMAH, AL MUGHNI 320-321 VOL. 7 (Cairo Library. 1968). See also Id.

200 Quran 4:35.

201 Some proponents of this view do not distinguish between arbitration and jurisdiction as will be presented later in chapter 4. See SAHIHAB ALDDIN 'AHMAD 'IIDRIS ALQURAAFI, ALDHDHAKHIRA 35 VOL. 10 (Aar Algharb Al'iislami First Edition ed. 1994). See also Hossain, JOURNAL OF PHILOSOPHY, CULTURE AND RELIGION, 5-6 (2013).

202 Al Quran 4:58.

same way that a contract is binding.[203] As a result, according to Islamic *Sharia*, there is a religious duty to enforce agreements, including arbitral awards, unless there is a conflict with the roots of Islamic *Sharia*.[204]

> O you who believe fulfil any contracts [that you make]...Fulfil God's agreement once you have pledged to do so, and do not break any oaths once they have been sworn to. You have set God up as a surety for yourselves.[205]

Hence, this view considers arbitration to be based on a contract and all the consequences of the contractual promises will apply to arbitration.

Still another view thinks that there are two types of arbitration, binding and non-binding. Supporters of this view believe that the word *Hakam*, which translates to English as "arbitrator", is used in the primary texts of Islamic *Sharia* both for conciliation that leads to non-binding decisions and for arbitration that leads to binding decisions.[206] According to Aseel Al-Ramahi:

> The word Hakam has been given different meanings. The word can be used in its broad sense to refer to an authorized person to dispose of rights, to settle differences between different persons by suggesting settlement or helping them to reach it, or by issuing a binding decision to settle the dispute. The agreement of the parties defines the type of authorization in each case.[207]

This view considers the type of arbitration to depend upon what the text in the contract between the parties says, because the term "arbitration" used in Arabic can mean binding and non-binding settlement procedures.

After reviewing these opinions regarding arbitration, it may appear that there is an immense wealth of different opinions and that most of these opinions are within a general understanding of the primary sources of Islamic *Sharia*. This ample room gives Muslim countries an excellent opportunity to develop and adapt their legal systems to the exigencies of time and place. Thus, the arbitral contract is recognized as valid under Islamic *Sharia* as long as its specific terms are not prohibited by Islamic *Sharia* as will be shown later in the study. Similarly, the

203 See ALQURAAFI, Aldhdhakhira 35. 1994. See also Hossain, JOURNAL OF PHILOSOPHY, CULTURE AND RELIGION, 5-6 (2013).

204 Al-Ramahi, 14 (2008). See also ALQURAAFI, Aldhdhakhira 35. 1994.

205 See Al-Ramahi, 14 (2008).

206 Id. at.17. Also see ANN BLACK, Modern Perspectives on Islamic Law 161-164. 2013.

207 Al-Ramahi, 17 (2008).

selection of arbitrators, the place of arbitration, the procedure, any time limits, the applicable rules, and the remuneration of the arbitrators will be discussed and explained in the third chapter.

3. The History of Commercial Arbitration Law in Saudi Arabia

At the beginning of the legal history of Saudi Arabia, no particular law comprehensibly regulated arbitration in the Kingdom. The process of regulating Saudi arbitration began with a few rules and passed through several stages.

a. The Commercial Court System Created in 1931[208]

The first stage of arbitration in the Kingdom of Saudi Arabia was through the Law of the Commercial Court System, which was promulgated by Royal Decree No. 32 in 1931. It was the first law that contained some clauses, namely clauses 493-497, that govern the arbitration process between parties wishing to settle their dispute through arbitration.[209] The clauses regarding arbitration were about aspects of form, the content of the arbitration agreement,[210] the appointment of the arbitrators,[211] the duration of the arbitration,[212] some of the procedures associated with the operation of arbitration, the possibility of challenging the arbitration award in front of the Commercial Court at the time,[213] and the need to approve the arbitration award by the Commercial Court before its implementation.[214]

b. The Saudi Labor Law of 1969[215]

The Saudi Labor Law of 1969, in Articles 183 and 184, permitted employers and workers to refer disputes between them to arbitration rather having them resolved by the Primary Committee competent to settle labor disputes.[216] The law also required that the arbitration agreement be ratified by the competent

---

208 The Commercial Court Law (1931). Available at Ministry of Commerce and Industry at: http://mci.gov.sa/LawsRegulations/SystemsAndRegulations/LawofCommercialCourt/22-2/Pages.

209 See BAAMIR, Shari'a Law in Commercial and Banking Arbitration: Law and Practice in Saudi Arabia 96-97. 2013.

210 The Commercial Court Law Art. 493. 1931.

211 *Id.* at. Art. 493, 496.

212 *Id.* at. Art. 493.

213 *Id.* at. Art. 495, 496.

214 *Id.* at. Art. 497.

215 This law was issued by Royal Decree No M/21 in 1969.

216 Saudi Labor Law Art. 183 (1969).

pre-primary committee before beginning the arbitration proceedings.[217] The law also dealt with conflicts in the appointment of arbitrators, in which event the President of the Primary Committee was competent to undertake the appointment.[218] This law provided that the award of the tribunal could be appealed to the Supreme Committee for the Settlement of Labor Disputes, unless the parties agreed in advance in the arbitration agreement that the award would be final.[219] In all cases, the arbitral award must be recorded before the Trial Committee for the settlement of the competent labor disputes during the week following the date of issuance.[220]

c. *Chambers of Commerce and the Industrial Law of 1980*[221]

The Chambers of Commerce and Industrial Law of 1980, which was issued by Royal Decree No. (M/6), showed in articles 5 and 37 the terms of reference of Chambers of Commerce to resolve commercial and industrial disputes by arbitration if parties so agree. Article 5 of this law stipulates that Chambers of Commerce and Industry specialize in the following matters: "(h) commercial and industrial dispute resolution by arbitration if the parties to the conflict agreed to forward it to them". In addition, the law Implementing Regulations of the Chambers of Commerce issued by the Minister of Trade No. 1871 in 1981 set out the rules and procedures that must be followed in articles 49, 50, 51, 52, 53, and 54 when doing arbitration between the disputing parties before the Chambers of Commerce.[222]

d. *The Arbitration Law of 1983*[223]

The Arbitration Law was issued by Royal Decree No. M/46 in 1983 to provide a fixed plan to create an independent system of private arbitration and to confirm the function of arbitration as a primary method of resolving disputes between parties. The law contained twenty-five articles and organized many aspects of arbitration that were overlooked by previous regimes. Executive regulations for

---

217 *Id.*

218 *Id.*

219 *Id.*

220 *Id.*

221 This law is available at the Ministry of Commerce and Industry website at http://mci.gov.sa/LawsRegulations/SystemsAndRegulations/Documents/a19.pdf.

222 The implementation regulations of this law are available at Ministry of Commerce and Industry website at http://mci.gov.sa/LawsRegulations/SystemsAndRegulations/SystemOfChambersOfCommerceAndIndustry/Pages/19-4.

223 This law was issued in 1983 but was replaced by a new law promulgated in 2012 as will be discussed later.

the implementation of this law were also issued by decision of the President of the Council of Ministers No. (7/2021) in 1985.[224]

The law and its implementing regulations included the latest arbitral principles prevailing at that time and addressed most of the issues related to the process of arbitration, such as the number of arbitrators, the method of appointment, the method of issuance of the arbitration award and its implementation. It also avoided most of the defects and criticism of the Saudi arbitration law in the previous stages.[225]

For the first time, the Saudi justice system was given broad authority to oversee the arbitration process. With the 1983 law, Saudi Arabia adopted the idea of a dual role for the state with respect to arbitration matters, which means that the state is an assistant and an associate in the arbitration process in addition to its traditional role of supervising its function. This model has been used successfully in many countries, such as France. However, the new law was criticized, especially because court supervision sometimes led to unexpected or even unfair outcomes. The situation was exacerbated by an unprecedented increase in the volume and diversity of commercial activity in the Kingdom, which saw, inter alia, the entry of many investors from various countries to exercise their activity in the Kingdom.[226]

The law was criticized, for example, because the adoption of the arbitration document by the competent judicial authority could take a long time. Delays could also be caused by one of the parties, such as when one refuses to appoint its arbitrator, the parties cannot or will not agree on the appointment of the sole arbitrator, or if one of the arbitrators withdraws before the start of the arbitration proceedings.[227] Also, there was no right to choose a foreign language, foreign law, or the principles of international trade as the substantive law to be applied, as will be discussed later in the study.

Per the above and other weaknesses, the Arbitration Law of 1983 met some of the needs of its time, but, after the commercial and industrial development in the Kingdom and the entry of many foreign investors to Saudi Arabia, it no longer met the aspirations and requirements of stakeholders. It was, therefore, necessary

---

224 See BAAMIR, Shari'a Law in Commercial and Banking Arbitration: Law and Practice in Saudi Arabia 117. 2013.

225 See Sayen, U. PA. J. INT'L ECON. L., 912-913 (2003).

226 See BAAMIR, Shari'a Law in Commercial and Banking Arbitration: Law and Practice in Saudi Arabia 119-122. 2013. Also see Sayen, U. PA. J. INT'L ECON. L., 912-913 (2003).

227 Id.

for a new arbitration law be issued that would go hand in hand with the commercial development in the Kingdom and would be more in step with the evolution of arbitration laws around the world. Thus, the Saudi ruler promulgated the current arbitration law by Royal Decree (M/34) in 2012, which will be discussed in the next parts of this study in more detail.

4. Recent Challenges and Attempts at Modernization

The new arbitration law issued by Royal Decree Number M/34 took effect in April 2012. That new law and the new enforcement law, known as the Royal Decree Number M/53, which followed the same year, were instituted to modernize the arbitration process in the Kingdom of Saudi Arabia. The new arbitration law is broad and is patterned after the United Nations Commission on International Trade Law (UNCITRAL) Model Law on International Commercial Arbitration.[228]

There were two primary reasons for the creation of the new arbitration law in the Kingdom: First, the old arbitration law in Saudi was criticized for being inconsistent with modern arbitration rules that were being practiced in other countries.[229] Second, when international tribunals had to refer to Saudi law, they sometimes found provisions that were incomplete or insufficient when applied to particular cases.[230]

When Saudi Arabia became a signatory of the 1958 United Nations Convention on Recognition and Enforcement of Foreign Arbitral Awards ("the New York Convention") in 1994, it made reservations regarding the recognition of arbitral agreements and the enforcement of foreign arbitral awards originating from another New York Convention state.[231] As a consequence, Saudi Arabia became known as a hostile country in matters that deal with the recognition of commercial arbitration agreements and enforcing foreign awards. Several international awards were rejected by Saudi courts for being incompatible with Islamic Sharia for reasons that will be addressed later in this study.[232] Since the reservation of compatibility with Islamic Sharia is a standard reservation made by Saudi Arabia

---

228 See Mithani, CORPORATE DISPUTE MAGAZINE, (2014).

229 See Saleem, AVAILABLE AT SSRN 2315728, 5 (2012).

230 See Arbitration between the State of Saudi Arabia and the Arabian American Oil Co., 27 ILR 117 - 1958. See also, Saudi Basic Industries v. Mobil Yanbu Pet, 866, 1, (Del: Supreme Court)., 866 A.2d 1 (Del. 2005).

231 Saleem, AVAILABLE AT SSRN 2315728, (2012)., 9.

232 *Id.* See also Nancy B Turck, *Arbitration in Saudi Arabia*, 6 ARBITRATION INTERNATIONAL, 922 (1990).

when ratifying international treaties and conventions and will not be abandoned, the study needs to analyze the legal, cultural and traditional role of religion in Saudi Arabia that may impact the enforcement of arbitration agreements and the recognition of foreign arbitral awards. This will be done in the next chapter dealing with Saudi courts.

Several factors or grounds are accepted by the New York Convention for a country to refuse to recognize and enforce foreign awards. The most common grounds include the invalidity of the arbitration agreement due to the incapacity of one of the parties, lack of adequate notice given to either party to the dispute, and problems with the tribunal acting beyond the scope of its authority as expressed in the agreement.[233] However, these grounds were often criticized for being mere procedural irregularities that did not affect the actual intention of the parties.[234] Another hindrance to the efficient settlement of disputes through arbitration was that the New York Convention allows contracting states to refuse to recognize or enforce an award if the action would be contrary to "public policy".[235] Some countries, namely the United States, Kuwait, and Syria, have adopted a narrow interpretation of the issue of public policy to maintain the intention of the parties to resort to arbitration and to avoid the abuse of the public policy defense by contracting states.[236] Not all countries have followed this example. Later, this study will discuss how Saudi courts have interpreted the public policy exception.

It is important to know the changes that took effect with the implementation of the new law. First, the new law has allowed arbitration to be in a language other than Arabic, as agreed upon by the disputing parties or as ordered by the arbitral tribunal. This significant change was made to avoid having to translate contracts and other legal documents from one language to another.[237]

The second change is that arbitral tribunals are now allowed to apply whatever substantive laws were agreed upon by the parties to govern the arbitration proceedings. The parties are given the option to choose the substantive law that

---

233 See Jan Paulsson, Delocalisation of International Commercial Arbitration: When and Why It Matters, 32 INTERNATIONAL AND COMPARATIVE LAW QUARTERLY (1983).

234 See Ray Y Chan, Enforceability of Annulled Foreign Arbitral Awards in the United States: A Critique of Chromalloy, The, 17 BU INT'L LJ (1999).

235 See Saleem, AVAILABLE AT SSRN 2315728, 9 (2012).

236 *Id.*

237 See Mithani, CORPORATE DISPUTE MAGAZINE, (2014).

will be applied even if such law is in a foreign language.[238] With this innovation in the arbitration proceedings, the parties will have the opportunity to choose a law that is deemed suitable to the nature of the contractual obligations undertaken by the parties.

Another change incorporated into the new law is that parties can now adopt any institutional set of arbitration rules of their choice, such as the International Chamber of Commerce (ICC) Rules of Arbitration. However, if the parties fail to stipulate the rules that will govern the arbitration proceedings, the new law provides a set of procedural guidelines to be followed in the arbitration.[239]

Another innovation in the new law is that the parties are no longer required to file an arbitration agreement that has to be approved by the court before the arbitration process can proceed. This enables the parties to have a free hand in deciding whether to go to court or to settle the dispute amicably. It also saves time by avoiding the delay caused by waiting for the court's approval. Another important and significant change in the new arbitration law requires the arbitral tribunal to render a decision no more than 12 months after the commencement of the arbitration.[240] The tribunal may extend the 12 month period for another six months or longer, provided that this power to extend was stipulated in the agreement made by the parties. Such a period is more realistic than the 90 day period set by the old arbitration law.[241]

The most significant development in the new law is that the local courts are precluded from re-examining the facts and the subject matter of the award, and the enforcement of foreign judgments and the arbitral awards has been assigned to the Executive Judge and no longer to the Board of Grievances.[242] Under the old law, enforcement of the award was most commonly hindered by the length of the procedures. The delegation to the Executive Judge of the enforcement of the arbitral award is expected to shorten the enforcement process and will facilitate the consistency of the decisions.[243] However, the courts still have the authority to

---

238 *Id.*

239 See *Id.*

240 *Id.*

241 *Id.*

242 There was no Executive Judge under the old Saudi law, which was one of the disadvantages of the old law. The study will extensively explain such differences between courts in chapter 2.

243 See Mithani, CORPORATE DISPUTE MAGAZINE, (2014).

review an award for compliance with Sharia.[244] For example, the local courts are obliged to strike down portions of the award that do not comply with Sharia principles, such as the prohibition against the application of interest and selling music tools that may have no consensus support among Islamic jurists, as will be discussed later.[245] In the following chapters, the study will analyze the application of the principles of Islamic Sharia by Saudi courts and their impact on the recognition and enforcement of foreign judgments and arbitral awards.

The new Saudi laws also provide clearer guidelines for the enforcement of arbitral awards locally and internationally. However, there is some ambiguity that should be addressed, such as the public policy matter. Before discussing the framework of the new srbitration law, the study needs to review the current Saudi judicial system and the possible effects on reinforcement and enforcement of commercial arbitration.

244 *Id.*

245 The study will discuss this issue in more detail in chapter 4.

Chapter 2

The Legal System of the Saudi Judiciary and its Potential Effects on Reinforcing and Enforcing Commercial Arbitration

The modernization of the Saudi arbitration environment is more in line with modern international norms of commercial arbitration rules, embodying several "arbitration-friendly" principles of the UNCITRAL Model Law, such as competence-competence and the autonomy of the arbitrating parties. However, the new Saudi arbitration environment is still subject to certain intricacies and obstacles presented by the Saudi municipal courts during the process of arbitration. Even more common are challenges at the enforcement stage of an arbitral award in the Kingdom of Saudi Arabia. Thus, addressing such challenges posed by the Saudi courts and finding solutions through analyzing and examining the Saudi court system will help to pave the way toward creating a more welcoming arbitration environment locally and internationally and a viable choice for parties who will otherwise continue to encounter an unwelcome environment in the Kingdom.

A. Importance of the National Judiciary in the Arbitration Process

It is well known that investors and traders prefer the method of arbitration to settle merchant disputes both in international and national fields.[246] Commercial arbitration has become more attractive because of its privacy, party control of the process and the international recognition and enforcement of its awards.[247] Arbitration offers the opportunity to settle disputes between parties using a private method that is binding and enforceable in general. Several years ago, the Kingdom of Saudi Arabia realized that it should establish a new arbitration law in line with the rules applicable elsewhere in the international community to attract foreign companies to invest in the Kingdom. It became very clear that its old law did not meet the real legal and investment needs.[248] Accordingly, on April 16, 2012, Saudi Arabia issued a new arbitration law, which was inspired by the

246 See ASSOCIATION, AAA Handbook on International Arbitration and ADR 169-172. 2010.

247 Id.

248 See Saleem, AVAILABLE AT SSRN 2315728, Article 25, 38, 55 (2012). Also, Turck, ARBITRATION INTERNATIONAL, 922 (1990).

UNCITRAL Model Law.[249] This law offers greater independence in the arbitral process, provides enhanced procedural powers of the arbitral tribunal, and clearer enforcement rules for arbitration agreements and awards. However, while the new arbitration law substantially limits the previous mandatory oversight of the local Saudi courts, parties still need to deal with Saudi courts at different stages during the arbitration process.[250]

Under the new law, the disputing parties will need Saudi courts during the arbitration process similar to the practice in other jurisdictions. For instance, the courts may be called upon to address issues like the appointment of arbitrators when the parties cannot agree, or if a party needs temporary or injunctive relief.[251] While this works quite well in most countries, we must remember that most judges in Saudi courts are trained only in Islamic Sharia, and they usually lack any particular legal, technical or commercial background.[252] In addition, most rules applied in Saudi courts can be found in books that were written by medieval Muslim jurists.[253] For this reason, the Kingdom of Saudi Arabia solved the lack of background in certain technical and commercial legal matters by establishing specialized tribunals in certain fields, consisting of specialists to settle disputes involving their specialties.[254] For the enforcement of foreign arbitral awards, no such specialized tribunals have yet been created. This study will present how the ordinary judges deal with issues related to arbitration in practice, and why there is a need for a different skill set to address arbitration-relted issues nationally and internationally.

---

249 Mithani, CORPORATE DISPUTE MAGAZINE, (2014).

250 Id.

251 Saudi Arabia, Arbitration Law Article 22 (2012).

252 While there are law schools and Sharia schools in Saudi Arabia, the law of the Saudi judiciary requires that each candidate have a degree from one of the Sharia colleges in the Kingdom of Saudi Arabia. By contrast, the graduates from the Saudi law schools can hold any legal position except being a judge as will be shown later in this chapter. See Karl, GEO. WASH. J. INT'L L. & ECON., 144-145 (1991). Also, Nancy B Turck, Dispute Resolution in Saudi Arabia, THE INTERNATIONAL LAWYER, 418 (1988).

253 See FRANK E VOGEL, ISLAMIC LAW AND THE LEGAL SYSTEM OF SAUDÍ: STUDIES OF SAUDI ARABIA 9 (Brill. 2000).

254 Several tribunals with judicial powers, referred to as "committees", have been created over time in the Kingdom of Saudi Arabia. These committees deal with specific issues regulated by royal decrees, such as labor and commercial law. The jurisdiction of each committee is determined separately by the decree that created it. One of them was created to resolve banking disputes; it is called "the Banking Disputes Settlement Committee." See BAAMIR, Shari'a Law in Commercial and Banking Arbitration: Law and Practice in Saudi Arabia 22-24. 2013.

The new Enforcement Law, which was issued through Royal Decree No. M/53 on July 3, 2012, represents a significant step toward aligning the law in the Kingdom with international standards and a facilitation of enforcement of arbitral awards. However, the recognition and enforcement of (foreign) arbitral awards continues to be in the hands of ordinary Saudi courts even though they have the reputation of being highly skeptical of the recognition and enforcement of arbitral awards.[255] This skepticism is thought to exist in all cases involving investors, foreign and national, as the result of which investors and traders try to avoid Saudi courts.[256] In fact, the new law does not provide clear guidance about public policy as applied in the Kingdom or the meaning of Islamic Sharia as applied in the courts, in spite of the fact that there are different schools and opinions about many issues. For instance, an award granting interest, which is prohibited under Sharia according to most Muslim jurists, will run into problems at the enforcement stage in a Saudi court. In such cases, the court will make a determination whether it is possible to sever the part of the award that does not comply with public policy, such as the award of interest, from the rest of the award. In the end, it is left largely to the discretion of the judge(s) whether the enforcement court may order that the entire issue of damages be reheard. In the alternative, it may choose to enforce the award but without the provisions on interest.[257]

No foreign party needs to understand the Saudi judicial system only for its arbitration procedures; however, a foreigner might be forced to defend a case in a Saudi court if sued by a Saudi plaintiff. Appearance in a Saudi court may also be required by the terms of an agreement, if one of the parties, having more bargaining power, imposes an exclusive choice of forum in favor of a Saudi court. According to Fabio Bortolotti: "The party in question wants to make sure that possible disputes will be decided under a well-known procedural system, by judges who use the same language, with the assistance of lawyers with whom the

---

255 See Faris Nesheiwat & Ali Al-Khasawneh, The 2012 Saudi Arbitration Law: A Comparative Examination of the Law and Its Effect on Arbitration in Saudi Arabia, 13 SANTA CLARA JOURNAL OF INTERNATIONAL LAW, 445-446 (2015). Also, Kristin T Roy, New York Convention and Saudi Arabia: Can a Country Use the Public Policy Defense to Refuse Enforcement of Non-Domestic Arbitral Awards, The, 18 FORDHAM INT'L LJ, 920-958 (1994).

256 Some cases show that foreign investors and Saudis alike try to avoid enforcing arbitral awards in Saudi Arabia by using some available tactics that help them to avoid Saudi courts, such as in the case of Islamic Investment Company of the Gulf (Bahamas) Ltd v. Symphony Gems NV and others. For more information about this case and subject matter, see BAAMIR, Shari'a Law in Commercial and Banking Arbitration: Law and Practice in Saudi Arabia 173-175. 2013.

257 See Arabia, Arbitration Law Article 55. 2012.

judge is familiar."[258] Hence, the study will consider extensively the Saudi judicial system before beginning to study the new arbitration law to give foreign businessmen and women a clear picture of Saudi courts. This will also help legal researchers and policymakers in Saudi Arabia to improve the judicial system, because national courts can exist without arbitration, but arbitration cannot exist without the national courts.

B. History of Courts in Saudi Arabia

Islamic Sharia, the primary source of legislation in the Kingdom of Saudi Arabia according to its Basic law,[259] was gradually developed during Islamic history by Muslim jurists and scholars and was accepted as the basis of law in most of the Muslim world during the Islamic history and until now in the some Muslim countries.[260] One of the significant areas in the Muslim world is the Arabian Peninsula, most of which is part of Saudi Arabia. Over the years, various parts of the Arabian Peninsula have been subject to various types of governments, which reflected the judicial styles and formats from one region to another.[261] By examining the reality of the Arabian Peninsula, the study found that some of its parts, like Hejaz, possessed the administrative structure established by the Ottoman Empire and were sophisticated in outlook both through their permanent contact with foreign Muslims partaking in the annual Haj[262] to Makkah City and through their long-standing position on the trade route between Asia and Europe. As a consequence, the Hejaz judiciary has always had a measure of procedural sophistication.[263] In other parts of Saudi Arabia, such as Najd, the form of its judiciary was affected by the tribal system and was shaped by customs and traditions without regard to form and procedure, because many tribes and clans in the Arabian Peninsula lived according to the pattern of the desert and its

258 FABIO BORTOLOTTI, DRAFTING AND NEGOTIATING INTERNATIONAL COMMERCIAL CONTRACTS: A PRACTICAL GUIDE 95 (International Chamber of Commerce. 2013).

259 The Basic Law of Government Article 1. 1992.

260 See VOGEL, Islamic Law and the Legal System of Saudí: Studies of Saudi Arabia 4-32. 2000.

261 See JAN MICHIEL OTTO, SHARIA INCORPORATED: A COMPARATIVE OVERVIEW OF THE LEGAL SYSTEMS OF TWELVE MUSLIM COUNTRIES IN PAST AND PRESENT 144-145 (Leiden University Press. 2010). Also, Hanson, ARAB LAW QUARTERLY, 281-285 (1987).

262 Haj (pilgrimage) is a mandatory religious duty for Muslims, and it is an annual Islamic pilgrimage to Mecca. Every adult, who is financially and physically capable of undertaking this duty, must carry it out in the Islamic religion at least once in the adult's lifetime. See FRANCIS E PETERS, THE HAJJ: THE MUSLIM PILGRIMAGE TO MECCA AND THE HOLY PLACES (Princeton University Press. 1994).

263 See Hanson, ARAB LAW QUARTERLY, 283 (1987).

customs, traditions and customs inherited among themselves, with little or no interaction with the outside world.[264]

As a result, in 1927, after King Abdul-Aziz established the Kingdom of Saudi Arabia, at least two different court systems existed. Najd had a simple system. The ruler appointed single judges to the major towns, and these judges were specifically called upon in cases that the local governor, called the Amir, could not resolve amicably. The local governor would refer such cases for adjudication according to Islamic Sharia. The judgments rendered by the judges were submitted to the governor for enforcement. Moreover, appeals were possible only through a complaint to the local governor, who would then refer the matter to senior Sharia scholars.[265]

By contrast, the King established a framework for the courts of the Hejaz, which was a more elaborate judicial organization. This structure contains multi-judge courts, summary and general Sharia courts, and instances of appeal. Because the Najdi judges were not familiar with this judicial organi,zation, this system remained in place only for the Hejaz area, until 1960, when it was implemented in the other areas of the Kingdom.[266]

Beginning in the 1930s, the new kingdom needed to regulate its affairs nationally and with other states by enacting laws. However, the senior scholars opposed the new legislation, and the Sharia judges refused to apply it, because it was man-made, as they saw it.[267] According to Frank Vogel: " the 'ulama' – senior scholars – were unlikely to develop rules by Ijtihad,[268] and the 'ulama' rarely supported

---

264 See ALBERT HOURANI, A History of the Arab Peoples: Updated Edition 113 (Faber & Faber. 2013).

265 See VOGEL, Islamic Law and the Legal System of Saudí: Studies of Saudi Arabia 87-89. 2000. Also, OTTO, Sharia Incorporated: A Comparative Overview of the Legal Systems of Twelve Muslim Countries in Past and Present 144-145. 2010.

266 See VOGEL, Islamic Law and the Legal System of Saudí: Studies of Saudi Arabia 87-91. 2000. OTTO, Sharia Incorporated: A Comparative Overview of the Legal Systems of Twelve Muslim Countries in Past and Present 144-145. 2010. Also Hanson, ARAB LAW QUARTERLY, 283-284 (1987).

267 See OTTO, Sharia Incorporated: A Comparative Overview of the Legal Systems of Twelve Muslim Countries in Past and Present 146. 2010. Also, VOGEL, Islamic Law and the Legal System of Saudí: Studies of Saudi Arabia 286. 2000.

268 Ijtihad means obtaining the rules from the primary sources of Islamic Sharia by using the secondary sources, and the practice of ijtihad extends to emerging issues depending on one or more of the secondary sources. This tool will be explained as applied in the Saudi court later in this study.

rapid modernization anyway. A famous story tells of 'ulama' opposition to introducing radio: Abdu al-Aziz was able to overcome their opposition only by having the Quran transmitted to him in their hearing thus proving that the invention was not satanic." [269]As a result, the Kingdom was forced to establish specialized tribunals in specific legal areas to adjudicate matters, and they were under the supervision of a particular ministry with jurisdiction over the tribunal's field. These tribunals included the Tariffs Committee in 1953, the Committee for Commercial Paper Disputes in 1963, and the Committee for the Settlement of Labor Disputes in 1969.[270]

In 1955, a significant step was taken to establish a new judicial institution, which was an administrative court called the Board of Grievances. The Board's duty was to hear and investigate complaints against government officials or governmental agencies filed by Saudi citizens.[271] This institution reported directly to and advised the King about each such case, because he decided how each case was resolved.[272] in 1960, the Hejaz and Najd systems were united under the new Presidency of the Judiciary located in Riyadh after some improvements in the Hejaz judicial system, which were applied to all areas of the Kingdom. Furthermore, the "Presidency of the Judiciary" remained responsible for different religious and legal issues. For example, this institution was in charge of the issuance of fatwas,[273] supervision of religious education, and the appointment of candidates for significant religious positions until 1975 as will be shown later.[274] Between 1970 and 1975, there were further modifications of the Saudi judicial system. The Supreme Judicial Council, the Council of Senior Saudi Scholars, and the Ministry of Justice were new institutions that assumed the tasks of the Presidency of the Judiciary. Moreover, the Judiciary Regulation granted the Sharia court in 1975 general jurisdiction to adjudicate all civil and criminal disputes except in the legal

---

269 VOGEL, Islamic Law and the Legal System of Saudí: Studies of Saudi Arabia 286. 2000.

270 See OTTO, Sharia Incorporated: A Comparative Overview of the Legal Systems of Twelve Muslim Countries in Past and Present 146. 2010.

271 The administrative judiciary in Saudi Arabia passed through several stages. See the administrative judicial website at: www.bog.gov.sa/AboutUs/Pages/Engender.aspx.

272 See OTTO, Sharia Incorporated: A Comparative Overview of the Legal Systems of Twelve Muslim Countries in Past and Present 147-148. 2010.

273 Fatwa is the term for a legal opinion or learned interpretation provided on matters related to Islamic Sharia, see chapter 1 for more details.

274 See VOGEL, Islamic Law and the Legal System of Saudí: Studies of Saudi Arabia 91-93. 2000. Also, OTTO, Sharia Incorporated: A Comparative Overview of the Legal Systems of Twelve Muslim Countries in Past and Present 147-148. 2010.

matters where the specialized tribunals were competent.[275] The Supreme Judicial Council operated under the direct authority of the King and sat at the top of the judicial pyramid, below which were the appellate courts in Riyadh City and Mecca City and smaller courts spread all over the Kingdom. The specialized tribunals were outside of the formal judicial system.[276] They were under the scope of the executive branch. The Supreme Judicial Council was granted judicial, administrative, and regulatory authority.[277]

In 2007, the Kingdom introduced a modern judicial system.[278] The King of Saudi Arabia issued Royal Decree M/78 to reform the judiciary and to create a new court system after the Saudi judicial system was criticized for being slow, arcane, lacking in the safeguards of justice and unable to deal with the modern world especially after the World Trade Organization approved of making the Kingdom a member after 12 years of negotiations.[279] In practice, however, the reforms have yet to be implemented totally, and the judicial system is still in reorganization. The changes included the creation of a Supreme Court, an appeals court for each province, and new specialist first-instance courts that comprise various types of general, criminal, personal status, commercial and labor courts.[280] Furthermore, the new law transferred the Board of Grievances' commercial and criminal jurisdictions to a restructured general judicial system.[281] As a result, the Sharia courts will be more specified, and the workload of the government's mini-tribunals will be transferred to the new courts.

---

275 See VOGEL, Islamic Law and the Legal System of Saudí: Studies of Saudi Arabia 92-93. 2000.

276 The study will explain the legal position of such tribunals when it addresses the structure of the Saudi judiciary.

277 See OTTO, Sharia Incorporated: A Comparative Overview of the Legal Systems of Twelve Muslim Countries in Past and Present 148-149. 2010.

278 The Law of the Judiciary (2007). The law is available on the Ministry of Justice website at: https://www.moj.gov.sa/ar. Also, see RICHARD CLARK, THE DISPUTE RESOLUTION REVIEW 664 (Law Business Research. 2013).

279 See VOGEL, Islamic Law and the Legal System of Saudí: Studies of Saudi Arabia 363-365. 2000. Also, Hossein Esmaeili, On a Slow Boat towards the Rule of Law: The Nature of Law in the Saudi Arabia Legal System, 26 ARIZ. J. INT'L & COMP. L., 32-34 (2009). Also, OTTO, Sharia Incorporated: A Comparative Overview of the Legal Systems of Twelve Muslim Countries in Past and Present 155. 2010.

280 The Law of the Judiciary, Articles 9, 15. 2007.

281 See OTTO, Sharia Incorporated: A Comparative Overview of the Legal Systems of Twelve Muslim Countries in Past and Present 155. 2010.

The new judicial law provides a significant improvement over the old laws and applies a modern form under Islamic Sharia, which could be a big step to improving the legal environment in Saudi Arabia. According to Kenneth Dam:

> A sound judiciary is key to enforcement. No doubt some technical laws can be enforced by administrative means, but a rule of law, in the primary economic sense of protecting property and enforcing contracts, requires a judiciary to resolve disputes between private parties. And protection against the state itself is made easier where the judiciary can resolve a controversy raised by a private party against the state based on constitutional provisions or parliamentary legislation.[282]

Although such reforms seem a great step, the question remains how in practice such modernization will affect the legal environment in Saudi Arabia, especially since the history of the Saudi judiciary showed that there was a radical rejection of or failure to embrace the new models in different stages since King Abdul-Aziz, the founder of the Kingdom, which forced him and the kings after him to create special tribunals outside of the judicial system to resolve various cases in different aspects, which is what the study will address after presenting the structure of the new judicial law in more detail.[283]

C. Structure and Evaluation of the Current Saudi Judiciary

The Supreme Judicial Council consists of the president and ten other members. The members of the Council are the Chief of the High Court, four full-time members with the rank of Chief of the Appellate Court appointed by the King, the Deputy Minister of Justice, the Chief of the Bureau of Investigation and Prosecution, and three members who have the qualifications required to be appellate judges, also appointed by the King. All members of the Council serve for a period of four years, renewable, except for the Chief of the High Court, the Saudi Deputy Minister of Justice, and the Chief of the Saudi Bureau of Investigation and Prosecution.[284] Under the Saudi Judiciary Law of 2007, the Supreme Judiciary Council does not have the duty to serve as the Kingdom's highest court, because the new law, unlike the old law, provides for a new High Court.[285] However, the Council continues to oversee administrative aspects of the judiciary, such as

282 KENNETH W. DAM, THE LAW-GROWTH NEXUS: THE RULE OF LAW AND ECONOMIC DEVELOPMENT 93 (Brookings Institution Press. 2007).

283 CLARK, THE DISPUTE RESOLUTION REVIEW 662. 2013.

284 The Law of the Judiciary Article 5. 2007.

285 Id. at, Article 6 and 11.

promotions, transfers, assignments, secondments, and training, and it monitors the proper discharge of their duties by established rules and procedures to ensure the independence of judges.[286]

1. The New Court System

The new law organized the courts by a new hierarchical structure as set out below in descending order:[287]

- High Court;
- Courts of Appeals; and,
- First-Instance or Trial Courts, which are comprised of:
  - General Courts;
  - Criminal Courts;
  - Personal Status Courts;
  - Commercial Courts; and,
  - Labor Courts.

a. The High Court

The new High Court has the previous Supreme Judicial Council's primary function as the highest authority in the judicial system. The High Court is seated in Riyadh City.[288] This court is comprised of a president, who has the qualifications required for the Chief Appellate Judge, and is appointed by a Royal Order, along with an appropriate number of judges holding the rank of Chief of the Saudi Appellate Court, who is appointed by a Royal Order on the recommendation of the Supreme Judicial Council.[289] The Court exercises its duty through specialized circuits as needed, which consist of three-judge panels except for the Criminal Circuit, which reviews judgments involving certain major punishments, such as the death sentence. The Criminal Circuit is composed of a five-judge panel. Chief

286 Id. at, Article 6.

287 CLARK, THE DISPUTE RESOLUTION REVIEW 664. 2013.

288 The Law of the Judiciary Article 10. 2007.

289 Id.

Judges of the Saudi High Court Circuits are appointed by the Supreme Judicial Council on the recommendation of the Chief of the High Court.[290]

The High Court also supervises the implementation of Islamic Sharia and Saudi regulations, which are consistent with the matters that fall within the general jurisdiction of the judiciary.[291] Furthermore, the Court reviews rulings issued by the Courts of Appeals in a variety of cases. These include cases that involve crimes punishable by death and certain other major crimes;[292] rulings of the Courts of Appeals that may be in violation of Sharia and/or laws issued by the King that are not inconsistent with Islamic Sharia; cases in which judgment was entered by a court that was not properly constituted as provided for by the Judiciary law and other rules; cases in which judgment was entered by an incompetent Court or Circuit Court; and finally cases that involve the failure to frame an incident or impropriety in its description of the case.[293]

b. Court of Appeals

The Court of Appeals hears appealable decisions and judgments from lower courts.[294] The Court issues its decision after hearing the litigants' arguments under the code of criminal procedure and the code of procedure before Sharia Courts.[295] The new Court of Appeals consist of the following circuits: Civil Circuits, Circuits, Criminal Circuits, Personal Status, Commercial Circuits, and Labor Circuits.[296] Each circuit court is composed of a president, who is appointed by the Chief of the Appellate Court, and judges who hold the rank of Appellate Judge.[297] These specialized circuit courts are comprised of three three-judge panels. However, the Criminal Circuit courts, which review matters involving certain major crimes, including those punishable by death, are comprised of five-judge panels.[298]

---

290 Id.

291 The Law of the Judiciary Article 11. 2007.

292 Id. at. Article 11.

293 Id.

294 The Law of the Judiciary Article 17. 2007.

295 Id. at. Article 17

296 Id. at. Article 16

297 Id. at. Article 15

298 Id. at. Article 15.

c. *First Instance or Trial Courts*

According to the new law, the First Instance Courts are established in the Kingdom's provinces, counties, and districts as needed.[299] There are different types of first instance courts: General Courts, Criminal Courts, Commercial Courts, Labor Courts, and Personal Status Courts.[300] The General Courts are established in the provinces and consist of specialized circuits, including Implementation Circuits, Approval Circuits, and Traffic Cases Circuits.[301] The law also gives the Supreme Judicial Council authority to determine whether a circuit should be composed of one or three-judge panels.[302] Moreover, the Criminal Court consists of the following specialized circuits: Qisas Cases Circuits (Retaliatory Punishment), Hudud Cases Circuits (Prescribed Punishments), Ta'zir Cases Circuits (Discretionary Punishment), and Juvenile Cases Circuits. The Criminal Court is normally composed of a three-judge panel except with regard to cases involving minor offenses, which will be specified by the Supreme Judicial Council and which are heard by a single judge.[303] Other types of courts in Personal Status, Commercial, and Labor consist of specialized circuits as needed and are composed of one or more judges as specified by the Supreme Judicial Council.[304]

---

299 Id. at. Article 18

300 See id. at. Article 19-23

301 Id. at. Article 19

302 Id.

303 Id. at Article 20

304 Id. at Article 21.

Chart 3: Structure of the New Court System

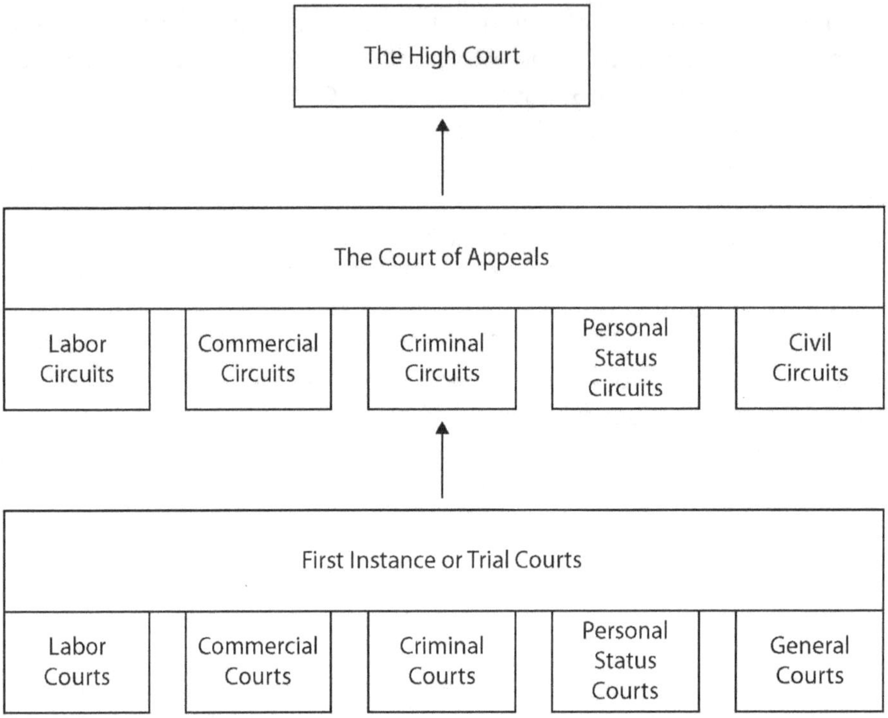

2. Board of Grievances Reform

Royal Decree M/78 brought about the overhaul of Saudi Arabia's Board of Grievances, an independent administrative, judicial commission responsible directly to the King.[305] The pyramidal structure of the new Board of Administrative Courts is parallel to the structure of the Judicial Courts.[306] The Board of Grievances consists of a president with the rank of minister, at least one vice-president, some assistant vice-presidents, and several judges.[307] Vice presidents are appointed by Royal Order from among those who possess the qualifications required to

305 law of the Board of Grievances Article 1 (2007).

306 Id. at article 5

307 Id. at article 2

become Chief of the Appellate Court.[308] The law stipulates that the Board of Grievances is based in the city of Riyadh.[309]

Furthermore, the new Board of Grievances Law establishes an Administrative Judicial Council, which consists of the president of the new Board, the Chief of the High Administrative Court, the most senior vice president of the Board, and four judges of the rank of chief of the Appellate Court appointed by Royal Orders.[310] The Council performs a number of administrative tasks similar to those of the Supreme Judicial Council.[311] The Administrative Judicial Council encompasses several committees, including the Jurisdictional Conflict Committee, the Judicial Disciplinary Committee, and the Department of Judicial Inspection.[312]

The Board of Grievances Law organizes the Board according to the following hierarchical structure as presented in the chart below:

High Administrative Court;

Administrative Courts of Appeals; and,

Administrative Courts.[313]

a. The High Administrative Court

The new High Administrative Court is comprised of a President holding the rank of minister, appointed by Royal Order, and an adequate number of judges, each having the rank of Chief of the Appellate Court. The latter are also appointed by Royal Order, but on the recommendation of the Administrative Judicial Council.[314] The High Court exercises its jurisdictions through specialized circuits as needed, which are composed of three-judge panels.[315]

Furthermore, the High Administrative Court has the competence to review rulings issued or upheld by the Administrative Courts of Appeals if the objection to the judgment involves a violation of Islamic Sharia provisions or any regula-

308 Id. at Article 3
309 Id. at Article 1
310 Id. at Article 4
311 Id. at Article 5
312 Id. at Article 15.
313 Id. at Article 8.
314 Id. at Article 10
315 Id. at. Article 9.

tions that do not contradict Sharia principles; faults in its implementation or interpretation; the entry of judgment from an incompetent court; the entry of judgment from a court not duly constituted as required by the Board of Grievances Law; fault in framing the incident or impropriety in its description; entry of a judgment contrary to another previous decision issued between the parties to the proceedings; or a jurisdictional conflict among the Board's courts.[316]

b. Administrative Courts of Appeals

The new law also establishes Administrative Courts of Appeals.[317] These courts hear appealable decisions from the lower Administrative Courts through Specialized Circuits composed of three-judge panels.[318] Moreover, they render their judgment after hearing the litigants' arguments according to stipulated law.[319]

c. Administrative Courts

The new law establishes Administrative Courts that function through specialized circuits, such as Administrative Circuits, Employment and Disciplinary Circuits, and Subsidiary Circuits.[320] According to the law, the courts are composed of either one or three-judge panels.[321] The Administrative Courts have jurisdiction to review the following cases:

(i) Cases related to the rights provided for in the Civil and Military Service and Pension Laws for government employees and independent public entities and their heirs and claimants;

(ii) Cases of objection filed by parties concerned by administrative decisions, where the reason for such an objection is a lack of jurisdiction, a deficiency in form, a violation or erroneous application and interpretation of laws and regulations, or abuse of authority. The rejection or refusal of an administrative authority to make a decision that it was required to make according to laws and regulations is considered to be an administrative decision;

(iii) Cases of compensation filed by parties concerned against the government and independent public corporate entities resulting from their actions;

---

316 Id. at. Article 11.

317 Id. at Article 8.

318 Id. at Article 12.

319 Id. at Article 12.

320 Id. at Article 8.

321 Id. at Article 9.

(iv) Cases filed by parties regarding contract-related disputes in which the government or an independent public corporate entity is a party;

(v) Disciplinary cases filed by the Bureau of Control and Investigation;

(vi) Other Administrative Disputes; and,

(vii) Requests for implementation of foreign judgments.[322]

Chart 4: Structure of the New Board of Grievances

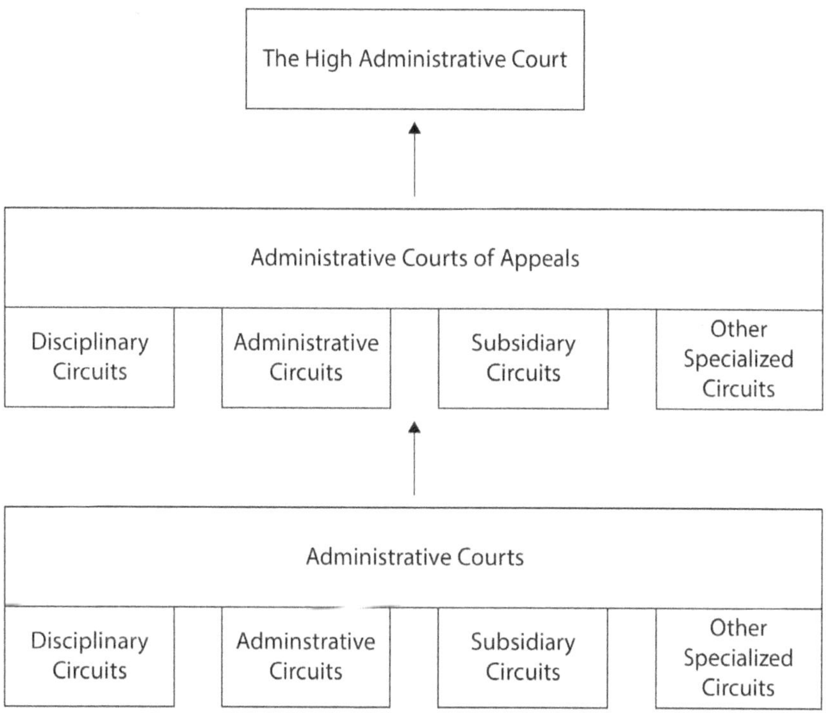

322 Id. at Article 13.

The new laws give the courts the authority to oversee all cases. For example, Commercial and Labor Courts will oversee disputes that had previously been handled by special committee tribunals at the Ministry of Commerce and Industry and the Ministry of Labor.[323] According to Article 25 of the Law of the Judiciary: "Courts shall have jurisdiction in all cases according to the rules outlined in the legal proceedings system and the system of criminal proceedings."[324] However, the Implementing Regulations of the Law of the Judiciary excluded three legal tribunals in three sectors, which are banks, the financial market, and customs. Furthermore, in 2012, Royal Order No. 37441 was issued regarding the formation of the first circle of the Appellate Committee of Banking Disputes and Irregularities.[325] Hence, not just the Banking Dispute Committee will remain, but also more than five years after the issuance of the new Judiciary Law, an appellate review level for this Committee was established, which means that the ruler regulates it as an independent court.

This begs the question why these committees remained even though they were previously criticized for their decisions, which were not always enforceable, and they also were challenged in the Saudi courts.[326] The tribunals always faced questions regarding their impartiality and independence, especially because they were technically under the executive authority.[327] The study needs to shed light on one such committee, which is the Committee for the Settlement of Banking Disputes, the most important legal committee in Saudi Arabia on account of its special nature.

3. The Committee for the Settlement of Banking Disputes

The Committee for the Settlement of Banking Disputes has been operating under the supervision of the Saudi Arabian Monetary Agency for three decades.[328] During this considerable time, this tribunal "committee" has evolved into a critical element for banks that need to enforce judgments against defaulting customers in the Kingdom. The tribunal's jurisdiction over banking disputes and its

---

323 See The Law of the Judiciary, Article 25. 2007.

324 *Id.*

325 Royal Order No. (37441), 2012

326 IBP USA, Saudi Arabia Company Laws and Regulations Handbook 62 (2008).

327 *Id.*

328 The history of this committee is available at Saudian Arabian Monetary Agency website: http://www.sama.gov.sa/en-us/about/pages/samahistory.aspx. See also, BAAMIR, Shari'a Law in Commercial and Banking Arbitration: Law and Practice in Saudi Arabia 179-184. 2013.

application of particular rules and principles to disputes, such as giving effect to the transaction agreed between the parties and upholding recognized, international banking practices, allows banking claims in the Kingdom to be enforced in a way that would not be possible in the general court system of the Kingdom for two main reasons:[329]

The first reason is that Saudi judges do not have the training required to deal with these types of disputes. Nancy Turck says that "the judges are trained only in Sharia and often have no technical background to understand a complex, highly technical case."[330] The study will shed additional light on this matter later. The other cause for creating this committee is that the legal right of the bank to collect interest is unacceptable under Sharia as applied in the Saudi courts. Abdurahman Bammmir says about this issue:

> It should be noted that the committee was established as a compromise between Sharia and economic interest in order to remove the burden from judges who faced a religious dilemma when deciding on disputes related to banking business. The dilemma occurred because of the gap between the legal right of the bank to collect the amount of interest in full, as stipulated in the agreement between the parties following the principle of pacta sunt servanda, on the one hand, and the fact that the whole transaction is unacceptable under Sharia on the other.[331]

As a result, this committee is the only authority in the Kingdom that recognizes charging interest as a valid legal practice.[332]

Since the Banking Dispute Committee was created in 1987, there have been elements of ambiguity around the Committee's procedural rules and the enforceability of the Committee's decision. However, in practice, the Committee has always borne many of the characteristics of a court, even if it is totally dependent

329 *Id.* at. 180-181.

330 Turck, THE INTERNATIONAL LAWYER, 418 (1988). See also, Karl, GEO. WASH. J. INT'L L. & ECON., 144-145 (1991). Also see VOGEL, Islamic Law and the Legal System of Saudí: Studies of Saudi Arabia 8-32. 2000.

331 BAAMIR, Shari'a Law in Commercial and Banking Arbitration: Law and Practice in Saudi Arabia 180. 2013.

332 See *id.* at. 149.

on other governmental bodies, such as the Ministry of the Interior, for the enforcement of its judgments.[333]

In 2012, the new Royal Order No 37441 clarified the status of the Committee's powers and processes.[334] According to the new Royal Order, the Committee has to establish Circuits as needed. Each circuit or committee consists of three members and an additional alternate member to allow for rotating members. The members must have legal qualifications and experience and be familiar with banking transactions. Moreover, at least one of the members must be Islamic Sharia qualified. All members are appointed for four years by Royal Order.[335]

The Committee shall hear disputes based on the information and evidence provided in the claim file and the agreements entered into between the disputing parties. The Committee's decisions must be made by majority, and there is a right to appeal within 30 days to the new Appellate Committee.

The new Appellate Committee created by the Royal Order consists of one or more circuits, as needed. Each Appellate Committee circuit consists of three members, at least one of whom must be Sharia qualified. The Appellate Committee is competent to hear objections filed against decisions of the Committee for the Settlement of Banking Disputes as stipulated in the Royal Order. The Appellate Committee renders decisions by majority, and its decisions are not subject to appeal before any other authorities.[336]

Furthermore, a new limitation period was issued. Claims will not be heard by the Committee if they are filed more than five years after the due date of the claimed amount or from the date when the claimant becomes aware of the event that is the subject of the application, unless there is a justification that is acceptable to the Committee.[337] Also, the Royal Order expressly gives the Committee the authority to freeze a debtor's bank- and investment accounts and entitlements at governmental authorities, restrict the debtor from dealing with national bodies and banks, and issue travel bans after its final judgment.[338]

333 See *id.* at. 179-181.

334 Royal Order No. 37441 dated 1 July 2012.

335 *Id.*

336 *Id.*

337 *Id.*

338 *Id.*

In sum, the Royal Order makes it eminently clear that the Committee for the Settlement of Banking Disputes is truly a court, and it is to be expected according to the provisions of the Royal Order that its circuits will expand the capacity of the system across the country to cover the increase of banking disputes in the Kingdom. However, establishing committees under executive supervision and outside of the judicial branch can compromise their independence. Michael Lindsey says:

> Middle Eastern countries are generally characterized by weak judiciaries, which are not independent from the executive branches of government. The judges in the region are often government employees working under the executive through the minister of justice. This gives the executive branch the power to interfere in the judicial process. Egypt and Lebanon, for example, have highly developed judiciaries but are often under pressure from the executive branches of their governments.[339]

No doubt, the existence the several committees in different legal areas raises serious inquiries about the quality of judges in the Kingdom especially after establishing a new judicial system and failing to depend on it and enforce it totally. Hence, the study will examine and analyze in the next part the qualifications, job performance, and training of Saudi judges in more depth.

D. Saudi Judges

The study will divide this subject into three main points:

1. Qualifications and Training

Since Islamic Sharia is the primary authority for Courts in Saudi Arabia, the Law of the Saudi Judiciary requires that each candidate for a judicial position has graduated from one of the Sharia colleges in the Kingdom of Saudi Arabia.[340] Although there are some law schools in Saudi Arabia, only Sharia graduates are qualified to be judges in Saudi Arabia with other requirements as stipulated by the Saudi law.[341] Hence, the Sharia schools in Saudi Arabia should be studied in more detail.

---

339 Radwa S Elsaman, Factors to Be Considered Before Arbitrating In the Arab Middle East: Examples of Religious and Legislative Constraints, 1 INT'L COM. ARB. BRIEF, 12-13 (2011).

340 The Law of the Judiciary, Article 31. 2007.

341 See Rayan Alkhalawi, Legal Education Reform in Saudi Arabia: A Case Study of Taibah University, 12-15 (2015).

Historically, the Kingdom of Saudi Arabia began opening Sharia schools at different times to meet different needs in the courts, education and other required governmental and non-governmental organizations starting with the Sharia College at Umm Al-Qura University in 1949. At the time, this was the only school that offered a legal education in the Kingdom in the form of a Sharia degree. Thereafter, different Sharia schools opened, including the Sharia College at the University of Dammam in 2013. Currently, there are thirteen Sharia schools in the Kingdom.[342]

The Sharia schools in Saudi Arabia depend in their teaching on the Hanbali School of Islamic jurisprudence by studying medieval texts that were written by the Muslim jurists in that era.[343] For example, the major textbook in the Sharia College at Al Imam Muhammad Ibn Saud Islamic University is Alrrud Almurabbae book for Mansour Al Bahuti, who died in 1641. This book consists of seven volumes, and it is a mandatory textbook, which is studied for all four years of study at the Sharia school.[344] As a result of the singular focus on Islamic jurisprudence, graduates of the Sharia schools lack knowledge about the country's regulations and laws, while they enjoy far-reaching implementations of legal systems of the past.[345] This explains the historic refusal of the Sharia judges to apply modern regulations, which was the one of the main reasons why the Kingdom was forced to create the legal administrative committees. It is clearly the result of the nature of their education.

The Kingdom tried to enable judges to attain the highest levels of education by creating an Institute of Public Administration in 1961,[346] and the Judicial Institutional Academy in 1966,[347] to train Saudi judges, enhance their expertise, develop their skills, and provide them the legal knowledge and skills they need in practice.[348] The law encourages the judges to join these institutions by stipulation in Article 43 by providing that graduation from one of these schools

342 See id. at, 8-12.

343 See VOGEL, Islamic Law and the Legal System of Saudí: Studies of Saudi Arabia 8-9. 2000.

344 See Al Imam Muhammad Ibn Saud Islamic University website at https://admission.imamu.edu.sa/programs/ProgramsLinks.

345 VOGEL, Islamic Law and the Legal System of Saudí: Studies of Saudi Arabia 363. 2000.

346 See Institute of Public Administration website available at http://www.ipa.edu.sa/Arabic/About/summary/Pages/default.aspx.

347 See Judicial Institutional Academy website available at https://sij.imamu.edu.sa/Pages/default.aspx.

348 *Id.*

is equivalent to four years of service in the courts.[349] In response to questions about the efficiency of these academic institutions to meet the judiciary requirements, especially after the new judiciary law, a reorganization of the Judicial Institutional Academy was approved in 2013 so that it would better serve the needs of the new judiciary law.[350] However, even this reform did not live up to the requirements of the judges, especially because the law of the judiciary stipulates that a holder of a Sharia certificate does not require additional training.[351] Consequently, the impact of these institutions cannot be tested easily in the Saudi legal practice.

As an important step forward, after realizing that graduates from Sharia schools are not sufficiently exposed to the country's contemporary laws and regulations, some programs were established in Saudi Arabia that combine both Islamic Sharia and law courses.[352] For instance, in 2010, Al-Imam Muhammad Ibn Saud Islamic University created a bachelor degree in law that is affiliated with the law program at the College of Sharia. Since it is part of the College of Sharia, the law program aims to teach the principles of law with Islamic Sharia[353]. However, it is still not clear if these types of programs will be overseen by the Sharia departments or by law schools. Presently, they are under evaluation as new programs, and the effort still needs time to see its results in the legal environment in the Kingdom. In addition to establishing specialized tribunals, the Kingdom established additional law schools to prepare specialists to work on different legal aspects in the state. Some of them are currently in public and private schools, which offer law degrees that give the right to practice law in Saudi Arabia but not to enter the judiciary. In spite of all efforts at bringing the two educational programs closer together, Islamic Sharia and law schools continue to have entirely different approaches in their curricula.[354]

349 The Law of the Judiciary. 2007.

350 See Judicial Institutional Academy website available at https://sij.imamu.edu.sa/Pages/default.aspx.

351 See The Law of the Judiciary, Article 31. 2007.

352 See Alkhalawi, 10 (2015).

353 For more information about this school, see its website at http://www.imamsh.org/i/?page_id=2036.

354 See Alkhalawi, 10 (2015).

2. Job Performance and Independence

The Saudi judiciary law clearly recognizes that an independent judiciary is the core to protecting the rights and freedoms of the people by providing a fair trial in an independent and impartial court system. Article 46 of the Saudi Basic Law of Governance states that "the judiciary shall be an independent authority and, in their administration of justice, judges shall be subject to no authority other than that of Islamic Sharia."[355] The same independence principle is embodied in many provisions of the Law of the Judiciary, which provides several safeguards. For instance, Article 1 of the Law of the Judiciary states that "judges are independent and, in the administration of justice, they shall be subject to no authority other than the provisions of Sharia and laws in force."[356] The same Article provides that "no one may interfere with the Judiciary."[357] Article 5 of the Ordinance concerning the Prosecution of Ministers prohibits any types of interference with judicial affairs and makes personal interference in the affairs of the judiciary a crime punishable by imprisonment for a term ranging from three to ten years.[358]

Furthermore, one of the significant characteristics of judicial independence is the protection of judges from removal from office or transfer or any act that might compromise their independence. Article 2 of the Law of the Judiciary states that "judges are not subject to removal from office except in the cases set forth herein."[359] In addition, Article 3 stipulates that "judges may be transferred to other positions only with their consent, and they are not subject to removal from office except in cases specified by the law, such as retirement."[360]

Moreover, special procedures are provided and safeguards needed to ensure the protection and independence of judges in conditions that warrant disciplining judges. The Law of the Judiciary states expressly that the Supreme Judicial Council is the only authority empowered to discipline a judge to ensure that the executive authority cannot interfere with the judicial system.[361]

---

355 The Basic Law of Government. 1992.

356 The Law of the Judiciary. 2007.

357 *Id.*

358 Ordinance Concerning the Prosecution of Ministers No/508 (1961). Available at the Bureau of Experts of the Council of Ministers website at: https://www.boe.gov.sa/ViewSystemDetails.aspx?lang=ar&SystemID=122&VersionID=152#M17986.

359 The Law of the Judiciary. 2007.

360 *Id.*

361 *Id.* at Article 59. 2007.

One of the most significant advantages of the new judiciary law is an application of the judicial independence principle, as evidenced by the limit imposed on the Ministry of Justice administrative power over the judiciary. According to the law, the right to supervise various aspects of the courts and judges was transferred from the Minister of Justice to the new Supreme Judicial Council. These aspects include judges' promotion, transfer, assignment, replacement, and training, and monitoring the proper discharge of their duties and other matters.[362] Hence, the new judicial system provides greater independence for judges and their adherence to Islamic rules clearly with adequate safeguards to protect them from an arbitrary transfer, dismissal, or legal action.

However, Kenneth Dam says: "Judicial independence does not depend solely on the structure of government and the judiciary's formal role within it. It also depends on the judges themselves."[363] Hence, how the Saudi judges exercise their considerable independence in the practice over cases is a factor for consideration. The study found that the courts in the Kingdom depend on the traditional approach taken by Muslim judges in the Islamic history. Accordingly, the study will examine the traditional Muslim judge in Islamic history in the next section.

3. Ijtihad in Saudi Courts

Unlike Western law, in Islamic Sharia, each case has to be viewed based on its own merit, and past decisions can be considered only as guidance for the new cases under most Muslim jurist opinions.[364] This position is still being maintained by some states like Malaysia[365] and Saudi Arabia.[366] Frank Vogel,who spent several months in the Kingdom of Saudi Arabia to study the Saudi judicial system, says: "We find that Saudi qadi (judge) is in fact given freedom to practice a broad Ijtihad and is not restricted to the Hanbali or any other school."[367] He also says:

362 *Id.* at. Articles 6 and 58.

363 DAM, The Law-Growth Nexus: the Rule of Law and Economic Development 111. 2007.

364 See Ata Ur Rehman, et al., The Concept of Independence of Judiciary in Islam, 4 INTERNATIONAL JOURNAL OF BUSINESS AND SOCIAL SCIENCE (2013). Also, Sa'id Adekunle Mikail & Mahamad Arifin, Application of Doctrine of Judicial Precedent in Shariah Courts, MALAYSIAN COURT PRACTICE BULLETIN (2014).

365 As the courts in Malaysia are divided into the three types and one of them is a Sharia court, the study addresses the Sharia court. See Mikail & Arifin, MALAYSIAN COURT PRACTICE BULLETIN, (2014).

366 *Id*

367 VOGEL, Islamic Law and the Legal System of Saudí: Studies of Saudi Arabia 107. 2000.

> "Saudi qadis (judges) do occasionally apply rules from other schools (in Islamic jurisprudence) when they believe that such rules are suited to the case before them".[368]

The functional and regulatory obligations of a Muslim judge have been clearly identified by Caliph Umar, the second leader of the Muslim state after Prophet Muhammad, to Abu Musa al-Ash'ari: "If you gave judgment yesterday and today, upon reconsideration, come to the correct opinion, you should not feel prevented by your first judgment from retracting... Use your brain about matters that perplex you and to which neither the Quran nor the Sunnah seems to apply."[369] Clearly, this letter is contrary to the doctrine of judicial precedent and endorses the duty of Muslim judges to make decisions based on their own personal interpretations. They are not prevented nor bound by their previous decisions. In addition, there is a rule upon which most Muslim jurists depend that provides that "Ijtihad cannot be revoked by another Ijtihad."[370] In fact, following this practice of the Saudi courts led to two significant consequences.

The first result is the difficulty in appointing enough competent judges who possess the qualification of exercising Ijtihad in deciding cases.[371] Historically, a Mujtahid must possess a number of important qualifications.[372] He must know enough Arabic so that he can understand both the Holy Quran and the Sunnah of the Prophet without having to rely on translations; he must possess an extensive, comprehensive knowledge of the Quran and the Sunnah; he must have a full understanding of the Quran's legal contents, understanding the particular texts that refer to legal rules and the incidence of abrogation in the Sunnah of the prophet; he must possess the ability to confirm the consensus of the Companions and the ability to understand fully the objectives of Islamic Sharia; he must be dedicated to protecting the Five Principles of Islam, which are life, religion, intellect, lineage, and property; he must be able also to distinguish strength and weakness in reasoning; and, finally, he must be known publicly as a sincere and good person.[373] In the history of Islam, the most famous scholars in Islamic Sharia

---

368 *Id.* at. 126.

369 Mikail & Arifin, MALAYSIAN COURT PRACTICE BULLETIN, 1-2 (2014).

370 *Id.*

371 See The Administrative Sheikh Ibrahim Hugail Chairman of the Saudi Board of Grievances and the Chairman of the Judicial Council (Al Majd TV ed., 2010) [Television interview].

372 Mujtahid is a person with the necessary knowledge and experience to exercise Ijtihad or Islamic jurisprudence.

373 MOHAMMAD HASHIM KAMALI, PRINCIPLES OF ISLAMIC JURISPRUDENCE 374-377 (The Islamic Text

were candidates to be appointed as judges;[374] in those days, the community was small, and people did not need many judges. However, nowadays, to achieve the goals of its legal system and the protection of the rights of its people, Saudi Arabia faces a shortage of judges in the Saudi courts, as the Chairman of the Board of Grievances, the Chairman of the Judicial Council, and the Administrative Sheikh Ibrahim Hugail stated during a television interview in 2010.[375]

The other significant obstacles within the Saudi judiciary system is that the decisions rendered by courts are random, because they do not follow the rule of stare decisis or a similar doctrine to bind judges to their prior decisions or to those issued by higher courts.[376] This obstacle forced the Kingdom to establish the specialized tribunals outside of the judicial system to assure investors, companies, and banks about their investing in the country as discussed earlier. Recently, the country started publishing previous court decisions in different volumes, which are available on the website of The Board of Grievances; however, for now they are not complete and additional cases are being added too slowly.[377] Publication of case law seems an extraordinary step for the Saudi judiciary. What needs to be remembered, however, is that past rulings do not mean that any other judge will rule the same way in the future or even explain why he is ruling differently. Nevertheless, having access to previous decisions may help to predict future outcomes.

E. Possible Solutions and Improvements

The Kingdom has tried during its history to balance between the sovereignty of Islamic Sharia as the constitution of an Islamic state and a modern and efficient legal system that enables its citizens and its international partners to pursue a broad range of personal and business ventures. However, in practice, the Kingdom established various types of courts; the Sharia courts on the one side, with a focus on family and criminal law, and the special tribunals with the Committee for the Settlement of Banking Disputes on the other. The different types of courts have at times been at odds and it is hard to see how they can

Society. 1991).

374 Rehman, et al., INTERNATIONAL JOURNAL OF BUSINESS AND SOCIAL SCIENCE, 72-73 (2013).

375 Chairman of the Board of Grievances and the Chairman of the Judicial Council. 2010.

376 See VOGEL, Islamic Law and the Legal System of Saudí: Studies of Saudi Arabia 107-165. 2000. Also see Karl, GEO. WASH. J. INT'L L. & ECON., 149-150 (1991).

377 These decisions are available at the Board of Grievances website at: http://www.bog.gov.sa/ScientificContent/JudicialBlogs/Pages/default.aspx.

merge into a unified court system in the foreseeable future. Similar obstacles have been encountered by other Muslim states, such as Malaysia, which has three types of courts, of which the Sharia court is one, none of which deal with civil legal aspects.[378] The study found that it is difficult to make Sharia courts oversee entire cases in the way it was done in classic Islamic history. However, the Ottoman Turkish Empire had an approach that may offer a potential solution for the Kingdom, because, like Saudi Arabia, the Ottoman Empire sought to apply Islamic Sharia in all aspects of life. Some modifications may be required, however.

The Mejelle Ottoman Turks made the first attempt to codify a part of the Islamic jurisprudence for the Islamic state. The Mejelle was the civil law of the Ottoman Empire in the late 19th and early 20th centuries. The Mejelle issued sixteen volumes containing 1,851 articles compiled between 1869 and 1876. It entered into force in 1877. Its design, structure and approach were clearly influenced by the earlier European codifications, in particular the French Code Civil and the German BGB. To facilitate the codification, the Ottoman codes were based only on the Hanafi School of Islamic jurisprudence, which was the official school of the Ottoman Empire.[379] A codification based on Western principles of legislative drafting as well as Islamic jurisprudence appears to be a useful proposal for Saudi Arabia. It can be improved beyond the accomplishments during the Ottoman Empire by basing the law on all of the Islamic schools instead of just the Hanafi School to better serve the modern needs in the legal environment in the Kingdom. However, because a change to the Ijtihad methods as applied in Saudi courts can only be successful after significant and successful reforms of legal education, which may take a long time, the Kingdom needs a temporary solution to deal with arbitration and ADR. This solution has to address the entire range of court involvement in ADR, beginning with assistance during the arbitration process and finishing with enforcement and recognition. After examining the problem, the study found that banking disputes, as explained earlier, faced the same type of challenges with Saudi courts and that the Kingdom provided a successful temporary solution. This solution was the establishment of a tem-

378 Mikail & Arifin, MALAYSIAN COURT PRACTICE BULLETIN, 3 (2014).

379 See BHALA, Understanding Islamic Law 1240-1247. 2011. For more information about the al majallah, see also Gemmell, SANTA CLARA J. INT'L L., 176-177 (2007). Najmaldeen K. Kareem Zanki, Codification of Islamic Law Premises of History and Debates of Contemporary Muslim Scholars, INTERNATIONAL JOURNAL OF HUMANITIES AND SOCIAL SCIENCE 2014. See also FM Goadby, The Moslem Law of Civil Delict as Illustrated by the Mejelle, 21 JOURNAL OF COMPARATIVE LEGISLATION AND INTERNATIONAL LAW (1939). See also Ya'akov Meron, Mejelle Tested by Its Application, The, 5 ISR. L. REV. (1970).

porary independent specialized committee (tribunal) for banking disputes. The study is proposing that Saudi Arabia take the same approach to arbitration and ADR, namely the establishment of a specialized and independent committee or tribunal to support ADR and arbitration until the courts are able to do so in a reliable and consistent way.

The proposed tribunal could operate under the Ministry of Commerce and Investment, which has experience in supervising different types of commercial disputes, including disputes involving commercial paper. The proposed tribunal would have jurisdiction over arbitration affairs and its application of mandatory rules, the arbitration agreement and the upholding of recognized international commercial arbitration norms and practices, which would likely allow arbitration awards to be recognized and enforced in a way that could not be possible were such cases to be submitted to the Saudi courts. Furthermore, like the banking disputes tribunal, the proposed tribunal should have the power to establish circuits as needed. Each circuit should be comprised of three members, and all members should have a legal qualification and experience and also be familiar with arbitration and ADR principles. In addition, at least one member must also be Sharia qualified to ensure that decision comply with general Islamic Sharia principles, as they are the primary source of law of the Kingdom of Saudi Arabia.

F. Conclusion

A state's legal framework represents a critical part of the international trade and investment system; decisions about significant investments in any foreign country necessarily require a certain level of knowledge and understanding about that country's legal system. In the case of Saudi Arabia, one of the most significant aspects is the Saudi judicial system and its court procedure. The Kingdom of Saudi Arabia has a dual judicial system comprised of the General Courts System and an independent administrative judiciary known as the Board of Grievances (Diwan Al-Mazalem); there are also several administrative Committees (mini-tribunals), which have jurisdiction over specific cases under the authority of different governmental bodies.

In 2007, the Kingdom started to implemented a modern judicial system by Royal Decree M/78 to reform the judiciary and to create a new court system after the Saudi judicial system was criticized domestically and internationally for being slow, arcane, lacking in safeguards of justice, and unable to deal with the modern world. However, the reforms have not yet been completely implemented, and the judicial system is still in the process of reorganization. The chapter shows that

Sharia as applied in the Saudi courts has a special nature that differs from the laws applied in a typical secular court. Consequently, it may be critical to potential foreign investors to understand how Saudi courts work, including the application of Sharia law. Choosing the right attorney and arbitral tribunal is crucial to assist and guide investors in how to comply with judgments and awards as required by the legal process in the Kingdom, including at enforcement stages.

Chapter 3

Arbitration in Saudi Arabia Under the New Arbitration Law in Comparison to International Arbitration Rules

As mentioned earlier, the Saudi ruler, to improve the legal system in the Kingdom for the investment environment, established a new Arbitration Law in 2012. The provisions of the new Arbitration Law, as will be seen in this chapter, are based on the UNCITRAL Model Law on International Commercial Arbitration.[380] The International Model Law covers all stages of the arbitral process and was initially adopted by the United Nations Commission on International Trade Law (UNCITRAL) in 1985. Since then, it has been amended several times.[381] The Model Law was primarily developed to help countries to modernize their arbitration rules and to achieve a level of harmonization between the countries in the global community.[382] Naturally, different states have taken different approaches toward this model. Some of them adopted it verbatim, such as Australia and Scotland,[383] while others, such as the Kingdom of Bahrain, adopted only the international commercial arbitration section.[384] Other states used it as a starting point for a proprietary drafting project, such as England.[385] The Kingdom of Saudi Arabia accepted those parts that did not violate Islamic Sharia as applied in the Kingdom and as will be explained more extensively later.

As a result, this chapter aims to identify the most significant features of the new Saudi arbitration system through the study of its statutory provisions. Our focus will be on the fundamentals and concepts of the arbitration process and its governing controls and the freedom of parties to the conflict in the selection of laws and rules that apply to arbitral tribunals when deciding the merits of the

---

380 This model law is available at: //www.uncitral.org/pdf/english/texts/arbitration/ml-arb/07-86998_Ebook.pdf.

381 See BORTOLOTTI, Drafting and Negotiating International Commercial Contracts: a Practical Guide 68-69. 2013. Also, MOSES, The Principles and Practice of International Commercial Arbitration 45. 2012.

382 *Id.*

383 See ASSOCIATION, AAA/ICDR Handbook on International Arbitration and ADR 21. 2006.

384 The law is available at the Ministry of Justice, Islamic Affairs and Awqaf in the Kingdom of Bahrain website at: http://www.moj.gov.bh/default9787.html?action=article&ID=941.

385 ASSOCIATION, AAA/ICDR Handbook on International Arbitration and ADR 21. 2006.

dispute. This study will also compare the new Saudi arbitration system with the international model and other international rules for international commercial arbitration.

The new Saudi law consists of eight sections containing fifty-eight articles. It begins with the general provisions which clarify the terms and definitions of the arbitration process and it ends with the part that determines the date of the validity of this system from the date of its publication in the Official Gazette.[386]

A. General Provisions of the New Saudi Arbitration Law

1. Definition of the Arbitration Agreement

In the first article of the new Saudi arbitration law, the Saudi ruler defines the arbitration agreement: "It is an agreement between two or more parties to refer to the arbitration all or some of certain disputes that have occurred or might occur between them concerning a particular regulatory relation, whether it is in the shape of a contract or not, whether the arbitration agreement appears as an arbitration condition mentioned in a contract or as an independent arbitration stipulation."[387] Under Article 7 of the UNCITRAL Model Law on International Commercial Arbitration, the arbitration agreement is explained as "an agreement by the parties to submit to arbitration all or certain disputes which have arisen or which may arise between them in respect of a defined legal relationship, whether contractual or not. An arbitration agreement may be in the form of an arbitration clause in a contract or the shape of a separate agreement."[388] Comparing the text of the definition of the arbitration agreement in the Saudi regime with the Model Law, it is clear that they are identical in all essential parts of the definition of the arbitration agreement, which can be separated into three points.

1) The nature of the arbitration agreement, which is dedicated to the principle of free will in resolving disputes that have arisen or which may arise between commercial parties. Consequently, the parties give up the right to have current or possible future disputes decided by national courts, which would be the normal procedure if the arbitration agreement did not exist.

2) The nature of the existing particular legal relationship, whether it is contractual or non-contractual.

386 Arbitration Law (Saudi Arabia 2012).

387 *Id.*

388 UNCITRAL Model Law on International Commercial Arbitration (2006).

3) Two types of arbitration agreement: one contained within the main contract, and the other contained within a separate agreement. The first type of arbitration clause continues to be valid even if the contract is not and allows an arbitration to proceed regardless of whether any of the parties argues that the contract is invalid. The second type of arbitration agreement can be concluded at the time when a dispute is already imminent and the parties, for whatever reasons, did not provide for ADR or arbitration in their original contract. This was confirmed by the Saudi Arbitration Law in Article 9, which provides: "The arbitration agreement may be precede any dispute whether the agreement is independent, self-contained, or contained in a particular contract..."[389] Hence, the text of the definition of arbitration in the Saudi regime is clear and specific to explain the nature of the arbitration agreement, and its modernization is identical to the modern international model for arbitration in the global community.

2. Scope of the Arbitration Law

Most jurisdictions in the different legal systems around the world exclude some types of subjects from arbitration. These matters usually involve fundamental principles of the legal system or the most fundamental notions of morality and justice.[390] According to Richard H. Kreindler:

> The question of arbitrability differs from country to country, but as a general rule it can be said that certain subject matters of a public nature are not arbitrable. Thus in most countries, claims related to labor, employment and family relationship are viewed as not arbitrable. For similar reasons, securities, antitrust and intellectual property claims have been considered non-arbitrable in some countries, although these are precisely where arbitration is in fact becoming more acceptable as an alternative to litigation.[391]

In this regard, the new Saudi Arbitration Law does not specify the types of arbitral disputes to which it applies; however, it determines the subjects to which it does not apply. Article 2 states:

> Without prejudice to provisions of Islamic Sharia and international conventions to which the Kingdom is a party, the provisions of this Law

389 Arbitration Law. 2012.

390 See BORTOLOTTI, Drafting and Negotiating International Commercial Contracts: a Practical Guide 64-67. 2013.

391 ASSOCIATION, AAA/ICDR Handbook on International Arbitration and ADR 5. 2006.

> shall apply to any arbitration regardless of the nature of the legal relationship subject of the dispute, if this arbitration takes place in the Kingdom or is an international commercial arbitration conducted abroad and the parties thereto agree that the arbitration is subject to the provisions of this Law. The provisions of this Law shall not apply to personal status disputes or matters not subject to reconciliation. [392]

It is apparent from the text that the Saudi Arbitration Law has limited the scope of the arbitration law, namely its applicability to all types of arbitration of whatever nature and form as long as the subjects are not personal status matters or matters in which reconciliation is not allowed. However, the Saudi law does not explain the types of issues that cannot be arbitrated. As arbitrability normally has a close link to public policy, the study will describe this issue more extensively in Chapter 4, where the enforcement of arbitration will be discussed.

Furthermore, the new Arbitration Law, for the first time, breaks the restriction that barred arbitration from being used to resolve domestic issues. Consequently, arbitration can now be used both for domestic and international business disputes. As a result, the Arbitration Law defines the situations in which arbitration is applicable to international disputes similar to the principles found in the Model Law.[393] The situations are:

A) If the main business center for each party is in more than one country when the parties conclude the arbitration agreement; if either party has several commercial centers, the center that is more attached to the dispute shall prevail; if either or both parties have no specific commercial center, their usual place of residence shall prevail;

B) If the main commercial centers for all of the arbitrating parties is located in the same country when the parties conclude the arbitration agreement, and one of the places listed below is outside of that country:

1) The arbitration venue as specified in or referred to in the arbitration agreement;

2) The place of implementation of a significant part of the commitments arising out of the business relationship between the two parties;

---

392 Arbitration Law. 2012.

393 UNCITRAL Model Law on International Commercial Arbitration, Article 1(3). 2006.

C) If the parties to the arbitration agreement agree to take recourse to an organization, permanent arbitration commission or an arbitration center, whose head office is located outside of the Kingdom of Saudi Arabia;

D) If the subject of the dispute covered by the arbitration agreement relates to more than one country. [394]

According to the general provisions, the new Saudi Law provides wide freedom to parties to choose the procedural rules they want to use and to agree about the extent to which the arbitration centers they wish to use locally or internationally are similar to the international model law for arbitration, provided that Islamic Sharia as applied in the Kingdom is not violated.

B. The Arbitration Agreement

According to the new Arbitration Law, the arbitration agreement can be entered into before a dispute arises or when a dispute has arisen. In the latter event, such an agreement is often referred to as a submission agreement.[395] Unlike some international rules,[396] the Saudi Law differentiates between the arbitration clause and the submission agreement by requiring that the submission agreement must define the nature of the dispute being submitted to arbitration; otherwise, the arbitration agreement will be void.[397] Furthermore, the arbitration agreement also can be in the main contract or independent of it.[398] Article 9 of the Law states:

> The arbitration agreement may be concluded prior to the occurrence of the dispute whether in the form of a separate agreement and stipulated in a specific contract. The arbitration agreement may also be concluded after the occurrence of a dispute, even if such dispute was the subject of an action before the competent court.[399]

Hence, the new Arbitration Law is flexible about submitting to the arbitration agreement, even if the dispute was already the subject of an action before a competent court.

---

394 Arbitration Law, Article 3. 2012.

395 *See id.* at, Article 9.

396 See New York Convention Article II (1958). See also UNCITRAL Model Law on International Commercial Arbitration, Article 7. 2006.

397 Arbitration Law, Article 9. 2012.

398 *Id.* at Article 9.

399 *Id.*

1. Requirement of a Written Agreement

Commercial contracts between parties can usually be oral or written in varying forms, such as faxes and emails, and the legal systems consider these kinds of forms differently. However, the arbitration agreement, under the New York Convention[400] must be in writing to be enforced. Similar to the New York Convention and the Model Law, the new Saudi Arbitration Law requires that the arbitration agreement be in writing. However, under what circumstances must the arbitration agreement be in writing under the new Saudi law?

The New York Convention, to which the Kingdom of Saudi Arabia acceded,[401] requires that the parties must sign an arbitration agreement, or they may exchange letters and telegrams. According to Margaret Moses:

> A number of interpretive issues are presented by the language of paragraph 2 (writing requirements in the New York Convention). First, does the signature requirement apply to both the contract containing the clause as well as to the submission agreement, or only to the submission agreement? Second, does the signature requirement also apply to the exchange of letters and telegrams? Different courts have taken different positions.[402]

As a result, in some cases, courts have strictly enforced the writing requirement even though disputing parties have manifested their agreement through conduct or trade practice, which may make it less effective and may not achieve its main goal of ensuring that such foreign awards are recognized and generally capable of enforcement globally in the same way as domestic awards. Furthermore, it does not consider the modern communication in the trade environment by electronic communication, which has become common place, such as

400 The International Convention on the Recognition and Enforcement of Foreign Arbitral Award, which is known as the New York Convention, was adopted by the United Nations on 10 June 1958 and entered into force on 7 June 1959. This Convention requires courts of contracting countries to give effect to private agreements to arbitrate and to recognize and enforce arbitration awards made in other contracting states. Widely considered the essential instrument for international arbitration, it applies to arbitrations that are not regarded as domestic awards in the country in which recognition and enforcement are sought. Though other international conventions apply to the cross-border enforcement of arbitration awards, the New York Convention is by far the most important. See http://www.uncitral.org/uncitral/en/uncitral_texts/arbitration/NYConvention.html.

401 See Contacting states at the New York Convention website http://www.uncitral.org/uncitral/en/uncitral_texts/arbitration/NYConvention.html.

402 See MOSES, The Principles and Practice of International Commercial Arbitration 21. 2012.

emails.[403] However, to modernize the New York Convention and harmonize the law among countries, the United Nations Commission on International Trade Law (UNCITRAL) amended Article 7 to align the model law with current practices in international trade. The new amendment does not require the signature, and, as long as the arbitration agreement is written in any form, it will be valid,[404] which will provide more flexibility in the trade environment instead of imposing a restricted form. Moreover, electronic communication is considered a written form of the agreement as shown in Article 7 of the Model Law.[405]

Unlike the old Saudi Arbitration Law, which was not as definitive or as expansive,[406] the agreement to arbitrate in the new law can be in different types, such as in print or electronic format. It can also be as simple as making reference to arbitration provisions found in another document, contract or international convention or by referring to the procedural rules of an arbitration institute or even ad hoc rules. It can also be by referral and reference to any document containing the arbitration clause, but the new law requires that such a referral be clear and unambiguous.[407]

In fact, the Saudi ruler did well to follow the Model Law as amended and by making written correspondence by mail, or by electronic means, sufficient evidence of the intention to arbitrate. This will make the Law more flexible and also complies with modern life in which the use of electronic methods of communications is most common. However, the agreement to arbitrate still has to be concluded by persons with full legal capacity, as Article 10 of the new Saudi Arbitration Law explains.

2. Full Legal Capacity of the Arbitrating Parties

According to Article 10, the full legal capacity to conclude the arbitration agreement comprises two major points.

---

403 See id. at.21 - 23.

404 UNCITRAL Model Law on International Commercial Arbitration. 2006.

405 Id.

406 Saud Al-Ammari & A Timothy Martin, Arbitration in the Kingdom of Saudi Arabia, 30 ARBITRATION INTERNATIONAL, 392 (2014).

407 Arbitration Law, Article 9(3). 2012.

a. *Full Legal Capacity*

One of the essential formal requirements for the arbitration agreement is that it be concluded by persons having the legal capacity to dispose of their rights or by their designees or by corporate persons.[408] Accordingly, the parties must be able to complete the disposal of the rights and perform all legal actions with regard to those rights, whether negatively or positively. According to Article 10 of the new Law, this condition is not required of the principal only, but extends to his agent and attorneys, who have entered into an agreement to arbitrate. Since the Saudi Arbitration Law does not specify the age for legal capacity, the study will look to other Saudi laws to see how the Saudi ruler has handled such matters. Most other Saudi laws provide for 18 years as the age of legal capacity. For instance, the Child Law protects "the child who has not yet reached the age of 18 years old."[409] The study proposes that the Saudi ruler specify the age for legal capacity in the new implementing regulations for the new Arbitration Law to be clear for foreign parties, who are not familiar with Saudi law, and, at the same time, resolve ambiguities about this issue that have arisen in the Saudi courts. It may surprise an international reader that this matter has different opinions in the Islamic jurisprudence,[410] which may open the door for Ijtihad (the process of legal reasoning through which the jurist derives the law from the Quran and the Sunnah of the Prophet Muhammad by independent reasoning)[411] as applied in the Saudi courts. This, in turn, can lead to unpredictable outcomes.

The person who is authorized to sign the arbitration contract for legal entities in the Kingdom depends on the type of legal entity involved. For instance, for joint stock companies, Saudi law provides in Article 82 that the Chairman of the Board of Directors represents the company before the courts, tribunals and third parties. He also has the authority to delegate some of his powers to one of the Board members or to a third party.[412] As a result, every legal entity has a different form of legal capacity depending on the Law of Companies.

---

408 Id. at. Article 10.

409 The Child Law Protection Art 1 (2014). See also Saudi Labour Law Art 2 (2005).

410 See BHALA, Understanding Islamic Law 541-543. 2011.

411 For more information about ijtihad, see the ijtihad section of Chapter 1 of this study and also ijtihad in the Saudi court in Chapter 2.

412 The Saudi Corporate Law, Article 82(1), Royal Decree No. M/3 (2015).

b. *Governmental Saudi Agencies and Ministries*

Since the early attempts to explore oil in the Kingdom of Saudi Arabia in the 1950s, the arbitration method was the primary way of resolving disputes between Saudi and foreign companies.[413] However, a significant action changed the attitude of the Saudi Government toward arbitration. The famous arbitration case of 1958 involving the Arabian American Oil Company, hereinafter referred to as "ARAMCO",[414] had a significant effect on the legal system of arbitration in Saudi Arabia. Greatly disappointed with the decision in that case, the Kingdom enacted resolution No. 58 in 1963, which prevented all government agencies and ministers from resorting to arbitration without prior approval from the Saudi Council of Ministers.[415] Hence, the absence of such approval of the Saudi Prime Minister renders an arbitration agreement void.

One of the disadvantages of the new Arbitration Law is that it has left this restriction on governmental agencies intact. Article 10 states: "Government bodies may not agree to enter into arbitration agreements except upon approval of the Prime Minister unless allowed by a special provision of law."[416] This restriction may deprive them of the advantage of using arbitration, as it is a useful method especially in the international community.

C. The Arbitration Tribunal

The crux of the arbitration process as a private method of dispute resolution is the arbitrator, who needs safeguards to comply with applicable national laws while achieving the goals of the parties in entering into arbitration. Frances Kellor, an early leader of the American Arbitration Association, describes the need for an effective arbitrator as follows:

> When an arbitrator is conscientious, painstaking and fair in arriving at his decision and bases that decision upon the proofs submitted; when he brings his competence and common sense to bear impartially upon the issue before him; when he follows the procedure laid down in the

---

413 See Sayen, U. Pa. J. Int'l Econ. L., 909-910 (2003).

414 This case related to the interpretation of the 1933 Concession Agreement between the Government of the Kingdom of Saudi Arabia and the Arabian American Oil Company, see Arbitration between The State of Saudi Arabia and The Arabian American Oil Co. 27 I.L.R. 117 (1963).

415 See Id. See also Al-Ammari & Martin, Arbitration International, 389 (2014).

416 Arbitration Law. 2012.

> arbitration law and in rules of procedure and makes each party feel that he has had a fair trial; then arbitration is a proceeding which commands confidence, and the award is one that satisfies justice.[417]

Hence, the Kingdom in the new Law set up significant safeguards as will be shown in the following points.

1. Appointment of Arbitrators

a. The Number of Arbitrators

The arbitration tribunal in commercial arbitration usually consists of a sole arbitrator or a three-arbitrator panel.[418] To resolve a dispute thorough international rules, the parties are usually free to choose the number of arbitrators. Having one or three arbitrators has advantages and disadvantages. For example, a single arbitrator could decide the outcome of the dispute quickly without having to confer with any other arbitrator at any stage of the arbitration, and a single arbitrator system is less expensive than a panel of three.[419] However, the three arbitrators bring more to the arbitration in terms of their collective experience and knowledge than a sole arbitrator. In addition, with three arbitrators, each party is able to choose an arbitrator who comes from a similar cultural or legal background, especially in international arbitration, where parties are, by definition, from different countries or even continents.[420]

In this regard, the new Saudi Law follows most of the international rules, which provide the parties the freedom to choose the number of arbitrators.[421] However, the Saudi law provides a safeguard against a potential road block that can arise in the arbitration process if the arbitrators cannot agree on a resolution of the dispute, because it requires that the number of arbitrators be an odd number. Otherwise, the arbitration shall be void.[422] Similarly, Article 12 of the ICC rules states: "The disputes shall be decided by a sole arbitrator or by three arbitra-

---

417 ASSOCIATION, AAA/ICDR Handbook on International Arbitration and ADR 81. 2006.

418 See MOSES, The Principles and Practice of International Commercial Arbitration 122-123. 2012.

419 See ASSOCIATION, AAA/ICDR Handbook on International Arbitration and ADR 72. 2006.

420 See MOSES, The Principles and Practice of International Commercial Arbitration 122-123. 2012.

421 See ICC Rules of Arbitration Article 12 (2012). Also, see ICDR Arbitration Rules Article 11and 12 (2014).

422 Arbitration Law Article 13. 2012.

tors."[423] Hence, the new Arbitration Law complies with most international standard rules in choosing the number of arbitrators.

However, if the parties cannot agree on the number of arbitrators, the international arbitration rules provide for a different solution. Some of them will appoint one arbitrator unless the matter seems particularly complex.[424] Other rules default to three arbitrators regardless of the circumstances.[425] In contrast, the new Saudi Law does not mention the possibility of a disagreement over the number of arbitrators between the parties. However, the Law, in Article 15(2), provides the competent court with the power to determine this issue according to the circumstances. The study does not see the difference between stating that the determination of the number of arbitrators depends on the complexity of the matter in dispute, as the ICC Rules provide, or failing to specify the number in the agreement and leaving it, as Saudi Law provides, for the competent court to decide. As a practical matter, either way, the court will usually evaluate the complexity of the case and then decide the appropriate number of arbitrators.

b. Qualifications

1) Knowledge and Experience

One of the significant advantages of arbitration is choosing the decision- maker who will resolve the dispute depending on the experience and understanding in a particular matter instead of a randomly selected judged in the national courts. For this issue, the Ministry of Justice in Saudi Arabia established a service to research the accredited arbitrators through its website quickly by searching by name in case the arbitrator is known or search by city. Then the researcher can query each arbitrator about his experience before choosing the arbitrator.[426]

2) Lawyers and Non-Lawyers

Many arbitration matters need specific knowledge and experience in a specific industry or science, which makes arbitration an excellent way to choose arbitrators from among many fields. However, according to Margaret L. Moses:

---

423 ICC Rules of Arbitration. 2012.

424 See ICDR Arbitration Rules Article 11. 2014. Also see ICC Rules of Arbitration 12(2). 2012.

425 See UNCITRAL Model Law on International Commercial Arbitration Article 10(2). 2006. Also see James E Meason & Alison G Smith, Non-lawyers in international commercial arbitration: gathering splinters on the bench, 12 NW. J. INT'L L. & BUS., 40 (1991).

426 This service is available at ministry of justice website at: https://www.moj.gov.sa/ar/eServices/Pages/Muhamah.aspx.

> There is also a risk that non-lawyers will not understand the basis for procedural or substantive rulings and that too much time may be lost educating them about the law. In addition, there have been occasional complaints about non-lawyers who lacked a judicial temperament, made editorial comments on the testimony, or openly ridiculed participants.[427]

As a result, the Saudi ruler was more flexible by combining the advantages of choosing a lawyer and non-lawyer in some particular circumstances. The Saudi Law divides the matter into different types depending upon the number of arbitrators involved. If there is one arbitrator, he must hold at least a university degree in Sharia or the law. If the arbitration tribunal has more than one arbitrator, it is sufficient that the chairman meets this requirement.[428] In this way, the Saudi Law allows what is common practice in international commercial arbitration, namely a choice of lawyers and non-lawyers to serve on the arbitration panel, especially in complicated cases, which need both of them.[429]

The Saudi Law requires that at least one arbitrator hold an Islamic Sharia degree if there is a single arbitrator or if he is the chair of an arbitration panel.[430] If the law of arbitration is Saudi law, this matter is not a problem, because Saudi law depends on Islamic Sharia. However, if the law is foreign, the parties may be disadvantaged because the arbitrator who holds an Islamic Sharia degree often has less sophisticated skills and experience in other areas of legal practice, which forced the Kingdom to create special tribunals outside of the judiciary to settle different types of legal matters. As a result, the study suggests that the Law should add experience in the relevant legal field as a condition to be met by the holder of an Islamic Sharia degree.

3) Reputation

Because arbitrating parties will not have a chance to appeal a decision on the merits they should choose an arbitrator whose integrity and abilities are beyond doubt. Hence, the Saudi Law requires that the arbitrator be of good conduct and reputation.[431] In practice, the arbitrating parties will gain this information from

427 MOSES, The Principles and Practice of International Commercial Arbitration 124. 2012.

428 See Arbitration Law, Article 14(3). 2012.

429 See Meason & Smith, NW. J. INT'L L. & BUS., (1991).

430 Arbitration Law, Article 14(3). 2012.

431 *Id.,* Article 14. The new Arbitration Law does not define the terms "good conduct and reputation" under this article. However, the implementing regulation of the old law de-

inquiries and investigations about potential arbitrators from previous arbitrating parties who chose a particular arbitrator.

4) Other Requirements

The new Arbitration Law reduced the requirements that had to be met by arbitrators under the old law. The old law and its implementing regulations also required that arbitrators be of full legal capacity and highly qualified as a Saudi judge, which means that the arbitrator had to be male and Muslim. Also, arbitrators had to be either Saudi citizens or non-Saudi Muslims with a professional designation.[432]

Article 14 of the new Arbitration Law requires that arbitrators must be of full legal capacity,[433] good conduct and reputation, and have a university degree in either Islamic Sharia or law. If the arbitral tribunal has more than one arbitrator, only the tribunal chair must meet the last requirements.[434] This means that the new Law avoids the requirements on arbitrators that are based on nationality, religion, gender or race, thereby joining most international rules. For example, Article 11(1) of the UNCITRAL Model Law states: "No person shall be precluded by reason of his nationality from acting as an arbitrator unless otherwise agreed by the parties."[435] However, in spite of this significant step by the new Law to comply with international rules and standards, there is still a risk that questions about religion and gender may be challenged in the Saudi courts based on the violation of Islamic Sharia, which always has to be respected pursuant to Article 2 of the new Law.[436] Because there is a debate about such matters between Muslim jurists, in particular, whether women and/or non-Muslims can serve as judges,[437] the

---

fined these terms as not having been convicted of a criminal offense or an offense involving moral turpitude, someone against whom a disciplinary decision of dismissal from a public office has not been issued, and someone who has not declared bankruptcy except if he has been rehabilitated. See Implementing Regulations of Arbitration Law, Article 4 (1983). Note that the study does not discuss this matter in more detail, because it is expected to be taken care of in the new implementation regulation for the new Law, as it was previously done with the old law.

432 See also Al-Ammari & Martin, ARBITRATION INTERNATIONAL, 392 (2014).

433 The study discussed the full legal capacity in the Saudi law in the legal framework of the arbitration agreement section of this chapter.

434 Arbitration Law, Article 14(3). 2012.

435 UNCITRAL Model Law on International Commercial Arbitration. 2006.

436 Arbitration Law. 2012.

437 See Faisal Kutty, Shari'a Factor in International Commercial Arbitration, The, 28 LOYOLA INT'L & COMP. L. REV., 52-56 (2006).

Saudi courts can challenge this matter based on Ijtihad as explained in Chapter 2. Hence, the safe way is to state explicitly in the Law or in the implementing regulations that a particular gender or religion is not required for an arbitrator. This was done, for example, in the Egyptian arbitration law.[438]

2. Obligations of Arbitrators

a. Independence and Impartiality

Two of the primary obligations of arbitrators in the international rules and the new Saudi Law are to be independent and impartial. However, what do independent and impartial mean? Impartiality, in general, means that the arbitrator is not biased and has no reason to favor one party over the other.[439] Independence means that the arbitrator has no financial interest in the case and does not depend on one of the parties financially, such as if he is employed by one of the parties.[440]

Most of the international rules set up specific provisions to deal with this case.[441] Among the rules that have gained wide acceptance within the international arbitration community are the IBA Guidelines on Conflicts of Interest in International Arbitration. These rules are commonly used as Guidelines when making decisions about prospective appointments and disclosures.[442] In addition, the rules provide precise instructions on independence that require arbitrators to disclose whether they have any past or present relationship with any party, directly or indirectly, or even with any of the parties' counsel, whether the relationship was financial, professional, social or otherwise. The rules also provide that certain more remote relations or issues do not require disclosure, thus

---

438 The article of the Egyptian law provides: "The arbitrator is not required to be of a given gender or nationality, unless otherwise agreed upon between the two parties or provided for by law." The Egyption Arbitration Law, Article 16(2), No. 27/1994 (1994).

439 For more information about such matters in international arbitration, see ASSOCIATION, AAA/ICDR Handbook on International Arbitration and ADR 86-89. 2006. See also, Leon Trakman, The Impartiality and Independence of Arbitrators Reconsidered, 6-9 (2007). Also, see MOSES, The Principles and Practice of International Commercial Arbitration 135-136. 2012.

440 For more information about such matters in international arbitration, see Trakman, 6-9 (2007). Also see, MOSES, The Principles and Practice of International Commercial Arbitration 135-136. 2012.

441 See ICC Rules of Arbitration, Article 11(2),(3). 2012. Also see ICDR Arbitration Rules, Article 13. 2014.

442 See IBA Guidelines on Conflicts of Interest in International Arbitration (2014).

providing clarity and certainty to both sides.[443] Furthermore, the UNCITRAL Model Law provides that arbitrators must immediately disclose all circumstances that may raise doubts about their impartiality and independence not just at the time of their appointment but also until the end of the arbitration proceedings.[444] The Saudi Law, in Article 16, follows the Model Law by stating: "An arbitrator shall have no vested interest in the dispute. He shall also, from the time of his appointment and throughout the arbitration proceedings, disclose to the arbitrating parties in writing any circumstances likely to give rise to justifiable doubts as to his impartiality or independence, unless he has already informed them thereof."[445] The study sees that the Model Law and the new Saudi law make the issues of impartiality and independence comprehensive by applying them to all types of doubts and during the entire arbitral process. These points will prevent any chance that an arbitrator may be challenged by one of the parties for illegitimate reasons, just to delay the arbitration process, for example.

b. Other Obligations

In addition to independence and impartiality, other obligations are imposed on arbitrators that are expressly or implicitly different from international rules. The most fundamental obligation is to issue enforceable awards. Of course, the primary goal of arbitrating parties is to get an enforceable arbitral award that resolves their dispute. According to Martin Platte:

> "Whichever way one prefers to look at it [...], it does not matter much whether the duty to render an enforceable award stems from contract, status or law. It is clear that, when the parties agree on arbitration as the method of resolving their dispute, they have in mind an award which they can enforce."[446]

Article 41 of ICC Rules expresses this obligation: "In all matters not expressly provided for in the Rules, the Court and the arbitral tribunal shall act in the spirit of the Rules and shall make every effort to ensure that the award is enforceable

443 *See id.* Also see ASSOCIATION, AAA Handbook on International Arbitration and ADR 133-137. 2010.

444 UNCITRAL Model Law on International Commercial Arbitration, Article 12(1). 2006.

445 Arbitration Law. 2012.

446 Martin Platte, An Arbitrator's Duty to Render Enforceable Awards, 20 JOURNAL OF INTERNATIONAL ARBITRATION, 308 (2003). See also MOSES, The Principles and Practice of International Commercial Arbitration 145-147. 2012.

at law."[447] Similar to the ICC, the LCIA states in Article 32.2: "For all matters not expressly provided in the Arbitration Agreement, the LCIA Court, the LCIA, the Registrar, the Arbitral Tribunal and each of the parties shall act at all times in good faith, respecting the spirit of the Arbitration Agreement, and shall make every reasonable effort to ensure that any award is legally recognized and enforceable at the arbitral seat."[448] Hence, the international rules expressly mention this obligation and consider it an ethical and moral obligation of arbitrators.

The new Saudi Law does not address this issue. However, it can be inferred from its articles that the arbitrator should care about the parties' goals in their agreement, which impose these moral and ethical obligations upon him implicitly.[449]

Another significant obligation on an arbitrator is to follow carefully the specific obligations imposed upon him by the arbitration agreement. In arbitration, the arbitration agreement is the primary source of law that every arbitrator must follow unless contradicted by a mandatory rule according to the applicable law stated in the contract.[450] According to Karl-Heinz Bockstiegel: "The principle of party autonomy is fundamental to arbitration in general and to international arbitration in particular."[451] He added that "the wide acceptance of party autonomy in national laws throughout the world might arguably be considered as leading to party autonomy being today a general principle of law."[452] One of the provisions that arbitrating parties may impose is not participating in *ex parte* communications with parties, unless a party is choosing its arbitrator pursuant to the agreement.[453] Most, if not all, international rules provide in various articles that the parties are free to agree in their arbitration agreement upon the rules of the arbitration. Article 19 of the UNCITRAL Model Law states that the arbitrating parties are free to agree on the procedure to be followed by the arbitral tribunal in conducting the proceedings.[454] The ICC similarly states that the arbitrating parties have the right to agree on the rules of law to be applied by the arbitral

447 ICC Rules of Arbitration. 2012.

448 LCIA Arbitration Rules (2014).

449 See Arbitration Law, Articles 15, 23, and 25. 2012.

450 See BORTOLOTTI, Drafting and Negotiating International Commercial Contracts: a Practical Guide 14-15. 2013. See also ASSOCIATION, AAA/ICDR Handbook on International Arbitration and ADR 82. 2006.

451 ASSOCIATION, AAA/ICDR Handbook on International Arbitration and ADR 115. 2006.

452 *Id.* at 117.

453 See MOSES, The Principles and Practice of International Commercial Arbitration 14-15. 2012.

454 UNCITRAL Model Law on International Commercial Arbitration. 2006.

tribunal to the merits of such dispute. The arbitral tribunal must also consider the provisions of the arbitration agreement between the parties and of any relevant trade usages. In addition, the arbitral tribunal must take the powers of an amiable compositeur or decide ex aequo et bono only if the arbitrating parties have agreed to give it those powers.[455] The new Saudi Law follows the international rules and the Model Law in this regard. One of the relevant articles is Article 25 of the new Law, which states that the arbitrating parties may agree on arbitration procedures to be followed by the arbitration tribunal in conducting the proceedings, including their right to subject the method to valid rules of any organization, agency or arbitration center within Saudi Arabia or abroad, unless such rules should conflict with the provisions of Islamic Sharia, which is a mandatory law in the Kingdom.[456]

In conclusion, the Kingdom's new Law complies with most international rules by given the arbitrating parties virtually unlimited rights to choose the applicable procedural and substantive rules.

Moreover, the Saudi ruler follows the UNCITRAL Model Law in requiring that arbitrators and the arbitral panel act with due care in treating the parties in arbitration equally and providing full opportunity to each party to show and present their case and its attachments.[457] Specifically, the Saudi Law states in Article 27 that arbitrating parties shall be treated equally and that they must have equal and full chances to present their cases or defenses.[458] In sum, the study concludes that the Saudi law complies with most international rules concerning the arbitrators' obligations to the arbitrating parties, which allows the international community to rely on the Saudi Law without reservations.

3. Challenges to an Arbitrator

In arbitration proceedings, one of the arbitrating parties may challenge an arbitrator at the time when the arbitral tribunal is constituted or at a later time, if facts become known that shed doubt on the independence and impartiality of the arbitrator.[459] The challenge may be based on the two principal grounds of

455 ICC Rules of Arbitration 21. 2012.

456 ICC Rules of Arbitration 21. 2012.

457 See UNCITRAL Model Law on International Commercial Arbitration Article 18. 2006.

458 Arbitration Law. 2012.

459 See Ilhyung Lee, Practice and Predicament: The Nationality of the International Arbitrator (with survey results), 31 FORDHAM INT'L LJ (2007). See also, MOSES, The Principles and Practice of International Commercial Arbitration 147. 2012.

conflict of interest or improper conduct of the arbitrator, such as having inappropriate ex parte communications with or benefits from one of the arbitrating parties or if the arbitration proceedings are not moving forward in a swift and efficient manner.[460] Most international rules provide for procedures for challenging an arbitrator to save the parties from unfair or dilatory actions and to ensure, as much as possible, that problems do not appear with a tribunal or an award at the enforcement stage.[461]

The rules in most international arbitration institutions provide the bases upon which the arbitrating parties may challenge an arbitrator. For instance, the LCIA Rules provide that the right to challenge is based upon justifiable doubts regarding aspects such as impartiality and independence, and the rules explain further that the arbitrator shall be considered unfit if he does not handle the case fairly or impartially or does nor conduct the arbitration proceedings with diligence.[462] Some international rules do not specify the basis upon which to challenge an arbitrator and leave them open, such as the ICC Rules. Article 14(1) of the ICC Rules states: "A challenge of an arbitrator, whether for an alleged lack of impartiality or independence, or otherwise, shall be made by the submission to the Secretariat of a written statement specifying the facts and circumstances on which the challenge is based."[463] However, the new Saudi Law closely follows the UNCITRAL Model Law about challenging an arbitrator, as stated in Article 12(2).[464] The new Saudi Law specifies two bases for a potential challenge to an arbitrator:

1) There are justifiable doubts about the impartiality or independence of the arbitrator; or

2) The arbitrator does not have the qualifications agreed upon in the arbitration agreement.

In addition to these conditions, under the new Saudi Law and the UNCITRAL Model Law, the arbitrating parties have the right to disqualify an arbitrator appointed by another arbitrator or in whose appointment he participated, if

---

460 Id.

461 See MOSES, The Principles and Practice of International Commercial Arbitration 147. 2012.

462 See the LCIA Arbitration rules Article 10.1, 10.2. 2014.

463 ICC Rules of Arbitration. 2012.

464 See UNCITRAL Model Law on International Commercial Arbitration. 2006. Also see Arbitration Law Article 16(3). 2012.

relevant reasons become known after the appointment of that arbitrator and not before.[465]

As a result, the Model Law and Saudi Law make it accurate and clear for arbitrating parties and arbitrators to determine the basis for challenging an arbitrator. If either of the two grounds were not known before but become known after the appointment of an arbitrator, this arbitrator can be challenged to prevent any simple ways of slowing or delaying the arbitration proceedings, to prevent unfair outcomes, to ensure enforceability of the award, and in general to save the parties and arbitral tribunal time, energy, and costs.

If an arbitrating party intends to challenge an arbitrator, it must follow the specified procedure carefully under the chosen law to avoid losing the right to challenge before the competent authority. Under the LCIA Rules, a party who intends to challenge an arbitrator must send a written statement to the arbitral tribunal within 14 days of becoming aware of any circumstances that would support a challenge.[466] The LCIA adds that the written statement must also be forwarded to the LCIA Court and all other arbitrating parties within the stated period of time.[467] The ICC Rules say that the submission must be sent to the Secretariat by stating the facts and circumstances upon which the challenge is based within 30 days from receipt of the notification of the appointment or confirmation of the arbitrator by the party or from the date the concerned matter was known from the facts and circumstances on which the challenge is based, if such date is after the receipt of such notification.[468] If the challenge is unsuccessful, most arbitration rules provide an opportunity to take the challenge to court, and the decision of the courts is usually not subject to appeal.[469] According to Article 13(3) of the UNCITRAL Model Law:

> If a challenge under any procedure agreed upon by the parties or under the procedure of paragraph (2) of this article is not successful, the challenging party may request, within thirty days after having received notice of the decision rejecting the challenge, the court or other authority specified in article 6 to decide on the challenge...[470]

---

465 See Id.

466 See LCIA Arbitration rules Article 10.3. 2014.

467 Id.

468 ICC Rules of Arbitration Article 14(1),(2). 2012.

469 See MOSES, The Principles and Practice of International Commercial Arbitration 148. 2012.

470 UNCITRAL Model Law on International Commercial Arbitration. 2006.

Saudi Law, which follows the UNCITRAL Model Law, divides this matter into two sections:

1) If the arbitration agreement includes a procedure for disqualifying an arbitrator, the agreed upon procedure must be followed.

2) If the arbitration agreement does not include such a procedure, specific procedures must be followed:

a) The party seeking to challenge the arbitrator must send to the arbitral tribunal a written statement explaining the grounds for the disqualification of the arbitration tribunal within five days of the date when the party first knows of the formation of the arbitration tribunal or any circumstances justifying such disqualification.

b) If the arbitrator who is sought to be disqualified does not recuse himself or the other party objects to the disqualification within five days from the date of submission thereof, the arbitration tribunal must decide on the disqualification matter within fifteen days from the date of receipt of such submission.

c) If the disqualification issue is not resolved by the arbitral tribunal, the party seeking disqualification may submit its petition to a competent court within thirty days after the tribunal denies the request for disqualification, and the relevant court decision must not be subject to appeal.[471]

The Saudi Law also provides a condition that a disqualification submission will not be accepted from an arbitrating party who has previously submitted a petition to disqualify the same arbitrator in the same arbitration on the same grounds.[472] As a result, the new Saudi Law follows the UNCITRAL Model Law with regard to challenges of an arbitrator, which is a marked improvement in the arbitration process in Saudi Arabia.

Article 16(2) of the Saudi Arbitration Law permits a challenge to an arbitrator by law even if neither arbitrating party requests it. The arbitrator is barred from considering or hearing a case for the same reasons for which a judge is prohibited from hearing a case by Saudi law.[473] Hence, the study will examine the statement of the grounds upon which a judge may be prevented from considering a case

---

471 See Arbitration Law, Article 17(1). 2012. And see UNCITRAL Model Law on International Commercial Arbitration, Article 13. 2006.

472 See Arbitration Law, Article 17(2). 2012.

473 *Id.*, at Article 16(2).

to know the grounds upon which an arbitrator can be prevented from considering an arbitration even without a request by either of the arbitrating parties.

According to Article 90 of the Saudi Procedure Law:

> A judge shall be forbidden to consider the case and hear it, even if not requested by one of the litigants in the following circumstances:
>
> A) If he is a spouse, relative, or in-law of one of the litigants until the fourth degree.
>
> B) If he or his wife have an existing dispute with one of the litigants in the case, or with his wife.
>
> C) If he is an agent, trustee, or presumptive heir for one of the litigants. Or if he is the spouse of the guardian, the values of one of the litigants. Or if he is a kinship or in-law until the fourth degree of such guardian or values.
>
> D) If he, his wife or his relatives, spouse's siblings or whom he is an agent or trustee, or values in it interest in the case.
>
> E) If he has issued a fatwa (the legal opinion or interpretation of Islamic Sharia), or pleaded for a litigant in the case, or written about it or expressed an opinion even if that was before he joined the judiciary. Or if he has reviewed it as a judge or an expert, or arbitrator, or had been a witness in, or engaged in any investigative procedures in that case.[474]

The Implementing Regulations of the Saudi Procedure Law explain that kinship and in-laws up to the fourth degree are:

> 1) First class: fathers, mothers, grandfathers, and grandmothers through the subsequent generations.
>
> 2) Second class: children and their children and their descendants through the subsequent generations.
>
> 3) Third degree: brothers and sisters whether full brothers and sisters or not, and their children and the children of their children through the subsequent generations.

474 Shari'ah Procedure Law (2013).

4) Fourth degree: uncles, aunts, and their children and maternal uncles and maternal aunts and their children.[475]

Moreover, the Implementing Regulations also show that litigation with the judge or his wife does not preclude the consideration of that case if the litigation arose after the case was assigned to him. As a result, what occurs after the start of the proceedings will not prevent the judge from considering the case. Consequently, a party cannot have a judge removed by filing a lawsuit against the judge or his wife during the consideration of the case. Moreover, having issues a fatwa prevents a judge from considering a case only if he was reviewing the same case. In addition, the Implementing Regulation explains that the judge is also prevented from hearing a case, if he wrote a lawsuit memorandum, answer, objection or consultation and the like in the interests of one of the disputing parties. If the judge is the relative or in-law of either or both of the disputing parties, he shall also be barred from reviewing the case. Finally, all of the conditions set forth in this Article of the Procedure Law shall prevent the judge from participating in the proceedings at all stages whether the judge and disputing parties are aware of the conflict or not.[476]

The reference to the qualifications required for a judge is actually a disadvantage of the new Saudi Arbitration Law. It leads to several consequences. First, it limits the autonomy of the arbitrating parties and their freedom to choose their arbitrator(s) by agreement, which is one of the significant advantages of arbitration over litigation for the international community. Second, it creates the possibility that a competent court may intervene to impose an arbitrator, if the parties cannot agree on one who complies with the legal requirements. This is a bigger issue than it may seem, especially since the decision of the competent court to appoint a certain arbitrator is not subject to appeal. As a result, this condition does not comply with the primary goal of arbitration, which is based on the full will of the arbitrating parties. For instance, even though the arbitrator may be a relative of either or both of the arbitrating parties, they may want the arbitrator to serve, because they trust him or her and are confident that his relationship will not affect the outcome of their dispute. Hence, it is better to refer to the will of the parties in choosing the arbitrator instead of setting up mandatory rules to achieve arbitration goals which do not comply with the modern trends of commercial arbitration rules in the global community.

475 Implementing Regulations for the Shari'ah Procedure Law, Article 7(1) (2014).

476 *Id.*, at. Article 94.

4. Failure or Inability to Act

The international arbitration rules also address the situation when an arbitrator does not act as he supposed to in moving the arbitration proceedings along efficiently or if he takes too long to issue the award.[477] The new Saudi Law again follows the international arbitration rules as they handle this matter. If an arbitrator becomes unable to perform his function or for other reason fails to act in a timely manner, there are two possible outcomes. Firstly, he may withdraw from his office, or the arbitrating parties may agree on removing him. Otherwise, any party may request the competent court or administrative authority in an international organization to replace the arbitrator, and the decision shall not be subject to appeal.[478] Only if the dismissal of the arbitrator is not attributed to any misconduct on the side of the arbitrator, will he be entitled to be compensated.[479]

5. Replacement of an Arbitrator

If an arbitrator's seat becomes vacant for any reason, for example if the arbitrator resigns, withdraws or is successfully removed, the international arbitration rules address this situation.[480] The new Saudi Law follows the international rules and especially the UNCITRAL Model Law by giving priority to the arbitration agreement if the arbitrating parties adopted specific rules for the issue. If the parties have not or cannot agree on how to resolve such a matter, the competent court will appoint the replacement arbitrator.[481]

The biggest question whenever an arbitrator has to be replaced is whether or to what extent the arbitration procedure has to be restarted or repeated. Most international arbitration rules refer this decision to the arbitral tribunal. According to Article 15(4) of the ICC Rules: "The arbitral tribunal shall determine if and to what extent prior proceedings shall be repeated before the reconstituted arbitral

---

477 Many jurisdictions and arbitration laws, such as the English arbitration act, Hong Kong's arbitration law, and the AAA arbitration rules, explicitly recognize that justice should not be delayed in the arbitration process. See ASSOCIATION, AAA/ICDR Handbook on International Arbitration and ADR 68-72. 2006.

478 See ICDR Arbitration Rules, Article 14(3),(4). 2014. Also see UNCITRAL Model Law on International Commercial Arbitration, Article 14(1). 2006. And see Saudi Arbitration Law, Article 18. 2012.

479 See LCIA Arbitration Rules, Article 10.7. 2014. Also see Saudi Arbitration Law, Article 18(2). 2012.

480 See UNCITRAL Model Law on International Commercial Arbitration, Article 15. 2006. Also see Saudi Arbitration Law, Article 19. 2012.

481 See Saudi Arbitration Law, Article 15. Also see ICC Rules of Arbitration, Article 15. 2012.

tribunal."[482] Similarly, the ICDR Rule states: "The arbitral tribunal shall determine if and to what extent prior proceedings shall be repeated before the reconstituted arbitral tribunal."[483] If two arbitrators remain on a three-person arbitral tribunal, some international arbitration rules state that the remaining arbitrators may decide to continue the arbitration proceedings, which is prudent especially if the departing arbitrator leaves the arbitral panel near the end of the arbitration proceedings[484].

However, the new Saudi Arbitration Law does not differentiate between an arbitral panel with three arbitrators and a tribunal with a sole arbitrator when it comes to repeating the arbitration proceedings after a petition to disqualify an arbitrator is granted, whether by the arbitration tribunal itself or by the competent court when considering an appeal. Hence, the Saudi Law requires that all previous arbitration procedures, including any arbitration award, be deemed null and void.[485] Again, the new Law provides mandatory rules that may waste the arbitrating parties' money, time and energy. It makes it impossible for the remaining arbitrators to complete the process or for a newly constituted tribunal to pick it up in the middle, even if the tribunal could otherwise do so with the full support of both parties. Instead of having a mandatory rule in this regard, Saudi law should leave the decision whether to start over or continue to the parties and the arbitral tribunal, because arbitration is based on the voluntary agreement of the parties and the arbitral panel is the closest to the case. Saudi law should limit itself to provide safeguards for the case that the parties cannot agree or the tribunal takes a decision that is unacceptable to at least one of them.

6. Arbitrator Immunity

One of the crucial issues relating to the arbitral tribunal is arbitrator immunity. The arbitrators are supposed to do their job in accordance with their duties and obligations. However, if the arbitrators fail in one or more of these duties, they may be liable to the arbitrating parties for any damage that results. There are two major arguments about this issue.[486]

---

482 ICC Rules.

483 ICDR Arbitration Rules, Article 15(2). 2014.

484 *Id.,* at Article 15(3). See ASSOCIATION, AAA/ICDR Handbook on International Arbitration and ADR 62. 2006.

485 See Saudi Arbitration Law, Article 17(4). 2012.

486 See Susan D Franck, Liability of International Arbitrators: A Comparative Analysis and Proposal for Qualified Immunity, The, 20 NYL SCH. J. INT'L & COMP. L. (2000).

One of the legal opinions is that the arbitrators should be granted broad immunity for several reasons. The arbitrators are performing a quasi-judicial duty. Consequently, they should be protected against suit by disgruntled parties. Without immunity, they may be intimidated during the arbitration process by either or both of the parties, which may affect an arbitrator's independence and lead to compromising the arbitral award and its finality. Moreover, without such immunity, many qualified individuals may be unwilling to serve as an arbitrator, which may adversely affect the arbitration method in general.

In contrast, others argue that the finality of arbitral awards must not be more significant than protecting the arbitrating parties from potential injustice inflicted by carelessness, fraud, or abuse of power by an arbitrator, who is protected by immunity.[487]

As a consequence of the differences of opinion, the immunity accorded to an arbitrator depends on the place of arbitration and the country in which a complaint arises. It is, therefore, necessary to look more closely how different international arbitration rules handle this issue.

The legal systems handle the immunity of arbitrators differently unless the acts are criminal in nature, such as accepting bribes, in which event all legal systems handle these situations under the criminal law of that country.[488] Most international arbitration rules deal with the immunity of arbitrators firstly by confirming the immunity of the arbitrators in their rules and provisions. For instance, Article 40 of the ICC Rules expressly provides the immunity not just of the arbitrators, but also of all of the following:

1) Individuals appointed by the arbitral tribunal;

2) The emergency arbitrator;

3) The Court, its members;

4) The ICC and its employees;

5) The ICC National Committees; and

487 See ASSOCIATION, AAA/ICDR Handbook on International Arbitration and ADR 92-94. 2006. See also MOSES, The principles and practice of international commercial arbitration 153-155. 2012.

488 See MOSES, The Principles and Practice of International Commercial Arbitration 154. 2012.

6) Groups and their staff and representatives. [489]

All of these individuals must not be liable to any individual for any act or omission in connection with the arbitration process, except to the extent that applicable law prohibits such limitation of liability.[490] Similar to this article, the ICDR states and the LCIA Rules add the case of deliberate wrongdoing as an exception to such immunity.[491] By proclaiming the immunity of the arbitrator, the rules allow the arbitrator to do his duty independently during the arbitration process.

Unlike most international arbitration rules and the rules in many jurisdictions, such as the United States,[492] the Saudi Arbitration Law does not contain any article, which protects the arbitrator from civil liability for mistakes that he may commit while carrying out his function in the arbitration process. In fact, the arbitrator's duty is the same as that of a judge. As a result, the arbitrator should be able to review and consider the dispute independently without fear of potential prosecution by one of the arbitrating parties who is dissatisfied with the arbitration award. Furthermore, without immunity, qualified arbitrators will be reluctant to arbitrate; they should instead be encouraged to participate in arbitration as discussed earlier. However, the judicial process is different from the arbitration process with regard to the safeguards that govern the legal process to reduce malpractice by the judiciary, such as correcting possible errors on appeal. As a result, the arbitrator has a higher chance of making errors than the court. Consequently, a restrictive immunity to exclude only deliberate wrong-doing by the arbitrator may be a middle position between concerns. In sum, inserting such text in the Saudi Arbitration Law to determine the responsibility of the arbitrator and providing restricted immunity would achieve a better balance between the needs of international commercial interests, private arbitrators, and public policy instead of exposing the arbitrator to the possibility of law suits just to disrupt the arbitration process, which may discourage the use of arbitration as a method of resolving deputes between investors and traders in the Kingdom.

489 ICC Rules of Arbitration. 2012.

490 *Id.*

491 See ICDR Arbitration Rules, Article 38. 2014. Also LCIA Arbitration Rules, Article 31. 2014.

492 See ASSOCIATION, AAA/ICDR Handbook on International Arbitration and ADR 92. 2006.

7. Costs and Fees

The arbitration process is not always less expensive than litigation. In this regard, Richard H. Kreindler says: "While each dispute (in arbitration) has its own dynamic and characteristics that contribute to costs involved, it is fair to say that certain arbitration proceedings may be as expensive as if they had taken place in the courts."[493] Arbitration costs include payment to the arbitrators, an administrative fee if the arbitration is under an arbitration institution, and other legal and administrative expenses.

In an institutional arbitration, usually, the institution will determine the cost and fees and will be paid some initial fees and costs in advance. For instance, Article 37(1) of the ICC Arbitration Rules states that the costs include the fees and expenses of the arbitrators and the ICC administrative expenses and that they will be set by the Court when the arbitration begins in addition to the fees and expenses of any experts appointed by the arbitral tribunal and the reasonable legal and other costs incurred by the parties to the arbitration. In ad hoc arbitrations, all parties should consult with the arbitrator(s) to agree upon the fees and expenses.[494] Similarly, Saudi Law refers this issue to the arbitration agreement between the arbitrating parties. Article 24(1) requires the arbitrating parties to enter into a separate contract upon the appointment of an arbitrator, which specifies the fees. It also requires that a copy of the contract shall be deposited with the agency specified in the Implementing Regulations of the Saudi Arbitration Law. However, if there is no agreement between the parties regarding the arbitrators' fees, Article 24(2) of the new Law refers this matter to the competent court, which should make a non-appealable decision regarding the issue. If the competent court appoints the arbitrators, the court shall determine their fees.[495] It remains to be seen whether this is workable in practice. The competent court may have quite different ideas about equitable fees from the arbitrators, in particular if the latter are internationally known and in high demand.

493 Id. at. 4.

494 MOSES, The Principles and Practice of International Commercial Arbitration 156. 2012.

495 Arbitration Law. 2012.

D. Competent Court Supervision and Assistance

As this chapter has shown in more than a few instances, participation of the judiciary can be essential during a commercial arbitration procedure to ensure that the arbitration is safe, fair and free from fraud, corruption, and violations of primary due process requirements, nationally and internationally. Although the arbitrating parties choose their arbitrator(s) and the rules that govern their disputes, the power of the court during the arbitration process is important to require or enforce or prevent acts over which the arbitral tribunal itself has no power. Such powers include, for example, enforcing the agreement to arbitrate and resolving challenges to an arbitrator for an alleged conflict of interest. Even before the arbitration process begins, one of the arbitrating parties may ask the court for emergency relief, such as maintaining the status quo until the outcome of the arbitration by ordering that disputed property not be sold. Furthermore, the court may assist if discovery is needed from witnesses who are not under the control of one of the arbitrating parties. The court also commonly rules on issues of vacating, recognizing, and enforcing the arbitration award, which will be presented in Chapter 4.[496] Usually, courts respect the arbitration parties' autonomy during its assistance; however, the court's participation can sometimes be helpful, while at other times it can be unhelpful interference during the arbitration process.

The old Saudi arbitration law expressly provided that the court would supervise the arbitration process, including appointing the arbitral tribunal where the arbitrating parties failed to agree upon the appointment of the arbitrators, and it could replace an arbitrator when needed.[497] The new Arbitration Law went a positive step further. It is similar to the UNCITRAL Model Law by allowing the arbitrating parties to choose their arbitral tribunal without the intervention of the courts.[498] Furthermore, it provides a detailed procedure for selecting an arbitral tribunal if the arbitrating parties have not done so in the arbitration agreement. Also, arbitral tribunals have the authority to rule on their jurisdiction by applying the doctrine of Kompetenz-Kompetenz. As a result, arbitral tribunals, if their powers are in question or being challenged, do not have to turn to the courts to

496 See William W Park, Judicial Supervision of Transnational Commercial Arbitration: The English Arbitration Act of 1979, 21 HARV. INT'L. LJ (1980). Also see MOSES, The Principles and Practice of International Commercial Arbitration 87-88. 2012.

497 Al-Ammari & Martin, ARBITRATION INTERNATIONAL, 392-393 (2014).

498 *See id.*

determine whether they have the power to proceed with the arbitration or not.[499] This section will study in some more detail the ways in which Saudi courts have an impact on the arbitration process and its possible results under the new Law, with emphasis on the following points:

1. Enforcement of an Arbitration Agreement

a. Scope of Judicial Review

There are two major arguments about the scope of judicial review at the time of enforcement of an arbitration agreement.[500] The first question is about the extent to which the court should consider the facts and circumstances in case an arbitrating party is seeking enforcement of an arbitration agreement. The New York Convention mandates recognition and enforcement of an agreement to arbitrate but does not say whether a complete review of the facts and circumstances is in order or merely a prima facie review to find a reasonable likelihood that the party bringing the suit had in fact previously agreed to arbitrate. Since the New York Convention is silent on the considerations courts should apply, in practice, the courts in different countries handle this issue in different ways. Those favoring complete review emphasize the need to ensure that an arbitration agreement is not defective in a way that may cause an award to be vacated, which would just be a waste of time and effort for parties and arbitrators. The others consider that prima facie review is sufficient and emphasize the need to prevent a party from engaging in dilatory and obstructionist tactics during arbitration proceedings.[501]

One of the major reasons why parties resort to arbitration, especially in international business and trade, is to reduce and limit the time required to resolve a dispute. Hence, the UNCITRAL Model Law permits only a prima facie review of an arbitration agreement. Article 8 requires that, if a court reviews an arbitration agreement, it shall refer parties to arbitration unless the agreement is found null and void, inoperative or incapable of being performed.[502] Hence, the Model Law tends to consider that prevention of dilatory and obstructionist conduct is more important than the risk that an arbitral award may be fatally flawed in a way that cannot be detected with mere prima facie review.

---

499 *See id.*

500 MOSES, The Principles and Practice of International Commercial Arbitration 87-88. 2012.

501 See *id.*

502 UNCITRAL Model Law on International Commercial Arbitration. 2006.

In the Saudi Law, the ruler does not explain the type of review that the court must make if an action is brought against an arbitration agreement. However, several cases show that Saudi courts tend to conduct a comprehensive review of the arbitration agreement and insist to hear from all parties. For instance, Case No 114/2/ق[503] was brought before the Saudi court in 2007, but the court did not accept the lawsuit after reviewing the facts and hearing from the defendant, who refused the claim because of the existence of an arbitration clause in the contract.[504] In my opinion, the new Saudi Arbitration Law could be better, if it clarified the extent of judicial review of arbitration agreements like the UNCITRAL Model Law instead of leaving it up to the court's consideration, which could waste the parties' time if the court undertakes a comprehensive review.

b. Kompetenz–Kompetenz[505]

Kompetenz–Kompetenz, or the competence to decide its competence, is a foundational principle recognized in most jurisdictions. This principle gives the arbitral tribunal authority to decide its own competence.[506] In other words, the arbitral tribunal has jurisdiction to decide its own jurisdiction. As a result, a court must refrain from hearing substantive arguments about the arbitrator's jurisdiction until after the arbitrators themselves have had an opportunity to do so and, according to this principle, at the first stage, the courts must limit their review to a prima facie determination of whether the agreement is not null and void, inoperative or incapable of being performed. The policy consideration involved in applying this principle is to give priority primarily to preventing delaying tactics in court by one of the parties. The arbitral process will be hindered if one of the parties can exploit the courts to create parallel proceedings for the sole purpose of interfering with the progress of the arbitration.[507]

---

503 (ق) is the Arabic letter.

504 This case is available at the Diwan Almazalim website at http://www.bog.gov.sa/ScientificContent/JudicialBlogs/Blog1428/Documents/. See also the case No 637/3/ق in 2009.

505 The idea originated in Germany, hence the spelling with "K". Nowadays, "competence-competence" is also being widely used.

506 See E. Gaillard & Y. Banifatemi, "Negative Effect of Competence-Competence: the Rule of Priority in Favour of the Arbitrators", in E. Gaillard & D. Di Pietro (Eds.) Enforcement of Arbitration Agreements and International Arbitral Awards: The New York Convention in Practice (London: Cameron May, 2008) 257-273. Also see MOSES, The Principles and Practice of International Commercial Arbitration 91-95. 2012. Also see ASSOCIATION, AAA/ICDR Handbook on International Arbitration and ADR 6-7. 2006.

507 See *id.*

For the reasons mentioned above, the UNCITRAL Model Law gives the arbitral tribunal authority to decide the validity of the arbitration agreement and to determine its own competence to hear the case in a preliminary question or in a final award. In addition, the Model Law limits the time to request a judicial determination of whether jurisdiction is proper by requiring that the request be made within thirty days after the arbitral tribunal decides its jurisdiction in the case.[508]

Similar to the UNCITRAL Model Law, the new Saudi Arbitration Law provides broad authority for the arbitral tribunal to decide its own competence and to apply the competence-competence principle. Article 20 of the new Law states that the arbitration tribunal has the right to decide all pleas related to its jurisdiction, including those based on an absence of an arbitration agreement, expiry or the nullity of such an agreement, or the non-inclusion of the disputed subject-matter in the agreement. In addition, the Article expresses that the appointment or participation in the appointment of an arbitrator by either party should not prevent the party from filing any such pleas. Moreover, the plea that the arbitration agreement does not include matters raised by the other party while the dispute is being reviewed must be raised immediately; otherwise, the right to raise such a plea shall terminate. The law also provides the arbitration with more authority to accept a late plea if it considers the delay justified. Moreover, according to this Article, the arbitration tribunal should decide on pleas challenging its competence before deciding on the subject of the dispute. However, it has the power to join the stated pleas to the subject and decide them both at the end together. Finally, if the arbitration tribunal decides to dismiss the plea, the plea may not be raised except through the filing of a case to nullify the arbitration award ending the entire dispute, which will be explained later.[509] Obviously, the new Arbitration Law embraces the modern trend to provide the arbitration tribunal wide power to review its competence. The additional details to reflect such authority are clearly following the UNCITRAL Model Law.

2. Anti-Suit Injunctions

An anti-suit injunction is an order issued by a court or arbitral tribunal that has personal jurisdiction over the opposing party and bars the party from commencing or continuing a proceeding in a foreign jurisdiction or forum. If a party does

508 UNCITRAL Model Law on International Commercial Arbitration, Article 16(3). 2006.

509 Arbitration Law. 2012.

not comply with such an order, the domestic court may issue a contempt of court order against that party. Recently, many jurisdictions have issued such orders to prevent oppressive and vexatious proceedings from opposing parties.[510] An example would be the investment arbitration case that involved the Swiss corporation SGS and the Government of Pakistan. SGS filed a claim at the International Centre for Settlement of Investment Disputes (ICSID) according to the bilateral investment protection treaty between Switzerland and Pakistan. The Government of Pakistan, however, requested an order from its own courts to enjoin SGS from pursuing the arbitral proceedings based on the wording of the arbitration agreement in the specific contract and its provision requiring that any arbitration should occur in Pakistan. In an order issued on 3 July 2002, the Supreme Court of Pakistan found that the bilateral treaty did not bind Pakistan in a case where the parties to a dispute had specifically agreed otherwise. Consequently, the Supreme Court granted Pakistan's request for an injunction and ordered that domestic arbitration should begin.[511]

Many countries recognize the need to save international arbitration from attempts at disrupting the arbitral process. Unfortunately, there is a recent trend to seek injunctions against arbitral proceedings in two different forms. One form occurs during the arbitral process to prevent an arbitral tribunal from reviewing and hearing the case; the other form occurs at the end of the arbitral process to obstruct the arbitral award from being enforced.[512] When injunctions are requested during arbitral proceedings, they are often directed against the claimant in the form of an order to suspend or terminate the arbitral proceedings. The order may also be directed against the arbitral tribunal itself challenging explicitly or implicitly the tribunal's authority to rule on its own jurisdiction.[513] An example would be the dispute that arose between the Hubco Corporation and the Water and Power Development Authority of Pakistan (WAPDA) relating to a US$1.8

---

510 See MOSES, The Principles and Practice of International Commercial Arbitration, 95-105. 2012.

511 There are more details about this case. However, the study here mentions the case only as an example of anti-suit injunctions in the municipal courts. For more information about this case, see Martina Polasek, SGS Société Générale de Surveillance SA v. Islamic Republic of Pakistan (ICSID Case No. ARB/01/13) Introductory Note, 18(1) ICSID REV. 290-2 (2003). See also Emmanuel Gaillard, Reflections on the Use of Anti-Suit Injunctions in International Arbitration, PERVASIVE PROBLEMS IN INTERNATIONAL ARBITRATION, 205 (2006).

512 See Emmanuel Gaillard, Reflections on the Use of Anti-Suit Injunctions in International Arbitration, PERVASIVE PROBLEMS IN INTERNATIONAL ARBITRATION, 203-215 (2006).

513 See id. Also see MOSES, The Principles and Practice of International Commercial Arbitration 95-105. 2012.

billion project to construct a power station in Pakistan. The agreement included an arbitration clause that required that disputes be resolved by ICC arbitration in London. In July 1998, during the arbitral process concerning the method of calculating the price of the electricity produced, WAPDA, deeming certain contracts to be illegal and claiming that fraud and corruption had obtained them, presented these questions to the Pakistani courts and asked them to order the claimant to suspend the arbitration. The courts granted this request and, in a judgment dated 14 June 2000, the Supreme Court of Pakistan upheld their decision, finding that the allegation of corruption rendered the matter non-arbitrable.[514]

The UNCITRAL Model Law also empowers municipal courts to perform some functions to confirm the conditions for granting and refusing the recognition and enforcement of foreign awards under Articles 35 and 36, respectively.[515] Furthermore, Article 17(2) empowers the arbitral tribunal to order interim measures for taking action that would prevent or even refrain action that would be likely to cause current or imminent harm or prejudice to the arbitral process itself.[516] This Article talks about the arbitral tribunal, but if this action is not likely to be enforceable by the arbitral tribunal, in particular if the opposite party refuses to cooperate, the tribunal may ask the court to enforce such interim measures via its police powers. Even if the local courts are not willing to support the arbitration, providing the arbitration tribunal such authority gives the party an advantage by allowing it to bypass a local injunction and to win an award from the arbitral tribunal that will be enforceable in other countries under Article 17H and I of the UNCITRAL Model Law as will explained later.[517] Saudi law gives the Saudi courts the authority to issue injunctions as they exist in other jurisdictions. For instance, Article 40(3) gives the competent court authority to stop an arbitration process if the arbitration award is not issued within the period provided in the arbitration agreement, unless the arbitrating parties agree to an additional period.[518] Interestingly, the Saudi courts have issued such injunctions in practice. For example, in Case No 1701/1/ق in 2007,[519] the court issued an order to prevent a

514 Gaillard, Pervasive Problems in International Arbitration, 205 (2006).

515 See UNCITRAL Model Law on International Commercial Arbitration. 2006.

516 *Id.*

517 *Id.*

518 Arbitration Law. 2012.

519 The case is available at http://www1.bog.gov.sa/ScientificContent/JudicialBlogs/Pages/default.aspx.

defendant from arbitrating outside of the Kingdom of Saudi Arabia according to the arbitration agreement upon the request of the plaintiff. This shows that Saudi courts have practiced this principle even under the old law, which is consistent with the recent trends in arbitration laws.

3. Interim Measures

Since arbitration tribunals do not have the police powers of the state to force the parties to do or not do certain things, most arbitration rules provide for the courts at the place of arbitration or the courts with jurisdiction over the parties and/or their assets to issue interim relief orders. This can be requested even before an arbitration procedure is formally launched without waiving the right to arbitrate. According to David E. Wagoner: "There is frequently a compelling need to seek interim relief (sometimes called conservatory and provisional measures) in connection with an international arbitration."[520] Hence, the role of the public courts is significant in this matter, as will be shown in the following points.

a. Types of Interim Measures

Either or both of the arbitrating parties may seek different kinds of interim measures. Some measure are procedural in nature, regulating the relationship between the parties during the arbitral proceedings or resolving issues concerning the production of documents, the protection of confidentiality, and costs. Other measures can be sought by one of the arbitrating parties asking for security for the claim itself, such as securing the evidence upon which that party depends to prove its case or even to prevent the defendant from hiding or removing assets, or from using the subject of the dispute, such as intellectual property.[521]

Unfortunately, there is no universal and precise definition for "interim measures". Therefore, the UNCITRAL Model Law provides a specific meaning for the term.[522] Article 17(2) of the Model Law states:

520 ASSOCIATION, AAA/ICDR Handbook on International Arbitration and ADR 145. 2006.

521 See William Wang, International Arbitration: the Need for Uniform Interim Measures of Relief, 28 Brook. J. Int'l L., 1072-1075 (2002). See also, Lee Anna Tucker, Interim Measures under Revised UNCITRAL Arbitration Rules: Comparison to Model Law Reflects Both Greater Flexibility and Remaining Uncertainty, 1 Int'l Com. Arb. Brief, 15-17 (2011).

522 See MOSES, The Principles and Practice of International Commercial Arbitration 105-107. 2012.

"An interim measure is any temporary measure whether in the form of an award or in another form, by which, at any time prior to the issuance of the award by which the dispute is finally decided, the arbitral tribunal orders a party to:

(a) Maintain or restore the status quo pending determination of the dispute;

(b) Take action that would prevent, or refrain from taking action that is likely to cause, current or imminent harm or prejudice to the arbitral the process itself;

(c) Provide a means of preserving assets out of which a subsequent award may be satisfied; or

(d) Preserve evidence that may be relevant and material to the resolution of the dispute."[523]

This article also shows that conservatory measures, which are intended to protect the ability of the parties to get a final award, are considered according to the UNCITRAL Model Law.

In addition to interim and conservatory measures, the UNCITRAL Model Law presents a specific regime for preliminary orders. According to Article 17C of the UNCITRAL Model Law, an arbitral tribunal has the authority to grant an initial order upon request by a party without notice of the request to any other party, if in the circumstances the arbitral tribunal finds that prior disclosure of the request might frustrate the purpose of the measure or lead to thwarting the requested protection, such as destroying evidence. Hence, this type of preliminary order may be sought by one of the arbitrating parties if the need for interim protection of rights is exceptionally urgent or when the element of surprise is essential.[524]

As a result, the differences between the interim measures appear according to Article 17C of the Model Law in the following points. The arbitral tribunal has authority to hear from one party and to issue such an order without giving notice to the other party. Such an order must be considered immediately after determination of the arbitration tribunal. In addition, the order expires after twenty

523 UNCITRAL Model Law on International Commercial Arbitration. 2006.

524 See id. Also see Tucker, INT'L COM. ARB. BRIEF, 19-22 (2011).

days, during which the tribunal must give the other party the opportunity to be heard. Such an order is not and cannot be enforced by a court, unlike the interim measures.[525] Without a doubt, this type of order is a practical solution provided by the Model Law to achieve justice in the arbitration process, mainly to preserve evidence under the control of one of the arbitrating parties.

The new Saudi law follows the Model Law in its approach to interim measures in most of its content. Article 22 of the Law provides that, upon a request by either of the arbitrating parties, provisional or precautionary measures may be granted before or during the arbitration process. In other words, in additional to interim and conservatory measures, the Saudi law provides the petitioner with the possibility of obtaining a preliminary order prior to the arbitration process, if certain circumstances so require. However, the Saudi Law differs from the Model Law regarding the preliminary order in two main aspects. First, the Saudi Law does not limit the time for preliminary and temporary orders. It also does not specify whether either order can be granted without prior notice to the adverse party, if there is reason to believe that the adverse party might try to frustrate the goals of the measure if given such notice.[526] Furthermore, the Law does not provide for a procedure to request an order of judicial delegation, to preserve the subject in dispute until the final arbitral award is issued.[527] The Saudi Law also does not define interim measures and does not refer to the definition in the UNCITRAL Model Law. Because the implementing regulation of the new Law has not yet been issued, and there are no published decisions from Saudi courts, it is difficult to know how the Saudi courts will interpret the new law in this regard.

b. Interim Relief Between the Arbitral Tribunal and the Court

Recently, international arbitration rules have come to assume that arbitrating parties will ask for interim relief from the arbitral tribunal first, and from the local courts only as a secondary remedy. This assumption appears in the 2012 ICC Rules and the 2014 LCIA Rules, which provide broad powers to arbitral tribunals to issue interim relief and at the same time limit the local courts' authority to do so to narrow circumstances. For example, Article 28 of the ICC Rules states: "The arbitral tribunal may, at the request of a party, order any interim or conservatory measure it deems appropriate. The arbitral tribunal may make the granting of any such measure subject to appropriate security being furnished by the requesting

525 See UNCITRAL Model Law on International Commercial Arbitration. 2006.

526 Arbitration Law. 2012.

527 Id. at. Article 22(2).

party..."[528] Similar to the ICC Rules, Article 25.1 of the LCIA Arbitration Rules provides the arbitral tribunal with wide-ranging power to grant such interim measures.[529] In addition to the broad powers to issue interim relief, most international arbitration rules preserve the arbitrating parties' ability to apply to the municipal courts for interim relief in limited circumstances. For instance, Article 28 of the ICC Arbitration Rules states: "Before the file is transmitted to the arbitral tribunal, and in appropriate circumstances even thereafter, the parties may apply to any competent judicial authority for interim or conservatory measures."[530] Similarly, Article 25.3 of the LCIA Rules says that, in exceptional cases and with the arbitral tribunal's authorization, the arbitrating parties may have recourse to the national courts.[531] Accordingly, the default position according to the international rules appears not only to permit but actually to prioritize recourse to the arbitral tribunal for interim relief in the absence of exceptional circumstances.

However, even if there is an emergency, resorting to the municipal courts in many cases may be more efficient and save time and energy for the petitioner instead of depending on a tribunal order, which is not self-executing.[532] According to Margaret L. Moses:

> There are practical reasons why a party might prefer to go to the court in the first instance, even if the tribunal has already been constituted. If the interim relief sought would ultimately require court assistance to be effectuated, such as attachment of a bank account, then going to court immediately could save time.[533]

As a result, if the requested relief is needed urgently, recourse to the municipal court could be the more efficient and effective way to obtain it.

The new Saudi Arbitration Law follows the recent international arbitration rules about interim relief before and after the arbitral tribunal is formed. Article 22(1) of the new Law authorizes a competent court to grant arbitrating parties

528 ICC Rules of Arbitration. 2012.

529 LCIA Arbitration rules. 2014.

530 ICC Rules of Arbitration. 2012.

531 LCIA Arbitration rules. 2014.

532 See ASSOCIATION, AAA/ICDR Handbook on International Arbitration and ADR 145-156. 2006.

533 MOSES, The Principles and Practice of International Commercial Arbitration 110. 2012.

provisional and precautionary measures before commencing arbitration proceedings upon the request of a party that believes that relief must be granted before commencing the arbitration process in the circumstances discussed earlier.[534] However, a request made during the arbitration proceedings and after the constitution of the arbitral tribunal will be granted according to the new Law upon the request of the arbitration tribunal, not the parties.[535] In other words, the arbitral tribunal has the power to review the interim measure request, and the Saudi law gives arbitrators wide authority over the arbitration process in line with the recent developments in international arbitration rules. In addition, the Saudi Law provides an exception when the parties have agreed, in which event the proceedings will be in accord with their agreement.[536] In sum, the Saudi law complies with the more recent evolution of arbitration rules in granting the interim relief in addition to its flexibility in such matters.

c. *Basis for Interim Measures*

The UNCITRAL Model Law also provides a basis for granting interim relief. The party requesting interim relief must present to the arbitral tribunal two conditions for granting interim measures. First, the party must satisfy the arbitral tribunal that harm not adequately remedied by an award of damages is likely to result if the measure is not ordered and that such harm substantially outweighs the harm that is likely to result to the party against whom the measure is directed if the measure is granted. In addition, a reasonable possibility of success on the merits of the claim must appear before the arbitral tribunal; however, the determination of this possibility must not affect the discretion of the arbitral tribunal in making any subsequent determination. Furthermore, the arbitral tribunal may request appropriate security in ordering the interim relief unless the arbitral tribunal deems that to be inappropriate.[537]

The Saudi Law does not specify a particular basis upon which to grant interim measures; instead, the law leaves the basis to the arbitration tribunal's discretion, which provides the arbitrator broad power in this regard. However, the law authorizes the tribunal to require the requesting party to provide sufficient financial guarantees for the execution of interim or conservative measures which

---

534 See Arbitration Law. 2012.

535 Id. at. Article 22(1)

536 Id.

537 UNCITRAL Model Law on International Commercial Arbitration Article 17 A. 2006. See also, MOSES, The Principles and Practice of International Commercial Arbitration 110-111. 2012.

could be necessary according to the nature of the dispute.[538] It would be better if the Saudi Law specified the grounds upon which the tribunal must depend to grant such interim measures and provisional orders to be more transparent to the requested party in advance.

d. Enforcement of Interim Measures

Since arbitration is voluntary and based on an agreement between business parties, the enforcement of orders issued by the arbitral tribunal depends on the good will and voluntary compliance of all disputing parties. In practice, the question of enforcement arises when one of the arbitrating parties refuses to comply with the arbitral tribunal's orders, because these orders are not self-executing in nature, which is a weakness of the arbitration process if there is no assistance from municipal courts in enforcing the arbitral orders. Although an arbitral tribunal could use negative procedural sanctions against a party who refuses to follow the order for interim measures, such as refusing to show necessary evidence to the tribunal, in most cases the enforcement of such orders needs the assistance of local courts. As a result, the position of municipal courts and national rules in the process of the enforcement of arbitral orders providing for interim measures is essential to the arbitration process. Matters are complicated by the fact that interim relief by an arbitral tribunal can take a number of different forms. Some orders are issued as an award or, to be precise, a partial award. If interim relief is provided in the form of an award, enforcement via the New York Convention, which was intended by its drafters to facilitate the recognition and enforcement of binding and final foreign arbitral awards, is possible. However, if the arbitral tribunal issues interim measures in a form other than an award, they cannot be recognized and enforced under the New York Convention.[539]

The UNCITRAL Model Law provides great solutions for both problems stated above regarding the issuance of interim measures relief. Firstly, Article 17H of the Model Law says that an interim measure issued by an arbitral tribunal must be considered binding and, unless otherwise provided by the arbitral tribunal, enforced upon application to the competent court regardless of the country in

538 See Arbitration Law Article 23(1). 2012.

539 See Natalija Kaminskiene, Application of Interim Measures in International arbitration: the Lithuanian approach, JURISPRUDENCIJA (2010). See also, ASSOCIATION, AAA/ICDR Handbook on International Arbitration and ADR 145-156. 2006.

which it was issued.[540] As a result, under the Model Law, no matter where enforcement of the arbitral award is sought, the competent court must consider it a binding decision. This is a great outcome, particularly when the place of arbitration is different from the place of enforcement, as long as the respective country or countries have duly implemented the Model Law. As a result, and in contrast to the New York Convention, the UNCITRAL Model Law takes a flexible view of the form of arbitral tribunal decisions issuing interim measures. Article 17 of the UNCITRAL Model Law allows interim measures to be taken in the form of an award or any other form.[541] Hence, the Model Law is a good example how to overcome the limitation in the New York Convention about enforcement of arbitral decisions other than "awards".

Furthermore, the UNCITRAL Model Law limits the grounds for refusing recognition and enforcement of interim measures as outlined in Article 17I and Article 36 of the Law. According to the stated Articles, the competent court may refuse to recognize and enforce an interim measure only in the following situations:

Firstly, at the request of the party against whom it is invoked if the court is satisfied that the refusal is based on:

A) In the following situations:

1) A party to the arbitration agreement was under some incapacity, or the agreement is invalid under the law to which the arbitrating parties have subjected it or, failing any indication thereof, under the legislation of the state where the award was made; or

2) The party against whom the award is invoked was not given proper notice of the appointment of an arbitrator or the arbitral proceedings or was otherwise unable to present his case; or

3) The award deals with a dispute not contemplated by or not falling within the terms of the submission to arbitration, or it contains decisions on matters beyond the scope of the submission to arbitration, provided that, if the decisions on matters submitted to arbitration can be separated from those not so submitted, that part of the award which contains decisions on matters submitted to arbitration may be recognized and enforced; or

540 See UNCITRAL Model Law on International Commercial Arbitration. 2006.

541 See Id.

4) The composition of the arbitral tribunal or the arbitral procedure was not in accordance with the agreement of the parties or, failing such agreement, was not in accordance with the law of the country in which the arbitration took place.[542]

B) The arbitral tribunal's decision with respect to the provision of security in connection with the interim measure issued by the arbitral tribunal has not been complied with.

C) The interim measure has been terminated or suspended by the arbitral tribunal or, where so empowered, by the court of the country in which the arbitration takes place or under the law of which that interim measure was granted.[543]

Secondly, if the court finds:

A) The interim measure is incompatible with the powers conferred upon the court unless the court decides to reformulate the interim measure to the extent necessary to adapt it to its own powers and procedures for the purposes of enforcing that interim measure and without modifying its substance.[544]

B) The subject matter of the dispute is not capable of settlement by arbitration under the law of this country.

C) The recognition or enforcement of the award would be contrary to the public policy of this country.[545]

The grounds for non-enforcement of interim measures issued by an arbitral tribunal are primarily the same as for non-enforcement of foreign arbitral awards under Article V of the New York Convention.[546] Hence, the study will explain this extensively in the enforcement chapter.

The Saudi Arbitration Law follows Article 39(5) of the UNCITRAL Model Law, which confirms that the arbitral tribunal has the authority to issue provisional or partial awards before making the final award that ends the entire dispute.[547] Furthermore, Article 52 confirms that these rendered awards have the authority of a judicial ruling and shall be enforceable as long as they are in accordance with

542 See Id at Article 36(1).

543 Id. at. Article 17I (1)

544 Id.

545 UNCITRAL Model Law on International Commercial Arbitration 36(1). 2006.

546 See New York Convention 1958.

547 Arbitration Law. 2012.

Saudi law.[548] As a result, the arbitral awards for interim measures relief will be handled according to the new law as the enforcement of final arbitral awards, which is explained in Article 50, and will be presented extensively in the enforcement chapter.[549] However, unlike the Model Law, the Saudi law does not define interim measures, which are granted by the arbitral tribunal through a non-award form. In fact, in the absence of the implementation regulation of the new law and cases that explain this matter, it is hard to imagine how the Saudi court will handle this issue. Hence, given the lack of support of the arbitration process by the Saudi court during its history, this gap may create a problem in enforcing these types of relief, such as delaying the process of arbitration if the adverse party argues about the relief. In sum, it would be better if the Saudi law set forth, as the Model Law does, any form of interim measures requested to be handled as an arbitral award, to cut off any gap that may delay the arbitration process.

4. Court Assistance in Obtaining Evidence

Court assistance in obtaining evidence is essential in the arbitration process as well as interim measures relief. Article 17 of the UNCITRAL Model Law defines, as presented previously, the conditions that must be met for measures to be called interim measures and preliminary orders; otherwise, they will be referred to as procedural orders.[550] Accordingly, there is a distinction between preserving evidence and obtaining it. In other words, preserving evidence is appropriate for interim measures relief; obtaining evidence is appropriate for procedural orders issued in the arbitration process by the arbitral tribunal, which may concern scheduling or delineate various obligations of the arbitrating parties that are not generally considered to be final as an arbitral order but may or may not be enforced by a competent court. [551]

Usually, in the commercial arbitration process, arbitrating parties will not resort immediately to the arbitral tribunal or to the competent court with approval from the tribunal. According to Margaret L. Moses:

---

548 Id.

549 Id.

550 See UNCITRAL Model Law on International Commercial Arbitration Article 17. 2006.

551 See MOSES, The Principles and Practice of International Commercial Arbitration 112-113. 2012. Also see ASSOCIATION, AAA/ICDR Handbook on International Arbitration and ADR 137-144. 2006.

> From a practical standpoint, the first step a party should take in trying to obtain documents would be to simply ask the other party for the information. If the other party does not cooperate, then a party could confer with both the other party and the tribunal, and the tribunal could suggest to the other party that it should produce the information. If this does not work, then a party may be able to persuade a tribunal to order the opposing party to produce documents or to produce witnesses under its control. If the tribunal agrees, the party subject to the order has a strong incentive to comply with the order, because arbitrators can draw adverse inferences from any noncompliance. Moreover, a party generally does not want a tribunal to think that it has reason to hide relevant information.[552]

As a result, resort to a competent court to enforce these kind of orders may not happen during the arbitration practice because the arbitrating parties generally comply.

However, if the evidence, such as documents and witnesses, are in the control of a third party, who is not subject to the arbitration agreement, the help of a municipal court will be essential in the arbitration process. Charles Owen Verrill says about this issue:

"More complex are the rules that determine opportunities to obtain discovery from persons that are not party to the arbitration (third-party discovery)."[553] Thomas H. Webster states: "To date, the discussion of these issues has been limited, but the issues are becoming more important as international arbitration and its relation with national courts evolves."[554] As a result, most national jurisdictions provide rules that govern obtaining evidence during the arbitration process with court assistance. For instance, the UNCITRAL Model Law, which many national laws adopted or, at least, take as guiding law, provides in Article 27, "[t]he arbitral tribunal or a party with the approval of the arbitral tribunal may request from a competent court of this State assistance in taking evidence."[555] Similar to the Model Law, Article 22(3) of the Saudi Arbitration Law states that the

552 MOSES, The Principles and Practice of International Commercial Arbitration 113. 2012.

553 Charles O Verrill Jr, Discovery From Non-Parties (Third-Party Discovery) in International Arbitration, 113 (2010).

554 Thomas H Webster, Obtaining Evidence from Third Parties in International Arbitration, 17 ARBITRATION INTERNATIONAL (2001).

555 UNCITRAL Model Law on International Commercial Arbitration. 2006.

arbitration tribunal may, as it deems fit, seek the assistance of the competent court in the arbitration proceedings, such as calling a witness or an expert, ordering the submission of a document or a copy thereof, reviewing the document, or any other proceeding, without prejudice to the right of the arbitration tribunal to conduct the proceeding independently.[556] Hence, the new Saudi law follows the modern arbitration law with regard to obtaining evidence that will or may be helpful during the process of arbitration.

E. Institutional Arbitration and Ad Hoc Arbitration

One of the advantages of the new Saudi Arbitration Law is that it allows arbitrating parties to use international or local arbitration institutions and their procedural rules. Ad hoc international arbitration rules are also an option for arbitrating parties, as long as the rules do not conflict with Islamic Sharia.[557] Thus, where a dispute arises between arbitrating parties, they are free to decide whether to refer and adopt the processes of a particular institution's rules or to tailor a different process on an ad hoc basis.

1. Institutional Arbitration

Institutional arbitration has several advantages for arbitrating parties. One of the better advantages is that institutional arbitration provides administrative functions, such as appointing an arbitrator in a timely way, moving the arbitration process along in a reasonable manner, and managing the payment of the legal fees and expenses.[558] Margaret L. Moses says: "From the arbitrator's point of view, it is an advantage not to have to deal with the parties about fees. The arbitral institution handles any issues of fees or payment."[559] Another benefit concerns issuing the arbitral award. An award issued by a well-known institution would be more credible before the international community and the municipal courts, which could protect the winning party from challenges against the award at the enforcement stage.[560] If the arbitrating parties consider institutional arbitration, they will have international arbitration centers and regional arbitration centers available to them. In international institutional arbitration, there are three globally well-known centers that administer commercial disputes:

---

556 Arbitration Law. 2012.

557 See id. at Article 3,5, 25(1).

558 See Wang, BROOK. J. INT'L L., 1063 (2002). Also see MOSES, The Principles and Practice of International Commercial Arbitration 9-10. 2012.

559 MOSES, The Principles and Practice of International Commercial Arbitration 9. 2012.

560 See id. at 9-10

a. *The ICC and the International Court of Arbitration*

The ICC, founded in 1923, is the oldest and most well-known arbitral center. The ICC headquarters in Paris, but it administers arbitrations all over the world. The ICC also has its own arbitration rules, which are used worldwide to resolve commercial disputes through arbitration. In addition to being flexible and autonomous, the ICC Rules have in their fundamental characteristics a "universal" character, meaning that they are intended for use in any country, under any law, and in accordance with any system of legal procedure. Its current rules have been in force since 1 January 2012. The ICC supervises and administers the arbitration process by helping to appoint arbitrators, receiving and distributing pleadings, and reviewing arbitral awards for technical accuracy. An ICC arbitration center differs from other arbitration institutions in several features. One of the best advantages is that every arbitral award is reviewed and scrutinized by the court before it is received by the arbitrating parties. The center does not have the power to modify or change the award; however it sends it back to the arbitral tribunal with comments, if necessary. Another advantage is that the ICC requires a document called the "term of reference", which lists a summary of the claims and relief sought, the place of arbitration, the rules, and other information pertaining to discovery or scheduling. This document helps the arbitrating parties to understand and know from the beginning the whole arbitration process. [561]

b. *The American Arbitration Association (AAA) and the International Centre for Dispute Resolution (ICDR)*

The AAA is another international arbitration center, which expands the number of arbitrations it handles yearly. It was founded in 1926. The AAA is an independent non-profit organization headquartered in New York with offices in many countries, such as Singapore and Bahrain. The AAA holds lists of arbitrators, and international arbitrations are regulated by the AAA Commercial Arbitration Rules. The current AAA version of arbitration rules was rendered effective on 1 June,

561 See ICC website for more information at: http://www.iccwbo.org/about-icc/organization/dispute-resolution-services/icc-international-court-of-arbitration/. Also see MOSES, the Principles and Practice of International Commercial Arbitration 11. 2012. Also see JASON FRY, et al., THE SECRETARIAT'S GUIDE TO ICC ARBITRATION: A PRACTICAL COMMENTARY ON THE 2012 ICC RULES OF ARBITRATION FROM THE SECRETARIAT OF THE ICC INTERNATIONAL COURT OF ARBITRATION; AUTHORS: J. FRY, S. GREENBERG, F. MAZZA, WITH THE ASSISTANCE OF B. MOSS; FOREWORD BY J. BEECHEY; PREFACE BY P. WOLRICH (ICC Publishing. 2012).

2014. The AAA rules are intended to provide effective arbitration services to global commercial transactions by using its administered arbitration.[562]

c. The London Court of International Arbitration (LCIA)

The London Court of International Arbitration (LCIA) is the international arbitration institution based in London, United Kingdom, offering the service of international arbitration. The institution is comprised of the Chamber of Commerce, the Corporation of the City of London, and the Institute of Arbitrators. The global center is considered the leading global forum for dispute resolution proceedings for disputing parties, irrespective of their location or even system of law. Although arbitration and the provision of formal arbitration tribunals are the institution's primary focus, the center is also active in mediation, which is a form of alternative dispute resolution (ADR). Furthermore, the international center has access to experienced arbitrators, mediators and experts from many jurisdictions, who collectively possess the widest range of expertise. Also, the LCIA International Arbitration Rules were revised on 1 October 2014. Similar to ICC and AAA arbitration, the LCIA is responsible for the supervision and administration of the procedure and in particular for the appointment of the arbitrators.[563]

d. Regional Arbitration Centers in the Middle East

In addition to the international centers that are available for arbitrating parties, some experienced arbitration centers are available in the Arabic region. In Egypt, the Cairo Regional Centre for International Commercial Arbitration (CRCICA) is one of the significant arbitration centers in the Middle East. The institution is an independent non-profit international organization founded in 1979 under the auspices of the Asian-African Legal Consultative Organization (AALCO). The Center is also considered an international organization, and its branches are endowed with all necessary privileges and immunities ensuring their independent functioning. Since its establishment, CRCICA adopted the arbitration rules of the United Nations Commission on International Trade Law (UNCITRAL) with some modifications approved by the General Assembly of the United Nations on 15 December 1976, and it amended its arbitration rules in 1998, 2000, 2002 and 2007 to ensure that it continues to reflect the best practice in the field of inter-

---

562 For more information, see the American Arbitration Association website at: https://www.adr.org/aaa/faces/s/about. See also Wang, BROOK. J. INT'L L., 1068-1069 (2002).

563 See The London Court of International Arbitration website at: http://www.lcia.org/LCIA/introduction.aspx. Also see id. at. 1069.

national institutional arbitration. The present CRCICA Arbitration Rules are based upon the new UNCITRAL Arbitration Rules as last revised in 2010, with some modifications emanating mainly from the Centre's role as an arbitral center and an appointing authority. They entered into force on 1 March 2011 and shall apply to arbitral proceedings that commenced after that date.[564]

One of the original arbitration centers is the Bahrain Chamber for Dispute Resolution (BCDR-AAA), which is an independent arbitration institution in partnership with the AAA. The BCDR-AAA is headed by its Chief Executive Officer and overseen by an international Board of Trustees. The center is staffed by bilingual lawyers trained at the headquarters of the AAA in New York and other venues with continuous training and professional development.[565]

Another experienced arbitration center is the GCC Commercial Arbitration Centre, which is an independent institution that has the authority to hear trade and resolve commercial disputes if one of the parties is a GCC national, including natural and corporate persons. Since 1995, the Centre has been based in the Kingdom of Bahrain, although it is not affiliated with the Kingdom's national legal system.[566]

Another regional center is the Dubai International Arbitration Centre (DIAC), which was established in 1994 as the center for commercial conciliation and arbitration. The DIAC center administers disputes by appointing arbitrators, choosing a venue and fixing fees of arbitrators and conciliators. DIAC contains arbitrators of the highest ability and professional competence from different countries and varied legal backgrounds. DIAC also has a directory of experts, who are highly recognized for their diverse knowledge and practical experience in the respective fields. The Center houses the latest facilities and equipment to host a variety of arbitration proceedings, such as spacious hearing rooms with adjacent retiring rooms, and a fiber optic network with a full range of electronic services including the internet and email access.[567]

564 See the Cairo Regional Center for International Commercial Arbitration website at: http://crcica.org.eg/.

565 See the Bahrain Chamber for Dispute Resolution (BCDR-AAA) website at: http://www.bcdr-aaa.org/en/about-us/.

566 See the GCC Commercial Arbitration Centre website at: http://www.gcccac.org/en/about-centre.

567 See the center website at http://www.diac.ae/idias/services/diac/.

The last center is the DIFC-LCIA. This Centre was established in 2004 in Dubai City. It is a joint venture between the Dubai International Finance Institution and the LCIA Center. The DIFC-LCIA Rules were updated to reflect the changes and improvements contained in the 2014 LCIA Rules. Under Article 16 of the DIFC-LCIA Rules, parties may select the seat of arbitration, failing which the seat must be the DIFC, ensuring that DIFC law will govern the procedural aspects of the arbitration.[568]

On 4 October 2016, the Kingdom physically established the Saudi Centre for Commercial Arbitration in a modern facility in Riyadh City, which was legally established by Council of Ministers decree No 2057 dated 14/6/1435H (corresponding to 15 March 2014), and is the first of its kind in Saudi Arabia. Soon after its establishment, the Center made an agreement with international arbitration centers such as International Center for Dispute Resolution (ICDR) to offer high quality training for its professional staff, including the case management of mediation and arbitration cases.[569] On 18 October 2016, the author visited New York and met Thomas M. Ventrone, Esq., Vice-President of the American Arbitration Association's International Centre for Dispute Resolution (ICDR) and its team, and was shown that there is significant cooperation with the Saudi Center and an ambitious plan from Saudi authorities to improve alternative dispute resolution in the Kingdom, and to meet international standards. Until now, as it is in the formation period, there is not enough information about the new Center, such as about its sufficient experience or competence, to appoint arbitrators or administer domestic or international commercial arbitrations. As a result, the Center cannot yet be relied on in the arbitration process until the picture becomes clearer in the future.

e. Selection of Applicable Procedural Rules

After the most experienced arbitration institutions internationally and regionally were presented, selecting an appropriate set of rules or arbitration body is an important and difficult step in the arbitration process. The institutions listed above provide varying levels of experience and qualifications for particular disputes. An international organization will not always be better than a regional center, especially if the latter brings together international and local experience through a joint venture with a global center. This mixed experience could be

---

568 For more information about the center and its rules, see its website at http://www.difc-lcia.org/Default.aspx.

569 For more information about such center see its website at: http://sadr.org/en

helpful especially at the enforcement stage. For example, in Saudi Arabia, there can be problems with the application of public policy which needs an experienced institution to make sure an award will be enforced in Saudi court to avoid arbitral awards to be challenged at the enforcement stage as will be seen later.

Different factors can help in choosing the arbitration institution, such as the applicable law and the venue of the arbitration, because these factors will usually be controlled by the arbitration agreement and by the law of the jurisdiction in which the parties are based or do business. Some factors should be considered when choosing the right institution. According to John B. Tieder: "At the risk of over-simplification, there are ten major factors to consider in determining which arbitral organization to select."[570] One of the most significant factors is that the arbitral tribunal can decide on its own jurisdiction. If the arbitral tribunal does not have the power to decide its own jurisdiction (competence-competence), it will lose one of the advantages of arbitration, which is to enable parties to bypass municipal courts. Another important factor is the availability of a diversity of arbitrators with regard to nationalities and qualifications. Parties should nominate arbitrators who are highly qualified yet do not share the same nationality as one of the parties. Otherwise, an arbitrator might be challenged for lack of neutrality. Another factor to take into consideration is the existence of a procedure to appoint an arbitrator if one party fails to appoint the arbitrator, because an arbitration cannot be allowed to flounder due to the failure of a party to appoint an arbitrator. Furthermore, a pre-hearing disclosure of evidence should be possible, i.e. the rules should allow an arbitrator or tribunal to require such disclosure. Moreover, the arbitral rules should allow the arbitral tribunal to appoint an independent expert instead of leaving it to the parties, which could waste time and money. Another important issue during the arbitration process is the appearance of both parties. Therefore, the rules must be clear about what should happen if one of parties fails to appear at the arbitration hearing. The arbitral award must also be carefully considered. The award should be reasoned and in writing to assure that it is based on appropriate contractual and legal principles. Only a well-reasoned award will survive a challenge before a municipal court. Furthermore, challenges against an award in court should be allowed only in limited circumstances. Otherwise, the benefit of arbitration as being final will be lost.[571] These are the most important factors that parties should consider in

570 ASSOCIATION, AAA/ICDR Handbook on International Arbitration and ADR 97. 2006.

571 Id. at. 97-100. Also see The NAFTA Secretariat website at: see https://www.nafta-sec-alena.org/Home/Alternative-Dispute-Resolution/Selecting-an-Arbit

selecting the arbitration institution. These factors will be clearer when the arbitration process is explained in the next section.

2. Ad Hoc Arbitration

In an ad hoc arbitration, the arbitrating parties have some advantages. The first is that the parties will not pay the fees and expenses of the administering institution like in institutional arbitration. The parties will also have the freedom to craft and tailor the rules that will govern the arbitration. Hence, if the parties decide to choose ad hoc arbitration, greater care needs to be given to identifying various procedural issues. A simpler alternative to trying to design a complete ad hoc procedural system is to designate one of the established procedural rule systems, such as the UNCITRAL Arbitration Rules. This needs co-operation from both arbitrating parties. One of the disadvantages of ad hoc arbitration is potential non-cooperation of one of the parties. This can present a significant problem in the arbitration process, and may require recourse to the municipal court to move the arbitration forward. This, in turn, can cost considerable time and money.[572]

F. The Arbitral Proceedings

The new Saudi Arbitration Law provides the arbitrating parties the freedom to rely on procedural rules of their choosing, as long as they do not conflict with the principles of Islamic Sharia. The liberty and autonomy of the parties is similar to the UNCITRAL Model Law, as will be presented in this section. In addition, when the arbitrating parties have not agreed on the procedural rules to be applied in the arbitration process, the new Saudi Arbitration Law sets forth a detailed arbitration procedure which includes features commonly used in international commercial arbitration practices in the different stages of the arbitration process, such as pleadings, witness statements, expert reports and hearings. Hence, this section will address the arbitral proceedings under the new Saudi Arbitration Law, comparing them with the international arbitration rules in a number of points.

---

ration-Institution.

572 See Wang, BROOK. J. INT'L L., 1063 (2002). Also see MOSES, The Principles and Practice of International Commercial Arbitration 9-10. 2012.

1. Initiation of the Arbitration Process

There are different types of international arbitration rules that address the procedure of commencing the arbitration process. One significant point at the beginning of arbitration is how to determine when the arbitration process begins. For example, does it begin when the claimant files a notice with the arbitration institution? Does it begin when the respondent receives the notice? Should the process be initiated by some other event? The two ways of handling this issue are by rules of limitations or by an arbitration agreement.

In addressing the issue of when the arbitration process begins, Article 4(2) of the ICC Arbitration Rules states that the date on which the request is received by the Secretariat of the Center shall be considered to be the date of the commencement of the arbitration.[573] Similar to the ICC Rules, Article 2 of the ICDR Rules and Article 1.4 of the LCIA Rules state that arbitration begins when the institution receives the arbitration request.[574] The UNCITRAL rules provide an option for the arbitrating parties to choose the rules that govern this matter; however, if the arbitrating parties do not agree, the date when the respondent receives the arbitration request will be deemed the beginning of the arbitration.[575] The new Saudi Arbitration Law follows the UNCITRAL Model Law in Article 26, which states: "The arbitration proceedings will begin on the day when one of the arbitrating parties receives the request for arbitration from the other party, unless the parties to the arbitration agree otherwise."[576] Clearly the Saudi Arbitration Law follows the Model Law verbatim regarding the time when the arbitration process commences.

Another point that should be addressed at the beginning of the arbitration is what the claimant must do to start the arbitration. For example, should the claimant file with the arbitration institution or submit to the other party or both a simple notice or a complete statement of the claim? In this regard, Article 4(3) of the ICC Rules states that the arbitration request must state the following:

> a) The name in full, description, address and other contact details of each of the parties;

573 ICC Rules of Arbitration. 2012.

574 ICDR Arbitration Rules. 2014. Also LCIA Arbitration rules. 2014.

575 UNCITRAL Model Law on International Commercial Arbitration Article 3(1). 2006.

576 Arbitration Law. 2012.

b) The name in full, address and other contact details of any person(s) representing the claimant in the arbitration;

c) A description of the nature and circumstances of the dispute giving rise to the claims and of the basis upon which the claims are made;

d) A statement of the relief sought, together with the amounts of any quantified claims and, to the extent possible, an estimate of the monetary value of any other claims;

e) Any relevant agreements and, in particular, the arbitration agreement(s);

f) Where claims are made under more than one arbitration agreement, an indication of the arbitration agreement under which each application is made;

g) All relevant particulars and any observations or proposals concerning the number of arbitrators and their choice in accordance with the provisions of Articles 12 and 13, and any nomination of an arbitrator required thereby; and

h) All relevant particulars and any observations or proposals as to the place of the arbitration, the applicable rules of law and the language of the arbitration. The claimant may submit such other documents or information with the request as it considers appropriate or as may contribute to the efficient resolution of the dispute.[577]

Article 2(3) of the ICDR Rules and Article 1.1 of the LCIA Rules impose similar requirements. However, unlike the other international arbitration rules, Article 1.1(iii) of the LCIA Rules and the Model Law require only a brief description of the claim when submitting the arbitration request.[578] Another difference is that a written arbitration notice must be directed to both the arbitration institution and the opposing party under the ICDR Rules,[579] while the ICC Rules and the LCIA Rules require that the notice be sent only to the arbitration institution.[580] Along with the request, the claimant must make an advance payment of administrative

577 ICC Rules of Arbitration. 2012.

578 LCIA Arbitration rules. 2014.

579 ICDR Arbitration Rules Article 2(1). 2014.

580 ICC Rules of Arbitration Article 4(1). 2012. Also, LCIA Arbitration rules Article 1.1. 2014.

expenses under the ICC Rules.[581] Similar to the international arbitration rules, the new Saudi Arbitration Law states in Article 30 that the claimant must send by the date agreed to by the arbitrating parties, or the one appointed by the arbitral tribunal, to the defendant and to each and every one of the arbitrators, a written statement of his claim, which includes the claimant's name and address, and the name and address of the defendant, and explain the facts of the claim, his requests and commitments, and any other matters that require the agreement of the parties.[582] As a result, the new Saudi law complies with international arbitration rules with regard to how arbitration is commenced.

The UNCITRAL Model Law also addresses when the statement is deemed legally to be delivered when there is no agreement between the arbitrating parties. Delivery occurs in such situations when it is made to the addressee personally, at his place of business, habitual residence or mailing address. If these conditions cannot be met after making a reasonable inquiry, a written communication is considered to have been received under the Model Law if it is sent to the addressee's last-known place of business, habitual residence or mailing address by registered letter or by any other means that makes a record of the attempted delivery. Moreover, the communication is deemed to have been received on the day it is so delivered, although the provisions of this article do not apply to communications in court proceedings.[583] Article 6 of the new Saudi law follows the Model Law in all meanings, and there is no difference between the applicable articles.[584]

Once the opposing arbitrating party receives the arbitration notice according to the arbitration rules, that party has a limited period of time to respond. The available time differs between different arbitration rules. For example, Article 5 of the ICC Arbitration Rules and Article 3 of the ICDR Rules state that the respondent shall submit an Answer within 30 days from the receipt of the arbitration request.[585] However, Article 2.1 of the LCIA Rules limits the period to

581 ICC Rules of Arbitration Article 4(4). 2012.

582 Saudi Arbitration Law. 2012.

583 UNCITRAL Model Law on International Commercial Arbitration Article 3. 2006.

584 Arbitration Law. 2012.

585 ICC Rules of Arbitration. 2012. Also ICDR Arbitration Rules. 2014.

28 days.[586] Article 30 of the new Saudi law refers the determination of this time period to the arbitration agreement or otherwise to the arbitral tribunal.[587]

Furthermore, the international arbitration rules often assume that certain (procedureal) rights have been waived if the respondent does not file a counterclaim within the time allowed. The same is true for any objections to the tribunal's jurisdiction, or an assertion that the tribunal is exceeding the scope of its authority.[588] For instance, Article 4 of the Model Law states:

> A party who knows that any provision of this Law from which the parties may derogate or any requirement under the arbitration agreement has not been complied with and yet proceeds with the arbitration without stating his objection to such non-compliance without undue delay or, if a time-limit is provided therefor, within such period of time, shall be deemed to have waived his right to object.[589]

Similarly, Article 2.1 of the LCIA Rules states:

> Failure to deliver a Response within the time allowed shall constitute an irrevocable waiver of that party's opportunity to nominate or propose any arbitral candidate. Failure to deliver all or any part of a Response within the time allowed or at all shall not (by itself) preclude the Respondent from denying any claim or from advancing any defense or cross-claim in the arbitration. [590]

In contrast, Article 20 of the Saudi law refers this issue to the arbitral tribunal to decide.[591]

As a result, unlike the old Saudi arbitration law, the new law provides arbitrating parties a high degree of autonomy for initiating arbitration proceedings without permission from the competent court. Article 9 of the old Saudi arbitration law specifically required the approval of the competent court for the commencement of an arbitration process.[592] Article 26 of the new law states: "The arbitration

---

586 LCIA Arbitration rules. 2014.

587 Arbitration Law. 2012.

588 See MOSES, The Principles and Practice of International Commercial Arbitration 160. 2012.

589 UNCITRAL Model Law on International Commercial Arbitration. 2006.

590 LCIA Arbitration rules. 2014.

591 Arbitration Law. 2012.

592 Arbitration Law (1983).

proceedings shall start from the day when one of the parties to the arbitration receives the request for arbitration from the other party, unless the parties to the arbitration agreed otherwise."[593] Hence, the new Saudi law follows standard international arbitration practice such that any arbitrating party can commence arbitration by serving notice on the opposite party without the involvement of the competent court.

2. The Pre-Hearing Process

Once the arbitral tribunal has been constituted, most international arbitration organizations require a significant process prior to the hearing.[594] According to David E. Wagoner, "a bad pre-hearing process makes a bad arbitration."[595] The pre-hearing process has three primary objectives.[596] The first is to set at an early stage the hearing dates and a procedural schedule embodied in a procedural order. For example, Article 24 of the ICC Arbitration Rules states that, during or following the preliminary conference, the arbitral tribunal shall establish the procedural timetable including those determinations that are considered provisional. The purpose is to organize the conduct of the arbitration.[597]

Another significant objective of the pre-hearing process is to identify the issues to be resolved by the tribunal and particularly those serious fact matters that require live testimony. In handling this matter, Article 23 of the ICC Arbitration Rules provides for a document called the Terms of Reference, which is based on the prior written submissions between the arbitrating parties. The Terms of Reference set forth the nature of the claims and defenses of the respective parties.[598] Moreover, after the Terms of Reference have been signed by the parties – or approved by the Court of the ICC, if any of the arbitrating parties refuses to take part in drawing up the Terms of Reference or to sign them – no party shall make new claims that fall outside of the limits of the Terms of Reference, unless authorized to do so by the arbitration tribunal, which will consider the nature of the new claims, the stage of the arbitration and other relevant circumstances.[599]

593 Arbitration Law. 2012.

594 See LCIA Arbitration Rules Article 14. 2014. Also see ICDR Arbitration Rules Article 4. 2014.

595 ASSOCIATION, AAA/ICDR Handbook on International Arbitration and ADR 73. 2006.

596 See id. Also, see MOSES, The Principles and Practice of International Commercial Arbitration 160-166. 2012.

597 ICC Rules of Arbitration. 2012.

598 See id. at Article 23

599 See id.

Furthermore, one of the preliminary matters that should be addressed in the pre-hearing process is the administration of the arbitration, which will organize and manage the arbitration process, such as that the examining of witnesses or the use of technology in the submission and exchange of documents.[600] In addition, if there is no agreement between the arbitrating parties about issues of rules, law, language, or place of arbitration, these issues will be addressed during this meeting.[601] Moreover, the deposit for expenses and fees will be discussed in an ad hoc arbitration, unlike the institutional arbitration, which will be required by the institution.[602] Because of the myriad of matters to be discussed at the preliminary meeting, the UNCITRAL Model Law provides a useful checklist entitled "UNCITRAL Notes on Organizing Arbitral Proceedings." This checklist can be helpful in addressing the preliminary matters in the initial meeting.[603]

Another issue that can arise during the pre-hearing process is whether the meeting before the hearing will be face-to-face or by other means, such as by telephone or video conferencing. Pierre Karrer, an arbitrator in Switzerland, explains the three factors that should be considered in choosing the type of preliminary meeting. Hence, he states:

> Whether to have a face-to-face initial meeting depends upon:
>
> 1) The size and complexity of the dispute;
>
> 2) The distance parties and counsel have to travel; and
>
> 3) Whether the arbitrators and counsel know one another.

Another factor is that sometimes clients want to come to a face-to-face conference to meet the arbitrators. Although telephone conferences are less expensive, if you are too cheap in the preliminary conference, you usually pay a price. [604]

---

600 See ASSOCIATION, AAA/ICDR Handbook on International Arbitration and ADR 74. 2006. See also, MOSES, The Principles and Practice of International Commercial Arbitration 161. 2012.

601 See MOSES, The Principles and Practice of International Commercial Arbitration 161. 2012.

602 See id.

603 This checklist is available at UNCITRAL website at: https://www.uncitral.org/pdf/english/texts/arbitration/arb-notes/arb-notes-e.pdf.

604 MOSES, The Principles and Practice of International Commercial Arbitration 160. 2012.

As a result, no one rule applies to all arbitration disputes when considering whether the parties should meet face-to-face with the arbitrator in a preliminary meeting, because different factors come into play.

The new Saudi Arbitration Law does not specify the procedures for the pre-hearing process. However, Article 25 provides the arbitrating parties with broad freedom to agree on the actions adopted by the arbitration tribunal, including the right to subject such actions to the valid rules of any institution, authority, or arbitration center in Saudi Arabia or abroad, such as the ICC Arbitration Rules and its Terms of Reference, which can save the parties time and costs by clarifying the procedure in advance.[605] However, the Saudi law requires that such rules cannot conflict with the provisions of Islamic Sharia. If the arbitrating parties cannot agree, the arbitral tribunal can choose the arbitration proceedings as it deems appropriate taking into account the provisions of Islamic Sharia and of this law.[606] As a result, the Saudi law provides the arbitrating parties an excellent opportunity to apply the best international rules for their own circumstances, which makes the Saudi law flexible in the arbitration field.

3. The Hearing

In international arbitration rules, holding a hearing in the arbitration process depends on the request[607] or demand of the arbitral tribunal on one of the arbitrating parties.[608] Saudi law also follows the international arbitration rules in providing full freedom to the arbitrating parties to decide about holding a hearing or simply having the tribunal resolve the dispute based on submitted documents alone. However, absent such an agreement, the arbitral tribunal has the authority to decide this matter.[609] Although the new law provides such wide freedom, the law sets some rules to make sure that the hearing is fair to the arbitrating parties. For example, Article 31 of the new law provides:

> A copy of all that is provided by one of the parties to the arbitral tribunal, such as notes, documents or other papers, shall be sent to the other party. Also, a copy of what is provided to the mentioned tribunal,

605 See ICC Rules of Arbitration Article 23. 2012.

606 Arbitration Law. 2012.

607 See ICDR Arbitration Rules Article 20(1). 2014.

608 See ICC Rules of Arbitration Article 25(6). 2012. Also see LCIA Arbitration rules Article 19.1. 2014.

609 Arbitration Law Article 25, 33(1). 2012.

> such as expert reports, documents and other evidence, that the arbitral tribunal can rely on when issuing its award, shall be sent to both parties.[610]

In discussing the arbitration hearing, the study needs to elaborate on various points in the hearing process as follows.

a. *Decisions on Procedural Issues*

If there is more than one arbitrator in the arbitration tribunal, all of the arbitrators confer regarding procedural issues, such as the disclosure of documents or time limitations for witness testimony, before rendering a decision, because such issues may delay the arbitration process and may impede the smooth operation of the arbitration process.[611] The international arbitration rules handle this issue by allowing the presiding arbitrator to decide procedural orders alone if the other members and all arbitrating parties agree.[612] For example, Article 29 of the UNCITRAL Model Law states:

> Decisions by the panel of arbitrators during the arbitral proceedings with more than one arbitrator shall be made, unless otherwise agreed by the parties, by a majority of all of its members. However, questions of procedure may be decided by the presiding arbitrator, if so authorized by the parties or all members of the arbitral tribunal.[613]

The Saudi law does not mention this issue, but it refers procedural matters to the arbitration agreement between the parties.[614] Hence, the agreement between the parties on such issues is the core in most international arbitration rules and the Saudi Arbitration Law.

b. *Seat of the Arbitration*

International arbitration rules provide the arbitrating parties the freedom to choose the seat of the arbitration. Absent agreement, the place of arbitration will be determined by the arbitral tribunal if it is ad hoc arbitration or by the arbitration institution if it is institutional having regard to the circumstances of the case,

---

610 Id. at Article 31.

611 See MOSES, The Principles and Practice of International Commercial Arbitration 167. 2012.

612 See LCIA Arbitration rules Article 14.6. 2014.

613 UNCITRAL Model Law on International Commercial Arbitration. 2006.

614 See Saudi Arbitration Law Article 25. 2012.

including the convenience of the parties.[615] Some arbitration rules provide a time limit for the arbitral tribunal to determine the place of arbitration. For example, the ICDR Rules provide that the tribunal must decide this aspect within 45 days after its constitution.[616] Furthermore, unless there is agreement between the arbitrating parties, the arbitral tribunal may, after consultation with the parties, conduct hearings, hold conferences, hear witnesses, inspect property or documents, or deliberate and meet at any location that it considers appropriate.[617] If the arbitral tribunal conducts a hearing at a place other than the place of arbitration, the arbitration will still be regarded as conducted at the place of arbitration, and any award will be deemed made at the place of arbitration.[618] Moreover, the law applicable to the arbitration agreement and the arbitration will be the law applicable at the seat of the arbitration,unless the arbitrating parties agree on the application of other laws or rules and such agreement is not prohibited by the law applicable at the arbitral seat. [619]

The new Saudi law follows the modern international arbitration rules regarding the seat of the arbitration matter. Article 28 of the new law states:

> The parties of the arbitration may agree on the place of the arbitration in the Kingdom or abroad. And if there is no agreement, the arbitral tribunal shall determine a place for the arbitration taking into account the circumstances of the claim, and the convenience of the site for both parties, without prejudice to the authority of the arbitral tribunal to meet at any place it deems appropriate for deliberation among its members, and to hear witnesses, or experts, or the parties to the dispute, or to preview the dispute, or to examine the documents, or review them.[620]

Hence, the Saudi courts are required under the new law to recognize and enforce arbitral awards from international venues outside of Saudi Arabia. However, in

---

615 See ICC Rules of Arbitration Article 18(1). 2012. Also, ICDR Arbitration Rules Article 17(1). 2014. Also, LCIA Arbitration rules Article 16.1 and 16.2. 2014. Also UNCITRAL Model Law on International Commercial Arbitration Article 20(1). 2006.

616 See ICDR Arbitration Rules Article 17(1). 2014.

617 See ICC Rules of Arbitration Article 18(2),(3). 2012. Also ICDR Arbitration Rules Article 17(2). 2014. Also, LCIA Arbitration rules Article 16.3. 2014. Also, UNCITRAL Model Law on International Commercial Arbitration Article 20(2). 2006.

618 See ICDR Arbitration Rules 17(2). 2014. Also see LCIA Arbitration rules Article 16.3. 2014.

619 See LCIA Arbitration rules Article 16.4. 2014.

620 Arbitration Law. 2012.

practice, these types of awards may face difficulties at the enforcement stage. According to Al-Ammari, Saud:

> The Saudi courts have traditionally been suspicious of arbitral awards issued outside of the country and Islamic region in general because of their concern that Sharia may not have been applied in the proceedings or in the arbitral award. One strategy that parties can, therefore, use to increase their ability to enforce an international arbitration award in Saudi courts is to select an arbitration venue in either Saudi Arabia, in a GCC country or in the Islamic world at large.[621]

In fact, as discussed in Chapter 2, the arbitrating parties may face difficulties in all stages of the arbitration process when issues come to the Saudi courts, not just at the enforcement stage. Some of the reasons were already discussed above. As a result, the new law regarding the seat of the arbitration complies with the modern arbitration rules, although the practice depends on how the Saudi courts will apply it.

c. Substantive Law of the Contract

The arbitrating parties under most modern international arbitration rules are free to choose the law that governs their disputes and contracts. For example, Article 21 of the ICC Arbitration Rules states: "The parties shall be free to agree upon the rules of law to be applied by the arbitral tribunal to the merits of the dispute. In the absence of any such agreement, the arbitral tribunal shall apply the rules of law which it determines to be appropriate."[622] The old Saudi law did not mention whether the arbitrating parties have the authority to choose the law to govern the contract and dispute.[623] In contrast, Article 38(1) of the new law states that the arbitral tribunal must apply the rules agreed upon by the parties to the arbitration on the subject of the dispute if they agree on the application of the law of a particular state. However, the chosen law must not conflict with the provisions of Islamic Sharia and public order in the Kingdom. If the parties have not agreed about the governing law, the tribunal shall apply the substantive rules of the law that it considers the most relevant to the subject of the dispute.[624] As a result, the new law gives broad freedom to choose the substantive law even if it is not one

---

621 Al-Ammari & Martin, ARBITRATION INTERNATIONAL, 394-395 (2014).

622 ICC Rules of Arbitration. 2012

623 See Al-Ammari & Martin, ARBITRATION INTERNATIONAL, 395 (2014).

624 Arbitration Law Article 38(1). 2012.

of the Islamic schools of jurisprudence as long as the law chosen does not contradict provisions in the primary sources of Islamic Sharia. In practice, there are some possible difficulties in choosing non-Saudi law as the applicable law in the arbitration contract. If the chosen law does not comply with Islamic Sharia as applied in Saudi courts, enforcement will be very difficult as will be explained extensively in the enforcement section.

d. Language of the Arbitration

Modern international arbitration rules give the arbitrating parties the freedom to choose the language or languages that apply during the arbitral proceedings. However, absent such agreement, the arbitral tribunal will determine the language or languages to be used in the process.[625] This agreement or determination, unless otherwise specified therein, should apply to every written statement by a party and to every hearing, award, decision and other communication by the arbitral tribunal.[626] Moreover, the arbitral tribunal may order that any documentary evidence or witness testimony will be accompanied by a translation into the language or languages agreed upon by the parties or determined by the arbitral tribunal.[627]

Because every document, witness testimony and legal argument should be translated for an arbitrator who does not speak the chosen language, the arbitration will become more costly and will take longer. The IBA Rules of Ethics for International Arbitrators, which were issued in 1987, require in Article 2.2 that an arbitrator should not accept an appointment if he does not have adequate knowledge of the arbitration language.[628] However, if the language of the arbitration is not known in advance, this IBA provision will not be effective. [629]

Unlike the old Saudi arbitration law, which required that the Arabic language must be the official language in the whole arbitration process at all its stages and also in all correspondence,[630] the new Saudi law is similar to the modern arbitration rules and provides the arbitrating parties the freedom to choose any

625 See ICC Rules of Arbitration Article 20. 2012. Also ICDR Arbitration Rules Article 18. 2014. Also, UNCITRAL Model Law on International Commercial Arbitration Article 22(1). 2006.

626 See UNCITRAL Model Law on International Commercial Arbitration Article 22(1). 2006. Also, see ICDR Arbitration Rules Article 18. 2014.

627 See UNCITRAL Model Law on International Commercial Arbitration Article 22(2). 2006.

628 IBA Rules of Ethics for International Arbitrators (1987).

629 See MOSES, The Principles and Practice of International Commercial Arbitration 169. 2012.

630 See Al-Ammari & Martin, ARBITRATION INTERNATIONAL, 395-396 (2014).

language that suits their needs.[631] The law also gives the arbitral tribunal the authority to determine the arbitration language absent agreement by the parties on this aspect.[632] Once a language is determined, it applies to the entire arbitration proceedings, including submission of data and written submissions and oral pleadings, every decision made by the tribunal, message oriented sent to or from it, and finally the award rendered by it.[633] Furthermore, similar to most modern arbitration rules, the Saudi law allows the arbitral tribunal to require that all or some of the written documents provided in the claim be attached to a translation into the language or languages used in the arbitration. Regarding multiple languages, the tribunal may confine the interpretation to some of them.[634] Otherwise, the new law provides that the default language in the arbitration is Arabic.[635] If a language or languages other than Arabic are involved, the law requires that the arbitration award be translated into the Arabic language and must be certified by an accredited authority to submit it to the Saudi court for enforcement.[636]

e. Legal Representation Requirements

Most jurisdictions do not require that lawyers who represent the arbitrating parties be admitted to the local bar, and some of them do not even require representatives to be lawyers or have any legal background.[637] In the Kingdom of Saudi Arabia, the new law does not mention who can legally represent the parties during the arbitration process. Hence, the Code of Legal Practice in Saudi Arabia must be considered as long as there are no exceptions about arbitration. Article 3 of the Code of Legal Practice in Saudi Arabia states:

> A person who practices law shall have his name included in the list of practicing lawyers and shall satisfy the following requirements:
>
> a) He must be a Saudi national. However, a non-Saudi shall be entitled to practice law subject to the terms of agreements concluded between the Kingdom and other countries.

631 Arbitration Law Article 29(1). 2012.

632 Id.

633 Id.

634 Id. at Article 29(2).

635 Id. at Article 29(1).

636 Id. at Article 53.

637 See MOSES, The Principles and Practice of International Commercial Arbitration 169. 2012.

b) He must be a holder of a degree from a Sharia college or a bachelor of law from one of the Kingdom's universities or an equivalent of any of these degrees obtained from abroad, or a post-graduate diploma in legal studies from the Institute of Public Administration.

c) He must have at least three years of practical legal experience. This period may be reduced to one year for a holder of a Master's degree in Sharia or law, or an equivalent of any of these degrees, or a post-graduate diploma in law for the graduates of a Sharia college. This requirement shall not apply to a holder of a doctorate in these fields of specialization.

d) He must be of good conduct and not under interdiction.

e) He must not have been subjected to any Hadd (Quranic prescribed punishment) or any other sentence in connection with a crime that impugns integrity, except where a minimum period of five years has expired since the execution of that sentence.

f) He must be a resident of the Kingdom.

The Minister of Justice shall cause to be prepared a declaration form to be signed by the applicant wherein he confirms that the requirements of paragraphs stated in (d), (e), and (f) of this article are complied with.[638]

As a result, the Saudi law does not differentiate between the arbitration process and other legal actions in the requirements for legal representation. This can be both positive and negative. For example, if the need arises during the arbitration process to go to court for assistance or to enforce arbitral awards, a local lawyer may be required to deal with the legal matters in the Kingdom. Under the current state of the law, the parties will already have one and save time and money. On the other hand, in international business arbitration, a party could need an international lawyer to help with the complicated international matters, who has knowledge of global commerce, which differs from local issues. In this case, the party will not gain an advantage by hiring the international lawyer, because the party will then have to hire both a local lawyer and an international legal consultant, which will be more costly.

---

638 Code of Law Practice (2001).

f. *The Flexibility of the Hearing Procedure*

Unlike hearings before courts, the flexibility of hearings in arbitration is clear under most modern international arbitration rules and practices.[639] The new Saudi law follows this trend, so that each of the arbitrating parties may amend his requests or the aspects of his defense, or he may complete them during the arbitration proceedings, unless the arbitration tribunal refuses to permit it, which may occur, for example, to prevent delays to the process or arbitral award.[640]

g. *Record of Proceedings*

Either or both of the arbitrating parties may require a verbatim record of the arbitration proceedings. Usually, the parties share its cost, which can be expensive, especially if it is provided on a daily basis.[641] The arbitration rules, including the Saudi law, leave this matter to the arbitration agreement.

h. *Technology*

The availability of modern technology to arbitrating parties and the arbitral tribunal can significantly improve the arbitration process and increase its speed, decrease its cost, and improve its efficiency. The types of technology range from from PowerPoint or video for the presentation of information to sophisticated database management systems. According to Thomas D. Halket:

> Software can analyze large amounts of documentary evidence in ways that would not be possible by hand; video technology is an alternative to traditional in-person hearing based procedures when those procedures prove to be overly costly or just plain impossible to implement; e-mail can be a reliable, secure, and fast means of party-panel communications, and on-line filing sites can provide safe, authoritative, and convenient repositories for all documents pertinent to an arbitration. Many technical aids are easily available at low or no cost and in a very real sense, they can be a win-win for the arbitral process. [642]

---

639 See ICDR Arbitration Rules Article 20(4). 2014. Also see MOSES, The Principles and Practice of International Commercial Arbitration 169. 2012.

640 Arbitration Law Article 32. 2012.

641 See MOSES, The Principles and Practice of International Commercial Arbitration 170. 2012.

642 Thomas D Halket, Use of Technology in Arbitration: Ensuring the Future Is Available to Both Parties, St. JOHN'S L. REV., 305-306 (2007).

As a result, the arbitral institutions and other related organizations realized the importance of technology in the arbitration process. Accordingly, they introduced rules and guidelines to deal with technology-related issues, such as E-documents under the IBA Rules on the Taking of Evidence in International Arbitration,[643] or the ICC Report on E- Discovery completed in August 2011.[644]

The new Saudi law acknowledges the need for technology in the arbitration process. Therefore, it opened the door to arbitrating parties to use and adopt any international rules or guidelines that pertain to how to apply technology in a modern and efficient way without specifying them or imposing any conditions on them.[645] In addition, Saudi Arabia recently issued two laws that govern all electronic disputes, the Electronic Transaction Law[646] and the Anti-Online Crime Law.[647] Hence, the Kingdom is ready to allow technology tools in arbitration proceedings. However, in practice, the use of technology needs to be evaluated, because the law is still new. Furthermore, because technology changes quickly, parties should refer to the international rules and guidelines, which usually accompany the latest changes in technology, instead of determining the relevant rules in the Saudi law, which can be too old for the fast changing technology. This is the best way for the Kingdom to keep up with international practice and the modern track.

i. Equal Treatment of the Parties

Most arbitration rules impose on the arbitral tribunal the duty to achieve fairness in dealing with the arbitrating parties. Hence, the rules assure two main things during the arbitration hearing: that parties be treated equally and that they be given a full opportunity to present their case.[648] Saudi law follows the modern rules in this regard.[649] However, applying equal treatment during the arbitration hearing does not always mean the same manner and can differ from case to case.

643 See IBA Rules on the Taking of Evidence in International Arbitration Article 3(3)(a)(ii) (2010).

644 See MOSES, The Principles and Practice of International Commercial Arbitration 170. 2012.

645 See Arbitration Law Article 5. 2012.

646 See The Electronic Transaction Law, No. M/18 (2007).

647 See The Anti Online Crime Law, No. M/17 (2007).

648 See UNCITRAL Model Law on International Commercial Arbitration Article 18. 2006. See also ASSOCIATION, AAA/ICDR Handbook on International Arbitration and ADR 75-76. 2006.

649 See Arbitration Law Article 27. 2012.

For example, the panel may decide not to give the parties the same amount of time to present their cases. In this regard, Margaret L. Moses says:

> Arbitrators must always use their common sense to ensure fairness and equal treatment. It may not always be fair to provide exactly equal time to the parties, because one side may have more witnesses or may have a much heavier burden of proof. Giving each side an equal opportunity to present its case fairly may, in fact, result in one side having more time than the other side.[650]

As result, treating parties equally in practice needs to be flexible in the view of the arbitral tribunal to ensure that each party is treated fairly if not equally.

j. Default of Appearance

With regard to appearing at arbitration and participating during the arbitration proceedings, the new Saudi law follows the UNCITRAL Model Law entirely.[651] A party may be defaulted in any of three possible situations. First, if, within the time period as agreed by the arbitrating parties or determined by the arbitral tribunal, the arbitration tribunal does not receive the statement of the claimant's claim, which contains the specific requirements stated in Article 23(1) of the Model Law,[652] the arbitral tribunal must terminate the arbitration proceedings. Secondly, if the respondent fails to communicate his statement of defense in accordance with the specific requirements stated in Article 23(1) of the Model Law, the arbitral tribunal must continue the proceedings without treating such a failure as an automatic win for the claimant; the claimant must still prove its claim during the process of arbitration. Lastly, if any of the arbitrating parties fails to appear at a hearing or to produce the required documentary evidence, the arbitral tribunal has the authority to continue the arbitration proceedings and issue the arbitral award based on the available evidence before it. In such a situation, the party who did not participate may challenge the arbitral award that was made against

---

650 MOSES, The Principles and Practice of International Commercial Arbitration 171. 2012.

651 See UNCITRAL Model Law on International Commercial Arbitration Article 25. 2006. Also see Arbitration Law Article 34,35. 2012.

652 Article 23(1) of the UNCITRAL Model Law states: "Within the period of time agreed by the parties or determined by the arbitral tribunal, the claimant shall state the facts supporting his claim, the points at issue and the relief or remedy sought, and the respondent shall state his defense in respect of these particulars, unless the parties have otherwise agreed as to the required elements of such statements. The parties may submit with their statements all documents they consider to be relevant or may add a reference to the documents or other evidence they will submit."

him. To avoid this possibility, the arbitral tribunal should try to make all possible efforts to provide the respondent with a fair chance to participate in the arbitration proceedings.[653]

k. Expedited Arbitration Proceeding

One of the main concerns in international arbitration is delay in the arbitration proceedings.[654] Consequently, the modern arbitration rules provide the parties with the right to shorten the arbitration proceedings, which is referred to as fast-track arbitration. For example, Article 38(1) of ICC Rules provides such a right; however, any such agreement entered into after the constitution of an arbitral tribunal will become effective only upon the approval of the tribunal[655] However, the arbitration institution could save the right to extend any time limit if it deems that it is essential to achieve the responsibilities under the rules,[656] in which event and as long as the rules permit, the institution will eliminate the purpose of an expedited arbitration proceeding in the first place. In fact, the fast track arbitration could guarantee the parties a speedy procedure, and the awards could be rendered within a short time through the more efficient process avoiding any unnecessary delays during the arbitration proceedings, which helps to save time and reduce cost. However, some flexibility to extend time limits is necessary where appropriate especially in international arbitration, in which lawyers may not be familiar with the applicable law or legal system.[657] Hence, short time limits for arbitration proceedings should be considered on a case-by-case basis depending on the circumstances.

The new Saudi Arbitration Law leaves the opportunity to the parties to choose what they think is best for them. The parties can take advantage of any modern

---

653 See MOSES, The Principles and Practice of International Commercial Arbitration 171-172. 2012.

654 See ASSOCIATION, AAA/ICDR Handbook on International Arbitration and ADR 67-79. 2006.

655 ICC Rules of Arbitration. 2012.

656 Id. at 38(2).

657 See Irene Welser & Christian Klausegger, Fast Track Arbitration: Just Fast or Something Different?, 259 AUSTRIAN ARBITRATION YEARBOOK (2009). Also see Mirèze Philippe, Are Specific Fast-Track Arbitration Rules Necessary?, PERMANENT COURT OF ARBITRATION/PEACE PALACE PAPERS, THE (HRSG.), ARBITRATION IN AIR, SPACE AND TELECOMMUNICATIONS LAW, DEN HAAG (2002). Also see MOSES, The Principles and Practice of International Commercial Arbitration 172. 2012.

arbitration rules because the new Saudi Law leaves these decisions to party autonomy without specifying requirements for them.[658]

4. Presenting Evidence

Generally, the arbitral tribunal under most modern international arbitration rules has the authority to manage the procedures for taking evidence between the arbitrating parties and to determine the admissibility and the weight of the presented evidence.[659] Similar to the current rules, the Saudi law provides such power to the arbitral tribunal.[660] However, the arbitral tribunal usually applies a flexible approach to establishing the facts presented in a case instead of using the rules of evidence that are part of the procedural law of the seat of the arbitration.[661] The study will explain this through the following points.

a. The IBA Rules on the Taking of Evidence

One of the significant points that faces international arbitration is the difference between legal systems in approaching evidence. Hence, especially important are the IBA Rules on the Taking of Evidence in International Arbitration (IBA Rules), which were adopted in 1999 and amended in 2010 and which provide flexible rules that try to find a compromise between various legal norms and practices in international arbitration. These Rules can be especially useful when the arbitrating parties and their representatives come from different legal cultures.[662]

---

658 See Arbitration Law Article 25(1), 38(2). 2012.

659 See ICDR Arbitration Rules Article 20(6). 2014. It states: "At any time during the proceedings, the tribunal may order the parties to produce documents, exhibits, or other evidence it deems necessary or appropriate." Also see ASSOCIATION, AAA/ICDR Handbook on International Arbitration and ADR 74-79. 2006.

660 See Arbitration Law Article 25(2),28,31,33,38(1). 2012.

661 See MOSES, The Principles and Practice of International Commercial Arbitration 172. 2012.

662 See ASSOCIATION, AAA/ICDR Handbook on International Arbitration and ADR 140. 2006. Also see IBA Rules on the Taking of Evidence in International Arbitration 2. 2010. The Committee that established the IBA Rules on the Taking of Evidence in International Arbitration is in the International Bar Association's Legal Practice Division. This panel focuses on the various aspects, such as laws, practice, and procedures relating to the arbitration of transnational disputes. Also, currently, the Committee has more than 2,300 members in 90 different countries, and membership has increased steadily. The Committee tries to share and provide details about the international arbitration files through publications and conferences. Information about this Committee is available on its website at http://www.ibanet.org/LPD/Dispute_Resolution_Section/Arbitration/Default.aspx

The IBA Rules contain mechanisms for the presentation of documents, witnesses of fact and expert witnesses, and inspections, in addition to conducting the evidentiary hearings. The IBA Rules also recommend the specific languages to add in the arbitration clause if the arbitrating parties want to adopt its rules. For example, it states that parties could choose the following languages:[663] "[In addition to the institutional, ad hoc or other rules chosen by the parties,] [t]he parties agree that the arbitration shall be conducted according to the IBA Rules of Evidence as current on the date of [this agreement/the commencement of the arbitration]." Moreover, one of the great advantages of the IBA Rules is that arbitrating parties and tribunals can choose to adopt them in whole or in part any time during the arbitration process. Parties can also consider them to be binding or use them as guidelines to develop their own procedures.[664] Some arbitrating parties prefer to use the Rules merely as recommendations to be more flexible and make the arbitral process responsive to the needs of a particular case. Others prefer the rules to be binding so that there will be less discussion about evidentiary issues during the arbitration process, which saves time and costs in arbitration.[665]

Similar to modern international rules, the arbitrating parties who chose the new Saudi law may need to use the IBA Rules. As stated earlier, the new Saudi Arbitration Law is open to international arbitration,[666] and allows participation by international parties from different legal norms and cultures. Hence, applying the IBA Rules can be helpful in addressing the issue of presenting evidence during the arbitration process. The arbitrating parties can decide whether to use those IBA Rules that they see to suit their needs as binding rules or as guidance.

b. *The Burden of Proof*

In international arbitral proceedings, most rules state that each party must demonstrate the facts with sufficient evidence.[667] For example, Article 27(1) of the UNCITRAL Model Law states: "Each party shall have the burden of proving the

663 See the IBA Rules on the Taking of Evidence in International Arbitration 2-3. 2010.

664 Id.

665 See MOSES, The Principles and Practice of International Commercial Arbitration 173. 2012.

666 See Arbitration Law Article 3. 2012.

667 See MOSES, The Principles and Practice of International Commercial Arbitration 174-175. 2012. Also see Caroline E Foster, Burden of Proof in International Courts and Tribunals, 29 AUST. YBIL (2010). Also see ASSOCIATION, AAA Handbook on International Arbitration and ADR 81. 2010.

facts relied on to support its claim or defense."[668] Similarly, Article 30(3) of the new Saudi law requires that both parties present the evidence that supports their claims.[669] However, the arbitrating parties can choose the rules that manage this issue in their arbitration agreement if they believe that a different rule will fulfill their needs better.

c. Documentary Evidence

The major types of evidence that parties rely on in international commercial arbitration are the supporting documents. Hence, each party is bound to produce to the other party the documents that the submitting party contends are in support of its position in the dispute.[670] Although most international arbitration rules explain this matter,[671] the most detailed set of international rules that manage the issue of documentary evidence and its production are the IBA Rules.[672] For example, Article 3(3) of IBA Rules explains the production of documentary evidence. It states:

> A Request to Produce shall contain:
>
> (a) (i) a description of each requested Document sufficient to identify it, or a description in sufficient detail (including subject matter) of a narrow and specific requested category of Documents that are reasonably believed to exist; in the case of Documents maintained in electronic form, the requesting Party may, or the Arbitral Tribunal may order that it shall be required to, identify specific files, search terms, individuals or other means of searching for such Documents in an efficient and economical manner;
>
> (b) a statement as to how the Documents requested are relevant to the case and material to its outcome; and
>
> (c) (i) a statement that the Documents requested are not in the possession, custody or control of the requesting Party or a statement

---

668 UNCITRAL Arbitration Rules (2010).

669 Arbitration Law. 2012.

670 See ASSOCIATION, AAA/ICDR Handbook on International Arbitration and ADR 142-143. 2006. Also see MOSES, The Principles and Practice of International Commercial Arbitration 175-178. 2012.

671 See ICDR Arbitration Rules Article 21. 2014. Also see LCIA Arbitration rules 22.1(iv),(v). 2014. Also UNCITRAL Arbitration Rules Article 27(3). 2010.

672 ASSOCIATION, AAA/ICDR Handbook on International Arbitration and ADR 142. 2006.

of the reasons why it would be unreasonably burdensome for the requesting Party to produce such Documents, and (ii) statement of the reasons why the requesting Party assumes that the Documents requested are in the possession, custody or control of another Party.[673]

One can infer from the stated article that the arbitral tribunal will order a party to produce the documents if the request contains a description of specific documents or classes of documents, and that tribunal has broad discretion to order such documents from the other party and evaluate the importance of such an order in proving the case.[674]

Similarly, the new Saudi law gives the arbitrating parties a wide opportunity to agree on any rules or guidelines that may govern the issue of producing documents. The Saudi law also follows the Model Law by providing court assistance in obtaining such documentary evidence from the other party or from non-parties with an importance of tribunal discretion in such manner similar to the Model Law, on condition that these rules must not conflict with the provisions of Islamic Sharia. [675]

d. Witnesses of Fact

Fact witnesses play an important role in international commercial arbitration. For instance, under the IBA Rules, witness statements are submitted to the arbitral tribunal and the other arbitrating parties during the arbitration process within the time ordered by the Arbitral Tribunal. The parties are also usually permitted to submit revised or additional witness statements, including statements from individuals not previously named as witnesses, so long as such revisions and additions respond only to matters stated in another party's witness statements, expert reports or other submissions that have not been previously presented in the arbitration.[676] Also, any individual can testify at the arbitration hearing,

673 IBA Rules on the Taking of Evidence in International Arbitration. 2010.

674 Also 21(4) of ICDR Rules explain: "The tribunal may, upon application, require a party to make available to another party documents in that party's possession not otherwise available to the party seeking the documents, that are reasonably believed to exist and to be relevant and material to the outcome of the case. Requests for documents shall contain a description of specific documents or classes of documents, along with an explanation of their relevance and materiality to the outcome of the case."

675 See UNCITRAL Arbitration Rules Article 27. 2010. Also see Arbitration Law Article 22(3),25. 2012.

676 IBA Rules on the Taking of Evidence in International Arbitration Article 4(6). 2010.

including a party itself, in accordance with the arbitral tribunal's discretion.[677] Furthermore, modern international arbitration rules allow a prior meeting with witnesses to discuss their prospective testimony with them. According to Margaret L. Moses: "In some countries, rules of professional conduct or case law prohibit prior meetings with witnesses. However, it is generally expected in international arbitrations that witnesses will be interviewed.[678] Also, the type of examination of the witnesses and the nature and extent of the arbitrator's intervention depend on the rules that arbitrating parties agree or otherwise on the arbitration tribunal's discretion according to the specific circumstances.[679]

The appearance and availability of witnesses occupy a significant place in the arbitration process. For example, under the IBA Rules, if one of the parties requests a fact witness or expert, the tribunal orders the witness to appear in person, unless the tribunal allows using technology, such as a video conference. If, without appropriate reason, the stated witness fails to appear to testify at the hearing, the arbitral tribunal will disregard any witness statement related to that evidentiary hearing by that absent witness unless the arbitral tribunal decides otherwise under the particular circumstances.[680] However, if a person who has evidence refuses to appear voluntarily at the arbitral tribunal's request, the arbitral tribunal can take whatever legal steps to obtain the testimony of that individual.[681] In addition, the arbitral tribunal has the authority at any time prior to and including the arbitration to order any party to provide the appearance for testimony at an evidentiary hearing of any person, including one whose testimony has not yet been offered.[682]

The new Saudi law provides two significant aspects regarding this subject. The first is providing arbitrating parties with extensive opportunities to govern fact witnesses under any international rules that they deem appropriate for their dispute.[683] Also, it provides assistance through the competent court according to what this tribunal considers fit for the proper functioning of arbitration, such as:

---

677 See MOSES, The Principles and Practice of International Commercial Arbitration 180-181. 2012. Also see ASSOCIATION, AAA/ICDR Handbook on International Arbitration and ADR 143-144. 2006.

678 MOSES, The Principles and Practice of International Commercial Arbitration 181. 2012.

679 See Id. at 181-184

680 See IBA Rules on the Taking of Evidence in International Arbitration Article 8(1),4(7). 2010.

681 See Id. Article 4(9).

682 See Id. Article 4(10).

683 See Arbitration Law Article 25(1). 2012.

call a witness or an expert with no prejudice to the right of the arbitral tribunal to conduct that independently.[684] In sum, the Saudi law is similar to the modern trend in respecting party autonomy with available assistance from the court to achieve the arbitration goals.

e. Expert Witnesses

In addition to fact witnesses, the arbitration may need the opinions of experts based on their expertise to resolve some highly technical issues. According to Karl-Heinz Bockstiegel: "The tribunal has the burden of making its own evaluation of disputed technical or scientific questions presented through expert opinion."[685] Because it is hard for the arbitral tribunal to decide whose testimony is more convincing when both parties present expert testimony,[686] most modern arbitration rules allow the arbitral tribunal to appoint one or more neutral experts to testify regarding the disputed matter.[687] Both the new Saudi law and the UNCITRAL Model Law require that the arbitral tribunal notify both parties about its appointment of an expert, unless they agree otherwise. However, the Model Law states that the expert report must be written, while Saudi law allows reports to be written, oral or both to be determined by the arbitral tribunal.[688] Moreover, the Model Law and Saudi law require that both arbitrating parties submit to the appointed expert the information related to the dispute and also allow him to examine and inspect documents, items or other material related to the dispute. During this process, the arbitral tribunal will resolve every possible dispute that may arise between parties or one of them and the expert in this regard, and the tribunal's determination is not subject to appeal by any method.[689] Furthermore, Saudi law and the Model Law confirm that the arbitral tribunal must allow the arbitrating parties to examine the documents relied upon by the expert in his report, and the expert may issue a final report after considering what both sides note about it. The arbitral tribunal must also hold a hearing to provide the parties with the opportunity to hear the expert's testimony and what is stated in the report.[690] Moreover, to assure the parties that the expert is independent, the

684 See Id. at Article 22(3).

685 ASSOCIATION, AAA/ICDR Handbook on International Arbitration and ADR 144. 2006.

686 See Id.

687 See ICDR Arbitration Rules Article 25(1). 2014. Also see UNCITRAL Arbitration Rules. 2010.

688 See UNCITRAL Arbitration Rules Article 29. 2010. Arbitration Law Article 36. 2012. See also ASSOCIATION, AAA Handbook on International Arbitration and ADR 88. 2010.

689 See UNCITRAL Arbitration Rules Article 29. 2010. Arbitration Law Article 36. 2012.

690 See Id.

UNCITRAL Model Law adds that, before accepting the appointment, the expert should describe his qualifications and state to the arbitral tribunal and the arbitrating parties that he is impartial and independent. The parties must have the opportunity to object to the expert's qualifications, impartiality and independence. The arbitral tribunal should also decide promptly whether to accept all of some of those objections. However, after an expert is appointed, an arbitrating party can object to the expert's qualifications, impartiality or independence only if that objection is for reasons of which the party becomes aware after the appointment has been made, in which event the arbitral tribunal must decide promptly what, if any, action to take.[691]

f. Suspension and Termination of Arbitration Proceedings

The new Saudi law also provides rules that apply if a matter is brought up during the arbitration proceeding, which is not within the authority of the arbitral tribunal. For example, if a party contends that a document presented to the arbitration tribunal has been forged, or penal proceedings have been taken for fraud or any other criminal action, the arbitration tribunal may consider and resolve the matter or it may determine that it is not necessary to decide the matter. The arbitral tribunal in such case can continue reviewing the dispute.[692] However, if the tribunal determines that the matter cannot be resolved and that it affects the resolution of the dispute, the proceedings must be stayed until a final decision is issued in this matter, which will lead to the suspension of the deadline for the issuance of the arbitration award. [693]

The arbitration proceedings end when the arbitral award is issued. However, in certain instances, the arbitration proceedings may end before the arbitral award is issued. The Saudi law and the UNCITRAL Model Law are identical in such cases.

1) If the arbitrating parties agree to end the arbitration process.

2) If the complainant leaves the dispute, unless the arbitration tribunal decides upon the request of the defendant that he has a serious interest in continuing the arbitration proceedings to settle the dispute.

3) If the arbitration tribunal deems for any other reasons the futility of continuing the arbitration proceedings or its impossibility.

---

691 See UNCITRAL Arbitration Rules Article 29(2). 2010.

692 Arbitration Law Article 37. 2012.

693 See id.

4) If the prosecutor does not provide without an acceptable excuse a written statement of his claim accordance with the provision of the Article 30(1) of the Model Law.[694]

The new Saudi law does not consider the death of one of the parties to the arbitration or his loss of eligibility to participate in the arbitration as causes that require ending the arbitration proceedings, unless it is otherwise agreed by a competent person and the other party to terminate the dispute, and the determined date for the arbitration is extended for thirty days, unless the arbitral tribunal decides to extend the period for a similar period or the arbitrating parties to the arbitration agree otherwise.[695]

g. *Closing the Hearing*

At the end of an arbitration hearing, the arbitral tribunal will declare closure of the hearing. Usually, before closing the hearing, the arbitral tribunal will ask the arbitrating parties if there is an further inquiry or proofs to offer, such as witnesses to be heard or submissions to make. Moreover, on its own initiative or upon the application of one of the parties, the arbitral tribunal may reopen the hearings at any time before the award is made in the presence of exceptional circumstances, such as if new evidence is discovered.[696] The new Saudi law does not mention how the arbitral tribunal shall close the hearing. This will be left to party agreement or following the above stated arbitration practice.

G. Conclusions

The arbitration process provided in the new Saudi Arbitration Law is comprehensively modernized and approximated to most international rules. First, unlike the previous law, the new Law clarifies the meanings of some terms, such as the term of the arbitration agreement. It states that the arbitration agreement is an agreement between two or more parties to refer to arbitration all or some of the particular disputes that have occurred or might occur between the parties concerning a certain contractual relation, whether it is in the form of a contract and whether the arbitration agreement appears as an arbitration condition mentioned in a contract or as an independent arbitration stipulation. Under the

---

694 See id. at Article 41. See also UNCITRAL Model Law on International Commercial Arbitration 32. 2006.

695 Arbitration Law article 41. 2012.

696 See UNCITRAL Arbitration Rules. 2010. Article 31; ICC Rules Article 27, 2010; ICDR Article 27, 2014.

new Law, there are no conditions about any particular nationality, gender, or religion, and only the chairman of the arbitral tribunal is required to have a legal or Sharia degree. Of special significance is that the new Law identifies the standards that make the arbitration international under the law, while the old law did not address to determine when to make the arbitration international. Moreover, there is clarity and precision in dealing with technical issues that may be mixed with confusion at all stages of the arbitral process. For example, the law provides clearly the authority of the arbitral tribunal to use any technical and legal experts to achieve the principle of balance among the members of the arbitral tribunal. In addition, unlike the old law, in which the court intervened during the arbitration process broadly, the role of the court has become supportive of the arbitration. Regulating the relationship between the arbitration process and the Saudi courts was the most difficult aspect that affected the arbitration process in the Kingdom. For example, the new Law does not require the adoption of the arbitration document by a court before the dispute can be subjected to arbitration, which was one of the obstacles that delayed the start of the arbitration process in the former regime, because it could take a court several months to act.

In addition to limiting the court's involvement in the arbitration process, the new Law provides the arbitral tribunal with more power in different parts of the arbitration. For example, Article 33(1) gives the arbitral tribunal the power to decide whether to hold a hearing or only to send memoranda and documents. Article 35 of the new law also gives the arbitral tribunal the authority to continue the arbitration proceedings in the event of default by the defendant and the defendant's failure to attend a meeting despite receiving notification to induce defendants to attend arbitration hearings and not to cause delays in procedures. Furthermore, the arbitral tribunal has the power to issue both procedures and precautionary measures provisional or conservatory as requested by the parties to achieve equality and justice between the parties until the issuance of the award that terminates the dispute. Moreover, the arbitration process will have guarantees of impartiality and fairness. If an arbitrator exhibits any lack of impartiality at any stage of the arbitration proceedings, the parties have the right to challenge the arbitrator.

Conversely, there are some points that should be clarified to reinforce the arbitration process in the Kingdom and to live up to the best legal and regulatory foundations. One of the disadvantages of the new Law is that it prohibits government agencies from using arbitration except under certain circumstances, which may deprive public sector companies of the opportunity to use arbitration or make them reluctant to resort to it. There are large state-owned businesses in the Kingdom that operate in the oil, energy, aviation, communications and other areas. If these governmental entities had the right to resort to arbitration directly with the contracting parties, it would be a significant incentive for foreign investors to deal with them, because arbitration provides unique advantages, such as confidentiality, speed, and professional specialists. Furthermore, the new Law needs to change some rules, such the rules that require arbitration proceedings to restart from the beginning if an arbitrator is replaced after the arbitration proceedings began. Some issues should be clarified by adding some rules. For example, the new Law does not address the scope of judicial review in the enforcement of an arbitration agreement and the basis for interim measures.

Moreover, some significant points should be considered about the arbitrator. First, according to Article 14 of the new Law, the arbitrator must have at least a university degree in law or Islamic Sharia to serve as the sole arbitrator or as the head of the tribunal. Most modern rules do not impose such requirements; in general, arbitration is not limited to those who have a background in legal or Islamic Sharia, but extends to all professionals, such as engineers, accountants, doctors and others. However, it is understood that the law requires that arbitrators have a legal background in case he serves as the sole arbitrator or as the head of the tribunal panel, because it complies with arbitration practice to prefer an arbitrator who has a legal background. However, it is not clear why an arbitrator must have an Islamic Sharia degree, as many who have such a degree have little knowledge of the legal field. Another issue is the immunity of arbitrators. The new Law does not address this subject, which may leave parties reluctant to participate in arbitration, because they cannot be confident that the arbitrator will faithfully perform his obligations.

Chapter 4

Arbitral Awards Between Saudi Law and International Rules

Arbitrating parties expect that the arbitration process will result in final and binding awards. To reassure foreign investors to invest in the Kingdom, the Kingdom signed the New York Convention in 1994. Despite accession to the New York Convention, Saudi Arabia has been described as a hostile country toward the recognition of arbitration agreements and enforcement of foreign awards, and many international awards have been rejected.[697] Hence, the Kingdom has tried to improve by reforming its arbitration regime. A new Enforcement Law came into effect in 2012 by Royal Decree No. M/53. The new Law, which replaced older provisions, and its possible impact on the enforcement of arbitral awards, should be examined in the context of domestic and international arbitration. In practice, how will the new enforcement law and the new arbitration law impact arbitral awards and avoid the flaws of the previous legislation? This study will address the arbitral award under the Saudi law by comparing it with modern trends in the international commercial arbitration practice.

A. Rendering an Enforceable Award

During the arbitration process, an arbitral tribunal issues different types of awards, such as partial awards and interim awards. In addition, during an arbitration the tribunal may issue certain directions and orders to manage and push the arbitration process to remain on track. The study will address this issue in several points.

1. Differences Between Orders and Awards

During the arbitration process, the arbitral tribunal makes different types of decisions. Some are related to administrative matters, such as discovery issues or places and times of hearings. These kinds of decisions are generally in the form of a procedural order. [698]

---

697 See Saleem, AVAILABLE AT SSRN 2315728, 9 (2012).

698 The terms orders and awards are used differently between the laws and rules. See JEAN-FRANÇOIS POUDRET & SÉBASTIEN BESSON, COMPARATIVE LAW OF INTERNATIONAL ARBITRATION 637-643 (Sweet & Maxwell. 2007).

Other decisions are considered more significant, such as determining the language and the seat of the arbitration when the arbitrating parties have not agreed to them.[699]

Another type of decision that an arbitration tribunal issue is the award, which decides contested matters in favor of the one or the others side. Between partial and interim awards and the final award, the tribunal has to decide on all claims made by either side, in particular who shall prevail and how much money, if any, must be paid.[700]

Some international rules allow an arbitral tribunal to issue conservatory and interim measures as "awards" or in the form of orders and decisions. For example, Article 28(1) of ICC Rules states:

> Unless the parties have otherwise agreed, as soon as the file has been transmitted to it, the arbitral tribunal may, at the request of a party, order any interim or conservatory measure it deems appropriate. The arbitral tribunal may make the granting of any such measure subject to appropriate security being furnished by the requesting party. Any such measure shall take the form of an order, giving reasons, or of an award, as the arbitral tribunal considers appropriate.[701]

Similar to the ICC, Article 24 of the ICRD Rules provides: "Such interim measures may take the form of an interim order or award...".[702] In contrast, the new Saudi law, which follows the Model Law, does not mention the form in which the tribunal must issue temporary measures, although they are called orders.[703]

Although some rules, such as the ICC Rules, provide power to the arbitral tribunal to issue a conservatory measure in any form, the ICC Rules and other modern rules, including the new Saudi law, distinguish between the two with respect to the procedure that must be followed. For instance, Article 29 of the Model Law states:

---

699 See UNCITRAL Arbitration Rules Article 18(1), 19(1). 2010. Also see ICC Rules of Arbitration Article 18, 20. 2012.

700 See POUDRET & BESSON, Comparative Law of International Arbitration 637-643. 2007.

701 ICC Rules of Arbitration. 2012.

702 ICDR Arbitration Rules. 2014.

703 See UNCITRAL Arbitration Rules Article 26. 2010. Also Arbitration Law Article 22(1). 2012.

> In arbitral proceedings with more than one arbitrator, any decision of the arbitral tribunal shall be made, unless otherwise agreed by the parties, by a majority of all its members. However, questions of procedure may be decided by a presiding arbitrator, if so authorized by the parties or all members of the arbitral tribunal.[704]

The Saudi law follows the Model Law exactly on this issue.[705] Moreover, usually orders are not reviewable by a competent court prior to the rendering of the final award, except that some orders can be challenged in court. Awards which have different procedures as will be presented later.

Although orders issued by arbitral tribunals are not usually reviewable by a competent court, most modern arbitration rules require the party who is challenging an order should express his objection to the arbitral tribunal to preserve his right to challenge the final award at the enforcement stage.[706] For instance, Article 32 of the UNCITRAL Model Law states:

> A failure by any party to object promptly to any non-compliance with these Rules or with any requirement of the arbitration agreement shall be deemed to be a waiver of the right of such party to make such an objection, unless such party can show that, under the circumstances, its failure to object was justified. [707]

Similar to the Model Law, the Saudi law states in Article 7:

> If one of the parties of the arbitration continues in the arbitration proceedings with knowledge of the occurrence of a violation of a provision of this law, which may be agreed to violating or due to a condition in the arbitration agreement, and does not object to this violation within the time limit agreed upon or within thirty days of his knowledge of the occurrence of the violation absent an agreement, shall be deemed to have waived his right to object. [708]

704 UNCITRAL Model Law on International Commercial Arbitration. 2006. See also ICC Rules of Arbitration Article 33. 2012.

705 Arbitration Law Article 39(1),(3). 2012.

706 See ICC Rules of Arbitration Article 39. 2012. Also see ICDR Arbitration Rules Article 28. 2014.

707 UNCITRAL Arbitration Rules. 2010.

708 Arbitration Law. 2012.

The difference between the Model Law and the Saudi law is that the Saudi law sets out a specific limit time, which is thirty days from obtaining knowledge of the occurrence of a violation, while the Model Law requires only that the objection be made "promptly". This means that the time limit will be up to the discretion of the arbitral tribunal or the competent court, depending on each particular situation.

Whether a decision of the arbitral tribunal is an award or order is important for several reasons. An award takes on res judicata effect, and can be executed with the help of the competent court, if the party against whom the award is issued does not comply voluntarily. If that party has assets in one of the contracting countries to the New York Convention, the award can be executed in that state under this Convention. Usually the municipal courts will consider actions based on a final award, which may be a partial award. The same is not true for decisions that take other forms.[709] The different kinds of arbitral awards will be presented in the following points.

2. Types of Awards

a. Final Award

Issuing the final award is the last duty of the arbitral tribunal, upon which the tribunal will be terminated except for some corrections or interpretation in some instances, as will be presented later.[710]Also, the final award refers to the award that resolves all of the disputes between the arbitrating parties.[711]The first advantage of the final award is that it can be enforced under the New York Convention, although it can be challengeable at that time by the losing party aiming to annul or vacate it according to the law of the situs.[712] This type of award will be more understandable after discussing partial and interim awards in the next section.

709 See MOSES, The Principles and Practice of International Commercial Arbitration 189-190. 2012. See also ASSOCIATION, AAA Handbook on International Arbitration and ADR 165-167, 213. 2010.

710 See MOSES, The Principles and Practice of International Commercial Arbitration 189-190. 2012.

711 See id.

712 See Id.

b. *Partial and Interim Awards*

Unlike the final award, partial awards resolve some, but not all, of the disputes between the arbitrating parties. Most modern international arbitration rules allow the arbitral tribunal to issue one or more partial awards, in particular if a certain disputed question can be settled ahead of other parts of the dispute.[713] For instance, Article 34 of the UNCITRAL Model Law provides that the arbitration tribunal may issue separate awards on different matters at various times.[714] Similarly, Article 29 of the ICDR Rules states: "In addition to making a final award, the arbitral tribunal may make interim, interlocutory, or partial awards, orders, decisions, and rulings."[715] Article 39(5) of the new Saudi law follows the international rules and provides: "The arbitral tribunal may deliver temporary awards, or in a part of the requests, before judging the award that ends the dispute, unless the parties to the arbitration agree otherwise."[716] The laws differ regarding whether the prevailing party can seek to confirm this type of award or the opposing party can challenge it.[717] The new Saudi law complies with the modern international rules in allowing partial awards to be confirmed, although, under the Saudi law, is not clear how the Saudi court will handle this issue in the absence of an implementation regulation. Consequently, this matter is vague under the new Saudi law.

Unlike the ICC and other international rules,[718] the UNCITRAL Model Law and the new Saudi law do not determine and discuss whether interim measures it will be in the form of an award or an order. In practice, the competent court will determine if an order is, in fact, an award depending on substantive factors.[719] Even if an interim measure is designated an award, such awards generally will not

---

713 See id. at 191.

714 UNCITRAL Arbitration Rules. 2010.

715 ICDR Arbitration Rules. 2014.

716 Arbitration Law. 2012.

717 See MOSES, The Principles and Practice of International Commercial Arbitration 191. 2012.

718 See ICC Rules of Arbitration Article 28(1). 2012.

719 See MOSES, The Principles and Practice of International Commercial Arbitration 191. 2012.

be considered a final award and will not be recognized and enforced under the New York Convention.[720] [721]

c. Consent Awards

Most modern arbitration rules allow arbitrating parties to resolve the dispute by agreement at any time during the arbitration proceedings.[722] The new Saudi law follows this recent trend in the international rules, as it states in Article 38.[723] Accepting the resolution of a dispute by agreement must occur before the award is made, and the agreement must be accepted by all of the arbitrating parties.[724] Unlike the Model Law and other international rules, the Saudi law does not explain clearly how the award should be issued when the parties settle their dispute by agreement. However, the Model Law explains this explicitly:

> The arbitral tribunal shall either issue an order for the termination of the arbitral proceedings or, if requested by the parties and accepted by the arbitral tribunal, record the settlement in the form of an arbitral award on agreed terms. The arbitral tribunal is not obliged to give reasons for such an award.[725]

Hence, the arbitrating parties have a choice. They can enter an award upon agreed terms or have the settlement recorded as a consent award. In practice, the arbitrating parties would be better advised in most cases to convert the settlement agreement into an award to take advantage of the enforcement provisions of the New York Convention if the disputes are not completely resolved, or if one of the parties does not perform as agreed.[726]

---

720 See Id. For more information about interim measures in international arbitration rules, see Gregoire Marchac, *Interim Measures in International Commercial Arbitration Under the ICC, AAA, LCIA and UNCITRAL Rules*, 10 AM. REV. INT'L ARB. 123-559 (1999).

721 Note: recognition and enforcement of an interim measure is outside the control of arbitration parties or tribunal, they are governed only by legislative provisions by the law of the country in which the measure must produce its effect. See Association for International Arbitration, Interim Measures in International Commercial Arbitration (Maklu Publishers. 2007).

722 See ICC Rules of Arbitration Article 32. 2012. See also UNCITRAL Arbitration Rules Article 36(1). 2010.

723 Arbitration Law. 2012.

724 See UNCITRAL Arbitration Rules Article 36(1). 2010.

725 Id.

726 See MOSES, The Principles and Practice of International Commercial Arbitration 192-193. 2012.

d. *Default Awards*

If the defendant fails to participate in the arbitration proceedings, most international arbitration rules authorize the arbitration tribunal to continue the proceedings and issue a default award based on the evidence before it.[727] The Saudi law follows the international rules and the Model Law regarding the issuance of a default award.[728] Article 35 states:

> "If one of the parties fails to attend one of the hearings after being notified or to provide any of the documents he is asked to bring, the arbitral tribunal may continue the arbitration proceedings and deliver an award concerning the dispute on the basis of the existing evidence."[729]

Hence, the arbitral tribunal should continue the proceedings; this means that the tribunal must not treat the failure to appear in itself as an admission of the claimant's allegations. The tribunal must review and handle the case depending on the available evidence before it. Nevertheless, were it not for the existence of the default award, defendants would be more likely to ignore the arbitration process, if their absence would prevent the process from progressing to a conclusion. Consequently, it is a great step that the Saudi law follows the modern trend to protect the arbitration method through such awards.

3. Validity of the Award

The validity of the arbitral award is of paramount importance to arbitration, since an invalid award renders the arbitration a useless exercise. An award is valid as the result of complying with chosen rules and situs laws, which affect the award at the enforcement stage. International arbitration rules and Saudi law set forth the requirements for the award to be valid, which will be discussed in the following points.

a. *Formal Requirements*

In addition to conforming to the arbitration agreement, chosen rules, and the applicable law, there are specific formalities that an arbitral award must meet

---

727 See POUDRET & BESSON, Comparative Law of International Arbitration 506-513. 2007. See also MOSES, The Principles and Practice of International Commercial Arbitration 193. 2012.

728 See UNCITRAL Model Law on International Commercial Arbitration Article 25. 2006.

729 Arbitration Law. 2012.

under international arbitration rules.[730] The new Saudi law follows the Model Law with regard to most of these requirements. These requirements are:

1) The award must be in writing.

2) The award must be final and binding. The Saudi law does not express this condition plainly. However, it could be understood from the whole of Article 42 that an award must be final and binding.

3) The award must be supported by legal reasons upon which the arbitral tribunal depended.

4) The award must be signed by the arbitrator. If there is more than one arbitrator, it is sufficient if the majority of the arbitrators sign, provided that the reasons why the minority did not sign must be recorded in the minutes of the claim.

5) The award must contain its date of issuance and the place of arbitration.

6) The award must be kept confidential, unless the arbitrating parties agree otherwise. Unlike the Model Law, the Saudi law requires that such agreement be in writing. In addition to the consent of the parties to make the award public, the Model Law adds as a second exception that the award may be disclosed if required by a legal duty or to protect a legal right. Although the Saudi law does not express this exception, it is understood from the whole the law that this exception is established as if the one of the parties refused the award or a part of it, as will be presented later.

7) The award must be communicated to all of the arbitrating parties.[731]

In addition to these stated requirements, the Saudi law requires that the arbitration award include the names of the parties and their addresses. It must also include the names of the arbitrators and their addresses, nationalities, and attributes. A summary of the arbitration agreement, a summary of the statements and requests of the arbitrating parties, their pleadings, their documents, a summary of the report of the experts, if any, the award text, the determination of

730 See ICC Rules of Arbitration Article 31. 2012. Also see ICDR Arbitration Rules Article 30. 2014.

731 UNCITRAL Arbitration Rules Article 34. 2010. Also Arbitration Law Article 42. 2012.

the arbitrators' fees, the expenses of the arbitration, and how they are distributed between the arbitrating parties, must all be included in the arbitral award under the Saudi law.[732]

As a result, the arbitrator has a heavy burden to make sure that such formalities are met under the law. However, the Saudi law does not explain the consequences if an award fails to meet any of the requirements as to form, such as omitting the date or place of arbitration. As a practical matter, the study found that the award remains valid, but the court may order that the missing information be inserted.

b. Communication

After an arbitral award is issued, the arbitral tribunal must deliver to each of the arbitrating parties an actual copy of the arbitration award under most, if not all, international arbitration rules.[733] The new Saudi Arbitration Law follows the modern rules in this regard, although it also states that a copy of the award must be delivered within fifteen days from the date on which the award was issued.[734] Most rules do not specify the exact period of time.[735] The fifteen-day requirement is significant, because, if any corrections need to be made, they can be done promptly.[736]

c. Time Limits

Most international arbitration rules set a time limit that must be met for the arbitral award to be valid.[737] For example, the ICC Rules requires the arbitral tribunal to render its final award within six months after the beginning of the arbitration, while other rules, such as the ICDR Rules, require that the award be issued within sixty days from the date when the hearing closes.[738] Because the stated period can expire before the tribunal has been able to issue the award, the international rules allow extending the time limit upon a reasoned request from

---

732 Arbitration Law Article 42(2). 2012.

733 See UNCITRAL Arbitration Rules Article 34(6). 2010. See also, ICC Rules of Arbitration Article 34(1). 2012. Also see ICDR Arbitration Rules Article 30(4). 2014.

734 See Arbitration Law Article 43(1). 2012.

735 See ICC Rules of Arbitration Article 34(1). 2012. Also see ICDR Arbitration Rules Article 30(4). 2014. Also UNCITRAL Arbitration Rules Article 34(6). 2010.

736 See MOSES, The Principles and Practice of International Commercial Arbitration 194. 2012.

737 See ICC Rules of Arbitration Article 30(1). 2012. See also ICDR Arbitration Rules Article 30(1). 2014.

738 See id.

the arbitral tribunal.[739] Saudi law follows the modern rules in setting a limit time and allowing the fixed time to be extended in the absence of an agreement between parties about it. Hence, Article 40(1) of the new law provides:

> The arbitral tribunal must issue the arbitral award terminating the whole dispute within the date agreed upon by the arbitrating parties, and if there is no agreement, the award must be delivered within twelve months from the time of commencement of the arbitration proceedings. The arbitral tribunal may, in all cases, decide to extend the duration of the arbitration, provided that such an extension shall not exceed six months, unless otherwise agreed to by the arbitrating parties to be over 12 months.[740]

As a result, the Saudi law provides the parties the freedom to agree on the time within which the award must be issued; otherwise if there is no agreement on such matter, the time limit is twelve months with the possibility for the tribunal to extend the deadline by another six months. In practice, putting a strict time can impose some risks on the arbitration process. According to Margaret L. Moses:

> Parties should be wary of placing strict time limits on the tribunal by express agreement, without any possibility of extension. The risk of having an inflexible time frame is twofold. First, the time period may run out before the tribunal has been able to issue an award, leaving the arbitrators with no jurisdiction to proceed. Second, the tribunal might be so rushed into meeting the deadline that the losing party could try to vacate the award on the grounds that it was not fully able to present its case. Thus, any time limits should be imposed only as guidelines, with the flexibility to extend them as needed.[741]

The old Saudi arbitration law required that the award be issued within 90 days from the date when the arbitration was commenced, unless the arbitrating parties had agreed otherwise in the arbitration agreement or the competent court or the arbitral tribunal itself extended the time for the award to be issued. If the time expired, any party was entitled to begin a separate proceeding in the competent court. As a result, this process allowed the parties to ignore the

---

739 See ICC Rules of Arbitration Article 30(2). 2012.

740 Arbitration Law. 2012.

741 MOSES, The Principles and Practice of International Commercial Arbitration 195. 2012.

arbitration process, which usually led to the arbitration agreement and award having no effect.[742] However, the new Saudi law provides flexibility by giving the parties the opportunity to determine the rule that fits their own circumstances and, in the absence of an agreement, by providing enough time and the possibility to extend it if necessary.

d. Concurring and Dissenting Opinions

Like most modern international rules, the Saudi law provides that, if the arbitral tribunal is formed of more than one arbitrator, the award must be issued by a majority of its members after confidential deliberation.[743] However, sometimes the views of the arbitral tribunal are divided, and the tribunal has difficulty reaching a decision by majority. In that event, some rules, such as ICC Rules, state that the president of the arbitral tribunal must make the award alone.[744] The Saudi law, in contrast, states that, if the views of the arbitral tribunal are divided and a majority is impossible to obtain, the competent court must appoint a casting arbitrator.[745] Moreover, most arbitration rules, including the Saudi law, do not mention dissenting or concurring opinions, but it is generally agreed that dissenting opinions would not be a part of the award to avoid giving the losing party an unfair advantage in a challenge against the award.[746]

4. Remedies and Costs

a. Potential Remedies Against an Award

One of the core matters that arbitrators should care about while issuing the award is the law of the place of arbitration. The jurisdictions vary widely in their approach to the remedies that an arbitral award may provide. In Saudi Arabia, the new law expresses clearly that arbitral awards must not violate Islamic Sharia or public policy.[747] In fact, it is not easy to determine what Islamic Sharia means as

---

742 See Al-Ammari & Martin, ARBITRATION INTERNATIONAL, 397 (2014).

743 See Arbitration Law Article 39(1). 2012. Also see UNCITRAL Arbitration Rules Article 33(1). 2010. See also ICC Rules of Arbitration Article 31(1). 2012. Also see ICDR Arbitration Rules Article 29(2). 2014.

744 See ICC Rules of Arbitration Article 31 (1). 2012.

745 Arbitration Law Article 39(2). 2012.

746 See MOSES, The Principles and Practice of International Commercial Arbitration 195. 2012. For more information about dissenting views in international commercial arbitration, see Lee, Ilhyung Lee, Introducing International Commercial Arbitration and Its Lawlessness, by Way of the Dissenting Opinion, 4(1) CONTEMP. ASIA ARBITR. J. 19-35 (2011).

747 See Arbitration Law Article 38. 2012.

applied in Saudi courts and the scope of the public policy under Saudi law. Hence, this issue will be discussed widely in the enforcement section of this study.

b. Costs of the Arbitration Proceedings

Another significant matter in the arbitration process is determining the costs and who has to bear them. The costs will usually be determined in advance. In Saudi Arabia, the arbitration law requires that an award include the determination of the arbitrators' fees, the expenses of the arbitration, and how they are distributed between the arbitrating parties.[748] The honoraria of the arbitrator(s), under Saudi law, have to be agreed upon in an independent contract when choosing the arbitrator.[749] The contract must determine the arbitrator fees and expenses, and a copy of the contract must be deposited with the authority as prescribed by the executive regulation of this law.[750] If the parties and arbitrators cannot reach agreement regarding the arbitrators' fees, the competent court must determine such fees.[751] There are no available cases that show how the Saudi courts will handle this matter and the allocation of those costs between the arbitrating parties. Moreover, the decision of the competent court is not subject to appeal in any way. If the competent court appoints the arbitrators, it must determine the arbitrators' fees.[752]

5. Confidentiality of the Award

Making the arbitral award public may affect either or both of the parties in different aspects. For example, Margaret L. Moses says: "When substantial amounts of money are at stake, this kind of disclosure could cause the stock prices of the parties involved to go up or down, depending on the result."[753] As a result, the international arbitration rules protect the parties through particular confidentiality rules, such as the LCIA Rules[754] or by giving a party the right to request confidentiality as provided in the ICC Rules.[755] These rules differ in handling sensitive matters between a broad protection of confidence, like the LCIA

748 Id. at. Article 42(2).

749 Id. at. Article 24.

750 Id.

751 Id.

752 Id.

753 MOSES, The Principles and Practice of International Commercial Arbitration 199. 2012.

754 See LCIA Arbitration rules Article 30. 2014.

755 See ICC Rules of Arbitration Article 22(3). 2012.

Rules[756], and providing minimum protection.[757] The Saudi law follows the modern rules in providing such protection to the arbitration award by preventing it or a portion of it from being published absent the written consent of the arbitrating parties.[758] However, it does not impose on the parties a confidentiality obligation as to information obtained during the arbitration, which could be more important to the parties in some cases than knowing the arbitral award itself. Reference is made to trade secrets and other confidential business information. This gap can be handled under the Saudi law through the adoption of one of the international rules that provides such protection. For example, the study found that the LCIA Rules provide high and broad protection in this regard. Article 30 of the LCIA Rules states:

> 30.1 The parties undertake as a general principle to keep confidential all awards in the arbitration, together with all materials in the arbitration created for the purpose of the arbitration and all other documents produced by another party in the proceedings not otherwise in the public domain, save and to the extent that disclosure may be required of a party by legal duty, to protect or pursue a legal right, or to enforce or challenge an award in legal proceedings before a state court or other legal authority.
>
> 30.2 The deliberations of the Arbitral Tribunal shall remain confidential to its members, save as required by any applicable law and to the extent that disclosure of an arbitrator's refusal to participate in the arbitration is required of the other members of the Arbitral Tribunal under Articles 10, 12, 26 and 27.
>
> 30.3 The LCIA does not publish any award or any part of an award without the prior written consent of all parties and the Arbitral Tribunal.[759]

As a result, even the Saudi law does not provide such broad protection for arbitrating parties; it gives ample room to take advantage of using any appropriate modern rule that fits the circumstances of the arbitrating parties.

---

756 See LCIA Arbitration rules Article 30. 2014.

757 See ICC Rules of Arbitration Article 22(3). 2012.

758 See Arbitration Law Article 43(2). 2012.

759 LCIA Arbitration rules. 2014.

6. Post-Award Proceedings

Usually, an arbitral tribunal tries to issue an award that is final and binding. However, on some occasions, the arbitral award may return to the tribunal to complete some matters. One of these situations arises if the award contains typographical or clerical errors. Most international rules provide a specific amount of time after the award is issued or received by the parties to correct any error in computation, any clerical or typographical error, or any error or omission of a similar nature on its own or in response to a request from one of the parties.[760] The Saudi law complies with the modern arbitration rules in this regard. Hence, Article 47 of the Saudi law states:

> 1) On its own or at the request of one of the litigants, the arbitral tribunal shall correct in its award each purely material misstatement, writing and calculation. The arbitral tribunal shall complete the correction without pleading within fifteen days following the date of the award or to deposit the request of correction depending on the circumstances.
>
> 2) The corrected decision shall be issued in writing by the arbitral tribunal, and the parties to the arbitration shall be notified thereof within fifteen days from the date of its issuance. If the arbitral tribunal exceeds its power in the correction, it is allowed to challenge the invalidity of the decision by a claim of invalidity to which the provisions of the 50th and 51st Articles of this law shall apply.[761]

The only difference between the Model Law and the new Saudi law in this regard is that the Model Law sets a 45 day limit on the amount of time that the arbitral tribunal has to correct the award from the date of its receipt of a request therefor from either or both of the parties or within 30 days after the issuance of the award if such correction is on its own initiative. The new Saudi law sets the frame time at 15 days in all cases.[762] This 15 day period provided by the Saudi law is not enough time in the business world, especially if the arbitral tribunal has more than one arbitrator, and they are from different countries. Hence, it would be

760 See ICC Rules of Arbitration Article 35(1). 2012. Also see LCIA Arbitration rules Article 27.1. 2014. Also UNCITRAL Arbitration Rules Article 38. 2010.

761 Arbitration Law. 2012.

762 See UNCITRAL Arbitration Rules 38. 2010. See also Arbitration Law Article 47. 2012.

better if the Saudi law followed the Model Law in this regard to provide more flexibility to the tribunal.

Moreover, the Saudi law also follows the Model Law in affording a chance to either of the arbitrating parties to request an additional arbitration award on claims made during the proceedings but overlooked or missing in the arbitration award. Such a request must be made within thirty days following the reception of the arbitration award.[763] One of the requirements for such a request is that the other party must be notified of this application at his address, which is shown in the arbitration award, before it is submitted to the arbitral tribunal.[764] The arbitration tribunal has sixty days from the date of submission of such a request to decide upon it, although the tribunal has the authority to extend this period by another thirty days if it deems necessary.[765]

Furthermore, like most modern international rules, the Saudi law stipulates the right of any party to the arbitration to request an interpretation of any ambiguity contained in the award.[766] Under the Saudi law and the Model Law, each arbitrating party has 30 days after the receipt of the arbitral award to request an interpretation of the award with notice to the other parties.[767] The explanation must be given in writing within 30 days under the Saudi law, while the Model Law requires that such interpretation be given within 45 days from the receipt of the request and that the interpretation form part of the award.[768] As a result, after the stated time has passed, the award cannot be changed, and the arbitration tribunal no longer has the authority, as the tribunal has no further jurisdiction. However, the UNCITRAL Model Law and the Saudi law provide an exception. When a competent court reviews an award, a party can ask the court to set aside the award if the request is based on serious reasons.[769] In this situation, the competent court must decide within fifteen days of receiving the request whether to issue a stay of execution, and it has authority to order a financial

763 Arbitration Law Article 48. 2012. Also see UNCITRAL Arbitration Rules Article 39. 2010.

764 Id.

765 Id.

766 See Arbitration Law Article 46. 2012. See also UNCITRAL Arbitration Rules Article 37. 2010. See also ICC Rules of Arbitration Article 35. 2012.

767 See UNCITRAL Arbitration Rules Article 37. 2010. See also Arbitration Law Article 46. 2012.

768 Id.

769 See Arbitration Law Article 54. 2012. Also UNCITRAL Model Law on International Commercial Arbitration Article 34(4). 2006.

guarantee or warranty from the requesting party.[770] The court must also judge the validity of such a claim within one hundred and eighty days from the date of its acceptance of the request.[771]

There are two significant differences regarding the filing of the arbitral award between the Saudi law and the UNCITRAL Model Law. First, the Saudi law places an obligation of the arbitral tribunal to file the issued award in the competent court, while the UNCITRAL Model Law puts this burden on the party who is relying on an award or applying for its enforcement.[772] Such filing must meet some requirements under the Saudi law. The arbitral tribunal must:

1) File the award.

2) Deposit an original of the award or a signed copy in the language in which it was issued.

3) Provide a translation into Arabic, certified by an accredited authority, if the award was issued in another language.

4) Do all of the above within fifteen days from the date when the original award was issued.[773]

One of the requirements that can put an arbitrating party at risk is the time frame for filling the award in the competent court along with the Arabic translation. It would be hard to meet such a limit time with the translation if the award was issued in a foreign language, especially if the arbitration was long, which could need more time and effort. Hence, it would be better if the Saudi law were more flexible with the time frame especially if it intends to showcase its support for international arbitration to attract foreign parties.

The second point is that the Saudi law requires that the arbitral award has to be filed in the competent court, whether the decisions in the arbitral award are carried out voluntarily by the parties or not and regardless whether the obligated party has assets in Saudi Arabia. This is unlike the UNCITRAL Model Law, which requires that such an award be filed just in case there is a need to seek enforce-

770 Arbitration Law Article 54. 2012.

771 Id.

772 See Arbitration Law Article 44. 2012. Also see UNCITRAL Model Law on International Commercial Arbitration Article 35(2). 2006.

773 Arbitration Law Article 44,43(1). 2012.

ment.[774] Because most arbitration awards are satisfied through voluntary compliance by the arbitrating parties involved in the dispute,[775] the requirement of filing a case with the court could waste time in the event that a party does not need to enforce the award. It may also compromise the confidentiality. Hence, it would be better if the Saudi law followed the UNCITRAL Model Law in this regard.

B. Challenges Against an Arbitral Award

Because an arbitral award is considered final and binding, modern arbitration rules generally make it difficult to set aside or vacate an arbitral award. Since one of the significant advantages of arbitration is the finality of the award, the new law in the Kingdom of Saudi Arabia follows the modern rules by supporting such finality while allowing some instances to be considered as exceptions to achieve balance between supporting the finality of the award and justice to the complaining party if his case may need further review.

1. Available Methods for Challenging an Arbitral Award

The new Saudi Arbitration Law follows the procedure of most commercial arbitration practices regarding attempts to set aside an arbitral award. An award is challenged by bringing an action to annul, set aside, or vacate the arbitral award in the competent court in Saudi Arabia.[776] One of the advantages of the new Saudi law is that it follows the international arbitration practice in putting the burden on the complaining party to submit the objection about the arbitral award instead of putting the burden on the winning party when he seeks to enforce the award as was the case in the old law.[777] The challenge must be based on the grounds upon which an arbitral award can be challenged as provided under the UNCITRAL Model Law and the new Saudi law and the New York Convention.

2. Potential Grounds for Challenging an Arbitral Award

Under the Saudi law and the UNCITRAL Model Law, the grounds for challenging the arbitral award fall into two main categories.

---

774 See id. at. Article 44. Also see UNCITRAL Model Law on International Commercial Arbitration Article 35(2). 2006.

775 See ASSOCIATION, AAA/ICDR Handbook on International Arbitration and ADR 158. 2006.

776 See Arbitration Law Article 49. 2012. Also see UNCITRAL Model Law on International Commercial Arbitration Article 34(1). 2006.

777 See Al-Ammari & Martin, ARBITRATION INTERNATIONAL, 400 (2014).

a. *Jurisdictional Challenges*

The challenge of jurisdiction can arise at the beginning of an arbitration or it can be raised after an arbitral award is rendered. To challenge jurisdiction at the outset of an arbitration, the challenging party must comply with a time frame. For example, the Saudi law and the UNCITRAL Model Law provide that a party has a right to challenge the lack of jurisdiction of the arbitral tribunal and that the appointment of an arbitrator or participation in such appointment should not eliminate the party's right to assert any of these defenses.[778] However, the Model Law requires that such a challenge be made within 15 days after the party has been notified of the appointment of the challenged arbitrator, while the Saudi law states that such a challenge must be made immediately.[779] Like many modern laws, if the allowed time expires, the party may lose the right to object.[780] However, the Saudi law offers an exception for the delay if there is an acceptable reason.[781] Furthermore, the Saudi law follows the Model Law in giving the party a right to challenge arbitral jurisdiction based on a claim that the arbitral tribunal exceeded its authority.[782] For example, Article 47(2) of the new law states: "If the arbitral tribunal exceeds its power in making the correction, it is allowed to challenge the invalidity of the decision by a claim of invalidity."[783] This right exists if the arbitral award deals with a dispute that was not contemplated by the terms of the arbitration agreement[784] and if the award decides matters beyond the scope of the submission to arbitration.[785] Moreover, the stated laws provide that, if the awards on issues submitted to arbitration can be separated from those not so submitted, only that part of the award that contains decisions on matters not submitted to arbitration can be set aside.[786]

---

778 Arbitration Law Article 20(2). 2012. Also see UNCITRAL Arbitration Rules Article 13(1). 2010.

779 Id.

780 See MOSES, The Principles and Practice of International Commercial Arbitration 205. 2012.

781 See Arbitration Law Article 20(2). 2012.

782 See UNCITRAL Model Law on International Commercial Arbitration Article 34(2). 2006. Also Arbitration Law Article 50(1). 2012.

783 Arbitration Law. 2012.

784 Id. at. Article 50(1). Also see UNCITRAL Model Law on International Commercial Arbitration Article 34(2). 2006.

785 Id.

786 See id.

b. Procedural Challenges

Another type of challenge recognized under the UNCITRAL Model Law and Saudi law is procedural.[787] The grounds that will support such a challenge are:

> 1) If there is no arbitration agreement or such an agreement is null and void, or revocable, or has become invalid due to expiry.
>
> 2) If one of the arbitrating parties at the time of the arbitration is incompetent or not entirely competent by the rules that govern his competence.
>
> 3) If one of the arbitrating parties is unable to present his defense because he was not actually notified of the appointment of an arbitrator or of the arbitral proceedings or any other reasons beyond his control.
>
> 4) If the arbitral tribunal is unlawfully constituted, or the arbitrators are selected in a way that violates the law or the arbitration agreement.

The new Saudi law adds a ground that is not mentioned in the Model Law:

> 5) If the arbitral tribunal does not take into consideration the conditions that must be met in the award to the extent that affects its content, or the award is based on false arbitration proceedings that have affected it.[788]

The grounds have not yet been tested in practice in the Saudi courts because the law was only adopted recently. However, in the practical view, it would be better if the Saudi law followed the grounds stated in the Model Law without adding the last ground. The last ground permits the competent court to review and consider the facts of the case, thereby creating opportunities to avoid the arbitral awards in the Kingdom based on alleged improper arbitration proceedings that adversely affected the award.

In addition to the grounds for a challenge asserted by a party, the competent court has the authority to hear a claim of invalidity against an award in both types

---

787 See Id.

788 See Id.

of challenges, jurisdictional and procedural, of itself without request from one of parties, if the competent court finds that:

> 1) The subject matter of the dispute is not capable of settlement under the law of Saudi Arabia;
>
> 2) The award is in conflict with the public policy of the country, specifically if the award is contrary to the provisions of Islamic Sharia or to the agreement of the arbitrating parties.[789]

In the latter cases, the party does not need to prove that such grounds exist, because the court will consider them on its own. These grounds will be explained extensively in the enforcement section below.

c. *Challenges Based on the Merits*

The general rule in arbitration is that the grounds for challenging an arbitral award should be limited to procedure, jurisdiction, irregularities, arbitrability, or public policy.[790] Saudi law adds that awards must not conflict with Islamic Sharia.[791]

The new Saudi law follows the modern trend in arbitration regarding limiting judicial review of arbitral awards and trying to avoid the past practice of intervening in arbitration matters by the Saudi court, which caused arbitrating parties to lose the benefits of arbitration by having to litigate their cases in the Saudi courts.[792] The new Saudi law provides specific instances that can be the basis for a challenge against an arbitral award.[793] The law not only states the grounds, it also confirms that the competent court can hear a challenge to the validity of an award, but it has no authority to examine the facts and subject of the dispute.[794]

---

789 See UNCITRAL Model Law on International Commercial Arbitration Article 34(2). 2006. Also see Arbitration Law Article 50(2). 2012.

790 See MOSES, The Principles and Practice of International Commercial Arbitration 207-208. 2012.

791 See Arbitration Law Article 50(1),(2. 2012.

792 See BAAMIR, Shari'a Law in Commercial and Banking Arbitration: Law and Practice in Saudi Arabia 137. 2013.

793 See Arbitration Law Article 50(1),(2. 2012.

794 See id. at Article 50(4).

However, while consider a challenge to the validity of an award, the court retains the authority to determine on its own if the award is in any way contrary to Islamic Sharia as it is applied in Saudi courts, which allows to it to review the facts and the subject from that perspective.

3. Time Limits

Most jurisdictions limit the time during which an application to set aside an award must be filed. The Model Law provides that the time is limited to three months from the date on which the arbitrating party filing the application received the award, or, if there was a request to correct and interpret an award or for an additional award, the time will begin from the date on which that request was disposed of by the arbitral tribunal.[795] The Model Law states in Article 34: "An application for setting aside may not be made after three months."[796] In contrast, the new Saudi law provides a shorter time. Article 51(1) of the Saudi law states: "The invalidity claim of the arbitration award is brought by any of the parties within sixty days following the date of notification of that party of the award."[797] Hence, the Model Law allows for three months, while the new Saudi law allows only for two months before a challenge to an award has to be filed. Moreover, the Saudi law adds that a waiver of the right to bring a claim of invalidity issued by a party prior to the delivery of the arbitral award does not preclude a court from accepting an invalidity claim after the award was issued.[798]

4. Effects of a Successful Challenge

After an arbitrating party challenges an arbitral award, the party will encounter two possibilities. The first is the party's effort to vacate the award will fail. Under Saudi law, the award is not subject to any further kind of appeal. Consequently, after the deadline for challenging the validity of the award has passed, the request for the execution of the arbitral award will be accepted, which will be explained in the enforcement section.[799]

---

795 See UNCITRAL Model Law on International Commercial Arbitration Article 34(3). 2006.

796 Id.

797 Arbitration Law Article 51(1). 2012.

798 See Id.

799 It is not necessary that a challenge to an award fail before enforcement of the award is sought. The winning party can request enforcement of the award after the deadline of suing for the invalidity of the arbitral award has passed. See id. at Article 51(2), 55(1).

The other possibility is that the competent court will decide to vacate the arbitration award. Saudi law provides that such a decision against an arbitral award may be appealed within thirty days from the day following the notification.[800] The law does not identify the court in which the appeal must be filed. However, the implementation regulation of this law may explain this question. If the appellate court does not vacate the arbitral award, then the status will be as though the first court did not nullify the award, and the winning party can proceed to enforce the award.[801] However, if the appellate court agrees with the first court's decision to vacate the arbitral award, the outcome is different.

If the appellate court vacates the award because it finds that the arbitration agreement itself was invalid, then the arbitration agreement is rendered invalid, and the parties can initiate a court action on the same arbitration issues.[802] If the award is vacated based on some significant procedural irregularity, then, under Saudi law, the arbitration agreement is still valid, unless parties agree otherwise.[803]

In the absence of such agreement by the parties, the Saudi law does not provide rules about whether the case will be reheard by the same or a new arbitral tribunal. A new arbitral tribunal may require the parties to start all over again, which is a substantial duplication of effort, time, and resources that will be a loss for both parties. In addition, the new law distinguishes between whether the award was vacated because the arbitration agreement was not valid and other reasons. However, it does not distinguish among the other reasons. For example, if the agreement was vacated, based on grounds of corruption, fraud, or arbitrator misconduct or partiality, it does not make sense to repeat the procedure with the same tribunal. For that, the arbitrating parties would be wise to include some sensible rules in their agreement.

One of the sets of rules that handle this situation clearly is the Uniform Arbitration Act (RUAA) as revised in 2000. Under RUAA, if the competent court vacates the arbitral award based on grounds other than an invalid agreement, the court may ask the arbitration parties for a rehearing.[804] However, if the basis for vacating the award is corruption, fraud, or arbitrator misconduct or partiality, the hearing shall

800 See id. at Article 51(2).

801 See id.

802 See id. at Article 50(3).

803 See id.

804 Uniform Arbitration Act (RUAA) §23(c) (2000).

be in a new arbitral tribunal.[805] If the grounds are based on a failure of the procedure, or the tribunal exceeding its powers, the rehearing may be before the tribunal that made the award or a new one.[806]

As a result, there is a gap in the new Saudi law, which the Saudi Ruler should resolve in the implementation regulation.

5. The Competent Court to Hear a Challenge

The new Saudi law clearly explains which Saudi court will adjudicate issues regarding the validity of an arbitration award, whether the arbitration is domestic or international. Article 1(3) of the new law defines the Saudi competent court as the court that has authority in law to judge the disputes that are being arbitrated.[807] In addition, there is a difference between domestic commercial arbitration and international commercial arbitration in determining which court has jurisdiction.[808] The Saudi court that has the competence to hear a challenge to the validity of the arbitral award and the matters that are referred to the court by Saudi law should be the Court of Appeals, which is originally competent to hear this type of dispute.[809]

Because Saudi law pays more attention to international commercial arbitration, which has a particular nature, it grants the jurisdiction over international commercial arbitration to the Court of Appeal, which is originally competent to hear such disputes in the city of Riyadh, although the parties have the right to agree on another Court of Appeal in the Kingdom.[810] Assigning consideration of international commercial disputes to a specialized court of appeal could lead to significantly positive results.

Creating such a specific court of appeals would allow the cases to be heard by experienced judges, who spent years adjudicating this type of disputes and by trained judges who have specific knowledge of the nature of international commercial arbitration. In the Kingdom, it is still not clear how this issue will be handled, because the judicial system is still under new formation. Of course, the stated difference between domestic and international disputes in the new law

---

805 Id.

806 Id.

807 Arbitration Law. 2012.

808 See id at Article 8.

809 See Id.

810 See Id.

reflects clearly that the Saudi Ruler realizes the importance of international commercial arbitration and its nature and that such international commercial disputes are usually governed by principles of international laws and customs,[811] which require specific knowledge not always available to regular Saudi judges.

C. Enforcement of an Arbitration Award

Before the Kingdom began reforming its regulations and laws related to arbitration, the arbitrating parties were required by law to bring actions for the enforcement of foreign judgments and arbitration awards before the Saudi court, which involved a long and rigid procedure, as the Saudi court would undertake a full review of the merits of each award, ensuring that the arbitral award complied with Islamic Sharia as it was applied in the Kingdom.[812] Furthermore, all relevant documents of the arbitration had to be submitted to the court in the Arabic language to allow for the review and the court re-examined the merits of each case.[813] An ICC case, Jadawel International v. Emaar Property PJSC (UAE), provides a good example that Illustrates the prior system. In 2006, Jadawel initiated arbitration, which was seated in the Kingdom of Saudi Arabia. The claim was about damages of US$1.2 billion based on a breach of contract by Emaar on a construction project. After lengthy arbitration had taken two years, the claim was finally dismissed, and Jadawel was ordered to pay legal costs. The award was then submitted to the Saudi court for enforcement. In its review, the court re-examined the merits of the case, and, not only did it decline to enforce the arbitral award, it reversed the award and ordered Emaar to pay damages to Jadawel.[814]

To respond to challenges and to improve its investment environment, the Kingdom issued, in addition to the new Arbitration law, a new Enforcement Law in 2012. On 28 February 2013, the new Enforcement Law came into effect in the Kingdom, replacing the relevant provisions of the 1989 Rules of Civil Procedure before the Saudi courts.[815] The new law has a particular impact on the enforcement of arbitral awards, whether domestic or international, in addition to aspects

811 The lex mercatoria are common customs, rules and principles between merchants in the international environment used to regulate their dealings. See BORTOLOTTI, Drafting and Negotiating International Commercial Contracts: a Practical Guide 135-139. 2013.

812 See Al-Ammari & Martin, ARBITRATION INTERNATIONAL, 402 (2014).

813 See Implementing Regulations of Arbitration Law Article 12,25,41. 1983.

814 See Al-Ammari & Martin, ARBITRATION INTERNATIONAL, 402 (2014).

815 This law issued by the royal decree No M/53. See Enforcement Law (2012).

of national and foreign judgments. This section will discuss and analyze the procedure for the enforcement of an arbitral award in the Kingdom under the new law.

1. Submission to the Court at the Seat of the Arbitration

The Saudi Ruler wanted to change the past picture about enforcement in the Kingdom by reassuring investors in Article 52 of the new Arbitration Law that the arbitration award delivered in accordance with this law will be authentic, authoritative, and enforceable.[816] The new Saudi law confirmed that arbitral awards will be enforced if they comply with the new Saudi law. In addition, the new Saudi law stated that the competent court does not have the authority to examine the facts and subject of the dispute as the old system permitted and which was a major obstacle to arbitration in the Kingdom as demonstrated in the ICC case.[817]

The new Arbitration Law requires that, to be executed, the arbitral award has to be submitted to the competent court after the expiration of the time permitted for challenges against the validity of the award,[818] which was discussed earlier, with the following attachments:

1) The original of the award or a certified copy of it.

2) A true copy of the arbitration agreement.

3) A translation of the arbitration award into Arabic certified by an accredited authority if it was issued in another language.

4) Proof of depositing the award with the competent court, and the deposited award must be the original copy of the award or a signed copy in the language in which it was delivered by the competent court within fifteen days from the date of issuance, with a translation into Arabic certified by an accredited authority if it was delivered in a foreign language.[819]

---

816 See Arbitration Law. 2012.

817 See id. at Article 50(4).

818 See id. at Article 55(1).

819 See id. at Articles 43, 44, 53. Note: Parties should be aware that depositing the arbitral award with the competent court after issuance, even if there is no need to enforce it, does not comply with international commercial practice as shown earlier. However, the most important point of which foreign parties should be aware is that the award must be translated into Arabic if it was issued in a foreign language within 15 days after it was

After satisfying these requirements according to the law, the competent court must verify the following points:

1) The arbitral award does not conflict with an award or decision issued by a court, committee or authority that has jurisdiction over the subject of the dispute in Saudi Arabia.[820] This requirement is logical, because it is impossible to enforce an award that conflicts with another award already issued by other judicial bodies in the Kingdom.

2) The arbitral award does not include anything that contradicts the provisions of Islamic Sharia and public order in the Kingdom. The law provides more flexibility on this point, because it allows the competent court to enforce those portions of the award that do not violate Islamic Sharia and to dismiss those portions that do violate Islamic Sharia.[821]

3) The award has been well and truly notified to the party against whom enforcement is being sought.[822]

These conditions in Saudi law, which allow an arbitral award to be enforced, whether it is domestic and international, are similar to those required by the New York Convention, so that they will be explained extensively later of this section. Moreover, the Saudi law does not allow an appeal of the order issued to execute the arbitration award. However, an order rejecting the execution may be appealed to the competent court within thirty days from the date of issuance of the order.[823]

2. Submission to the Enforcing Court

If an arbitral award meets the requirement of the new Arbitration Law as stated above, the arbitral award will be enforced by the competent court, which completes the first stage of getting the award enforced in the Kingdom. The second step needs to follow the rules that are set up in the new enforcement law for taking actual enforcement to the award.

issued. Hence, it is better to make the translation a priority, especially if the case is long and the right translator may be hard to obtain in time.

820 See Id. at Article 55(2).

821 See id.

822 See id.

823 See id. at Article 55 (3).

According to the Royal decree No M/53, 2012, the Saudi judicial authority must customize enforcement circuits in the public courts in the main cities and provinces.[824]

These circuits undertake the implementation of decisions or orders of the competent quasi-judicial committee, such as the banking dispute committees according to the system of implementation.[825] In addition to judgments, decisions, and orders issued by the courts, the enforcement court is responsible for executing arbitral awards that have obtained an executive order from the competent court in accordance with the new Arbitration law. [826]

What remains a concern is the fact that an arbitral award may be at risk in the implementation stage if the implementing court reviews the award to ensure that it is not contrary to the provisions of the public order in the Kingdom.[827] Hence, the arbitral award will be reviewed to make sure that it complies with Islamic Sharia and public order twice, at the competent court and again at the implementing court. The enforcement law could be a significant step to assure that the arbitral award is executed. In particular, the fact that the precise extent and content of Islamic Sharia and public order as applied in the Kingdom are not defined could make the enforcement of awards less certain and could subject their enforcement in the future to the same problems that characterized past practice. Although all decisions of an enforcement judge are final, decisions regarding enforcement disputes and claims of insolvency are subject to appeal, and the determination of the appellate court shall be final.[828] This is the last stage of implementing the domestic arbitral award.

The enforcement law requires that international arbitration awards comply with all requirements in the new Arbitration law and all requirements in the new Implementation law. It also stipulates additional requirements.[829] Inter alia, the law states that the application of this system must not conflict with any international treaties or conventions associated with states, bodies, and organiza-

824 Enforcement Law. 2012.

825 See id.

826 See id. at Article 9(2).

827 See id. at Article 11.

828 See id. at Article 6.

829 See id. at article 11, 12.

tions.[830] Therefore, the study needs to analyze the requirements introduced via international conventions and treaties and their practice in the Kingdom.

3. International Arbitration, Recognition and Enforcement in the Kingdom

Of great concern to foreign investors in the Kingdom is the possibility of having to enforce arbitral awards in Saudi Arabia.[831] If voluntary compliance is not forthcoming, then enforcing an award may prove a most difficult task in the Kingdom.[832] Saudi Arabia has sought to become an arbitration-friendly jurisdiction by reforming its laws as explained earlier and also by entering into international conventions and treaties that aim to achieve the uniform enforcement of such awards in all countries.[833] Among the international conventions most relevant to enforcing international arbitration awards is the New York Convention. Accordingly, this section discusses some of the issues and procedures pertinent to recognition and enforcement of awards under the New York Convention as applied in the Kingdom of Saudi Arabia.

a. Background

International commercial arbitration requires the systematic and efficient enforcement of international arbitral awards. To achieve uniformity among countries in matters of international commercial arbitration, the New York Convention requires all signatories to recognize and enforce both arbitration agreements and foreign arbitral awards.[834] The New York Convention arose as the result of dissatisfaction with the previous conventions, the Geneva Protocol on Arbitration Clauses of 1923 and the Geneva Convention on the Execution of Foreign Arbitral Awards of 1927.[835] As a result, the ICC issued a first draft convention in 1953. The ICC's action was taken over by the United Nations Economic and Social Council (ECOSOC), which produced an amended draft convention in 1955.[836] That draft was discussed during a conference at the United Nations Headquarters in May-June 1958, which led to the establishment of a new convention, which was called the New York Convention for the Recognition and

830 See id. at Article 94.

831 See Saleem, AVAILABLE AT SSRN 2315728, (2012).

832 See id.

833 See id.

834 See MOSES, The Principles and Practice of International Commercial Arbitration 211. 2012.

835 See the history of New York Arbitration Convention, which is available at its Website at http://www.newyorkconvention.org/travaux+preparatoires/history+1923+-+1958.

836 See id.

Enforcement of Foreign Arbitral Awards.[837] When the New York Convention was initially promulgated, many countries were hesitant to become signatories because they were concerned that the rules of the New York Convention were in conflict with their own national laws.[838] Article V(b) of the New York Convention, however, allows a signatory to decline to enforce a foreign arbitral award if it finds the award contrary to its public policy. This provision, together with increased recognition by international investors of an actual global commercial market, has led many countries to adopt the New York Convention and to embrace the Convention's foreign arbitral award enforcement policies.[839]

During the 1950s, Saudi courts refused to enforce many international arbitral awards, because they found that the awards were degrading and disrespectful to Islamic Sharia, which is the primary source of law in the Kingdom.[840] However, the Kingdom of Saudi Arabia entered into the New York Convention on 19 April 1994.[841] Upon adoption, Saudi Arabia became the ninety-fourth party to the Convention, which requires all signatories to recognize and enforce arbitration agreements and awards issued by other member nations.[842]

As a result, it was expected that the Kingdom would become more attractive to investors in the modern global community, and the study will examine whether the Kingdom's adoption of the New York Convention has indeed advanced the successful application of international commercial arbitration by foreign investors in the Kingdom.

b. Principles Governing Recognition and Enforcement

According to Article III of the New York Convention, each contracting state must recognize international arbitral awards as binding and enforce them by the rules of procedure of the state upon which the award is relied and also under the conditions stated in the articles of the Convention.[843] Hence, the Convention distinguishes between recognizing and enforcing arbitration awards. Reco-

---

837 See id.

838 Roy, FORDHAM INT'L LJ, 925-926 (1994).

839 See id. at 920-930

840 See id. at 920-924

841 See the list of contracting states at New York Arbitration Convention at http://www.newyorkconvention.org/list+of+contracting+states.

842 See id.

843 See New York Convention 1958.

gnizing an award means acknowledging that it is valid and binding.[844] Thus, the award will have an official legal status, as the result of which the award cannot be re-litigated or arbitrated.[845] Saudi Arabia recognizes international arbitral awards in the new Arbitration Law and Enforcement Law as long as they comply with its rules.[846] However, to accept such an award, Saudi law requires that the arbitral tribunal deposit the original copy of the award or a signed copy in the language in which it was delivered by the competent court within 15 days with a translation into Arabic certified by an accredited authority if it was performed in a foreign language as stated earlier.[847] The term of enforcement frequently used for the purpose of execution, which is obtained under the legal process of the authorizing jurisdiction, is explained in the following points.

c. Requirements for Enforcement

The scope of the New York Convention is international awards as provided explicitly in Article I(1) of the Convention, which refers to two types of awards:

> 1) Arbitral awards that are made in the territory of a State other than the State in which the recognition and enforcement of such arbitral awards are sought.
>
> 2) Arbitral awards that are not considered domestic awards in the State in which their recognition and enforcement are sought.[848]

The nature of the first type as international awards issued between states is clear; however, the definition of a domestic award is not provided in the Convention, which leads to different determinations between states about the second type. Thus, many countries enforce only the first type of awards, such as Japan and the Netherlands, and other states, like the United States, apply this Convention even if the arbitration involved citizens of the United States as non-domestic awards, if the relationship involves property located abroad, envisages performance of enforcement abroad, or has some other reasonable relation with one or more foreign states.[849] Similar to the United States, Saudi law considers some awards as non-domestic, even if they are between Saudis in the following instances:

844 MOSES, The Principles and Practice of International Commercial Arbitration 212-213. 2012.

845 See id.

846 See Arbitration Law Article 3,8(2). 2012.

847 See id. at article 43, 44.

848 New York Convention 1958.

849 See MOSES, The Principles and Practice of International Commercial Arbitration 213. 2012.

1) If the headquarters of both parties to the arbitration lie in more than one country at the time of the arbitration agreement; if one party has more than one business center, this depends mainly on the center that is most relevant to the subject of the dispute, and if one or both arbitrating parties do not have a certain business center, it depends mainly on their usual residential address.

2) If the headquarters of both arbitrating parties lie in the same country at the time of the arbitration agreement, and one of the following places lies outside of that country:

a) the venue of the arbitration procedures as assigned in the arbitration agreement or the agreement refers to how to assign the venue;

b) the place of execution for an essential part of the obligations arising from the trading affairs between both parties;

c) the place most relevant to the subject of the dispute.

3) If both parties agree to resort to an organization or a permanent arbitration authority, or an arbitration center that lies outside of the Kingdom.

4) If the arbitration subject included in the arbitration agreement is related to more than one country.

Hence, the Convention provides one type of international awards that all contracting states are bound to recognize and enforce, namely awards made in the territory of a State other than the State where the recognition and enforcement of such awards are sought. Other arbitral awards that are not considered domestic awards have different determination between laws, which leads to differences in their recognition and enforcement.

In addition to determining the scope of the Convention, the Convention allows states to make two reservations.[850] The first is allowing any contracting state on the basis of reciprocity to declare that applying the Convention to the recognition and enforcement of awards will be only in the territory of another contracting State.[851] That reservation is adopted by many contracting states, one of which is the Kingdom of Saudi Arabia, which has declared: "On the basis of

850 See New York Convention Art. I(3). 1958.

851 See id.

reciprocity, the Kingdom declares that it shall restrict the application of the Convention to the recognition and enforcement of arbitral awards made in the territory of a Contracting State."[852] In addition to this reservation, the Saudi Ruler states in the Enforcement law that the enforcement judge must not enforce an international award except on the basis of reciprocity.[853] The only difference between the new enforcement law and the replaced rules is that the party who was seeking enforcement under the old law had to show that the jurisdiction that issued the international award will, as a matter of reciprocity, enforce an award of the Kingdom. The new Law states clearly that the enforcement judge must find such reciprocity ex officio.[854] For example, in one case under the old law, a Saudi court requested from a party, who was seeking enforcement of an arbitral award in the Kingdom, a specific example of enforcement of a Saudi judgment in an American court. The party was unable to provide such an example. Then the party provided the Saudi court with an opinion from the legal office of the United States Department of State, which confirmed that American courts recognize and enforce Saudi judgments. However, the Saudi court was not satisfied by such proof and refused to recognize and enforce the international arbitration award issued in the United States.[855] It is not clear how the Saudi court will handle this matter under the new Law, but the new Law is a good step toward saving the arbitrating parties time and energy by leaving this responsibility to the court. As a result, according to the limitation of reciprocity that Saudi Arabia has adopted in the past, it would be better if the arbitrating parties, who aim to enforce an award in the Kingdom, consider the place of arbitration to avoid obstacles at the enforcement stage arising out of reciprocity issues.

The second allowed reservation under the New York Convention is that a contracting state may declare that the Convention will be applied only to differences arising out of legal relationships, whether contractual or not, that are considered commercial under the national law of the state making such a declaration.[856] Saudi Arabia is not among the forty-four countries that have made this reservation. Theoretically, since the term "commercial" is not defined, its definition will differ from country to country. As a result, the practice in international arbitration

852 Such reservations are available at New York Convention website at: http://www.newyorkconvention.org/list+of+contracting+states.

853 Enforcement Law Article 11, 12. 2012.

854 See Al-Ammari & Martin, ARBITRATION INTERNATIONAL, 404 (2014).

855 See id.

856 New York Convention Article I (3). 1958.

between states will not be uniform, which can cause the Convention to lose one of its goals.[857] However, in practice, the commercial reservation, in general, has not caused real problems, because the courts tend to interpret the term "commercial" broadly. In addition, there is a tendency by some states to rely on the broad description of a commercial term as is provided in conjunction with the UNCITRAL Model Law, which provides a kind of unity among the states that adopt such a tendency.[858]

d. Enforcement Procedures

The New York Convention does not provide specific rules about the procedure for enforcement, but leaves this matter to be handled by the contracting states in accordance with their own rules,[859] except for some requirements stated in Article IV as follows:

> 1) The party who is applying for recognition and enforcement of the arbitral award must, at the time of the application, provide:
>
> > a) The duly authenticated original arbitral award or a duly certified copy thereof;
> >
> > b) The original agreement or a duly certified copy thereof.
>
> 2) If the arbitral award or agreement is not made in an official language of the state in which the award is relied upon, the arbitrating party who is applying for recognition and enforcement of the award must produce a translation of these documents into that language. The translation must be certified by an official or sworn translator or by a diplomatic or consular agent.[860]

Article 53 of the new Saudi Arbitration Law states the same requirements as the Convention as explained earlier.[861]

In addition to the above-stated requirements, the Convention requires that contracting states not impose more onerous terms or higher service fees or charges on the recognition or enforcement of arbitration awards to which this

---

857 See MOSES, The Principles and Practice of International Commercial Arbitration 214. 2012.

858 See van den Berg, Albert Jan. The New York Convention of 1958: An Overview. 5 (2013).

859 New York Convention Article III. 1958.

860 Id. at Article IV.

861 See Arbitration Law. 2012.

Convention applies than are imposed on the recognition or enforcement of domestic awards.[862] The Saudi law does not differentiate between domestic and international awards in the conditions or fees in the course of enforcing arbitration awards, and most of the conditions imposed by Saudi law are similar to those found in other Convention states. However, the Saudi Enforcement law differentiates between local and international awards issued within the Kingdom on one hand, and international awards that have come from a foreign state, in the enforcement and recognition stage. The international awards that have come from another country do not need to go to the competent court of appeal like other arbitral awards for ratification but can be enforced directly through enforcement courts.[863] Hence, enforcement of international awards issued from a foreign state will face only one stage, while other awards will face two stages, one before the competent court and another at the enforcement court, which make them harder to enforce than the first type.

e. *Grounds for Non-Enforcement under the NY Convection*

Grounds for not enforcing an arbitral award under the New York Convention are the same as the grounds set forth in the Saudi law and the UNCITRAL Model Law.[864] The Convention provides specific grounds for not enforcing an arbitral award, which means that the award must be enforced by the contracting party, unless there is one of the stated grounds.[865] Such grounds are not based on the merits, so the facts and the law in the case cannot be reviewed under the Convention. However, the grounds for not enforcing an award are based on the arbitrating parties' will as stated in the arbitration agreement and on the integrity of the arbitration process, such as fairness of the procedure and for each side having sufficient opportunity to present its case. [866]

862 See New York Convention Article III. 1958.

863 See Enforcement Law article 9. 2012.

864 See id. at Article 11. See New York Convention, Article V. 1958. See also, UNCITRAL Model Law on International Commercial Arbitration Article 35, 36. 2006. See also, Arbitration Law Article 55. 2012.

865 See New York Convention Article V. 1958.

866 See ASSOCIATION, AAA/ICDR Handbook on International Arbitration and ADR 157-175. 2006. See also MOSES, The Principles and Practice of International Commercial Arbitration 217. 2012.

The first defense that an arbitrating party can assert is comprised of the following:

- Incapacity of the party; or
- Invalidity of the arbitration agreement.

The determination of incapacity or invalidity will be in accordance with the law that was chosen by the arbitrating parties, or, if no law was chosen, it will be in accordance with the law of the country in which the award was made.[867] Under the Saudi Arbitration Law, there is no determined age of legal capacity. However, in returning to other Saudi laws that handle the matter, such as the Child Protection Law, the study found that 18 years is generally deemed to be the age of legal capacity.[868] In legal entities, legal capacity will be in the hands of the person who is authorized to sign the arbitration contract for legal entities according to the type of company. For instance, in the joint stock company, the Chairman of the Board of Directors represents the company before the courts, tribunals and third parties.[869] Hence, every legal entity has a different form of legal capacity, which depends on the applicable law of companies. Although the Convention refers the rules of incapacity and invalidity to the applicable law, it provides the standard that the arbitration agreement must meet to be valid. In the arbitration agreement, which must be in writing, the arbitrating parties undertake to submit to arbitration all or any differences that arise or that may arise between them with respect to a defined legal relationship, whether contractual or not, concerning a subject matter capable of settlement by arbitration.[870] The Convention also states that the term "agreement in writing" under the Convention must include an arbitration clause in a contract or an arbitration agreement, and it must be signed by the arbitrating parties or contained in an exchange of letters or telegrams.[871] The study presented in Chapter 3 how Saudi law handles this matter.

The second ground for not enforcing an arbitral award under the New York Convention is not giving an arbitrating party a full opportunity to present his side of the disputed case.[872] This defense can be based on a lack of notice of the appointment of the arbitration tribunal or of the arbitration proceedings or on

867 New York Convention Article V(1). 1958.

868 See The Child Law Protection. 2014. Also see Saudi Labour Law article 2. 2005.

869 See the Saudi Corporate Law article 82(1). 2015.

870 See New York Convention Article II. 1958

871 Id.

872 See id at article V(1)(b)

the basis that the party was otherwise unable to present his case.[873] One of the famous cases based on this ground is Iran Aircraft Industries v. Avco Corp.,[874] Avco Corporation (Avco) entered into a contract with Iran Aircraft Industries for the repair and replacement of helicopter engines. A dispute between the parties arose, and an arbitral tribunal denied Avco's claims. The United States Court of Appeals for the Second Circuit denied enforcement of the award. In so ruling, it found that the tribunal's award was subject to the defenses to enforcement provided in the New York Convention, because Avco had been "unable to present its case" within the meaning of Article V(b) of the Convention. In the opinion of the court, Avco did not have the chance to present its case in a meaningful manner. One of the judges had approved a method of proof, which was proposed by Avco, which was a submission of Avco's audited accounts receivable ledgers. However, another judge later asked for the actual invoices to substantiate Avco's claim. Thus, Court concluded on appeal that Avco was misled regarding the evidence that it was required to submit and thus was deprived of the opportunity to present its case.[875]

The third defense an arbitrating party can assert concerns actions by the arbitral tribunal that exceed its authority.[876] This ground can take different forms, such as that the arbitration award deals with matters not within the scope of the arbitration agreement, or that it contains decisions on issues beyond the framework of the arbitration agreement.[877] However, if decisions on matters that were submitted to arbitration can be separated from those that were not, the parts of the arbitration award that contain decisions on matters submitted to arbitration can be recognized and enforced.[878] In international commercial arbitration, the defense based on the ground of exceeded authority has rarely succeeded,[879] and the study did not find a case in the Saudi courts that has addressed this issue.

Article V(d) of the New York Convention provides that the grounds for not enforcing an arbitration award include the composition of the arbitration authority, that the arbitration procedure did not comply with the arbitration

873 Id.

874 Iran Aircraft Industries v. Avco Corp., 980 F. 2d 141 (2nd Cir 1992).

875 For more information about this case, see Cindy Silverstein, Iran Aircraft Industries v. AVCO Corporation: Was a Violation of Due Process Due, 20 BROOK. J. INT'L L. 443 (1993).

876 New York Convention Article V(1)(c). 1958.

877 See id.

878 See id.

879 See MOSES, The Principles and Practice of International Commercial Arbitration 221. 2012.

agreement, and that the arbitration was not in accordance with the law of the state in which the arbitration took place.[880] The defense on these grounds is not often successful in international commercial arbitration, and they are rarely asserted in international arbitration.[881]

The fifth defense is that the arbitration award is not yet binding on the arbitrating parties or that it has been set aside or suspended whether by the competent authority or under the law of the country in which the award was made.[882] Hence, the award must be binding and unappealable so as to be fully enforceable as explained under the Saudi law earlier. However, the municipal courts have discretion to enforce an arbitral award even if the award was vacated in another jurisdiction, because the Convention uses the word "may" instead of "must" if the defenses arise that could create a loophole in applying the Convention between contracted states, and at the same time it provides an advantage to enforce the vacated award in the countries that can enforce such awards such as France, and unlike the Kingdom of Saudi Arabia.[883]

The last two defenses under New York Convention are those that permit the court to refuse recognition and enforcement of an arbitral award by itself without a request from an arbitrating party.[884]

Subject matter not arbitrable: Not all subject matters are capable of arbitration, and some matters can be arbitrated in one country but not in another country.[885] The New York Convention refers to the law of arbitrability only from the perspective of enforcing the award. It requires the competent court to look to its own rules to determine whether the subject of dispute is arbitrable.[886] Hence, determination of the law governing arbitrability is significant and crucial.

Under Saudi law, the issue of the arbitrability of the subject matter is vague. The provisions of Saudi law provide two types of disputes that cannot be arbitrated:

a) The personal status;

---

880 New York Convention 1958.

881 MOSES, The Principles and Practice of International Commercial Arbitration 222. 2012.

882 New York Convention Article V(1)(e). 1958.

883 See MOSES, The Principles and Practice of International Commercial Arbitration 222-226. 2012.

884 New York Convention Article V(2). 1958.

885 See MOSES, The Principles and Practice of International Commercial Arbitration 226-228. 2012.

886 New York Convention Article V. 1958.

b) Issues that cannot be reconciled.[887]

The first type is clear but the second one is not. The implementing regulations of the old arbitration law mention the second type by provided three instances of disputes that cannot be reconciled:[888]

1) Hadd (plural: Hudud) refers in Islamic Sharia to unchangeable punishments directly prescribed by primary sources of Islamic Sharia, which is considered as the right of God (Allah).[889]

Hudud are specified both in their quantity and quality by Allah for the public interest and individuals. Muslims can neither amend nor annul Hudud. According to the majority of Muslim scholars, Hudud crimes are the following:

a) Zina (unlawful sexual intercourse);

b) Theft;

c) Qazf (false accusation of Zina);

d) Drinking intoxicants;

f) Hirabah (highway robbery);

g) Baghy (rebellion); and

h) Riddah (apostasy).[890]

Once the offender is convicted of a Hudud crime, the judge has no choice other than to impose the prescribed punishments, neither more nor less, even if the victim consents to mitigation or removal of the punishment.[891]

2) Lian: This dispute involves a husband who accuses his wife of adultery without supplying witnesses.[892] The Quran governs such a dispute in four verses:

---

887 See Arbitration Law Article 2. 2012.

888 Implementing Regulations of Arbitration Law Article 1. 1983.

889 See Hossain, JOURNAL OF PHILOSOPHY, CULTURE AND RELIGION, 7-8 (2013).

890 See id.

891 See id.

892 See JAMAL J NASIR, THE ISLAMIC LAW OF PERSONAL STATUS 159-161 (Brill Archive. 1990).

والذين يرمون أزواجهم ولم يكن لهم شهداء إلا أنفسهم فشهادة أحدهم أربع شهادات با للهإنه
لمن الصادقين

And those who accuse their wives [of adultery] and have no witnesses except themselves – then the witness of one of them [shall be] four testimonies [swearing] by Allah that indeed, he is of the truthful.[893]

والخامسة أن لعنت الله عليه إن كان من الكاذبين

And the fifth [oath will be] that the curse of Allah be upon him if he should be among the liars.[894]

ويدرؤا عنها العذاب أن تشهد أربع شهادات بالله إنه لمن الكاذبين

But it will prevent punishment from her if she gives four testimonies [swearing] by Allah that indeed, he is of the liars.[895]

والخامسة أن غضب الله عليها إن كان من الصادقين

And the fifth [oath will be] that the wrath of Allah be upon her if he was of truthful.[896]

Hence, this dispute is explicitly addressed in the Quran, which states that the husband must swear four times that his accusation against the wife is real, followed by a fifth oath in which he invokes the wrath of God (Allah) upon himself if he is lying. Then, the wife may neutralize the claim by responding to it with four oaths of her own. The fifth oath of which calls upon her the wrath of God (Allah) if her husband is telling the truth. If she refuses to take the oath, she is presumed guilty and subject to the punishment for adultery. However, if she takes the oath, she is declared innocent and permanently divorced from her husband. As a result, her husband forfeits any paternity claims over children born after their sworn

893 Quran 24:6.
894 Quran 24:7.
895 Quran 24:8.
896 Quran 24:9.

oaths.[897] The first and second instances are not relevant to international commercial arbitration, but foreign parties should understand such instances, especially since the Saudi arbitration law is not limited to commercial disputes as explained in Chapter 3.

3) Any subject related to public policy

Article V(b) of the New York Convention authorizes the competent court to refuse recognition and enforcement of an arbitral award if doing so would be contrary to the public policy of that state.[898] This defense should only arise if enforcing the award in question would violate the forum country's most basic notions of morality and justice.[899] The term "public policy" is not defined in the Convention, so that each state applies it differently. Some tend to narrow its scope to achieve the Convention's goal of enforcing international awards in a uniform way among states. Other countries interpret this defense broadly to protect national political interests.[900] The United States applies a narrow interpretation. The Second Circuit Court of Appeals affirmed the enforcement of an arbitral award against an American company stating:

> We conclude, therefore, that the Convention's public policy defense should be construed narrowly. Enforcement of foreign arbitral awards may be refused on this basis only where enforcement of such an award would violate the forum country's most basic notions of morality and justice.[901]

However, a Turkish court in 1995 refused to enforce an ICC award that was based on Turkish substantive law, because the tribunal did not use both Turkish substantive law and Turkish procedural law, which violates Turkish public policy even though there is no material difference in the procedural law of Turkey and the procedural law that applied.[902] Hence, the absence of a specific definition of "public policy" in the Convention creates a broad loophole in practice between contracting states, which can lead to unjust and improper results.

---

897 See NASIR, The Islamic Law of Personal Status 159-161. 1990.

898 New York Convention 1958.

899 See MOSES, The Principles and Practice of International Commercial Arbitration 228-229. 2012.

900 Id.

901 Parsons & Wh. Ov. Co., Inc. v. SOCIETE G. DE L. DU P.(R.), 508 F.2d 969 (2d Cir. 1974).

902 MOSES, The Principles and Practice of International Commercial Arbitration 228. 2012.

The issue of public policy is different under Saudi law. Islamic Sharia as applied in the Saudi court is considered part of the public policy in the Kingdom.[903] However, public policy principle cannot be specified in the Saudi courts for two main reasons. First, there are not enough published cases. Saudi Arabia has begun to release a few of the cases, but there are still not enough to establish a clear picture of the meaning of public policy in the Kingdom.[904]

Even if the Kingdom had enough published cases, the principle of stare decisis is not recognized in the Saudi courts, which makes it hard to predict future decisions even if the facts are the same as or very close to the facts of the previous case.[905] Hence, Ijtihad as applied in the Saudi court without binding precedents provides the court the power to refuse any award if the court considers the award to be against public policy or Islamic Sharia even if the subject is not settled among Muslim jurists. For example, in Case Number 3375/1 / ق of the year 1424 h,[906] a Saudi court refused to enforce a foreign judgment for payment of a specific amount of money. The court based its decision on the fact that the judgment was connected with revenue from singing and music, and the Kingdom of Saudi Arabia recognizes as highest legal authority the Book of Allah and the Sunnah, which, in the opinion of the judges, forbid song and music. Although the court acknowledged that there is a debate between Muslim jurists whether singing is indeed forbidden, it would not change the decision, because it made the decision based on judges personal faith. This case provides a clear picture of how Ijtihad as applied in Saudi courts can lead to unpredictable outcomes in the process of recognition and enforcement of an international award.

In effect, Article V(2)(b) of the New York Convention provides a safe harbor in which the Kingdom can refuse to recognize or enforce an international arbitral award that is contrary to its public policy or Islamic Sharia and maintain its history and religious beliefs. However, this creates a problem for foreign investors and contractors who choose to do business in the Kingdom. While ratification of the

903 See Al-Ammari & Martin, ARBITRATION INTERNATIONAL, 402-405 (2014).

904 The Saudi courts have begun to publish some of cases at its website at http://www.bog.gov.sa/ScientificContent/JudicialBlogs.

905 See Al-Ammari & Martin, ARBITRATION INTERNATIONAL, 405 (2014). For more information about the principle of stare decisis, see Frank Emmert, *Stare Decisis: A Universally Misunderstood Idea*, 6(2) LEGISPRUDENCE 207-27 (2012). Available at: https://papers.ssrn.com/sol3/papers.cfm?abstract_id=2052660.

906 ق is the Arabic letter and 1424 h is the Muslim calendar. Such case is available at Diwan Almazalim website at: http://www.bog.gov.sa/ScientificContent/JudicialBlogs/1430/Documents/.

New York Convention and adoption of the new Arbitration law were intended to give the international community security in commercial contracts with Saudi Arabia and confirmation that disputes will be adjudicated fairly, Saudi courts will find it easy to reject international arbitral awards under New York Convention's Article V (b) as shown earlier. In the end, the Kingdom may not be required to enforce any more international arbitral awards than it did prior to its 1994 accession to the New York Convention.[907]

There are different proposals to resolve the public policy problem in the Convention, such as a proposal to establish a new international court, a new convention, a new organization or even determining international public policy with which all contracting states must comply, and such proposals have been discussed extensively in other sources.[908] Independently of potential international reforms, the study found that the Kingdom of Saudi Arabia must review its handling of the public policy matter to achieve the purpose of the New York Convention.

The Kingdom can give the New York Convention greater effect if it chooses to give Article V(b) a more narrow reading. For example, American courts, as in the previous example, have held that all New York Convention defenses should be given a narrow reading so that they are effective only when enforcement of an award would violate the most fundamental notions of justice.[909]

The Kingdom of Saudi Arabia, with its need to gain the confidence of the international commercial community, may choose to give the public policy defense set forth in Article V(2)(b) of the New York Convention a similarly narrow reading, which undoubtedly requires reviewing Ijtihad as it is applied in the Saudi courts and which conflicts with the predictability of decisions and obstructs efforts to put the Kingdom on track with the international community.

D. Conclusions

The new Saudi Enforcement Law is a significant step toward harmonizing Saudi law with the international community and its standards. This new Law also facilitates enforcement of international and domestic arbitral awards with the creation of a specific authority and specific procedures applicable to such

907 See Roy, FORDHAM INT'L LJ, 953-955 (1994).

908 For more information about such proposals, see ASSOCIATION, AAA/ICDR Handbook on International Arbitration and ADR 50-52. 2006.

909 See Roy, FORDHAM INT'L LJ, 953-955 (1994).

enforcement, which was absent in the past. In theory, the enforcement court will not review the merit of the dispute. However, in practice, the new Enforcement Law still provides that enforcement must not violate public policy in the Kingdom and as long as this is broadly interpreted, it could be obstructive especially for awards issued by foreign arbitrators who are not versed in Saudi law or Islamic Sharia as applied in the Saudi courts.

The meaning of "public policy" is not clear in the Saudi courts, and Islamic Sharia applies it through Ijtihad that is not bound by any precedent decisions. This makes enforcement of an arbitral award unpredictable as long as any Saudi judge or court could decide that some element of the dispute is not in line with Saudi public policy as understood or interpreted by that judge or court. The problem is potentially reduced by the rule that enforcement judges may refuse to enforce only that part of an award that conflicts with public policy – say the granting of interest on monetary claims – instead of the entire award, unless that part is not severable from the rest of the arbitral award. It remains to be seen, whether this will make a big enough difference. In a nutshell, the new Saudi Enforcement Law remains a significant step toward international legal principles, but it needs to review the public policy matter to make the recognition and enforcement of international awards more predictable at the final stages of the arbitration process.

Chapter 5

Choice of Saudi Law as the Applicable Substantive Law and the Impact on International Arbitration Agreements

When negotiating international commercial contracts, a crucial matter that the parties should consider carefully is the choice of the governing law that will be used and applied to interpret the contract and to determine the rights and obligations that flow from it. It is common in international arbitration that parties choose as the applicable law in their contract the law of the domicile of one of the parties. For example, in the Chromalloy case, a contract involved an American company as one party. The other party was Egyptian. Egyptian law was chosen as the applicable law.[910] However, choosing Saudi law as the applicable law in a contract invites different challenges that have arisen in international arbitration cases or even in the municipal courts as will be addressed in this study, together with possible solutions within the new Saudi arbitration regime. Foreign investors, who usually are not very familiar with the laws and rules of Muslim countries, such as Saudi Arabia, should know these solutions before entering into such agreement.

A. Overview

Choosing Saudi law as the applicable law in a commercial arbitration agreement means that Islamic Sharia will be applied, as it is the primary source of law in the Kingdom of Saudi Arabia.[911] An example is provided by *National Group for Communications & Computers v. Lucent Technologies International*.[912] National Group and Lucent Technologies agreed that Saudi law should govern the terms of their dispute. The Court acknowledged that to judge the case, it would first have to determine how Saudi law would decide the claim for loss of the plaintiff's Projects Department. In doing so, the Court analyzed tenets of Islamic Sharia. In

910 See MATTER OF CHROMALLOY AEROSERVICES (ARAB REPUBLIC), 939 F. Supp. 907 (D.C. 1996).

911 See Arbitration between the State of Saudi Arabia and the Arabian American Oil Co., 27 I.L.R. 117 (1958).

912 NATIONAL GROUP FOR COMMUN. AND COMPUTERS LTD. v. LUCENT TECHNOLOGIES INTERN. INC., 331 F. Supp. 2d 290 (D.N.Y. 2004).

its opinion, the Court recited some rules from the Basic Law of the Kingdom of Saudi Arabia, which is equivalent to the constitution in other countries. Those rules provided that, in cases brought before them, the courts must apply Islamic Sharia according to its primary sources, the Quran and the Sunna, and the rules issued by the Saudi Ruler that do not contradict the Quran or the Sunnah of the Prophet Muhammad.[913]

However, early arbitration cases demonstrate that some international arbitral tribunals denied that Islamic Sharia, which is used in some countries, such as Qatar and Saudi Arabia, is adequate and sophisticated enough to govern complex commercial disputes. One of the famous international arbitration cases in which this matter was raised is the dispute between Aramco and Saudi Arabia. The arbitral tribunal stated: "In view of the insufficiency of Muslim law as interpreted by the school of Imam Ahmed Ben Hanbal... and as the law in force in Saudi Arabia contains no determined rule concerning oil exploration... it is necessary to resort to the general principles of law..."[914] A similar decision was reached in a case in Qatar, where the arbitral tribunal held: "I need not set out the evidence before me about the origin, history and development of Islamic law as applied in Qatar or as to the legal procedure in this country. I have no reason to suppose that Islamic law is not administered there strictly, but I am convinced that this law does not contain any principles which would be sufficient to interpret these particular contracts."[915] In the case of Petroleum Development (Trucial Coasts) Ltd. v. Sheikh of Abu Dhabi, Lord Asquith acted as an arbitrator in a dispute arising out of a contract executed in Abu Dhabi. He arrived at the same conclusions about Islamic Sharia as the applicable law.[916]

Even if the arbitral tribunal tries to apply Islamic Sharia as the applicable law, judicial interpretation and enforcement of contracts could raise legal problems, especially since Sharia is unfamiliar to most judges around the world.[917] Furthermore, there are different schools inside Islamic Sharia, so that there is no single authoritative interpretation of Islamic Sharia or doctrine,[918] which creates difficul-

---

913 See id.

914 (1963) 27 I.L.R. 117 Aramco case.

915 Ruler of Qatar v. International Marine Oil Co. Ltd., 20 I.L.R. 534 (1953).

916 Arbitration Between Petroleum Development (Tmcial Cod) LTD and the Shiekh of Abu Dhabi, 1 INT'L & COMP. L.Q. 247 (1952).

917 See Charles P Trumbull, Islamic Arbitration: a New Path for Interpreting Islamic Legal Contracts, 59 VAND. L. REV. (2006).

918 See BHALA, Understanding Islamic Law 391. 2011.

ties for judges in attempting to interpret the contract and apply it. This occurred in the Shamil Bank case, where the tribunal found considerable controversy and then difficulty in applying Islamic Sharia to matters of finance and banking; as a result, it concluded that it is improbable that the disputing parties were truly asking the Court to get into issues of Islamic religion and orthodoxy even though the Court agreed that there might be general consensus in Islamic Sharia upon some of the principles of the presented case.[919] Hence, this study will now address challenges of Saudi law (Islamic Sharia) as an applicable law in international commercial contract arbitration and possible solutions.

B. Saudi Law as Applicable Law

Determining the applicable law means that substantive contractual issues, such as interpretation, validity, rights of disputing parties, performance, breaches and remedies, that are derived from a contract will be ruled based on the chosen law.[920] The courts selected by the parties or an arbitral tribunal appointed to review the dispute will apply the law chosen by the parties, and, if the parties fail to choose, most tribunals determine the substantive law that they consider the most relevant to the subject of the dispute based on the presented aspects and circumstances.[921] For instance, Article 21(1) of the ICC Arbitration Rules states: "The parties shall be free to agree upon the rules of law to be applied by the arbitral tribunal to the merits of the dispute. In the absence of any such agreement, the arbitral tribunal shall apply the rules of law which it determines to be appropriate."[922] Similar to the ICC, the Saudi law provides in Article 38(1):

> 1) Taking into account the non-violation of the provisions of Islamic Sharia and public order in the Kingdom, the arbitral tribunal, during the hearing of the dispute, shall:
>
> a) Apply the rules agreed upon by the parties of the arbitration on the subject of the dispute, and if they agree on the application of a law

919 See Shamil Bank of Bahrain EC v. Beximco Pharmaceuticals Ltd, 2004 E.W.C.A. Civ 19 (2004).1784, 1793, 1800-1801. For more information about this case, see Julio C Colon, Choice of Law and Islamic Finance, 46 TEX. INT'L LJ, 414-415 (2011).

920 See BORTOLOTTI, Drafting and Negotiating International Commercial Contracts: a Practical Guide 20-23. 2013. See also MOSES, The Principles and Practice of International Commercial Arbitration 67-68. 2012.

921 See BORTOLOTTI, Drafting and Negotiating International Commercial Contracts: a Practical Guide 26. 2013.

922 ICC Rules of Arbitration. 2012.

of a particular state, the substantive rules shall be followed without those of dispute-of-laws, unless agreed otherwise.

b) If the parties of the arbitration do not agree on the statutory rules applicable to the subject of the dispute, the tribunal shall apply the substantive rules in the law that it considers the most relevant to the subject of the dispute.[923]

The stated articles presented two major principles relevant to choosing the applicable law: party autonomy and mandatory law.

Arbitrating parties are free to choose a national or a state law to govern their contract, and they can also choose other sets of rules, such as the United Nations Convention on Contracts for the International Sale of Goods (CISG), and/or general principles of law, or equitable principles. As a matter of fact, parties can even agree that different parts of the contract will be governed by different laws or write their own rules altogether.[924] This autonomy is supported by the Saudi law as stated in Article 38 of the new Arbitration Law. However, the mandatory law principle puts some limits on the principle of party autonomy. Such restrictions commonly involve laws that regulate matters of public policy within a given state,[925] or according to Islamic Sharia, such as in the Kingdom of Saudi Arabia.[926] For example, in Saudi Arabia, the parties cannot choose a rule that permits and regulates interest, because iterest is forbidden as applied in the Kingdom as will be presented later in this chapter.

Although arbitrating parties have ample autonomy to choose the law or rules that apply to their commercial contracts and subsequently the arbitration process, this freedom comes with inherent risks when choosing inefficient law as the applicable law that will govern substantive contractual issues. One of the famous examples is the Aramco case where Saudi law was the applicable law; however, the arbitral tribunal considered Saudi law insufficient because it did not contain sufficiently detailed rules concerning oil exploration. As a result, and in spite of a clear choice by the parties, the tribunal resorted to general principles of law.[927]

---

923 Arbitration Law. 2012.

924 See MOSES, The Principles and Practice of International Commercial Arbitration 73-78. 2012.

925 See ASSOCIATION, AAA Handbook on International Arbitration and ADR 74-78. 2010.

926 See Arbitration Law Article 38. 2012.

927 See (1963) 27 I.L.R. 117 Aramco case.

Therefore, arbitrating parties should be careful when choosing Saudi law as the applicable law, especially for foreign investors who are not familiar with Islamic Sharia as applied in the Kingdom. Saudi law is very different from the secular laws applied in other states and may not provide business partners with some of the advantages they might expect, including a full set of legal remedies. The differences in the Saudi law as applied by the tribunal may frustrate at least some of the intentions parties had when entering into their contract in the first place. Hence, the study will now address challenges parties may face when choosing Saudi law as the applicable substantive law.

C. Differences Between Islamic Sharia and Secular Law

1. The Characteristics of Islamic Sharia

Islamic Sharia differs from secular laws in several aspects. First, Islamic Sharia derives its legitimacy from Allah (God) and not from one of the authorities of the country, as does secular law.[928] Hence, the violation of Islamic Sharia or one of its rules is not merely an infringement of the law or the social order, but it is a transgression against Allah's will, which warrants punishment not just in life on earth but also in the afterlife.[929] Thus, Muslims view Islamic Sharia as a religious duty, with which they must comply even in the absence of state enforcement, because Islamic Sharia appeals to the religious conscience of the individual.

The second difference is the interpretation of Islamic Sharia. As Islamic Sharia derives its authority from Allah, Islamic Sharia must be interpreted by religious scholars rather than by authorities of the state.[930] The religious scholars do not purport to create laws but to provide their understanding of God's will based on analysis of the primary sources of Islamic Sharia.[931] As a result, Islamic Sharia consists of a series of scholarly opinions intended to explain principles and rules of Islamic Sharia. Differences in these scholarly opinions led to the development of different schools of Islamic jurisprudence.[932] Muslim jurists use the primary sources of Sharia to arrive at rules, along with secondary sources as scholarly consensus, analogous reasoning, and policy-related considerations, such as

928 See Trumbull, VAND. L. REV., 630-633 (2006).

929 See id.

930 See id.

931 See BHALA, Understanding Islamic Law 334-335. 2011.

932 See id. at 391.

public interest, precautionary measures, and custom.[933] One of the Saudi scholars summarized this matter at an American university, where he stated:

> Broadly defined, the Sharia consists of everything written by Muslim jurists throughout the centuries . . .Narrowly construed, the Sharia is confined to the undoubted principles of the Quran, what is true and valid of the Sunnah, and the consensus of the community represented by its scholars and learned men during a certain period and regarding a particular problem, provided there was such a consensus.[934]

However, such scholarly opinions may differ or even contradict each other, even if they generally agree on the core principles of Sharia. Despite such differences, scholarly opinions are considered valid interpretations of Sharia as long as they are based on the sacred sources and developed according to accepted methods in Islamic jurisprudence.[935]

Moreover, unlike secular law, Islamic Sharia consists of the legal and moral value of particular acts. According to Nadia E. Nedzel:

> Islamic law (sharia) does not distinguish between moral and legal obligations, because it regards law and religion as intimately connected... [M]odern common law distinguishes between law and morality and recognizes that one might be morally obligated but not legally obligated to do or not do something. One well-established principle of common law is that generally there is no duty to rescue another person, even if the potential rescuer realizes that some action on his or her part is necessary for the other's protection or aid unless there is a special relationship between the two parties." [936]

Hence, the moral and ethical objectives of the primary sources of Islamic Sharia play a core role in the process of legal analysis, unlike in secular laws.

Such differences show that Islamic Sharia is not really a law in the modern sense, because it lacks many of the characteristics that we nowadays consider essential to law. For example, secular laws enacted by a state are backed by the enforce-

933 See id. at 390-391.

934 Quoted in Colon, TEX. INT'L LJ, 417 (2011).

935 See BHALA, Understanding Islamic Law 391. 2011.

936 NADIA E. NEDZEL, LEGAL REASONING, RESREARCH, AND WRITING FOR INTERNATIONAL GRADUATE STUDENTS 32-33 (Wolters Kluwer Law & Business. 2012).

ment authority of the state. Also, the law is publicly accessible, generally applicable, and consistent.[937] In contrast, Islamic Sharia does not strive for stability, predictability, or consistency. The goal of Islamic Sharia is to draw as near as possible to Allah's actual evaluation of each particular event via the process of Ijtihad. According to Raj Bhala: "Ijtihad connotes a personal struggle to find the truth through study of the sacred sources and Sharia. The struggle is to interpret the will of God (Allah) and how best to submit to it."[938] Because people have an imperfect and incomplete understanding of Allah's will, Islamic Sharia accepts the necessity of uncertainty and values the search for divine truth over stability and predictability.[939]

2. Consequences for Litigation

a. *Stare Decisis*

One of the main obstacles when choosing Saudi law as applicable law in a contract is that Saudi courts do not follow the rule of stare decisis or a similar doctrine to bind courts to their prior decisions or to those issued by higher courts.[940] Therefore, the fact that a Saudi judge issued a particular ruling in the past does not mean that he or any other court will rule the same way in the future, even if presented with an identical set of facts.[941] For instance, in *National Group for Communications & Computers v. Lucent Technologies International*, the Court was to ascertain how a Saudi judge would resolve the dispute if it were brought in a Saudi court. The Court stated: "Saudi Arabian judges are not bound by judicial precedent ... and the concept of stare decisis does not exist. Instead, judges must strive for the divine truth for each case that confronts him, without being bound by past opinions, even his own."[942] Although Saudi Arabia has recently started to publish court decisions,[943] this will be of little help in predicting

---

937 See Trumbull, VAND. L. REV., 630-633 (2006).

938 BHALA, Understanding Islamic Law 335. 2011.

939 See Trumbull, VAND. L. REV., 630-633 (2006). Also see BHALA, Understanding Islamic Law 335. 2011.

940 See Karl, GEO. WASH. J. INT'L L. & ECON., 149-150 (1991). See also Rehman, et al., INTERNATIONAL JOURNAL OF BUSINESS AND SOCIAL SCIENCE, (2013). Also see Mikail & Arifin, MALAYSIAN COURT PRACTICE BULLETIN, (2014).

941 See id.

942 NATIONAL GROUP FOR COMMUN. AND COMPUTERS LTD. v. LUCENT TECHNOLOGIES INTERN. INC. 331 F.Supp.2d 290 (2004).

943 Saudi Arabia began publishing some judicial decisions, which are available on the Board of Grievances website at:

future outcomes. However, because most judges around the world are neither trained nor obligated to strive for divine truth in each case that confronts them, which is called Ijtihad in Islamic Sharia, this creates problems for judges who are attempting to interpret Islamic Sharia and its doctrines.

b. Evidence

Another difference that should be considered is the production of evidence.[944] Under Saudi law, the burden of proof is on the proponent of a statement, which must be met by producing live testimony or documentary evidence.[945] Live testimony means the testimony of eye-witnesses - Shahada.[946] There are many details about such evidence in Islamic jurisprudence.[947] In short, the essential proof is eye-witness testimony, and other kinds of evidence are less significant.[948] Direct testimony is what Saudi courts want to hear, and there is no hearsay rule,[949] which complies in this point with the practice of international arbitration.[950] In addition, in financial matters, a party must produce two male witnesses or one male and two female witnesses to prove a case.[951] Female witnesses are of inferior value. Moreover, non-Muslims may testify but only against other non-Muslims.[952]

If the claimant can produce the required witnesses, and their testimony supports the claim, the claimant will win, as long as the defendant cannot present at least equally valuable contradicting testimony.[953] On the other hand, if the applicant cannot produce such witnesses, he can require the defendant to take an oath,

---

http://www.bog.gov.sa/ScientificContent/JudicialBlogs/Pages/default.aspx.

944 For details about evidence in the litigation proceedings under the civil law and common law see, ASSOCIATION, AAA Handbook on International Arbitration and ADR 49-59. 2010.

945 See Karl, GEO. WASH. J. INT'L L. & ECON., 150-151 (1991). Also see Joseph L Brand, Aspects of Saudi Arabian Law and Practice, 9 BC INT'L & COMP. L. REV., 12-13 (1986).

946 See Id. Note: the Muslim jurists set up some conditions that witnesses characteristics must meet to be approved see such as that he must be a Muslim, have full legal capacity, and integrity. See for more information QUDAMAH, Al Mughni 144-147. 1968.

947 See id. at, 242-289.

948 See Brand, BC INT'L & COMP. L. REV., 12 (1986).

949 See id.

950 See ASSOCIATION, AAA Handbook on International Arbitration and ADR 50. 2010.

951 See QUDAMAH, Al Mughni 133-134. 1968.Note: Some cases that are not financial matters permit one male or one male plus two females, while some of them require four male witnesses. For more details see id. at, 130-132.

952 Id. at. 147. See also Brand, BC INT'L & COMP. L. REV., 12 (1986).

953 Brand, BC INT'L & COMP. L. REV., 12-13 (1986). See also Karl, GEO. WASH. J. INT'L L. & ECON., 150-151 (1991).

and if the defendant refuses, the plaintiff's allegations are considered established.[954] If the defendant denies the claim undertaking the oath, the defendant will win unless the plaintiff can prove the allegations through other evidence.[955] Such an oath is used in a civil case relating to money or property.[956]

As in the common law and civil law systems, Islamic Sharia presumes on the criminal side that one is innocent until proven guilty, while the burden of proof is on the claimant in a civil case, though it can shift with the presentation of claims and defenses.[957] Moreover, in the Saudi court, documentary evidence does not carry as much weight as the testimony of eye witnesses. Documentary evidence is considered to be a presumption of fact, so it must be proved by witness testimony or by admission.[958] Furthermore, modern scientific evidence has been little known and used in Saudi courts until recent times.[959] Such evidence is used mostly in the testimony of handwriting and fingerprint experts.[960] Other evidence that is utilized in Saudi courts is expert testimony.[961] It is well applied, recognized and favored, especially on such typical issues as the fairness of a sale or rental agreement or the custom of a certain locality or the adherence by a building contractor to an architect's specifications.[962] In sum, Saudi courts extensively permit the introduction of different types of evidence, but testimony is the most influential evidence during litigation, and the Court has broad powers to evaluate it.

954 See id.

955 See id.

956 See Brand, BC INT'L & COMP. L. REV., 12-13 (1986).

957 See id. For more information about the burden of proof under Saudi law in civil matters, see Jean-Benoit Zegers, Foreign Investment Protection in Saudi Arabia, 9(1) Y.B. ISLAMIC MIDDLE E. L. 65-87 (2002). For more details about the burden of proof under Saudi law in criminal matters, see Elizabeth Peiffer, The Death Penalty in Traditional Islamic Law and as Interpreted in Saudi Arabia and Nigeria, 11(3) WM. & MARY J. WOMEN & L. 507-39 (2004).

958 See Brand, BC INT'L & COMP. L. REV., 12-13 (1986). See also Karl, GEO. WASH. J. INT'L L. & ECON., 150-151 (1991).

959 See Brand, BC INT'L & COMP. L. REV., 12-13 (1986).

960 See id.

961 See id. For more information about expert testimony under Saudi law and also traditional Islamic Sharia, see Moore Jr, Richter H., Courts, Law, Justice, and Criminal Trials in Saudi Arabia. 11(1-2) INT'L. J. COMP. APPL. CRIM. JUSTICE 61-7 (1987).

962 See Brand, BC INT'L & COMP. L. REV., 12-13 (1986).

3. Traditional Legal Doctrines

Although the Kingdom of Saudi Arabia has used and applied modern forms of commercial regulations, as have most Middle East states, the Saudi legal system remains firmly rooted in the Islamic tradition of Sharia. Principles of Islamic Sharia have an influence on virtually every commercial transaction.[963]

The most significant Islamic Sharia doctrines that appear in modem commercial dealings are the prohibitions of Riba and Gharar, which will be presented and discussed in the following points.

a. The Prohibition of Riba (Usury)

The concept of Riba in Islamic jurisprudence is wide and has many details that cannot be considered in this section, but they are discussed extensively in numerous books by other researchers.[964]

Riba is translated literally as "usury" or "unjust".[965] While Muslim jurists agree that Riba is prohibited, there is debate over what it is and whether it should be equated with all forms of banking interests.[966] For the purposes of this chapter, the study will present only what Saudi courts have adopted and applied from among Muslim jurists' opinions about Riba.

Riba is mentioned and forbidden in different verses of the Quran and in many sayings of the Prophet Muhammad.[967] For example, one verse of the Quran states:

---

963 For more information about influence of Islamic sharia on business laws in the kingdom, See Karl, GEO. WASH. J. INT'L L. & ECON., 150-151 (1991).

964 For more information about Riba in Islamic Sharia, see BHALA, Understanding Islamic Law 667-701. 2011. Also, see ANN BLACK, Modern Prespectives on Islamic Law 181-185. 2013.For more information about Riba in transactions, see Barbara L. Seniawski, Riba Today:Social Equity, the Economy, and Doing Business Under Islamic Law, 39 COLUM. J. TRANSNAT'L L. 701 (2000).

965 See BHALA, Understanding Islamic Law at 668. See also Karl, GEO. WASH. J. INT'L L. & ECON., 151-152 (1991).

966 See BHALA, Understanding Islamic Law 668. 2011. (Note: Riba is not restricted just to the idea of banking interest. There are other types of Riba. For example, in case number of appeal 363/2 /? 1434H the court decided that compensation for delaying payment is a type of Riba that is prohibited under Sharia as applied in the Kingdom. However, for the purpose of this book, the study focuses on the best known type of Riba, which is the banking interest.

967 See Quran 2: 275-280.

ٱلَّذِينَ يَأْكُلُونَ ٱلرِّبَوٰا۟ لَا يَقُومُونَ إِلَّا كَمَا يَقُومُ ٱلَّذِى يَتَخَبَّطُهُ ٱلشَّيْطَٰنُ مِنَ
ٱلْمَسِّ ذَٰلِكَ بِأَنَّهُمْ قَالُوٓا۟ إِنَّمَا ٱلْبَيْعُ مِثْلُ ٱلرِّبَوٰا۟ وَأَحَلَّ ٱللَّهُ ٱلْبَيْعَ وَحَرَّمَ ٱلرِّبَوٰا۟ فَمَن جَآءَهُۥ مَوْعِظَةٌ
مِّن رَّبِّهِۦ فَٱنتَهَىٰ فَلَهُۥ مَا سَلَفَ وَأَمْرُهُۥٓ إِلَى ٱللَّهِ وَمَنْ عَادَ فَأُو۟لَٰٓئِكَ أَصْحَٰبُ ٱلنَّارِ هُمْ فِيهَا خَٰلِدُونَ

> Those who consume Riba cannot stand on the Day of Resurrection except as one stands who is being beaten by Satan into insanity. That is because they say, trade is just like Riba. But Allah has permitted trade and has forbidden Riba. So, whoever has received an admonition from his Lord and desists may have what is past, and his affair rests with Allah. But whoever returns to usury those are the companions of the Fire; they will abide eternally therein.[968]

Under Saudi law, all types of banking interests are prohibited. For instance, the law governing the Monetary Agency (SAMA) explicitly prevents SAMA from receiving or paying interest. Article 2 of its Charter says: "The Saudi Arabian Monetary Agency shall not pay nor receive interest."[969] In a similar manner, Article 6 states: "The Agency shall not charge any interest on its receipts and payments..."[970] Saudi courts also deem that all types of banking interests conflict with Islamic Sharia.[971] In addition to extending the prohibition of Riba to banking interests, the Saudi courts have treated similarly other instances, such as gambling and bargains, where one party receives money without giving something of equal value to the other party.[972]

In sum, most Islamic jurists consider charging interest to be oppressive and exploitative as a mechanism that transfers wealth from the poor to the rich and that thereby creates a greater disparity in the distribution of wealth and an idle class in the community.[973] Hence, the contracts that involve interest, such as those for investment or financing, will not be enforced in Saudi courts.[974] Banks

968 Quran 2:275.

969 Charter of the Saudi Arabian Monetary Agency (1957).

970 Id.

971 See case No. ق/1/2496, 1425H is the Arabic date, and ق is the Arabic letter. Available at Diwan Al Mazalim website at: http://www.bog.gov.sa/ScientificContent/JudicialBlogs/Blog1427/Documents/.

972 See Karl, GEO. WASH. J. INT'L L. & ECON., 151-152 (1991).

973 See id. Also see BHALA, Understanding Islamic Law 669. 2011.

974 See Karl, GEO. WASH. J. INT'L L. & ECON., 151-152 (1991).

in Saudi Arabia have confronted this problem and have been unable to collect interest due on their loan agreements, which forced the Kingdom to establish the Committee on Banking Disputes, under the authority of the Saudi Arabian Monetary Agency, by Royal Order[975] No. 729/8 (1987).[976] Although the Charter of SAMA explicitly prevents SAMA from receiving or paying interest as shown earlier, the Banking Dispute Committee decides more flexibly on banking interest. The only explanation, upon which the Committee of Banking Disputes depends, is the Saudi Banking Control Law promulgated by Royal Decree No. M/5 of 1966, which is completely silent on the issue of interest.[977] Based on this, interest is prevented in Saudi Arabia except in banking disputes according to Royal Decree No. M/5 of 1966. In the other cases, such as enforcement of foreign judgments or arbitral awards granting, inter alia, interest on late payment, the Saudi courts have remained unwilling to enforce claims that involved interest. In some cases, the courts have used equitable remedies to restore the disputed parties to the status quo ante.[978]

b. The Prohibition of Gharar (Gambling, Betting, and Contracts with Uncertain Outcomes)

Another major Islamic legal doctrine that is applied in Saudi courts is Gharar (the prohibition of risk or uncertainty in commercial dealings).[979] Every financial transaction involves risk, and the types of risk varies, such as country risk, credit risk, currency risk, insolvency risk, legal risk, or even political risk.[980] However, in Islamic Sharia as applied in Saudi Arabia, Gharar means any contract that involves speculation, such as gambling, which is void under Gharar. More importantly,

975 Note: Legislation in the Kingdom is enacted in different forms, the most common of which are Royal Orders, Royal Decrees, Council of Ministers Resolutions, Ministerial Resolutions and Ministerial Circulars. The difference between a royal order and a royal decree is that the former reflects the consideration of the King only without any prior resolution from any other Saudi authorities. In contrast, a royal order is discussed and approved by the legislative authorities (the Shura Council and the Council of Ministers) before being issued by the King. see See AHMED A. BIN BAZ, POLITICAL AND CONSTITUTIONAL LAW OF SAUDI ARABIA 264 (2000).

976 See BAAMIR, Shari'a Law in Commercial and Banking Arbitration: Law and Practice in Saudi Arabia 179-184. 2013.

977 See id.

978 See Karl, GEO. WASH. J. INT'L L. & ECON., 151-152 (1991). See also case No. ق /1/2496, 1425H is the Arabic date and ق is the Arabic letter. Available at Diwan Al Mazalim website at: http://www.bog.gov.sa/ScientificContent/JudicialBlogs/Blog1427/Documents/.

979 See Karl, GEO. WASH. J. INT'L L. & ECON., 153 (1991).

980 See BHALA, Understanding Islamic Law 653-654. 2011.

Gharar also covers events that might not occur, or transactions in which the gain of each party is not clearly defined at the time the contract is made.[981] Hence, any contract that leaves open either the amount or the date of payment or that is tied to a fluctuating standard, such as market price or the prime rate of interest, could considered void for Gharar because of the inherent uncertainty or risk. This is also true of most insurance contracts because the event, for which insurance is bought, might never occur. However, Muslim jurists differ between major and minor Gharar; some allow minor Gharar.[982] They also set conditions to determine whether Gharar is present under Islamic Sharia. According to Professor Al Darir:

> To know whether a contract is invalidated:
>
> 1) The Gharar must be excessive.
>
> 2) The contract that is potentially affected must be a commutative financial contract.
>
> 3) The Gharar must affect the principal component thereof.
>
> 4) If a commutative contract contains excessive Gharar but meets a need that otherwise cannot be met, then the Gharar does not invalidate the contract.[983]

Under these conditions, insurance contracts can be accepted because they meet a need that cannot otherwise be met. However, this is only one of many opinions on the subject. As a result, based on stated conditions, the discretion of the court about the existence of Gharar in the contract and its impact on the contract will be a crucial issue in this matter.

4. Modern Strategies for Accommodating the Prohibition of Riba

The prohibitions of Riba and Gharar, as applied in Saudi courts, may cause problems for modern commercial transactions. However, some methods are used to accommodate such traditional doctrines. Most strategies for accommodating Riba and Gharar in the past and in modern time used, for example, by Islamic financial organizations, are based on legal fictions (Hiyal), which means "tricks."[984]

---

981 See Karl, GEO. WASH. J. INT'L L. & ECON., 153 (1991).

982 See BHALA, Understanding Islamic Law 657-658. 2011.

983 Quoted in Id. at 657.

984 See id. at. 707, 708-729. See also, ANN BLACK, Modern Perspectives on Islamic Law 185-190. 2013.

Such Hiyal are utilized to fulfill objectives that cannot be accomplished directly through Islamic Sharia rules.[985] Hiyal enable companies and individuals to arrive safely at desired results and at the same time conform to Islamic Sharia as applied in the Saudi courts. Some Islamic scholars refuse such Hiyal.[986] However, for the purposes of this chapter, the study will not discuss the debate between Muslim jurists. Instead, it will present the strategies as used in the real world and practice, especially by Islamic financial institutions, to guide foreign investors and their attorneys in the Kingdom. The groups of lawful Hiyal include many methods used in financial transactions. The first set of Hiyal address the prohibition of Riba.

a. The Double Sale (a bai al inah)

The double sale, also known as a "buy-back", is one of the financing techniques used to circumvent Riba in Islamic Sharia and to comply with the rules that Muslim jurists have established over centuries.[987] In the double sale transaction, a seller (lender) sells an asset to a buyer (the borrower) on credit (payment later within a fixed time) for a fixed price (the loan amount) plus a profit element, which is called the interest amount in non-Islamic finance transactions. The seller (lender) immediately repurchases the asset from the buyer (borrower) in cash for the fixed price.[988] As a result of such double transaction,

1) the asset returns to the lender, and he owns it;

2) the borrower gets to use the asset without having the cash;

3) the borrower has an obligation to pay the asset's original purchase price from the first sale plus the profit element (interest), and it will usually be in installments as applied in the Islamic financial institution;

4) the profit (interest) results from the sale, not from the loan, which complies with Islamic Sharia. [989]

---

985 See Karl, GEO. WASH. J. INT'L L. & ECON., 153-154 (1991).

986 The Islamic schools debate about using Hiyal, See BHALA, Understanding Islamic Law 707. 2011.

987 See Ayub, Muhammad Ayub, UNDERSTANDING ISLAMIC FINANCE 230 (England, John Wiley & Sons 2009). See also, Karl, GEO. WASH. J. INT'L L. & ECON., 153-154 (1991).

988 See id.

989 See AYUB, UNDERSTANDING ISLAMIC FINANCE 230. 2009.

This transaction has been rejected by many Islamic jurists as a legal contrivance intended to overcome the forbidden Riba and therefore a violation of Islamic Sharia principles.[990]

Islamic financial institutions differ regarding the extent to which they adopt this device.[991]

b. Tripartite Sale (Tawarruq)

Tawarruq is another financial instrument that is used to get cash and at the same time to avoid a conflict with Riba. In this transaction, a buyer purchases a commodity from the seller on a deferred payment basis and then sells the same product to a third party (buyer) on a cash payment basis.[992] When the buyer gets the cash from the second transaction, he pays the first seller usually on an installment basis as Islamic banks have practiced.[993] This is also controversial among Muslim scholars.[994] Some of them see it as not Sharia-compliant because of the absence of any real economic activities and, therefore, as a method of creating interest, which is prohibited in Islamic Sharia.[995] On the other hand, some of them accept it, because it is based on two valid legal sales contracts,[996] and in practice most Islamic banks have adopted it, such as the United Arab Bank[997] and Bank Muaamalat of Malaysia.[998]

c. Single Purchase Loans (Murabaha)

This transaction is usually used to get financing to buy a commodity that is not in conflict with Islamic Sharia rules. Here, the lender (usually the bank) purchases the product from the seller for cash and then sells the product to the buyer (customer) on the deferred payment basis usually in installments.[999] The

990 See ABDULLAH IBN QUDAMAH, AL MUGHNI 132-133 VOL. 4 (1968).

991 See AYUB, Understanding Islamic Finance 230. 2009.

992 See Mohammed Obaidullah, Islamic Financial Services, 109 (2005).

993 See id.

994 See id. at 109-110

995 See id.

996 See id.

997 Information about Tawarruq product is available at the bank website at http://www.uab.ae/islamic-banking/tawarruq.

998 See the bank website for more information about this product at http://www.muamalat.com.my/business-banking/corporate-banking/financing/tawarruq.html.

999 See Obaidullah, 73-80 (2005). See also BHALA, Understanding Islamic Law 727-729. 2011. Also see Karl, GEO. WASH. J. INT'L L. & ECON., 155 (1991).

difference between the prices the lender (buyer) pays to the first seller and the price the lender sells to the second buyer is profit (Murabaha), which in non-Islamic banks is called interest.[1000] Furthermore, the lender (bank) must actually physically possess the product in the custom, such as having a certificate of title or bill of lading.[1001] Most Islamic scholars accept such transactions,[1002] and most Islamic banks deal with Murabaha, such as the Dubai Islamic Bank. [1003]

d. Mudaraba (Sleeping or Silent Partnership)

Another financing product that is widely used and complies with the Islamic financial doctrine is known as Mudaraba.[1004] A Mudaraba project is a contract that is based on a partnership in which one partner is the financier (the investor-customer in the bank), and the other partner (the fund manager, working partner, or the bank) invests the capital in a particular economic activity.[1005] The second partner usually has experience in investment and operating venture capital in economic activities, such as the banks and specialized financial institutions.[1006] The main difference between the Mudaraba and financial products in non-Muslim financial institutions is that both parties agree in advance about sharing the profit and loss (PLS) deposit or participatory deposit.[1007] Hence, there is no guarantee about the capital or getting the profits, which is based on the economic activity, unless the second partner (Mudarib, fund manager) acts negligently or engages in misconduct. Most Muslim scholars accept this financial contract,[1008] and most Islamic financial institutions practice it, such as the Dubai Islamic Bank.[1009] In sum, most Islamic financial institutions say that they are Riba free based on this same principle of Mudaraba, which avoids collecting interest on its loans as done by conventional financial institutions.

1000 See id.

1001 See Karl, GEO. WASH. J. INT'L L. & ECON., 155 (1991).

1002 See Obaidullah, 73-80 (2005). Also see BHALA, Understanding Islamic Law 727-729. 2011.

1003 For more information about Murabaha in Islamic banks, see the bank website at: http://www.dib.ae/corporate-banking/products-and-services/murabaha.

1004 See Obaidullah, 52 (2005). Also see Karl, GEO. WASH. J. INT'L L. & ECON., 155-156 (1991).

1005 See Obaidullah, 52 (2005). See also BHALA, Understanding Islamic Law 708-727. 2011.

1006 See id.

1007 See Obaidullah, (2005). 52.

1008 See BHALA, Understanding Islamic Law 708-727. 2011.

1009 See the bank product at its website at: http://www.dib.ae/corporate-banking/products-and-services/mudaraba.

5. Modern Strategies for Accommodating the Prohibition of Gharar

a. *Insurance*

An insurance contract is considered by traditional Islamic Sharia as Gharar dealing because of the uncertainty whether the adverse event will materialize.[1010] In addition, some Muslim scholars see the insurance contract as gambling, because the policyholder will benefit from paying an amount of premiums only if there is a loss, which is uncertain.[1011] As a result, insurance was rejected at several international Islamic meetings, such as at the 1976 First International Conference on Islamic Economics and again in 1986 by the Islamic Fiqh Academy.[1012] However, the Islamic Fiqh Academy concluded that a cooperative or mutual forms of insurance can be legal under Islamic Sharia.[1013] Cooperative insurance, which is called Takaful in Islamic Sharia, acquires its capital from a pool of individual premiums and charitable donations. Thus, by paying such premiums, a policyholder becomes a partner in the insurance company, and the company invests the paid premium. If a loss occurs, the subscriber files and collects on the claim. However, if there is no loss, the policyholder gets back all premiums and any gain on the investment.[1014]

The Kingdom of Saudi Arabia recognizes the important role of insurance companies in the economic environment and in commerce and industry. However, the Kingdom chose cooperative insurance to operate in the state, to comply with Islamic Sharia.[1015] The first Saudi legislation regulating insurance was promulgated as the Control of Cooperative Insurance Companies Regulation, Royal Decree No. M/32 of 31 July 2003, which entered into force on 20 November 2003 and which took effect with the publication of its Implementing Rules on 23 April 2004.[1016] The first article of the Saudi Law on the Supervision of Cooperative

---

1010 See Ahmed A Al-Ghadyan, Insurance: The Islamic Perspective and Its Development in Saudi Arabia, 14 ARAB LAW QUARTERLY, 333 (1999). See also BHALA, Understanding Islamic Law 807-818. 2011.

1011 See Al-Ghadyan, ARAB LAW QUARTERLY, 333 (1999).

1012 See Karl, GEO. WASH. J. INT'L L. & ECON., 156-157 (1991).

1013 See id.

1014 See BHALA, Understanding Islamic Law 807-818. 2011.

1015 See Cooperative Insurance Companies Control Law, Saudi Arabia, Jul. 31, 2003, Royal Decree No. M/32 Article 1 (2003).

1016 For more information about the history of insurance in Saudi Arabia and its framework, see the Saudi Arabian Monetary Agency website at http://www.sama.gov.sa/en-US/Insurance/Pages/AboutISD.aspx.

Insurance Companies states: "Insurance in the Kingdom shall be undertaken through registered insurance companies operating in a cooperative manner as it is provided within the article establishment of the National Company for Cooperative Insurance promulgated by Royal Decree M/5 dated 17/5/1405 H, and in accordance with the principles of Islamic Sharia." As a result, conventional commercial insurance has been in an area of uncertainty under Islamic Sharia as applied in the Kingdom, so that commercial insurance companies may face a challenge when a case is brought before Saudi courts or at an enforcement stage in the Kingdom.[1017]

b. Deferred Delivery Sale (Salam) Contracts

As discussed above, Islamic Sharia has rejected Gharar, and the interpretation against uncertainty disfavors executor contracts for future payment and delivery of goods. However, under Islamic jurisprudence, a Salam contract is a recognized device that allows for the sale of goods not yet present or existing, or for the delivery of goods to be made at a future date.[1018]

The Salam contract in Islamic traditional jurisprudence is defined as one in which goods are to be delivered in the future for a price paid in the present (immediately).[1019] As a result, the essential requirements for a valid Salam contract are:

1) That the price is paid immediately upon signing the contract, and

2) That the goods are delivered on a specified, fixed date.

There are more details in Islamic jurisprudence about a Salam contract,[1020] but for the purpose of this chapter, this is the basic concept of this contract.

1017 For more details about how Saudi courts handle such cases, see James R Silkenat, et al., The ABA Guide to International Business Negotiations: a Comparison of Cross-cultural Issues and Successful Approaches 908-909 (American Bar Association 2009). Note: As stated earlier, in addition to the general Saudi courts and the Board of Grievances, other different specialised tribunals (committees) have subject matter-specific or participant-specific jurisdiction. One of these tribunals is the Insurance Dispute Committee under the Saudi Arabian Monetary Agency (SAMA), which is similar to the SAMA Committee for the Resolution of Banking Disputes explained in chapter 2 of this book.

1018 See Obaidullah, 95-99 (2005). See also Karl, GEO. WASH. J. INT'L L. & ECON., 158 (1991).

1019 See id.

1020 See Obaidullah, 95-99 (2005).

6. Other Issues in Contract Law

To align with international standards and to facilitate the enforcement of contracts, on July 3, 2012, Royal Decree No. M/53 issued the Saudi Enforcement Law, which represents a significant step with the creation of the particular jurisdiction and specific procedures applicable to enforcement. If a contract meets the requirement of the new enforcement law and does not conflict with Sharia as applied in the Kingdom, the contract will be enforced by the enforcement court. Article 9 of the Saudi Enforcement Law provides: "No forcible execution may be carried out except by an execution document of a right for a specified amount at the time of payment.

Execution documents are: ...

> 5) Authenticated contracts and writs, ...
>
> 8) Contracts and other papers, which have the power of the execution document under the law." Article 13 of such law also provides:
>
> "Official instruments enforced in any foreign country may be ordered to be enforced in Saudi Arabia on the same conditions as are laid down in the law of that country for enforcing official instruments executed in Saudi Arabia, on the basis of equal treatment."

The enforcement law should normally guarantee that a contract can be executed in the Kingdom.

However, one important aspect to know about Saudi contracts is that they are governed under Sharia in general, except for those contracts that are under particular laws and rules, such as the labor law and the companies law, which are codified. Even if there is a codification of particular types of contracts, such as labor contracts, general Sharia rules must be followed. For instance, Article 4 of the Saudi labor law states: "In applying the provisions of this Law, the employer and the worker must comply with the requirements of the provisions of the Islamic Shariah."[1021] Hence, to understand the potential impact of Islamic Sharia on a contract, it must be understood what this term means in the Arabic language. In Arabic, a contract is called Aqd, and the term means "knitting", "tying", or "joining", and it carries a broader meaning than the term "contract"

1021 The Saudi Arabian labor law issued by a Royal Decree No. M/46 of 05/06/1436 H, 2015

carries at common law.[1022] According to Professor Hussain: "The definition of contract (al-aqd) is similar to that in the common law, but is wider in that it includes dispositions that are gratuitous as well as endowments and trusts."[1023] As a result, "contract" in Islamic Sharia means a legal understanding of any kind, which includes gratuitous loans and gifts that are regarded as binding contracts under Islamic Sharia.[1024] Moreover, a contract may contain an agreement or assent between the parties, and it may also refer in Islamic Sharia to a unilateral juridical act, such as when a husband repudiates a marriage without his wife's consent.[1025] The concept of "contract" under Islamic Sharia, therefore, needs to be discussed in somewhat greater detail.

a. Interpretation of Contract Terms

Under Islamic Sharia, a contract must determine the types of goods delivered, the services performed, the method of payment and the amount for the sale or services as agreed by the parties.[1026] Such consideration (Badal) must be lawful, and any goods or services to be delivered must not involve anything that is forbidden in Islamic Sharia, such as alcohol, pork, or Riba.[1027] Furthermore, contractual conditions that conflict with the essence of the contract are void under Islamic Sharia. For instance, in a trusteeship, any stated term that holds the trustee liable for loss or damage to the property being held by him in trust is considered contrary to the essence of the trusteeship contract.[1028] As a result, the terms of the contract under Islamic Sharia must be specified and, at the same time, not contain anything that is contrary to Islamic Sharia and its purposes whether in the stated service or goods or in the consideration.

b. Remedies for Breach of Contract

Rescission of a contract is needed under specific circumstances, for example, when the seller fails to perform as agreed by delivering merchandise that is defective or in an incorrect quantity. In addition, unforeseen circumstances may prevent one of the parties from completing the contract. In common law, these

---

1022 See Karl, GEO. WASH. J. INT'L L. & ECON., 158 (1991).
1023 BHALA, Understanding Islamic Law 531. 2011.
1024 See id. at 531-533.
1025 See Karl, GEO. WASH. J. INT'L L. & ECON., 158 (1991).
1026 See id. at 158-159.
1027 See BHALA, Understanding Islamic Law 540-541. 2011.
1028 See Karl, GEO. WASH. J. INT'L L. & ECON., 158-159 (1991).

doctrines take the form of rights, such as the right of rescission or the right of cancellation. In Islamic Sharia, such rights are known as Khiyar and Faskh.[1029]

In accordance with Islamic Sharia as applied in the Saudi courts, remedies for the breach of a contract are restricted to direct and actual damages.[1030] The courts in the Kingdom do not recognize, for example, an economic loss of chance, interest, potential profits and other speculative awards that would usually be available under secular laws or international rules.[1031] The frame of reference in Islamic Sharia is that future situations are viewed as being neither predictable nor controllable, and they are known only to Allah (God).[1032] Specific performance and injunctive relief are also unavailable as judicial or adjudicative remedies, and, in any event,[1033] courts in the Kingdom are also precluded from awarding consequential damages based on anticipated profits.[1034]

As a result, contracts that involve a continuous supply of goods are not subject to full liability in Saudi courts if there is wrongful termination; the only available award is reparation for immediate damages.

In sum, when drafting a contract to which Saudi law is applicable or that will be enforced in the Kingdom's courts, a party should take care regarding Riba and Gharar. Hence, the terms of the contract should not provide a sense of any unfair dealing in gain, risk, speculation, or uncertainty in the agreement between the parties. It is also preferred that the contract language be as certain and immediate as possible and that it provide a clear procedural framework for the

1029 See BHALA, Understanding Islamic Law 584. 2011. See case number of appeal 2309/2 /س of 1433H, available at: https://www.bog.gov.sa/ScientificContent/JudicialBlogs/1434/Pages/default.aspx.

1030 See BHALA, Understanding Islamic Law 584. 2011. See case number of appeal 2309/2 /س of 1433H, available at: https://www.bog.gov.sa/ScientificContent/JudicialBlogs/1434/Pages/default.aspx.

1031 See Karl, GEO. WASH. J. INT'L L. & ECON., 160-162 (1991). In international business contract See Unidroit Principles of International Commercial Contracts Article 7.4.1-13 (2010).

1032 See Karl, GEO. WASH. J. INT'L L. & ECON., 160-162 (1991). See no. of appeal judgment 319/1 of 1434 H, available at: https://www.bog.gov.sa/ScientificContent/JudicialBlogs/1434/Pages/default.aspx.

1033 See Silkenat, et al., The ABA Guide to International Business Negotiations: a Comparison of Cross-cultural Issues and Successful Approaches 908. 2009.

1034 See Karl, GEO. WASH. J. INT'L L. & ECON., 160-162 (1991). See no. of appeal judgment 319/1 of 1434 H, available at: https://www.bog.gov.sa/ScientificContent/Judicial-Blogs/1434/Pages/default.aspx.

contracting parties' relationship. Finally, the rights and obligations of the contracting parties must be presented plainly.

7. Differences in Tort Law

Saudi law handles cases that contain claims based on wrongful acts against the person or property of another according to Islamic jurisprudence.[1035] Islamic Sharia handles tort claims as claims of one private party against another. Consequently, no official prosecution is involved, and no punishment is implemented on behalf of the public or its protection.[1036] The same elements in the common law of tort, which are wrongdoing, causation, and harm, apply to all tort cases.[1037]

However, the Kingdom does not have a statutory tort law. Consequently, Islamic Sharia principles apply.[1038] Therefore, when deciding tort cases, Saudi courts need to consider, interpret, and apply such principles to each instance individually.[1039] Because Islamic Sharia consists of different schools of thought, and all of them are equally valid, and since the Saudi courts do not follow stare decisis, as presented earlier, Saudi judgments are highly unpredictable.[1040] As a result, Saudi court decisions in tort cases are unclear and inconsistent, which make the tort system in the Kingdom strongly in need of extensive reform, especially since the country wishes to encourage foreign investment, which needs a predictable and modern legal system.

D. Summary: Consequences of the Application of Saudi Law for the Interpretation of Contracts

As discussed above, the differences between Islamic Sharia and secular laws are many and they impact different aspects of contractual relations. Because of these differences, Islamic Sharia as the applicable law can create difficulties in judicial interpretation, especially when, in negotiating or applying the terms of a contract, the parties or the court is not familiar with Islamic Sharia doctrines. For instance, an American judge may be called upon to decide whether some slight

---

1035 See Othman Talbi, Tort Reform in Saudi Arabia: Obstacles and Solutions, 10-13 (2015).

1036 See BHALA, Understanding Islamic Law 1286. 2011.

1037 See Talbi, 10-13 (2015). See the case number of appeal 1207 /ق of 1434 H, available at: https://www.bog.gov.sa/ScientificContent/JudicialBlogs/1434/Pages/default.aspx.

1038 See Talbi, 10-13 (2015).

1039 See id.

1040 See Mikail & Arifin, MALAYSIAN COURT PRACTICE BULLETIN, (2014).

uncertainty in a contract violates the prohibition of Gharar under Islamic Sharia, in determining whether a party to a contract can avoid the contract.

1. Interpretation of Contracts under Secular Laws

Interpretation of a contract is the process by which a court seeks to ascertain the meaning of the language used by the parties in determining their intentions and the legal effect of the contract.[1041] The determination of the contracting parties' intentions is the principal objective when interpreting a contract.[1042] As Article 4.1(1) of UNIDROIT[1043] Principles of International Commercial Contracts states: "A contract shall be interpreted according to the common intention of the parties."[1044] However, sometimes a contract's language leads to varying meanings, which makes it difficult for the court to discover the intent of the parties from the mere words themselves and their arrangement within the contract. Hence, the law has developed doctrines of construction for interpreting contracts based on the circumstances of each case.

a. If the Language of the Contract Is Plain and Unambiguous

If the words of a contract are plain, the prevailing meaning of the language will take effect unless another intention is manifested in light of the circumstances of the contract.[1045] However, in many situations, some words in a contract need to be interpreted.[1046] According to Mr. Justice Holmes: "A word is not a crystal, transparent and unchanged, it is the skin of a living thought and may vary greatly in color and content according to the circumstances and the time in which it is used."[1047]

1041 See E. ALLAN FARNSWORTH, CONTRACTS 439 (Aspen Publishers Fourth Edition ed. 2004).

1042 See Patrick S Ottinger, Principles of Contractual Interpretation, 60 LA. L. REV., 766 (1999).

1043 UNIDROIT is the International Institute for the Unification of Private Law. It is an independent intergovernmental organization, and has its seat in the Villa Aldobrandini in Rome. The purpose of the institution is to study methods and needs for modernizing, harmonizing and coordinating private and in particular commercial law as between countries and groups of States and to formulate uniform law instruments, principles and rules to achieve those objectives. For more information see the institution's website at: http://www.unidroit.org/about-unidroit/overview.

1044 Unidroit Principles of International Commercial Contracts. 2010.

1045 See Ottinger, LA. L. REV., 766 (1999). See also, Unidroit Principles of International Commercial Contracts Article 4.3. 2010.

1046 See FARNSWORTH, Contracts 441. 2004.

1047 See id.

b. If a Term in the Contract Is Ambiguous or Leads to Various Interpretations

In such a case, the court will consider all circumstances surrounding the transaction, such as oral statements, the course of performance between the disputing parties, and the general custom and usages of trade.[1048]

c. If the Intent of the Disputing Parties Is Still Not Discoverable

At this stage, the court may resort to statutory or common law rules to fill the gaps of the contract.[1049] In sum, the plain language will prevail in general; however, if one of the disputing parties asserts an interpretation that is different from the plain meaning or such meaning indicated from the context of the contract, he must provide a proof of the asserted meaning.

2. Interpretation of Contracts under Islamic Sharia

The well established doctrines of construction aid the court in interpreting secular contracts. However, with Islamic contracts, certain challenges may hinder judicial and arbitral tribunal interpretation, as can be illustrated with several examples. One such difficulty is that tribunals and some courts, especially non-Islamic courts, will face difficulties determining and examining the meaning of Islamic terms. According to Charles P. Trumbull:

> When asked to interpret Islamic legal contracts, judges should keep in mind several guidelines. First, judges themselves should not apply Saudi law to a contract dispute. Saudi law is generally inaccessible to U.S. judges, except perhaps to a Muslim judge. U.S. judges cannot look to statutes, case law, or precedent to determine the Saudi law to be applied to the case. Furthermore, they do not have the requisite knowledge of the sacred sources, nor are they capable of performing the Ijtihad that Saudi judges must perform in making legal determinations under Saudi law.[1050]

Usually, the courts conduct two approaches when seeking to prove and interpret foreign law. The first is proving it as law, which involves research by the judge or submissions by counsel with expertise in that law. Secondly, courts rely upon the

---

1048 See id. at 453-454. See also Unidroit Principles of International Commercial Contracts Article 4.3. 2010.

1049 See E Allan - Jr Farnsworth, William F Young - Sanger, Carol, Contracts, Cases & Materials 432-433 (Foundation Press Seventh Edition ed. 2008).

1050 Trumbull, Vand. L. Rev., 646 (2006).

testimony or reports of experts.[1051] However, in an Islamic Sharia case, there is no single authoritative interpretation of Islamic law or doctrine, which creates difficulties in interpreting such terms and endorsing one Islamic school's interpretation of Islamic Sharia over another as explained in the Shamail Bank case.[1052]

Secondly, religious scholars should determine Islamic contractual rights and obligations, because Ijtihad requires it, as explained earlier in this chapter.[1053] Hence, such a determination should be made only by Islamic jurists, who are trained in Islamic jurisprudence and who can determine the parties' intention to abide by Islamic Sharia in the performance of their contract. For example, in National Group for Communications & Technology v. Lucent Technology Int'l, National Group for Communications and Computers Ltd., (NGC),[1054] the disputing parties agreed to be bound by Saudi law. When they agreed that Saudi law governs their agreement, they intended to be ruled by Islamic Sharia, which is accessible only to qualified Islamic jurists, such as Saudi judges, who are trained to adjudicate cases according to Islamic jurisprudence. Actually, in such a case, parties cannot reach a mutual understanding of the applicable rules to be applied, because Saudi law is unmodified and reflects the personal conscience of a single judge or arbitrator by his Ijtihad. Thus, a judicial determination of Saudi law by an American judge, for example, who is not trained in Islamic jurisprudence, may not achieve the parties' intent. In Saudi Basic Industries Corporation v. Mobil Yanbu Petrochemical Company,[1055] the appellants challenged the American trial judge's qualifications to engage in a legal analysis under Saudi law, which depended on Islamic Sharia. In that case, Dr. Frank E. Vogel, who was appointed as an expert in Saudi law, opined that this Court could not credibly engage in the Ijtihad process. He stated: "Ijtihad requires for its credibility qualifications which on the very face of things, neither Professor Hallaq, myself or, with respect, any U.S. Court possesses."[1056] However, the Court refused this challenge, because the challenge was brought after receiving an adverse jury verdict and further, the appellant chose to file this dispute in a United States

1051 See ASSOCIATION, AAA Handbook on International Arbitration and ADR 7-9. 2010.

1052 See SHAMIL BANK OF BAHRAIN EC V. BEXIMCO PHARMACEUTICALS LTD, 2004 E.W.C.A. Civ 19 (2004) at 1800.

1053 See Trumbull, VAND. L. REV., 630-633 (2006).

1054 NATIONAL GROUP FOR COMMUN. AND COMPUTERS LTD. V. LUCENT TECHNOLOGIES INTERN. INC., 331 F. Supp. 2d 290 (D.N.Y. 2004).

1055 SAUDI BASIC INDUSTRIES V. MOBIL YANBU PET., 866 A.2d 1 (Del. 2005).

1056 Id.

court.[1057] The other challenge is that, in arbitration, for example, the arbitral tribunal that does not have knowledge of Islamic Sharia and the Ijtihad process can see that Islamic Sharia is not adequate and sophisticated enough to govern complex commercial disputes, such as in the Aramco case.[1058] However, the trained judge or arbitrator in Ijtihad in Islamic Sharia can rule cases by using different tools in Islamic jurisprudence, such Qiyas (deductive analogy)[1059] and Urf (custom).[1060] Parties, who contractually agree to the application of Saudi law, and thus Islamic Sharia, might willingly submit to a Muslim arbitrator or judge to rule over their dispute because of their desire to abide by Islamic Sharia. A ruling by a religious authority is more likely to yield a result that is in accordance with Islamic Sharia and its purposes than a ruling by a non-Muslim judge or arbitrator. However, the study found in stated cases that is hard to find such type of judge or expert in Saudi law. Even when the parties found one, the outcome can be unpredictable in the absence of the stare decisis principle, as shown earlier. This puts any party agreeing to have their contract governed by Saudi law at risk of unpredictable outcomes. Hence, the study will offer some proposals for foreign investors how to contain the problem.

E. Proposals for Foreign Investors Coming to Saudi Arabia

Parties who contractually agree that Saudi law, and thus Islamic Sharia, will govern their contractual disputes often file in a non-Sharia court or a non-Muslim arbitral tribunal because of difficulties in finding efficient tribunals that have experience in Islamic Sharia as applied in the Kingdom of Saudi Arabia. Moreover, some foreign investors like to choose one of the efficient laws, such as English law, to govern their disputes without violating Islamic Sharia principles, because their disputes concern the Islamic financial field, for example, or because they will have to enforce awards in the Saudi courts. An efficient solution is combining the law of a state and the general principles of Islamic Sharia, which means that the chosen state law is subject to disputes and that, in cases of conflict, Islamic Sharia will prevail.[1061] For instance, the law of England is a preferred choice of law for contracts involving Islamic financial transactions, and all deals are permissible

---

1057 Id.

1058 See Aramco case (1963) 27 I.L.R. 117

1059 See BHALA, Understanding Islamic Law 319-320. 2011.

1060 Urf is an Arabic term referring to the custom of a given society. Most Islamic scholars consider the Urf in society as a legitimate rule if it does not conflict with the primary sources of Islamic Sharia. See KHELAF, eulim 'usul alfaqqih. 89-90.

1061 See Colon, TEX. INT'L LJ, 415-417 (2011).

unless shown to contravene Islamic principles.[1062] Most arbitration in Islamic finance is done using combined laws, meaning under one nation's laws subject to Islamic Sharia.[1063]Although the Saudi legal system differs in nature from the modern rules as presented earlier in the study, the new arbitration law provides an opportunity to arbitrating parties to agree to any particular national law to govern their disputes without conflicting with Islamic Sharia, which means that Saudi law supports a combination of national law and general principles of Islamic Sharia. Article 38(1) of the Arbitration Law provides:

> 1) Taking into account the non-violation of the provisions of the Islamic Sharia and public order in the Kingdom, the arbitral tribunal, during the hearing of the dispute, shall:
>
> a) Apply the rules agreed upon by the parties to the arbitration on the subject of the dispute, and, if they agree on the application of a law of a particular state, the substantive rules shall be followed without those of dispute-of-laws, unless agreed otherwise.[1064]

This is a helpful opportunity for foreign investors in the Kingdom to choose the law with which they and their lawyers are familiar. Hence, arbitrating parties who are more comfortable with English or American laws, for example, will be advantaged by this solution. Furthermore, this opportunity allows them to take advantage of the most modern process and procedures of the management of disputes instead of being involved with the Saudi law that is based on traditional Islamic Sharia, which does not comply with many modern legal processes as presented in this chapter.[1065]

In conclusion, Saudi law as applicable law in a contract means that Islamic Sharia must be followed and applied. International tribunals and municipals courts around the world face difficulties when resolving contractual disputes that require interpretation of a disputed Islamic legal term or the application of Islamic

---

1062 See Anna Rogowska, English Law in Saudi Arabia, 27 ARAB LAW QUARTERLY (2013). See also Colon, TEX. INT'L LJ, 415-417 (2011).

1063 See Colon, TEX. INT'L LJ, 415-417 (2011).

1064 Arbitration Law, 2012.

1065 Note: Not all countries accept this proposal and may consider it like choosing two applicable laws that are not allowed under some laws. Hence, the parties need to contact an expert in the country to which they plan to submit disputes. For more information about this issue, see Colon, TEX. INT'L LJ, (2011). See also, SHAMIL BANK OF BAHRAIN EC V. BEXIMCO PHARMACEUTICALS LTD, 2004 E.W.C.A. Civ 19 (2004) at 1800.

Sharia. Naturally, contracts that involve Islamic Sharia vary widely in their purpose, specificity, and complexity. Western courts and arbitrators cannot interpret and apply Saudi law to a contract dispute, because Saudi law is based on the tradition of Islamic Sharia and is generally inaccessible to secular judges, except perhaps to an arbitrator or a judge who is trained in Islamic Sharia, because there are no statutes, case law, or precedents to determine the Saudi law to be applied to the case. This differs dramatically from secular law in various aspects as explained in this chapter. Furthermore, most judges and arbitrators do not have the essential knowledge of the sacred sources, nor are they capable of performing Ijtihad as applied in the Saudi courts, which must be done to determine a legal matter under Saudi law.

Furthermore, it is difficult for secular tribunals to determine the meaning of disputed Islamic legal terms, because such terms do not have a single, commonly accepted meaning known to all Islamic schools. The precise meaning of Islamic legal terms can be known only to Allah (God). However, Muslim jurists strive to approximate God's meaning for these terms, but they may disagree on their respective conclusions. However, the different meanings are regarded as equally valid under Islamic Sharia. As a result, judges should defer the interpretation of Islamic legal terms to a religious expert, and the disputing parties may mutually understand that an Islamic legal scholar would resolve the meaning of disputed terms according to Ijtihad principles.

Although Saudi law does not comply with modern legal systems in its nature and formation, the new Arbitration Law provides an outlet for arbitrating parties to choose with which they and their attorneys are familiar. Hence, arbitrating parties can bring their disputes to any secular court or arbitral tribunal and can take advantage of international arbitration centers without encountering the difficulties described earlier when choosing Saudi law. As a result, this opportunity opens the door for foreign and local investors to take advantage of the most modern process and procedures in managing disputes instead of being involved with Saudi law, which is based on traditional Islamic Sharia, which does not comply with some of the modern legal doctrines, as presented in this study.

Chapter 6: The Development of Saudi Arbitration in Light of the Needs and Customs of the International Commercial and Business Community

It is time to review the various aspects of the arbitration process in the Kingdom of Saudi Arabia to examine, discuss, evaluate, and present the possibility of finding a route to alining it better within the international community. To achieve the stated goal, the study conducted different approaches, such as literature review, analysis of the primary sources of Saudi law, Islamic Sharia and international arbitrational rules, principles, and guides, interviews with legal experts in the Kingdom and the international arbitration centers, such as the AAA and the ICDR in New York City. After the examination of arbitration in the Kingdom through previous approaches, the study concludes in this chapter by summarizing the current legal system of arbitration in the Kingdom and by recommending functional reforms to improve the Saudi arbitration environment.

A. Summary of the Analysis

The study shows that, although the Kingdom of Saudi Arabia has tried to reform its arbitration regime, there are still significant challenges to be confronted on the road to reinforcing arbitration in the Kingdom and making it attractive to the international community. The challenges were addressed in five chapters. The first chapter discussed a major issue that should be addressed when considering arbitration in Saudi Arabia, which is presented by the primary sources law in Saudi Arabia, which significantly impact the whole arbitration process.

The first primary source is Islamic Sharia, which is derived from the Quran and the Sunnah of Muhammad. The second source is the laws and rules issued by the King, although, to be a valid and primary source, these must not be contrary to the primary sources of Islamic Sharia. The study shows how the Kingdom follows modern legal systems in the adoption of its laws. For example, the Kingdom took the distinction between public and private law developed in French law, which is similar to the separation of issues in which the state is a party and other matters in private law. In addition, the majority of Saudi codes were inspired by the French system via Egypt, which has been the conduit for the reception of French laws into the Islamic culture in the Kingdom. For example, the Saudi Company Law, promulgated on 21 July 1965, was copied from the Egyptian code that was, in turn, taken directly from French law. In addition, the new Arbitration Law was inspired by the UNCITRAL Model Law upon which most modern laws around the world depend. Other examples show the Kingdom's trend to modernize its laws and rules. However, the Kingdom has faced difficulties with the primary source, Islamic Sharia, because Islamic Sharia as applied in Saudi Arabia is not codified. Consequently, this has led to considerable variation in its interpretation and application, which has affected the entire legal system in Saudi Arabia due to its uncertainty and unexpected outcomes. The chapters of this study have discussed at length this challenge and its impacts.

The first chapter also provides an overview of Commercial Arbitration Law in Saudi Arabia, and it discusses four main points: the concept of arbitration, the history of arbitration in Arabic communities, the history of commercial arbitration law in Saudi Arabia, and the challenge of enforcement. Hence, that section shows the historical role of arbitration as a dispute resolution mechanism in the Arabic region. From the overview it is clear that the Saudi arbitration environment has faced some different challenges that have affected its reputation regarding arbitration and the legal system. For instance, it has been described as a hostile country toward recognizing arbitration agreements and enforcing foreign awards. In particular, arbitration has suffered from a lack of support by the Saudi courts in the course of the arbitration process. Moreover, some international arbitration cases demonstrate that arbitral tribunals denied that Saudi law was adequate and sufficiently sophisticated to be the applicable law to govern complex commercial disputes. Consequently, many lawyers around the world nowadays avoid identifying Saudi law as the applicable substantive law and rely on international trade rules instead. However, on 8June 2012, the Kingdom issued its long-awaited reform of the arbitration law. The new Saudi Arbitration Law (Royal Decree No. M/34) replaced the Arbitration Law of 1983 (Royal Decree No. M/46). The new law instituted a variety of reforms to Saudi Arabia's arbitration system. The chapter presents an overview about how the new law could be part of a broader and continuing modernization of the Saudi legal environment. Based on this overview, such modernization needs to be examined and evaluated regarding four points, each of which is provided in a separate chapter: the legal system of the Saudi judiciary and its impact on arbitration (Chapter 2), the arbitration process (Chapter 3), arbitration awards (Chapter 4), and Saudi law as applicable substantive law (Chapter 5).

Arbitration has faced challenges in the national courts in the Kingdom and a lack of support during the arbitration process and at the enforcement stage. Indeed, most international awards were refused recognition and enforcement. Consequently, the Saudi judiciary and possible impacts on arbitration are examined and addressed in Chapter 2. To achieve the goal, the chapter discusses three major points: the historical perspective, the courts' structure, and the quality and independence of the judiciary.

The Kingdom has a dual judicial system consisting of Sharia courts, which are the courts of general jurisdiction and which hear both criminal and civil matters. Further, various other specialized tribunals (committees) are under the supervision of competent ministries or governmental agencies, such as the Committee for the Settlement of Banking Disputes, which is under the supervision of the Commerce Ministry. In 2007, King Abdullah initiated major reforms to the Saudi judiciary and the courts. The new Law of the Judiciary reorganized the existing structure and jurisdiction of the Saudi judicial system. These reforms have produced the structure of the modern courts and provide for the quality and independence of the judiciary. However, arbitration still faces significant challenges in practice that the new reforms have not resolved.

The first challenge is the difficulty of appointing enough competent judges who possess the qualification to exercise Ijtihad according to Islamic Sharia. Historically, some high requirements must be in the mujtahid, which only a small number of Muslim jurists can meet. Quite often,the most famous Islamic scholars and jurists were candidates to be judges. However, the community was small, and people did not need as many judges as are now required. Since the high qualifications of a mujtahid are not easily met, Saudi Arabia faced an insufficient number of judges in the Saudi courts.

Furthermore, Sharia schools competent to train Saudi judges focus on the traditional way for teaching Islamic Sharia and do not provide a legal education. Consequently, their graduates have no training in the application of modern laws and rules. Nevertheless, Sharia judges enjoy far-reaching powers to interpret all laws, including modern laws, according to their understanding of Sharia and this creates unpredictable and sometimes undesirable outcomes. The historic refusal of Sharia judges in the judiciary to apply modern regulations was one of the main reasons for the Kingdom to create legal administrative committees staffed with judges who are both trained in Sharia and in modern law.

The other significant challenge within the Saudi judiciary system is that judges do not have to follow a rule of stare decisis or a similar doctrine to bind courts to their prior decisions or to those issued by higher courts or even just to explain why a case is decided differently from a similar earlier case. This problem was the other main reasons why the Kingdom was forced to establish the specialized tribunals outside of the judicial system to assure investors, companies and banks of some level of predictablility of the law applied to commerce and investment in the country. For the same reason, the Kingdom began to publish previous decisions in different volumes, although past rulings still do not mean that any other judge must or will rule the same way in the future. For that reason, they are ultimately of little help in predicting future outcomes.

Chapter 3 of the study examines the new Arbitration Law and its compliance with international arbitration norms by examining the general provisions of the new Arbitration Law on the arbitration agreement, the arbitration tribunal, competent court supervision and assistance, institutional arbitration and ad hoc arbitration, and the arbitral proceedings. The study shows that the new Saudi law provides a significant step toward aligning the Kingdom more with international rules. The new Law supports party autonomy by allowing the parties to choose any language, substantive law, and even procedural rules. Moreover, the new law has become more flexible, so that the arbitrator no longer has to have a particular nationality, gender, or religion. Also, it is no longer required for each arbitrator to be a graduate from a legal or Islamic Sharia school, as long as the chair of a tribunal or a sole arbitrator has that qualification. Furthermore, clarity and precision in dealing with technical issues have appeared in the new Law. For instance, the new Law states expressly the power of the arbitral tribunal to call on technical and legal experts to achieve the principle of balance in members of the arbitral tribunal. Furthermore, unlike the old law, the new Law reduces the intervention by the municipal courts during the arbitration process, and the role of the competent court has become supportive of the arbitration process.

Another benefit of the new Law is that the arbitral tribunal has more power in different aspects of the arbitration. For instance, the arbitral tribunal has authority to decide between holding a hearing or relying instead on memoranda and documents submitted by the arbitrating parties. It also has the power to continue the arbitration proceedings in the event of a default by the defendant by failing to attend or participate in a meeting despite proper notification, in an effort to induce the defendant to attend arbitration hearings and not to cause delays in procedures. Moreover, the arbitral tribunal can issue procedural orders and precautionary measures on a provisional or conservatory basis as requested by the arbitrating parties. The arbitration process also has guarantees of impartiality and fairness at every stage of the proceedings of arbitration, and the arbitrating parties have the right to challenge the arbitrator.

The chapter also addresses some disadvantages of the new law. One is that it prohibits government agencies from participating in arbitration except with certain controls, which may deprive public sector companies of using arbitration, or it may make them reluctant to resort to it. This, in turn, could lead foreign investors to be reluctant to deal with public companies, as arbitration provides unique features, such as confidentiality, speed, and professional specialists. Further, the law requires that an arbitrator must have at least a university degree in law or Islamic Sharia to serve as the head of the tribunal or to serve as the only arbitrator. Most international arbitration rules do not impose such requirements, because arbitration is not limited to those with a background in legal or Islamic Sharia but extends to all professionals such as engineers, accountants, doctors and others. In addition, the law requires the Islamic Sharia degree even though Sharia schools do not provide training in the legal field. Another disadvantage is that the new Law does not provide immunity for arbitrators, which may cause interested individuals to be reluctant to enter in this arena, because they will be exposed to potential liability.

Chapter 4 of the study examines and evaluates the new Enforcement Law 2012 and the accession by Saudi Arabia to the New York Convention in 1994 along with the new Arbitration Law and its impact on the arbitral awards in the Kingdom. The discussion covers the following points: the issuance of an arbitration award, challenging an arbitration award, and enforcing the award. The chapter explains why Saudi Arabia has been described as hostile toward recognizing arbitration agreements and enforcing foreign awards, and why many international awards have been rejected. Further, the chapter shows the importance of reforming the arbitration award process, the enforcement regime in the Kingdom of Saudi Arabia and how it can avoid the flaws of the previous legislation. The study addresses the arbitral award under Saudi law in comparison with modern trends in the international commercial arbitration practice.

The chapter presents the significance of the new enforcement law in harmonizing Saudi law with the international community and its standards. The new law provides a facilitation of enforcement of international and domestic arbitral awards with the creation of a specific authority and specific procedures applicable to enforcement, which was absent in the past. However, Saudi law still does not provide a clear definition of "public policy" and how it will be applied in the Saudi courts. Public policy is the entry point of Islamic Sharia into all commercial transactions and all enforcement procedures, and the application of Islamic Sharia through Ijtihad is not bound by any precedent decisions. This makes the occurrence of a conflict between an arbitral award with Saudi public policy unpredictable. However, the law does allow the enforcement court to enforce those parts of an award that are not contrary to public policy and to not enforce those parts that are contrary to public policy unless the parts cannot be severed. The study concludes that the new Saudi Enforcement Law remains a significant step toward international legal principles, but it needs to be reviewed and to provide a more precise meaning for the public policy aspect.

Chapter 5 of the study discusses possible challenges that may arise from choosing Saudi law as the applicable substantive law governing a commercial transactions and the consequences this may have during arbitration and the solutions available according to the new Arbitration Law. This chapter examines the issue through the following points: the concept of applicable law, the differences between Islamic Sharia and secular law, contract interpretation and application, and a proposed solution for foreign investor in the Kingdom.

The chapter presents the importance of the applicable law for a commercial agreement and how choosing Saudi law as the applicable law means that Islamic Sharia will be applied. However, it demonstrates that international tribunals and municipals courts around the world face difficulties when resolving contractual disputes that require the interpretation of a disputed Islamic legal term or the application of Islamic Sharia. Western courts and most international arbitrators face difficulties when interpreting and applying Saudi law to a contract dispute, because these tribunals cannot look at statutes, case law, or precedent to determine the Saudi law to be applied to the case, unlike they do for the interpretation and application of secular laws. More specifically, most courts and arbitrators do not have the essential knowledge of the sacred sources, nor are they capable of performing Ijtihad as applied in the Saudi courts, to determine a legal matter under Saudi law.

Another challenge that faces international tribunals is determining the meaning of disputed Islamic legal terms, because such legal terms do not have a single accepted meaning known to all Islamic schools of Muslim jurisprudence. The precise meaning of an Islamic legal term is known only to Allah (God). Hence, Muslim jurists and scholars can only strive to get close to God's understanding of these terms, which leads to different meanings. However, all definitions provided by Muslim jurists are regarded as equally valid under Islamic Sharia, even if they are incompatible with each other, as long as they comply with principles of interpretation of Islamic Sharia. As a result, courts will refer to a religious expert to interpret such terms, and different experts may render different opinions. This, in turn, leads to difficulties in deciding who is most competent to render such services to the court.

Although Saudi law does not comply with modern legal systems in some of its core features, Chapter 5 shows how the new Arbitration Law handles this matter and provides more flexibility by offering an outlet for arbitrating parties to choose the law with which they are familiar. Hence, arbitrating parties can bring their disputes to any Western courts or international arbitral tribunals and get the advantage of the international arbitration centers without enduring the difficulties that arise when Saudi law is chosen as the applicable law for a contract. As a result, this opportunity opens the door for foreign investors to choose the law with which they are familiar and also for both local and international companies to take advantage of the most modern laws that will help them to achieve their commercial needs and goals.

Finally, the chapter offers a proposal for foreign investors who like to choose one of the more efficient laws, such as English law, to govern their disputes without violating Islamic Sharia principles, because they may need to enforce such awards in a Saudi court. One of the efficient solutions is combining another country's law with general principles of Islamic Sharia, which means that the chosen state law is subject to disputes and that, in cases of conflict, Islamic Sharia will prevail as explained more extensively in Chapter 5.

After this overview of the study, Chapter 6 provides recommendations for reinforcing the Saudi arbitration environment to align it further with the international arbitration community. These recommendations will be presented in the final sections.

B. Recommendations for Further Reforms of Saudi Arbitration Law

After a long journey researching Saudi arbitration law and practice and comparing it with international commercial norms through different approaches, the study found that there are various aspects that should be improved and rethought to reinforce Saudi law and make it more relevant and effective for the domestic and the international community.

1. Rethinking Islamic Sharia as Applied in the Kingdom

Islamic Sharia is applied through Islamic fiqh (jurisprudence), which is the human process to understand the primary sources of Islamic Sharia (the Quran and the Sunnah of Prophet Mohammed). Islamic jurisprudence was expanded and developed by interpretation (Ijtihad) by Islamic jurists and implemented through the rulings (verdicts) of jurists and judges on questions and cases presented to them, which produced different schools and various opinions through the history of Islamic jurisprudence. In Saudi Arabia, the Mujtahid (in the courts, this will be the judge) can apply any rules and views of jurisprudence by using Ijtihad tools as explained in Chapter 1 without being bound by precedents. Of course, such Ijtihad has resulted in inconsistent verdicts, which sometimes occur within the same case and in even in the same court or that are issued by the same judge.

Applying Islamic Sharia in this manner has adversely affected Saudi arbitration in three ways. Understanding the provisions of the law is one of the significant impacts. For example, Article 2 of the new Arbitration Law states: "Without prejudice to the rules of the Islamic Sharia..." Yet, how can the parties know the rules of Islamic Sharia if the rules are not codified? Secondly, at the recognition and enforcement stage, the law also states that the arbitral award must not conflict with Islamic Sharia, essentially subjecting even foreign arbitral rewards to review on the merits. The third problem arises when parties choose Saudi law (Islamic Sharia) as the applicable substantive law for the contract. In all these instances, there is uncertainty as to which rules of Islamic jurisprudence will be applied and used. This, in turn, defeats the purpose of the terms of the contract. The question of contradictions among jurists and judges' opinions and verdicts and the need for codification of Muslim law first arose in the early history of Islamic Sharia.[1066] However, the study will show the closest example to the Kingdom's position, which could suit it more than other forms. This is the "Majallah al-Ahkãm al-'adliyyah" (1876 CE), which is also called al Majallah.[1067]

Codification of Islamic jurisprudence reached an advanced stage with the issuance and production of the compilation of al Majallah (1869-1876 CE).[1068] This collection was derived from the best available understanding Islamic Sharia and applied in most territories ruled by the Ottomans, except Egypt.[1069] It had become the official code of civil law to entire countries ruled under the Ottoman Empire, even for a period after their independence. The government constituted a panel of several top ranking Muslim jurists (1822-1895 CE) and entrusted them with the task of compiling a book on Islamic fiqh (jurisprudence) in a methodical form, which should be quite convenient to reach, free from disputes in the opinions, be

---

1066 See Zanki, INTERNATIONAL JOURNAL OF HUMANITIES AND SOCIAL SCIENCE. 2014.

1067 For more information about the al Majallah, see id. See also Gemmell, SANTA CLARA J. INT'L L., 176-177 (2007).

1068 See Zanki, INTERNATIONAL JOURNAL OF HUMANITIES AND SOCIAL SCIENCE. 2014.

1069 See id.

an authoritative reference on all well-known pronouncements and decisions, and be available and undertandable to anyone. This compilation was finalized in 1876 CE.[1070]

The form of al Majallah is in a modern code's shape, and it consists of 1,851 articles, which are divided into an introduction and sixteen books.[1071] In drafting the code, the committee never stepped outside the limits of the Hanafī School's opinions and the rules taken from Hanafī sources. However, in later years, the al Majallah was amended several times to be more modern and to go beyond the Hanafī School. It took various principles from other Islamic schools. Substantively, the Majallah covered both more and less than a European Civil Code.[1072] It applies to contracts, such as sales, employments, guarantees, debts, etc. and some tort matters, but not to non-contractual obligations and other areas of private law, such as marriage, divorce, inheritance, and various aspects of a real property.[1073]

The Majallah could be a great example for Saudi Arabia to follow with regard to codifying Islamic jurisprudence by using the advantages that the Majallah offered while avoiding its disadvantages through the following points:

> 1) Codification of Islamic Sharia in the area where there is no code (Saudi Arabia has different laws in the various aspects) without being restricted to a specific school of Islamic jurisprudence.
>
> 2) Taking advantage of modern laws and codes, such as international guidelines, as long as they do not conflict with the rules that have consensus between Islamic jurisprudence and that should be adopted.

In producing such a codification, Saudi Arabia would gain the advantages of the modern laws and rules while keeping the primary sources of Islamic Sharia as the main references of the codification and without letting Ijtihad, as applied currently in Saudi courts, contradict with each other. This reform could attract foreign investors when they see a clear code that leads to predictable outcomes and uniformity between decisions.

1070 See id.

1071 See id.

1072 See id.

1073 See id.

2. Reinforcing the new Arbitration Law

In examining the new Arbitration Law, three aspects should be reconsidered as follows:

a. Clarifying the Meaning of Some Terms of the Law

1) The age of full legal capacity

The new law does not specify the age of full legal capacity. The study returned to other Saudi laws to see how the Saudi Ruler has handled this matter and found that 18 years of age is the age of legal capacity in most Saudi laws, such as in the Child Protection Law. The study proposes that the age for legal capacity be specified in the implementing regulations for the new Arbitration Law, which have not yet been promulgated. Such a regulatory provision would be transparent for foreign investors, who are not familiar with the legal system in the Kingdom and with Saudi laws. It would also avoid the possibility of differences about this issue in the Saudi courts, as this issue has different opinions in Islamic jurisprudence, which may open the door for Ijtihad, as applied in the Saudi courts, to lead to differences in outcomes.

2) Subject matters that are not arbitrable

Saudi law provides two types of disputes that are not arbitrable:

- personal status,
- issues that cannot be reconciled.

The first type of dispute is determined, but the second is not. The implementing regulations of the old arbitration law provided three examples of disputes that cannot be reconciled. Leaving this question open to interpretation could lead to problems at the enforcement stage in the Saudi court. Hence, the study suggests the the Ruler should determe all types of disputes that cannot be arbitrated to make it clear to the parties before they enter into an arbitration agreement to avoid wasting time and cost.

3) Public policy

Islamic Sharia as applied in the Saudi court is part of the public policy of the Kingdom. However, the meaning of public policy has not been specified in the Saudi courts for two main reasons. Firstly, there are not enough published cases. The Kingdom has begun to release a few of the cases, but there are not enough cases to define public policy clearly in the Kingdom. Even if more cases were published, however, the principle of stare decisis is not followed in the Saudi courts as explained in the study, which makes it hard to predict a future decision even if the same facts arise in a new case. Hence, Ijtihad as applied in the Saudi courts, without binding precedents, provides the courts power to refuse any award if the court considers such award to be against public policy or Islamic Sharia. This is the subject of much debate between Muslim jurists. The Kingdom can give public policy fuller effect if it specifies the meaning of public policy in the implementation regulation. Without doubt, this will require reviewing Ijtihad as applied in Saudi courts, which conflicts with the predictability of decisions. We may safely expect resistance against reforms that would put the Kingdom closer to the customs and rules applied by the international community. However, one could ask how the unpredictable outcomes in courts are reconciled with the prohibition of uncertain outcomes (Gharar) in contracts.

b. Changing Some Rules

1) Rules preventing governmental bodies from participating in arbitration

One of the disadvantages of the new Law is that it prohibits government agencies from using arbitration except in certain situations, which may deprive public sector companies the opportunity to participate in arbitration or make them reluctant to resort to it. Hence, the study suggests that allowing governmental corporations and agencies to resort to arbitration directly with the contracting parties may enable them to enjoy the benefits of arbitration, especially in dealings with the global community, which is a significant incentive for foreign investors to deal with them, because arbitration provides unique benefits, such as confidentiality, speed, and professional specialists.

2) Requirements that arbitrators have an Islamic Sharia degree

In the new Arbitration Law, the arbitrator must have at least a university degree in law or Islamic Sharia if he is the head of the tribunal and he is the only arbitrator. In examining international arbitration rules, this study found that most modern rules do not limit arbitrators to those who have a background in law or Islamic Sharia, but extend the opportunity to be chosen by the parties to a dispute to all professionals, such as engineers, accountants, doctors and others. However, most commentators suggest that an arbitrator should have a legal qualification if he is the sole arbitrator or the head of a panel of arbitrators. However, as shown in the study, the need for expertise in arbitration practice can be satisfied not only via selection of an arbitrator who has a legal background but also with specially trained non-lawyers. In any case, the requirement of having an

Islamic Sharia degree should not continue, as many with this degree lack knowledge of the legal field. Moreover, one of the main reasons why the Kingdom established specialized independent tribunals outside of the authority of Saudi courts in different legal aspects, such as banking disputes, was because judges in the Saudi courts who got their training from Sharia schools lacked training in the law as discussed in Chapter 2 of the study. As a result, the study suggests that Saudi Law should adds requirements of experience or getting training in law for an Islamic Sharia degree holder before practicing as arbitrator.

3) Repeating the arbitration proceedings

When an arbitrator is replaced for any reason, the question arises whether the newly appointed replacement arbitrator must begin the arbitration proceedings all over again or whether he can pick up where his predecessor left off in the proceedings. Most international arbitration rules refer this decision to the arbitral tribunal as shown in Chapter 3. If two arbitrators are left after the third arbitrator is removed or resigns, some international arbitration rules state that the remaining arbitrators can decide to continue the arbitration proceedings without a replacement arbitrator, which, of course, is preferred especially if the vacancy occurs near the end of the arbitration proceedings. However, the new Saudi Arbitration Law does not differentiate between an arbitral panel of three arbitrators and a sole arbitrator with regard to repeating the arbitration proceedings. It provides a mandatory rule that all previous arbitration procedures, including any arbitration award, be deemed null and void, and that the proceedings have to be repeated from the beginning. This rule is too inflexible and may waste the time and energy of the arbitrating parties if the remaining arbitrators see that nothing major could affect the process of arbitration if they continue and the parties so agree. The study suggests that allowing the arbitral panel to decide whether to start over or to continue where they left off when the arbitrator left is the best way to handle this matter, because the arbitral panel is the closest to the case and has lived with the case for a while, unless the arbitrating parties decide otherwise.

4) Time frame for filing the arbitral award

One of the requirements that can put an arbitrating party at risk if the award is issued in a foreign language is the time frame for filing the arbitral award in the competent court. Any award has to be filed within fifteen days from the date of issuance, along with a certified translation into Arabic from an accredited translating authority. It will be difficult to meet this time limit, especially if the award is lengthy and has to be translated from a language where translators are not easily available. Hence, it would be better if the Saudi law were more flexible in this regard.

5) Filing the arbitral award in the competent court

The Saudi law requires filing or each and every arbitral award in the competent court, whether the arbitral award needs to be enforced or is carried out voluntarily by the parties. In contrast, the UNCITRAL Model Law requires the award to be filed only if there is a need for enforcement.[1074] Since most arbitration awards are satisfied through voluntary compliance of the arbitrating parties involved in the dispute, the requirement that every award must be filed as a case in court will waste time if the prevailing party does not need to enforce the award. It can also compromise the confidentiality of the award. Hence, it would be better if the Saudi law followed the UNCITRAL Model Law in this regard.

6) Differences between an international arbitral award issued in a foreign state and other awards in the enforcement procedure

The Saudi Enforcement Law differentiates at the enforcement and recognition stage between local and international awards that were issued in the Kingdom and international awards that were made in a foreign state. International awards that were issued in a foreign country do not need to go to the competent court of appeal like other arbitral awards for ratification, but can be enforced directly through enforcement courts. Hence, the enforcement of an international award issued in a foreign country will face one stage to enforce the award, while other awards will face two stages, one before the competent court and another at the enforcement court. This makes awards issued in the Kingdom harder to enforce. The Enforcement Law states that the implementation court must ensure that the award does not include anything that is contrary to the provisions of public order in the Kingdom. Hence, domestic arbitral awards will be reviewed twice to ensure compliance with Islamic Sharia and public order: once at the competent court and again by the enforcement judge. Given the fact that each and every Saudi judge can potentially apply his own understanding of Sharia for the review of a case, this is not only a procedural hurdle. Since one of the main the goals of the new Arbitration Law is to facilitate the procedure for arbitrating parties, the study suggests that the arbitral enforcement procedure should be reduced to filing with the enforcement court without differentiating between the types of arbitration awards.

1074 See UNCITRAL Model Law on International Commercial Arbitration Article 35(2). 2006.

c. *Adding Some Rules*

1) Online arbitration and use of technology

The new law does not mention online dispute resolution (ODR), which is an avenue of settling disputes that uses and applies technology to facilitate the resolution of disputes at lower cost to the parties. Although this method of arbitration is still unknown in the Kingdom, since the new Law is more open to international arbitration, the Kingdom could face challenges about this type of arbitration if the law does not address it and the Saudi courts are not familiar with it. The new law allows parties in the arbitration agreement to use technology, and new laws issued recently about electronic transactions and electronic crimes could cover many disputes about online arbitration and the use of electronics and technology during the arbitration process. However, this developing area would evolve in the Kingdom more smoothly if it were mentioned in the law or its implementation regulation expressly to provide the arbitrating parties and arbitration tribunal more confidence when using this type of arbitration.

2) Clarifying provisions about the gender and religion of arbitrators

Unlike the old law, the new Arbitration Law no longer mentions requirements that an arbitrator has to have the high qualification of a Saudi judge, which meant that the arbitrator had to be male and Muslim. However, despite the absence of such requirements about religion, gender, and even nationality in the new law, this issue is being debated by Muslim jurists and in Saudi courts, as shown in Chapter 2. Each case has to be viewed based on its own merit, and there are no binding past decisions, which means that the court can choose any opinion in Muslim jurisprudence to apply in a case before it. To reduce the risk of an arbitration award being challenged in Saudi court based on an arbitrator's religion or gender, the study suggests that the Saudi Ruler state expressly that no particular religion, gender, or nationality is required for a person to serve as an arbitrator under the new law.

3) Immunity of arbitrators

One of the crucial issues relating to the arbitral panel is arbitrator immunity. Proclaiming arbitrators immune from liability actually offers significant motivation to arbitrators to perform their duties independently during the arbitration process. The arbitrator is doing a quasi-judicial duty, so he should be protected from being sued by disgruntled parties. Without such immunity, arbitrators may be intimidated during the arbitration process if either of the arbitrating parties is not pleased with the outcome, which may affect the arbitrator's independence and may disrupt the finality of the arbitral award. Moreover, without such immunity, many qualified individuals may avoid serving as an arbitrator, which may adversely affect the arbitration method in general. Different legal systems handle immunity of arbitrators differently, but all draw a clear line when criminal acts are concerned, such as accepting bribes. All legal systems handle these situations under criminal law in the country in which the arbitration is taking place. Thus, giving arbitrators immunity does not give them protection from prosecution for crimes. Also, most international arbitration rules deal with the immunity of the arbitrator in their articles, such as the ICC Arbitration Rules as shown in Chapter 3. In contrast, unlike most international arbitration rules, the new Saudi Arbitration Law does not contain any article that presents protection from civil liability to the arbitrator for mistakes that he may commit while carrying out his function in the arbitration process. Because court proceedings are different from arbitration proceedings with regard to safeguards, such as the possibility of correcting possible errors on appeal, the arbitrator has a higher chance of making incorrigible errors than the court. Implementing a limited immunity that protects the arbitrator from all liability except those caused by deliberate wrongdoing may be a middle ground between these concerns. Hence, the study suggests providing a limited immunity to the arbitrator against all claims arising out of arbitration, except for claims that allege deliberate wrongdoing by the arbitrator and to the extent that such a prohibition is allowed by the applicable law. This limited immunity will achieve a balance between the independence of arbitrators and a fair arbitration process instead of leaving the door open to the possibility of a suit against an arbitrator, which may well be motivated by the goal to just disrupt the arbitration process and the enforcement of the award.

4) The scope of judicial review in the enforcement of an arbitration agreement

In the Saudi law, the Ruler does not explain the type of review by the court if an action is brought that is the subject of an arbitration agreement before the court. However, several cases show that Saudi courts tend to review the arbitration agreement in a comprehensive way and hear from all parties, as shown in Chapter 3. The study recommends that the new Arbitration Law restrain the extent of judicial review of the arbitration agreement instead of leaving it up to the court's consideration, which can waste the parties' time if the court decides to undertake a comprehensive review.

5) Basis for interim measures

Unlike the UNCITRAL Model Law, the Saudi law does not specify a particular basis for granting interim measures but leaves it to the arbitration tribunal's discretion, which provides the arbitrator with broad powers in this respect. Among other powers, the law gives the tribunal the authority to require the requested party to provide sufficient financial guarantees before the execution of interim measures. It would be better if the Saudi law specified the grounds that must exist for the tribunal to grant interim measures, for the requesting party to supply security, and for cases when provisional orders must be notified to the affected party in advance.

6) Special protocols for consumer disputes

As noted earlier, unlike the judiciary system in the courts, the arbitration process provides little opportunity to conduct discovery, making it difficult for some types of disputes in which one of the parties is weaker than other party, such as consumers disputes. Less sophisticated parties and parties that will not be "repeat customers" for arbitrators may face difficulties vindicating their rights in arbitration because they lack many of the crucial process protections that exist in the justice system. The AAA has addressed this aspect of the process in its newly adopted Consumer Due Process Protocol, in which it has developed standards and procedures for the equitable resolution of consumer disputes.[1075] The new Saudi Arbitration Law does not mention special requirements for these types of disputes. Accordingly, the study suggests adding special principles for consumer disputes to Saudi Law that will identify minimum due process standards that embody the concept of fundamental fairness for a weaker party in compliance with recent trends in international arbitration rules and to take advantage of such norms in the Protocol in global institutional arbitration. In addition to achieving better balance for such type of disputes, this would educate consumers about the differences between arbitration and ADR on the one side and the court process on the other side, so that they can make decisions based on knowledge about whether to submit their claims to ADR.

1075 The due process standards of the Consumer Due Process Protocol and the Consumer Arbitration Rules of the American Arbitration Association (AAA) available at its website at: https://www.adr.org/aaa/faces/aoe/gc/consumer/registrywelcome?

7) Effects of a successful challenge to an arbitral award

If a court vacates an arbitral award because the arbitration agreement itself was invalid, the parties can initiate a court action on the same issues. By contrast, when an award is vacated based on some significant procedural irregularity, the arbitration agreement is still valid and the parties have to return to arbitration, unless the parties agree otherwise. In the absence of an agreement between the parties, Saudi law does not specify whether the case will be returned to the same tribunal or not.[1076] On the one hand, a new arbitral tribunal may require that the proceedings begin all over again, which would be a substantial duplication of effort, time, and resources and a loss for both parties. On the other hand, one of the parties may have lost faith in the old tribunal because of the procedural irregularity and may prefer the additional expenses over having to deal with the same tribunal again. The new law differentiates between whether the award is vacated because the arbitration agreement is not valid and for other reasons. However, it does not distinguish among the other reasons if the award is vacated, for example, because of corruption, fraud, or arbitrator misconduct or partiality.[1077] As long as the Law is not amended, it is better if the arbitrating parties attach some rules about these possibilities in their agreement.

As noted above, one of the best sets of rules in this regard is the RUAA as revised in 2000. Under the RUAA, if the competent court vacates the arbitral award based on grounds other than an invalid agreement, the court may request a rehearing. However, if the award is vacated based on corruption, fraud, or arbitrator misconduct or partiality, the hearing shall be in a new arbitral tribunal. Also, if the decision is based on a failure in the procedure or in the tribunal acting in excess of its powers, the rehearing may be before the tribunal that made the award or a new one.[1078] As a result, there is a gap in such a case in the new Saudi law. It would be better if the Saudi Ruler filled the gap by the same stated rule.

8) Confidentiality of arbitration

The Saudi law follows modern rules in protecting the arbitration award by providing that no part of the award shall be published unless the arbitrating parties consent thereto in writing. However, it does not impose on the parties a confidentiality obligation as to information obtained during the arbitration,

---

1076 See Arbitration Law article 50. 2012.

1077 See id.

1078 Uniform Arbitration Act (RUAA) 23(c). 2000.

which could be more important to parties in some cases than knowing the arbitral award itself, since it may include trade secrets and other confidential information. The Saudi law can fill this gap by adopting one of the international rules that provides such protection. For example, the study found that the LCIA Rules, in Article 30.1, provide high and broad protection in such matters, as explained in chapter 3 of this study.[1079]

9) Parallel proceedings

One of the main risks in international arbitration is that the same dispute may result in parallel proceedings before different arbitral tribunals, national courts or even between an arbitral tribunal on one side and a national jurisdiction on the other. This is not uncommon and always leads to conflicts between the authorities in the outcome and their decisions and awards. While there is no unified solution to this matter, different procedural mechanisms have been developed through some international conventions to avoid or mitigate the undesirable impacts of such parallel proceedings.[1080]

Although the Saudi law provides expressly for an antisuit injunction and also has rules about refusing enforcement of an arbitral award if it conflicts with a prior award or decision issued by a court, committee or authority that had jurisdiction on the subject of the dispute in the Kingdom of Saudi Arabia,[1081] there is silence about such matters if a conflict happens with a foreign court or international arbitral tribunal. In addition, because of the lack of available cases about such matters in the Kingdom, it is hard to imagine how Saudi court would handle such an issue. Hence, the study suggests adding clear rules and procedures for parallel proceedings which are already in another jurisdiction, to deny enforcement of a judgment when a parallel action exists that involves the same disputing parties and subject matter in another court or tribunal. In addition, the Kingdom could consider such a parallel proceeding part of public policy, which means that it can be considered under the New York Convention.

d) Attracting foreign international arbitration centers

As shown in the study, although the new Arbitration Law broadly complies with the most modern arbitration rules, the Kingdom of Saudi Arabia still does not have experienced arbitration centers. One the most significant steps in en-

1079 LCIA Rules 2014.

1080 See ASSOCIATION, AAA Handbook on International Arbitration and ADR 169-172. 2010.

1081 See Arbitration Law article 55(2)(a). 2012.

couraging investors to resort to arbitration or ADR methods is the existence of institutional arbitration as shown in Chapter 3, which has been lacking in the Kingdom until now. The study suggests that the existence of branches of international arbitration centers would significantly facilitate applying the new law and would bring the advantage of know-how transfer to accelerate the development of high quality domestic arbitration options in the Kingdom.

3. Developing Other Forms of ADR

Chapter one of the study shows that, in addition to binding arbitration that investors and companies are looking for, there are other types of ADR that have proven their value internationally. Mediation and conciliation may be preferred in some situations, when the parties need to maintain an amicable relationship between them. Although mediation and conciliation are deeply rooted in the Arabic culture and the Islamic religion, they were not officially developed in the Kingdom. Hence, the study sees that the development of the Saudi legal system should not stop at arbitration. Other means of dispute resolution that are successfully applied internationally, provide different styles of alternative dispute resolution and address different commercial and social needs. These include combined procedure mediation-arbitration, negotiation/mediation/ arbitration, or just mediation as a stand-alone procedure.[1082] Without doubt, they should be included among the opportunities offered to parties, especially foreign traders and investors that is used to working with these types of dispute resolution mechanisms. Also, after examining relevant rules, the study suggests that the Kingdom may take advantage of the UNCITRAL Conciliation Rules[1083] or modern ADR rules in international institutions such as ICC[1084] and ICDR,[1085] which contain the most advanced practice in such arena.

4. Reforming Legal Education in Saudi Arabia

As the study shows in Chapter 2, Islamic Sharia schools in the Kingdom are the only place where students may study to become a judge in the Saudi courts according to the Saudi judicial system. Of course, there are various legal educa-

---

1082 For more details about such types of ADR, see ASSOCIATION, AAA Handbook on International Arbitration and ADR 221,285, 309, 322-325, 328, 412-414. 2010.

1083 UNCITRAL Conciliation Rules (1980). Such rules are available at the United Nations Commission on International Trade Law website at: http://www.uncitral.org/uncitral/en/uncitral_texts/arbitration/1980Conciliation_rules.htm.

1084 Available at the ICC International Chamber of Commerce website at: http://www.iccwbo.org/products-and-services/arbitration-and-adr/mediation/rules/.

1085 Available at ICDR International Center for Dispute Resolution website at https://www.icdr.org/icdr/faces/i_search/i_rule/i_rule.

tion institutions in the Kingdom where students can study to become a judge, such as the Higher Judicial Institute, but graduates are not required to take a position as a judge in the country. Hence, the study will focus on how to reform and develop the education system in the Islamic Sharia schools.

Most aspects of developing the legal system depend on reforming legal education. For example, it is hard to imagine rethinking Islamic Sharia as it is applied in Saudi courts, and the Ijtihad principle as applied in those courts, without reforming the legal education that has produced them. Hence, the study suggests the following possibilities of improving the legal education system in the Kingdom:

a. Adjusting the Curriculum of Sharia and Law Schools and Other Training Courses

The largest part of the curriculum and courses in Islamic Sharia should remain, as it provides a foundation to understanding the principles of Islamic Sharia and how it works and is applied. However, various courses in different legal aspects should be added, such as specialized ADR courses in the international and national fields.

b. Attracting Foreign Experience

Even if the Kingdom offers modern legal courses and changes the current curriculum, it cannot depend on current local knowledge alone, which is build on traditional approaches, if the Kingdom wants to bring about a rapid opening of dispute settlement procedures for international parties and rules. Chapter 2 also shows that there are difficulties in reforming the legal system and legal education and internationalizing local knowledge and experience. Hence, the study suggests attracting foreign legal experience through teachers, professors, trainers, and retired judges to work in Islamic Sharia schools, and using them to transfer modern knowledge and expertise, especially with regard to international law and commerce.

c. Adding Some Legal Courses in the English Language

The English language is the global language of trade and business today. Although the United Nations adopted Arabic as an official language,[1086] Saudi lawyers and researchers still need English to access many of the specialized research platforms, treaties and conventions. For example, the New York

1086 See United Nations website at http://www.un.org/en/sections/about-un/official-languages/.

Convention does not provide an authentic translation in Arabic,[1087] which imposes some barriers and obstacles to access its provisions directly. In addition, knowing English presents an opportunity for Saudi lawyers and researchers to connect with huge numbers of foreign researchers, centers, and recently established websites in the legal field. Hence, the study suggests adding some legal courses especially in the international field, taught in the English language. A good example is the Law Department at the Sharia College at the Al-Imam Muhammad ibn Saud Islamic University - the Alhsaa branch - which customized 30% of its courses in the English language.[1088] This is a significant step toward opening the door for its students to connect with the international community in the future.

d. Establishing Research Centers for Arbitration and ADR

These type of centers could provide local and easy access to international knowledge and experience and reinforce the legal environment in the Kingdom by transferring the most modern practice to the country and its education community through conferences, joint seminars, training, or even by specialized researche projects and publications.

5. Establishing a Temporary Independent Specialized Committee or Tribunal for Arbitration and ADR

Reforms of legal education and changes to the culture and practice of Ijtihad, as applied in Saudi courts, will need a long time to take hold and bring about comprehensive improvements to the legal environment in the Kingdom. Accordingly, the Kingdom needs a temporary solution to deal with arbitration and ADR issues beginning with assistance during the arbitration process and ending with the recognition and enforcement stage so that awards can be processed efficiently and the challenges in the current position as discussed in chapters 2, 3, and 4 will be overcome. After examining this area, the study found that banking disputes, as explained in Chapter 2, faced the same type of challenges with Saudi courts, and the Kingdom provided a temporary solution in the form of the Banking Dispute Committees. The solution has been successful and it appears that it could also be implemented successfully to arbitration and ADR disputes. As a result, the study proposes establishing a temporary independent specialized committee (tribunal) for Arbitration and ADR.

1087 See New York Convention website at http://www.newyorkconvention.org/new+york+convention+texts.

1088 See the Collage website at http://www.imamsh.org/i/?page_id=2036.

The proposed tribunal could operate under the Ministry of Commerce and Investment, which has experience in supervising different types of commercial disputes, such as commercial paper disputes.[1089] The proposed tribunal should be given jurisdiction over arbitration affairs and its application of mandatory rules and the arbitration agreement, and the upholding of recognized international commercial arbitration norms and practices, would allow arbitration awards to be recognized and enforced in a way that could not be possible were such cases to be submitted to the Saudi courts, as shown in Chapter 2 of the study. Furthermore, like the banking disputes tribunal, the proposed tribunal could establish circuits for the committee as needed. Each circuit may sit as three members, and all members should have legal qualification and experience and be familiar with arbitration and ADR principles. Also, one member of each tribunal should be Sharia qualified to ensure compliance with general Islamic Sharia principles.

C. Outlook

A state's legal framework represents a critical part of the international trade and investment system; investment decisions in any foreign country necessarily require a certain level of knowledge and understanding about that state's legal system. In the case of Saudi Arabia, this includes aspects such as court procedure, the extent to which alternative dispute resolutions are effective and awards are enforced, and procedures for the enforcement of judgments, in addition to other characteristics affected by reforms envisaged in the framework of Vision 2030 to attract international investment in-country.[1090] The Kingdom of Saudi Arabia has a dual judicial system comprised of the General Courts System and an independent administrative judiciary known as the Board of Grievances (Diwan Al-Mazalem); there are also several Administrative Committees (mini-tribunals), which have jurisdiction over specific cases under the authority of different governmental bodies. In 2007, the Kingdom implemented a modern judicial system by Royal Decree M/78 to reform the judiciary and to create a new court system after the Saudi judicial system was criticized domestically and internationally for being slow, arcane, lacking in safeguards of justice, and unable to deal with the modern world. In addition, the Saudi government also renewed its efforts to be accepted by the World Trade Organization as a member after 12 years of negotiation and debate. Royal Decree M/78 established new courts and circuits and transferred the Board of Grievances' commercial and criminal

1089 For more information about the disputes for which the Ministry of Commerce and Investment is responsible, see the Ministry of Commerce and Investment website at: http://mci.gov.sa/en/ServicesDirectory/Pages/8-8.aspx .

1090 These goals have been listed at the Saudi vision website at: http://vision2030.gov.sa/en

jurisdictions and the workload of the government's mini-tribunals to a restructured general judicial system, causing the Sharia courts to become more specific in jurisdiction. In practice, however, the reforms have not yet been completely implemented, and the judicial system is still in the process of reorganization.

To align with international standards and to facilitate enforcement of arbitral awards, on July 3, 2012, Royal Decree No. M/53 issued the Saudi Enforcement Law, representing a significant step with the creation of a particular jurisdiction and specific procedures applicable to enforcement. Also, Article 38(1) of the Saudi Arbitration Law provides an opportunity for arbitrating parties to agree to any particular law of a state to settle their disputes, which is of great help to foreign investors in the Kingdom, because they can choose a law that is familiar to them. In addition, on October 4, 2016, by Decree No. 2057, dated 14/6/1435H (corresponding to March 15, 2014), the Council of Ministers established the Saudi Center for Commercial Arbitration (SCCA), the first of its kind in Saudi Arabia, in Riyadh City. The Center coordinates with other international arbitration centers, such as the International Centre for Dispute Resolution (ICDR), to offer specialized training for its professional staff, including case management of mediation and arbitration cases.[1091] Furthermore, as reported in the newspaper Okaz (January 18, 2017), the Saudi Minister of Justice has officially requested the implementation courts to stop receiving referrals on paper and to accept only electronic representations and orders. Through this proposal to make the courts "paperless," the Minister aims to speed up the delivery of judicial outcomes, thereby reducing the time and expenses involved in the judicial process.[1092] All of these steps have contributed to improvement in the efficiency of dispute settlement and enforcement procedures for foreign investors in Saudi Arabia.

Also critical to potential foreign investors is to understand how Saudi courts work, including the application of Sharia. Choosing the right attorney and arbitral tribunal is crucial to assist and guide investors in how to comply with judgments and awards as required by the legal process in the Kingdom, including at enforcement stages. This challenge can be surmounted, however, putting parties who have filed for arbitration in a good position, in cases were modern arbitration practices are offered (particularly in the enforcement stages of a case), and the arbitral tribunal has knowledge of both Saudi law and international practice. The SCCA provides such services to assist foreign investors. The Center can also

1091 For more information about the Center, see its website at: http://www.sadr.org/index.php?file=index.php&module=&id=&lang=en. The website is available in both English and Arabic.

1092 See http://okaz.com.sa/article/1521892/.

benefit international business investors by helping them find the right arbitrator with the specifically required experience,[1093] giving them more confidence in the entire legal process, including the enforcement stage.

1093 See its website at: http://sadr.org/en/

Appendix A

Glossary

A bai al inah: a double sale, also known as "buy-back"; this is one of the financing techniques used to circumvent Riba in Islamic Sharia and to comply with the rules established by Muslim jurists. In a double-sale transaction, a seller (lender) sells an asset to a buyer (borrower) on credit (payment to be made before a fixed period) for a fixed price (the loan amount) and a profit element, which is called the "interest amount" in non-Islamic financial transactions. The seller immediately repurchases the asset from the buyer in cash for the fixed price.

A royal order and a royal decree: the former reflects the consideration of the King alone without any prior resolution from other Saudi authorities, while a royal decree is discussed and approved by the legislative authorities (the Shura Council and Council of Ministers) before being issued by the King.

Al Mutawatir: one of the types of Sunnah (including teachings, deeds, and sayings) propounded by the Prophet Muhammad, which is indubitable because it is widely known and backed by numerous references.

Ayat: a verse of the Quran.

Baghy: rebellion.

Fatwa: the legal opinion or interpretation of Sharia.

Fiqh: Islamic jurisprudence.

Gharar: risk/uncertainty, specifically, in financial products, wherein details concerning the conditions of sale are unknown or uncertain.

Haj: (pilgrimage) is a mandatory religious duty for Muslims; it refers to an annual Islamic pilgrimage to Mecca, which every adult, who is financially and physically capable, must perform at least once in a lifetime.

Hakam: an arbitrator.

Hejaz: a region to the west of present-day Saudi Arabia.

Hirabah: highway robbery.

Hiyal: "legalistic trickery" in Islamic jurisprudence.

Hudud: the unchangeable punishments prescribed by the primary sources of Islamic Sharia, which are considered mandated by God (Allah). Both the quantity and quality of punishments are specified in the Hudud.

Ijma: consensus of opinion.

Ijtihad: independent reasoning, which refers to the thorough exertion of a jurist's mental faculties in finding a solution to a legal issue.

Istihsan: an Arabic term for juristic "preference." Literally, it means "to consider something good." Some Muslim scholars use it as one of the secondary sources of Sharia to express their preference for particular judgments over other possibilities.

Istishab: a situation that existed previously is presumed to continue even in the present until the contrary is proven.

Kaaba: a cuboid building at the center of the sacred mosque in Mecca City in the Kingdom of Saudi Arabia. Muslims face the Kaaba when performing their prayers from any part in the world.

Lian: a dispute in which a husband accuses his wife of adultery without supplying witnesses.

Madhhab: a school of thought within Islamic jurisprudence.

Maqasid: purposes that are derived from the primary sources of Sharia.

Maslahah mursalah: any type of public interest that can be advantageous, provided there is no relevant legislation in the Quran and the Sunnah regarding this, and it is of public benefit, such as building prisons, bridges, and so on.

Mudaraba: a partnership or a financing scheme that is widely used and is compliant with the financial doctrine of Islam. A Mudaraba is a partnership contract in which one partner is the financier (the investor-customer in the bank) and the other partner (the fund manager, working partner, or bank) invests the capital provided by the financier in economic activity. The second partner usually has the relevant experience in investment and operating the venture capital in economic activities like banks and specialized financial institutions. The main difference between the Mudaraba and the financial schemes of non-Muslim financial institutions is that, in the latter, both parties agree in advance about sharing the profit and loss (PLS). However, in the Mudaraba, there is no guarantee of receiving capital or profits from the economic activities because they depend entirely on the second partner (Mudarib; fund manager), unless there is negligence or misconduct.

Murabaha: a single purchase loan; a transaction made to obtain finance to buy a commodity, a principle not in conflict with Islamic Sharia. Here, the lender (usually, the bank) purchases the product from the seller for cash and then sells the product to a buyer (customer) on a deferred payment basis, usually in installments. The difference between the price the lender (buyer) pays to the first seller and the price the second buyer pays to the lender sells is profit (Murabaha), which in non-Islamic banks is called "interest." Furthermore, the lender must physically possess the product, such as by having a certificate of title or bill of lading.

Najd: the central geographical region of Saudi Arabia.

Qazf: false accusation of Zina.

Qisas: punishment equivalent and proportionate to the crime that has been committed, such as death penalty for murder.

Qiyas: deductive analogy.

Quran: the book of revelations from Allah (God) to Prophet Muhammad through the angel Gabriel (Jibril) given over a period of 23 years.

Riba: usury.

Riddah: apostasy.

Sahaba: Prophet Muhammad's companions.

Salam: deferred delivery sale contract under Islamic jurisprudence; a Salam contract is a recognized instrument that allows the sale of goods not yet manufactured or not yet existing for delivery on a future date. Traditional Islamic jurisprudence defines it as a contract in which goods to be delivered in the future are paid for in the present.

Shahada: testimony or witness.

Shar'u man qablana: the body of divine rules that were legislated to the people through the revelation to prophets before Prophet Muhammad.

Shura: Arabic word for "consultation".

Sulh: reconciliation; in Sharia, it means an "amicable settlement".

Sunnah: the teachings, practices, deeds, traditions, and sayings of Prophet Muhammad (PBUH), which form the second source of Islamic Sharia.

Tawarruq: a tripartite sale; a financial instrument that is used to obtain cash and, at the same time, avoid conflict with Riba (usury). In this transaction, a buyer purchases a commodity from the seller on a deferred payment basis and then sells the same product to a third party (buyer) on cash payment basis. When the buyer gets the cash from the second transaction, he pays the first seller, usually on an installment basis, like Islamic banks do.

Ttazir: punishments applicable to the offenses for which no punishment is specified in the primary sources of Sharia.

Ulama: those recognized as scholars or authorities in the "religious hierarchy" of Sharia.

Urf: the customs of a given society.

Zakat: one of the five pillars of Islamic religion; it is the amount of money that must be donated by an individual based on the wealth and assets possessed by the individual.

Zina: unlawful sexual intercourse.

Appendix B

Arbitration Law of Saudi Arabia (2012) [1094]

Royal Decree No M/34, dated 24/5/1433 AH (corresponding to 16/4/2012 AD) concerning the approval of the Law of Arbitration

With the help of Allah the Almighty,

We, Abdullah Ibn Abdul Aziz Al Saud, King of the Kingdom of Saudi Arabia,

Based on Article 70th of the Saudi Statute, issued by the Royal Decree No. (A/90), dated, 27/8/1412 AH,

And based on Article 20th of the Council of Ministers law, issued by the Royal Decree No. (A/13) dated 03/03/1414 AH,

And based on Article 18th of the Law of Ash-Shura Council issued by the Royal Decree No. (A/91) dated 27/08/1412 AH,

And having reviewed the Decree of Ash-Shura Council No. (99/77), dated 21/02/1433 AH,

And having reviewed the Decree of the Council of Ministers No. (156), dated 17/05/1433 AH (corresponding to 9/4/2012AD),

We hereby decree the following:

Firstly: The approval of the Law of Arbitration with the attached form.

Secondly: His Highness the Deputy Prime Minister, the Ministers and the Chairmen of the concerned independent bodies shall take this Decree into action, each under his competence.

Abdullah Ibn Abdul Aziz Al Saud

The Law of Arbitration

Part 1 – General Rules

Article 1

The following expressions shall have the meaning assigned to them, unless the context requires otherwise:

1) The Arbitration Agreement: It is an agreement between two or more parties to refer to the arbitration all or some of certain disputes that have occurred or might occur between them concerning a certain regulatory relation, whether it is in the shape of a contract or not, whether the arbitration agreement appears as an arbitration condition mentioned in a contract, or as an independent arbitration stipulation.

1094 Source: http://www.wipo.int/edocs/lexdocs/laws/en/sa/sa057en.pdf = http://www.idc.gov.sa/en-us/RulesandRegulations1/Arbitration%20Law.pdf.

2) The Arbitration Authority: It is the individual arbitrator including its team of arbitrators that judge in the dispute referred to the arbitration.

3) The Competent Court: It is the court of the regulatory authority to judge in the disputes that are agreed to be under arbitration.

Article 2

Without prejudice to the rules of the Islamic Sharia and the rules of the international conventions in which the Kingdom is included as one of its parties, the provisions of this law are valid for any arbitration, whatever the nature of regulatory relation of the dispute is, if the arbitration is conducted inside the Kingdom, or if it is a commercial international arbitration held abroad, and its parties agreed that it shall be subject to provisions of this law.

The provisions of this law are not valid for the disputes of the personal status or the matters that cannot be reconciled.

Article 3

According to this law, the arbitration shall be international if its dispute is related to the international trade, and this occurs in the following matters:

1) If the headquarter of both parties of the arbitration lies on more than one country at the time of the arbitration agreement; if one party has more than a business center, it depends mainly on the most relevant center to the subject of the dispute, and if one or both parties do not have a certain business center, it depends mainly on their normal residence address.

2) If the headquarter of both parties of the arbitration lies on the same country at the time of the arbitration agreement, and one of the following places lies outside that country:

a) The place of the arbitration procedures as assigned in the arbitration agreement, or referred to its way of assignation.

b) The place of executing an essential side of the obligations arising from the trading affairs between both parties.

c) The most relevant place to the subject of the dispute.

3) If both parties agree to resort to an organization or a permanent arbitration authority, or an arbitration center lies outside the Kingdom.

4) If the arbitration subject included in the arbitration agreement is related to more than one country.

Article 4

In the cases this law allows the parties of the agreement to choose the assigned procedure to be followed in a certain matter, this ensures their right to permit others to choose this procedure, and the others referred to in this subject are every individual, authority, organization or an arbitration center in the Kingdom of Saudi Arabia or abroad.

Article 5

If the parties of the arbitration agree to subject their relationship to the provisions of any document (a model contract, or an international convention or others), they shall act under the provisions of this document, for including special provisions of arbitration and that shall not be contrary to the provisions of the Islamic Sharia.

Article 6

1) If there is no special agreement between the parties of the arbitration regarding the notifications, then the notification shall be delivered to the addressee personally – or his representative – or sent to the mailing address specified in the contract subject of the dispute, or specified in the charter party of the arbitration, or in the document governing the relationship covered by the arbitration.

2) If the notification could not be delivered to the addressee in accordance with the paragraph (1), the delivery is considered achieved if it was done by a registered letter to the last workplace, or usual place of residence, or postal address known to the addressee.

3) The provisions of this Article shall not apply to the judicial notifications concerning the invalidity of the arbitration award before the courts.

Article 7

If one of the parties of the arbitration continues in the arbitration proceedings – with his knowledge of the occurrence of a violation of a provision of this law, which may be agreed to violating or due to a condition in the arbitration agreement – and does not provide an objection to this violation within the time limit agreed upon, or within thirty days of his knowledge of the occurrence of the violation in case of no agreement, this is counted as a waiver of his right for objection.

Article 8

1) The jurisdiction to hear the action of the invalidity of the arbitration award and the matters referred to the court by the law shall be to the competent court and concluded to the Court of Appeals that is originally competent to hear the dispute.

2) If the arbitration is commercial and international whether in the Kingdom or abroad, so the jurisdiction shall be to the Court of Appeal which is originally competent to hear the dispute in the city of Riyadh, unless otherwise agreed by the parties of the arbitration for another court of appeal in the Kingdom.

Part 2 – Arbitration Agreement

Article 9

1) The arbitration agreement may be earlier to the dispute, whether it is independent, self-contained, or contained in a particular contract. Also, the arbitration agreement may be later to the dispute, even if there is a suit concerning it before the competent court. In

this case, the agreement shall specify the issues covered by the arbitration, or the agreement is null and void.

2) The arbitration agreement shall be written, or it is null and void.

3) The arbitration agreement is considered written if it is included in a document issued by the parties of the arbitration, or if it is included in their exchanged documented correspondences, or telegrams, or other means of electronic communication, or written. And the indication in some contract or the referral in it to a document that includes a condition of arbitration is considered an arbitration agreement. It is also considered in effect of a written arbitration agreement all referrals – in the contract – to the provisions of a model contract, or an international agreement, or any other document containing an arbitration conditions only if the referral is clear in considering this condition a part of the contract.

Article 10

1) It is valid to agree on arbitration only for those who have the disposition of their rights whether a natural person – or his representative – or a legal person.

2) It is not permissible for governmental authorities to agree on arbitration only after the approval of the Prime Minister, unless there is a text of the special laws that allows it.

Article 11

1) The court, to which a dispute with an arbitration agreement is brought, shall judge with the inadmissibility of hearing the claim if the defendant refutes by that before any request or defense in the claim.

2) Bringing the suit referred to in the preceding paragraph shall not deviate from starting the arbitration proceedings, or continuing, or delivering the arbitration award.

Article 12

Subject to the provisions in the paragraph (1) of the ninth Article of this law, if it is agreed on arbitration during the hearing of the dispute before the competent court, it shall decide to refer the dispute to arbitration.

Part 3 – Arbitral Tribunal

Article 13

The arbitral tribunal shall be constituted of one arbitrator or more, provided that the number of the arbitrators shall be an odd number or the arbitration is null and void.

Article 14

The arbitrator shall

1) be legally competent;

2) be of good conduct and behavior;

3) hold at least a college degree in Islamic legislation knowledge or regular knowledge. And if the arbitral tribunal is made up of more than one arbitrator, it is sufficient that the head of the tribunal has this condition.

Article 15

1) The parties of the arbitration may agree on the choice of the arbitrators, if they do not agree, the following shall be done:

a) If the arbitral tribunal consists of a single arbitrator, the competent court chooses him.

b) If the arbitral tribunal consists of three arbitrators, each party shall choose an arbitrator for him, and then the two arbitrators agree to choose the third arbitrator. If one of the parties does not appoint an arbitrator within fifteen days following the reception of an application concerning that from the other party, or if the two appointed arbitrators do not agree on choosing the third arbitrator within fifteen days following the date of the appointment of the most recent of them, the competent court undertakes choosing him at the request of this who is concerned about acceleration, and this is to be done within fifteen days from the date of submitting the application. And the arbitrator chosen by the appointed arbitrators or chosen by the competent court shall be the president of the arbitral tribunal. And these provisions shall apply in the case of the formation of the arbitral tribunal of more than three arbitrators.

2) If the parties of the arbitration do not agree on the procedures of choosing the arbitrators, or one the parties violated them, or the appointed arbitrators do not agree on some matter where agreement is required, or if the other fails to perform what is entrusted to him in this regard, the competent court undertakes - at the request of whom is concerned about acceleration - to do the procedure, or the required work, unless it is provided in the agreement for how to complete this procedure or work.

3) The competent court shall take into account the arbitrator is to be chosen according to the conditions stipulated in the agreement of the parties, and the conditions required by this law, and the court issues its decision by choosing the arbitrator within thirty days from the date of submitting the application.

4) Without prejudice to the provisions of the 49th and 50th Articles of this law, the decision of the competent court concerning the appointment of the arbitrator in accordance with the paragraphs (1 and 2) of this Article is not subject to appealing independently by any way of appeal.

Article 16

1) The arbitrator shall not have an interest in the dispute, and – since his appointment and throughout the arbitral proceedings – he shall declare – in writing – to the parties of the arbitration with all the circumstances that would raise justified doubts about his impartiality and independence, unless he had already done that.

2) The arbitrator shall be prohibited from considering the claim and hearing it – even if either of the parties of the arbitration did not request that – in the same situations in which the judge is prohibited.

3) No arbitrator may be rebutted only if some circumstances raise serious doubts about his impartiality or independence, or if he is not in possessing qualifications agreed upon by the parties of the arbitration, without prejudice to the provisions of the 14th Article of this law.

4) It is not permissible for any of the parties of the arbitration to request to rebut the arbitrator appointed by him or he participated in that appointment except for reasons that appeared after the appointment of the arbitrator.

Article 17

1) If there is no agreement between the parties of the arbitration on the procedures of rebutting the arbitrator, the rebutting request shall be submitted – in writing – to the arbitral tribunal stating the reasons for that rebuttal within five days from the date of the learning of the caller of the rebuttal with the formation of the tribunal, or with the circumstances justifying the rebuttal. If the arbitrator – rebutted against – does not withdraw, or the other party does not approve the request of rebutting withinfive days from the date of submission, the arbitral tribunal shall decide on it within fifteen days from the date of receiving it. And, in case the request is rejected, the requester may submit his request to the competent court within thirty days, and the award of that case is not subject to appealing by any methods of appeal.

2) The rebuttal shall not be approved from this who has previously submitted a request to rebut the same arbitrator in the same arbitration, for the same reasons.

3) The rebuttal before the arbitral tribunal shall result in stopping the arbitration proceedings. And the appeal against the issued award of the arbitral tribunal to reject the rebuttal request shall not result in stopping the arbitration proceedings.

4) If it is awarded to rebut the arbitrator – whether by the arbitral tribunal or by the competent court when considering the appeal – this results in considering what would have been done of the arbitration proceedings – including the arbitration award – as none.

Article 18

1) If the arbitrator could not perform his task, or did not perform, or refrained from performing it leading to unjustified delay in the arbitration proceedings, and he did not withdraw, and the parties of the arbitration failed to agree to dismiss him, the competent court may dismiss him at the request of either parties with an award that is not subject to appealing in any way of appeal.

2) Unless the arbitrator is appointed by the competent court, he may be dismissed only with the agreement of the parties of the arbitration, without prejudice to the provisions of the paragraph (1) of this Article. And the dismissed may ask for compensation unless the dismissal is due to reasons of his side.

Article 19

If the arbitrator's task ended with his death, or rebuttal, or dismissal, or withdrawal, or disability, or any other reason, an alternative arbitrator shall be appointed in accordance with the procedures that have been followed in the selection of the arbitrator, whose task has ended.

Article 20

1) The arbitral tribunal shall judge the defenses of its non-competence, including the defenses based on the absence of an arbitration agreement, or its fall, or its annulment, or its lack of coverage of the subject of the dispute.

2) The defenses shall be revealed to the lack of jurisdiction of the arbitral tribunal in accordance with the dates referred to in the paragraph (2) of the 30th Article of this law.

The appointment of an arbitrator or participation in his appointment shall not result in the fall of his right to present any of these defenses. The defense of the lack of inclusion, of the arbitration agreement to the matters raised by the other party during the hearing of the dispute, shall be revealed immediately or this right shall be prescribed. In all cases, the arbitral tribunal may accept the late defense if it considers that the delay was due to an acceptable reason.

3) The arbitral tribunal shall judge the defenses referred to in the paragraph (1) of this Article before judging the subject, and it may annex them to the subject to judge them both together. If it awarded with rejecting the defense, the appeal shall not be done except by suing the invalidity of the arbitration award that terminates the whole dispute in accordance with the 54th Article of this law.

Article 21

The arbitration condition contained in a contract is considered a separate agreement from the other conditions of the contract. The invalidity of the contract – which includes the arbitration condition – or its revocation or termination shall not result in the invalidity of the arbitration condition which is included in the contract if this condition is true in itself.

Article 22

1) The competent court may command that interim or conservatory measures shall be taken at the request of one of the parties of arbitration before incepting the arbitration proceedings or at the request of the arbitral tribunal in the course of the arbitration proceedings. These procedures may be withdrawn in the same way, unless the parties of the arbitration agree otherwise.

2) The competent court may, at the request of the arbitral tribunal, command a judicial acting.

3) The arbitral tribunal may request from the concerned authority to help it with the arbitration proceedings according to what this tribunal considers fit for the proper functioning of arbitration, such as: call a witness or an expert, or the command to bring

a document, or a copy of it, or see it, or otherwise, with no prejudice to the right of the arbitral tribunal to conduct that independently.

Article 23

1) It is permissible for the parties of the arbitration to agree that the arbitral tribunal may – at the request of one of them – command either of them to take what he sees of provisional or conservatory measures required by the nature of the dispute. The arbitral tribunal may obligate the party that requires taking such measures to provide an appropriate financial guarantee for the execution of this procedure.

2) If the party, against whom the command is issued, failed to execute it, the arbitral tribunal may – at the request of the other party – authorize this party to take the necessary measures to execute it, and without prejudice to the right of the tribunal or the other party to request from the competent authority to mandate the party that against whom the command is issued to execute it.

Article 24

1) When choosing the arbitrator, an independent contract shall be concluded with him stating his fees, and a copy of the contract shall be deposited with the authority prescribed by the executive regulation of this law.

2) If there is no agreement reached between the parties of the arbitration and the arbitrators to determine the arbitrators' fees, the competent court shall determine these fees. That court shall judge by issuing a decision that is not subject to appealing in any way of the ways of the appeal. And if the appointment of the arbitrators is done by the competent court, it shall determine the arbitrators' fees.

Part 4 – Executing the Arbitration

Article 25

1) The parties of the arbitration may agree on the actions adopted by the arbitral tribunal, including their right to subject these actions to the valid rules in any organization, or authority, or arbitration center in the Kingdom or abroad, provided they do not violate the provisions of the Islamic Sharia.

2) If there is no such agreement, the arbitral tribunal may – taking into account the provisions of Islamic Sharia, and the provisions of this law – choose the arbitration proceedings as it deems appropriate.

Article 26

The arbitration proceedings shall begin from the day when one of the parties of the arbitration receives the request for arbitration from the other party, unless the parties of the arbitration agreed otherwise.

Article 27

The parties of the arbitration are treated equally, and each of them shall have the full and equal opportunity to display his claim or defense.

Article 28

The parties of the arbitration may agree on the place of the arbitration in the Kingdom or abroad. And if there is no agreement, the arbitral tribunal shall determine a place for the arbitration taking into account the circumstances of the claim, and the convenience of the place for both parties, without prejudice to the authority of the arbitral tribunal to meet at any place it deems appropriate for deliberation among its members, and to hear witnesses, or experts, or the parties of the dispute, or to preview the dispute, or to examine the documents, or review them.

Article 29

1) The arbitration is performed in Arabic unless the arbitral tribunal decides or the parties of the arbitration agree on another language or other languages. And the rule of the agreement or decision shall apply on the language of data and written submissions and oral pleadings, as well as on every decision taken by the arbitral tribunal, or a message oriented by it, or an award rendered by it, unless the agreement of the parties or the decision of the arbitral tribunal provides otherwise.

2) The arbitral tribunal may decide that all or some of the written documents provided in the claim shall be attached by a translation into the language or languages used in the arbitration. In the case of multiple languages, the tribunal may confine the translation to some of them.

Article 30

1) The prosecutor shall send within the agreed date between the parties, or the one appointed by the arbitral tribunal, to the defendant and to each and every one of the arbitrators, a written statement of his claim, that includes his name, address, and the name of the defendant, and his address, and explain the facts of the claim, and his requests, and commitments, and any other matter that requires the agreement of the parties shall be mentioned in this statement.

2) The defendant shall send during the date agreed upon between the parties, or who is appointed by the arbitral tribunal, to the prosecutor and to each and every one of the arbitrators a written rejoinder of his defense in response to what came in the statement of claim. His rejoinder may contain any application related to the subject of the dispute, or he may stick to a right emerging of him intending to defend by set-off. And he has that right even at a later stage of the proceedings if the arbitral tribunal considers that the circumstances justify the delay.

3) Each one of the parties may attach to the statement of the claim or his rejoinder to it - as the case may be - copies of the documents on which he relies on, and he may refer to all or some of the documents, and the evidences that he intends to provide. This shall not prejudice the right of the arbitral tribunal at any stage in the proceedings in the request for the original documents or documents on which any of the parties of the claim rely on, or copies of them.

Article 31

A copy of all what is provided by one of the parties to the arbitral tribunal; notes, documents or other papers, shall be sent to the other party. Also, a copy of what is provided to the mentioned tribunal; expert reports, documents and other evidences that the arbitral tribunal can rely on when issuing its award, shall be sent to both parties.

Article 32

Each of the parties of the arbitration may amend his requests – or the aspects of his defense – or complete them during the arbitration proceedings, unless the arbitral tribunal decides not to accept that in order to prevent delaying the award of the dispute.

Article 33

1) The arbitral tribunal holds hearings to enable both parties to explain the subject of the claim presented, present their evidences and proofs. The tribunal may suffice with written notes and documents, unless the parties of the arbitration agree otherwise.

2) The parties of the arbitration shall be notified, at their addresses registered with the arbitral tribunal, of the date of any hearing of oral pleading, and the date of sentencing, and any meeting of the arbitral tribunal for the purposes of the review of the dispute, or other matter, or to examine the documents, before holding the hearing well in advance.

3) The arbitral tribunal shall write down a summary of what is going on in the hearing in the minutes signed by the witnesses or experts and attendees of both parties, and their representatives, and the members of the arbitral tribunal. And a copy of this summary shall be handed to each party, unless the parties of the arbitration agree otherwise.

Article 34

1) If the prosecutor does not provide – without an acceptable excuse – a written statement of his claim in accordance with the paragraph (1) of the 30th Article of this law, the arbitral tribunal shall terminate the arbitration proceedings, unless the parties of the arbitration agree otherwise.

2) If the defendant does not provide a written rejoinder to his defense in accordance with the paragraph (2) of the 30th Article of this law, the arbitral tribunal shall continue the arbitration proceedings, unless the parties of the arbitration agree otherwise.

Article 35

If one of the parties fails to attend one of the hearings – after being notified – or to provide any of the documents he is asked to bring, the arbitral tribunal may continue the arbitration proceedings and deliver an award concerning the dispute on the basis of the existing evidences.

Article 36

1) The arbitral tribunal may appoint one expert or more, to provide a written or oral report to be proved in the minutes of the hearing regarding certain issues determined by the decision of them. And both parties shall be notified of that unless they agree otherwise.

2) Both parties shall submit to the expert the information related to the dispute, and enable him to inspect and examine what he may demand of documents, items or other money related to the dispute. And the arbitral tribunal judges in every dispute arises between the expert and one of the parties in this regard with an award that is not subject to appealing by any methods of appeal.

3) The arbitral tribunal shall send a copy of the expert's report once deposited to each of the parties and give the opportunity to express his opinion on it. Both have the right to review and check the documents relied upon by the expert in his report. The expert issues his final report after reviewing what the parties' notes about it.

4) The arbitral tribunal, after the submission of the report of the expert, may decide on its own, or at the request of one of the parties of the arbitration, to hold a hearing to hear the words of the expert and give the opportunity for both parties to hear and discuss him in regards to what is stated in his report.

Article 37

If a matter is brought up, during the arbitration proceedings, that is out of the mandate of the arbitral tribunal or an appeal of forgery in a document presented to them, or penal proceedings have been taken for forgery, or any other penal act, the arbitral tribunal may continue considering the dispute, if it considers that judging this matter or in the document forgery or the other penal act is not necessary to judge the subject of the dispute, or the proceedings shall be stayed until a final award is delivered in this regard, and this results in the suspension of the deadline for the issuance of the arbitration award.

Part 5 – Settlement Procedures of the Arbitral Claim

Article 38

1) Taking into account the non-violation of the provisions of the Islamic Sharia and public order in the Kingdom, the arbitral tribunal, during the hearing of the dispute, shall:

a) Apply the rules agreed upon by the parties of the arbitration on the subject of the dispute, and if they agree on the application of a law of a particular state, the substantive rules shall be followed without those of dispute-of-laws, unless agreed otherwise.

b) If the parties of the arbitration do not agree on the statutory rules applicable to the subject of the dispute, the tribunal shall apply the substantive rules in the law that it considers the most relevant to the subject of the dispute.

c) The arbitral tribunal shall take into account, when judging the subject of dispute, the conditions of the contract of the dispute, and take into account the current norms in the type of treatment, and customs, and the usual dealing between the parties.

2) If the parties of the arbitration agree expressly to authorize the tribunal to reconciliation, it may judge in accordance with the applicable rules of justice and fairness.

Article 39

1) The award of the arbitration tribunal, formed of more than one arbitrator, is issued by the majority of its members after confidential deliberation.

2) If the views of the arbitral tribunal are branched and it has become not possible to get the majority, the competent court shall appoint a casting arbitrator.

3) Awards of penal matters may be issued by the arbitrator, who heads the tribunal, if the parties of the arbitration made remarks in writing, or being authorized by all the members of the arbitral tribunal, unless the parties of the arbitration agree otherwise.

4) If the arbitral tribunal is mandated to reconciliation, it shall be judged unanimously.

5) The arbitral tribunal may deliver temporary awards, or in a part of the requests, before judging the award that ends the dispute, unless the parties of the arbitration agree otherwise.

Article 40

1) The arbitral tribunal shall deliver the award terminating the whole dispute within the date agreed upon by the parties of the arbitration, and if there is no agreement, the award shall be delivered within twelve months from the date of commencement of the arbitration proceedings.

2) The arbitral tribunal may – in all cases – decide to extend the duration of the arbitration and this extension shall not exceed six months, unless otherwise agreed by the parties of the arbitration (over 12 months).

3) If the arbitration award is not delivered within the time limit referred to in the preceding paragraph, any one of the parties of the arbitration may request the competent court to issue an order to identify an additional period, or the termination of the arbitration proceedings, and any of the parties then may appeal to the competent court.

4) If an arbitrator is appointed instead of another arbitrator in accordance with the provisions of this regulation, the deadline of the award shall be extended for thirty days.

Article 41

1) The arbitration proceedings end when delivering the award that terminates the dispute, or the decision of the arbitral tribunal to end the proceedings in the following cases:

a) If the parties of the arbitration agree to end the arbitration.

b) If the prosecutor leaves the arbitration dispute, unless the arbitral tribunal decides upon the request of the defendant that he has a serious interest in continuing the proceedings to settle the dispute.

c) If the arbitral tribunal sees for any other reasons the futility of continuing the arbitration proceedings or its impossibility.

d) An order of termination of the arbitral proceedings is issued in accordance with the provision of the paragraph (1) of the 34th Article of this law.

2) The arbitration proceedings shall not end with the death of one of the parties of the arbitration, or his loss of eligibility – unless otherwise agreed by a competent person and the other party to end the dispute – but the determined date for the arbitration is extended for thirty days, unless the arbitral tribunal decides to extend the period time for a similar period, or the parties of the arbitration agree otherwise.

3) Subject to the provisions of the 49th, 50th and 51st Articles of this law, the tribunal task shall end at the end of the arbitration proceedings.

Article 42

1) The arbitration award shall be in writing and it should be justified, and signed by the arbitrators. In the case of the formation of the tribunal of more than one arbitrator. It is sufficient to have the signatures of the majority of the arbitrators, provided that the reasons of not signing of the minority shall be recorded in the minutes of the claim.

2) The arbitration award shall include the date of the pronouncement, place of issuance, the names of the litigants, their addresses, the names of the arbitrators, their addresses, nationalities, attributes, a summary of the arbitration agreement, summary of the statements and requests of the parties of arbitration, their pleading, their documents, a summary of the report of the experts – if any – the award text, the determination of the arbitrators' fees, the expenses of the arbitration, and how they are distributed between the parties without prejudice to the 24th Article of this law.

Article 43

1) The arbitral tribunal shall deliver each of the parties of the arbitration a true copy of the arbitration award within fifteen days from the date of issuance.

2) The arbitration award shall not be published or a portion of it thereof except with the consent of the parties of the arbitration in writing.

Article 44

The arbitral tribunal shall deposit the original copy of the award, or a signed copy in the language in which it was delivered by the competent court within the period set forth in the paragraph (1) of the 43rd Article of this law, with a translation into Arabic certified by an accredited authority if it was delivered in a foreign language.

Article 45

If the parties of the arbitration agree during the arbitration proceedings to a settlement to end the dispute, they may request to verify the conditions of the settlement before the arbitral tribunal which shall, in this case, deliver an award that includes the conditions of the settlement and end the proceedings. And this award shall have the power of the awards of the arbitrators at execution.

Article 46

1) Each of the parties of the arbitration may request from the arbitral tribunal within thirty days following the reception of the arbitration award to interpret any ambiguity that came in his award. The requester for interpretation shall inform the other party, on the address described in the arbitration award, with this request before it is submitted to the arbitral tribunal.

2) The interpretation shall be issued in writing within thirty days following the date of submitting the request of interpretation to the arbitral tribunal.

3) The interpretation award is considered an integral part of the arbitration award, which it interprets and it is subject to its provisions.

Article 47

1) The arbitral tribunal shall correct what lies in its award of purely material mis-statement, writing or calculation, and this is done through a decision issued on its own, or at the request of one of the litigants. And the arbitral tribunal shall conduct the correction without pleading within fifteen days following the date of the award, or to deposit the request of correction depending on the circumstances.

2) The decision of correction shall be issued in writing by the arbitral tribunal, and it shall be notified to the parties of the arbitration within fifteen days from the date of its issuance. And if the arbitral tribunal exceeds its power in the correction, it is allowed to stick to the invalidity of the decision by a claim of invalidity on which the provisions of the 50th and 51st Articles of this law shall apply.

Article 48

1) Each of the parties of the arbitration, even after the expiry of the arbitration deadline, may request the arbitral tribunal within thirty days following the reception of the arbitration award to deliver an additional arbitration award on the requests made during the proceedings and that the arbitration award has overlooked. And the other party shall be notified of this request on his address shown in the arbitration award before it is submitted to the arbitral tribunal.

2) The arbitral tribunal shall deliver its award within sixty days from the date of sub-mitting the request, and it may extend this period for thirty days if it deems it necessary.

Part 6 – Invalidity of the Arbitration Award

Article 49

The arbitration awards delivered in accordance with the provisions of this law are not subject to appealing in any way of appeal, except suing for the invalidity of the arbitration award in accordance with the provisions set forth in this law.

Article 50

1) The claim of the invalidity of the arbitration award is rejected, except in the following cases:

a) If there is no arbitration agreement or the agreement is null and void, or revocable, or has become null due to expiry.

b) If one of the parties of the arbitration agreement, at the time of conducting, is incompetent, or not completely competent in accordance with the rules governing his competence.

c) If one of the parties of the arbitration is unable to present his defense because of not being truly notified of appointing an arbitrator or of the arbitral proceedings, or any other reason beyond his control.

d) If the arbitration award excludes any application of the statutory rules that the parties of the arbitration agree to apply to the subject of the dispute.

e) If the arbitral tribunal is constituted or the arbitrators are appointed in a way violating this law or the agreement of the parties.

f) If the arbitration award judges matters that are not covered by the arbitration agreement, however, if it is possible to separate the parts of the award on the matters that are subject to the arbitration from the parts on the matters that are not subject to it, the nullification shall occur to the parts that are not subject to the arbitration only.

g) If the arbitral tribunal does not take into consideration the conditions that shall be met in the award to the extent that affects its content, or the award is based on false arbitration proceedings that have affected it.

2) The competent court that hears the claim of invalidity delivers an award of its own with the invalidity of the arbitration award if it contains what is contrary to the provisions of the Islamic Sharia and public order in the kingdom, or what is agreed upon by the parties of the arbitration, or it finds that the subject of the dispute is of the matters that may not be arbitrated under this law.

3) The arbitration agreement is not valid after the competent court delivers its award of invalidating the arbitration award; unless the parties of the arbitration have agreed on that, or an award is delivered with invalidating the arbitration agreement.

4) The competent court hears the suit of the invalidity in the cases referred to in this article, without having the right to examine the facts and subject of the dispute.

Article 51

1) The invalidity claim of the arbitration award is brought by any of the parties within the sixty days following the date of notification of that party of the award, the waiver of the invalidity prosecutor of his right to bring the claim before delivering the award of the arbitration does not preclude from accepting the claim.

2) If the competent court delivers an award that supports the arbitration award, it shall order it to be executed, and this award is not subject to appealing in any way of appeal.

But if it delivered an award with the invalidity of the arbitration award, this award may be appealed against within thirty days from the day following the notification.

Part 7 – The Authentication and Execution of the Awards of the Arbitrators

Article 52

Subject to the provisions set forth in this law, the arbitration award delivered in accordance with this law will be authentic and authoritative, and it is enforceable.

Article 53

The competent court or its representative issues an order with the execution of the arbitrators' award, and the request to execute the award shall be submitted and attached with the following:

1. The original of the award or a certified copy of it.
2. A true copy of the arbitration agreement.
3. A translation of the arbitration award into Arabic certified by an accredited authority if it was issued in another language.
4. The proof of depositing the award with the competent court and in accordance with the 44th Article of this law.

Article 54

Bringing the claim of invalidity shall not result in a stay of execution of the arbitration award. However, the competent court may order a stay of execution if requested by the invalidity prosecutor in the declaration of his claim and the request is based on serious reasons. The competent court shall judge in the request for a stay of execution within fifteen days from the date of submitting the request. If the court orders a stay of execution, it may order to provide a financial guarantee or warranty, and if it orders a stay of execution, it shall judge in the invalidity claim within one hundred and eighty days from the date of the issuing this order.

Article 55

1) The request for the execution of the arbitration award shall not be accepted unless the deadline of suing the invalidity of the award has passed.

2) The order to execute the arbitration award in accordance with this law shall be done only after verifying the following:

a) It does not conflict with an award or decision issued by a court or committee or authority that has the jurisdiction on the subject of the dispute in the Kingdom of Saudi Arabia.

b) It does not include what is contrary to the provisions of the Islamic Sharia and public order in the Kingdom, and if it is possible to fragment the award of the violation part, it is possible to execute the remaining part which is not violating.

c) It has been well and truly notified to the convicted.

3) It is not permissible to appeal against the order issued to execute the arbitration award. The order of rejecting the execution may be appealed against before the competent authority within thirty days from the date of issuance.

Part 8 – Final Provisions

Article 56

The Council of Ministers shall issue the Implementing Regulation of this law.

Article 57

This law replaces the arbitration law, issued by the Royal Decree No. (M/46), dated 12/07/1403 AH.

Article 58

This law comes into force after thirty days from the date of its publication in the Official Gazette.

Appendix C

Execution Law to the Arbitration Law of Saudi Arabia [1095]

(Issued by Royal Decree No. M/53 of 13 August 1433 AH, the Resolution of the Council of Ministers No. 261 of 12 August 1433 AH and the Circular of the Minister of Justice No. 13/T/4687 of 10 September 1433 AH)

Article 1

The following words and expressions, wherever they occur in the law, shall have the meanings given opposite to each of them unless otherwise required by the context.

Law: This Execution Law.

Executive Regulations: The executive regulations of the present law.

Minister: Minister of Justice.

Execution Judge: Chief of the execution department and judges, execution department judge and the judge of the court who undertakes the duties of the execution judge, as the case may be.

Chief: Chief of the execution department, judge of the execution department or judge of the court who undertakes the duties of the execution judge, as the case may be.

Execution Officer: The person assigned to carry out execution procedures in accordance with the provisions of the law.

Judicial Papers Informant: The court usher, the requestor of execution or the person or firm licensed by the Ministry of Justice to report announcements, appointments, orders and judicial documents required for execution.

Judicial Sale Agent: The person licensed by the Ministry of Justice to sell the assets of the debtor to repay the debt to the creditor.

Decisions: Procedures and orders taken by the execution judge except his judgments on disputes.

Execution Disputes: Claims that may arise as a result of execution and that relate to the fulfillment of validity conditions which the execution litigation parties or others may file.

1095 Source: http://www.alnogaithan.com/en/wp-content/uploads/downloads/2014/04/Execution-Law.pdf

Part One

Chapter One – Authorities of the Execution Judge

Article 2

With the exception of the judgments and decisions issued on administrative and criminal cases, the execution judge shall have the authority of forcible execution and supervision assisted by the sufficient number of execution officers pursuant to the provisions of the Law of Procedure before Sharee'ah Courts unless otherwise provided for in the present law.

Article 3

The execution judge shall have the authority to decide on execution disputes whatever their value is in accordance with the provisions of the summary court. He shall also have the authority to take decisions and issue orders related to execution. He may order seeking the help of police and concerned force, order embargo on travel and lifting the same, order detainment and release, order disclosure of assets and consider claims of insolvency.

Article 4

The territorial jurisdiction of the execution judge, as the case may be, shall be as follows:

1. In the circle of the court, which issued the execution document,
2. In the territory of the authority where the writ was created,
3. In the domicile of the debtor, and
4. In the place of the real estates or moveable property of the debtor, the executive regulations determine the provisions necessary for this article.

Article 5

In case of multiple execution departments, the execution judge, who has undertaken the first execution procedure, may supervise execution and distribute its result. He may also deputize the execution judge at another execution department to act on the debtor's property. The executive regulations determine the provisions necessary for the same.

Article 6

All decisions taken by the execution judge shall be final. All his judgments on execution disputes and claims of insolvency may be challenged by way of appeal and the judgment issued by the court of appeal shall be final.

Article 7

If any aggression, resistance or attempt to hinder execution, the execution judge shall take all precautionary measures and may order concerned authorities to provide necessary assistance.

Execution officers may not break doors or locks by force to effect execution unless they seek the permission of the execution judge. Minutes shall be signed in this respect.

Chapter Two – Execution Document

Article 8

1) The execution department in every general court shall undertake execution and its procedures. More than one department may be constituted when needed.

2) The single judge in the general court shall undertake execution and its procedures.

3) Foreign judgments, orders and writes shall be executed by one judge or more, as needed. The Supreme Judicial Council may, when necessary, create special courts for execution.

Article 9

No forcible execution may be carried out except by an execution document of a right of a specified amount at the time of payment. Execution documents are:

1. Judgments, decisions and orders issued by courts,
2. Awards of arbitrators initialed by orders of execution in accordance with the law of arbitration,
3. Reconciliation minutes issued by authorized departments or approved by courts,
4. Commercial papers,
5. Authenticated contracts and writs,
6. Judgments, court orders, awards of arbitrators and authenticated writs issued in a foreign country,
7. Ordinary papers the contents of which are admitted in whole or in part, and
8. Contracts and other papers, which have the power of the execution document under the law.

Article 10

Judgments may not be forcibly executed while it is permitted to challenge them unless they are covered by summary execution or such summary execution is prescribed by relevant laws.

Article 11

Notwithstanding the provisions of treaties and conventions, the execution judge may not enforce any court judgments and orders passed in any foreign country except in cases of equal treatment and after verifying the following:

1. That the Saudi courts are not competent to hear the case in respect of which the court judgment or order was passed and that the foreign courts which passed it are competent in accordance with the international rules of jurisdiction set down in the laws thereof.

2. That the litigants to the case in respect of which the judgment was issued were duly summoned, properly represented and enabled to defend themselves.

3. That the court judgment or order has become final in accordance with the law of the court that passed it.

4. That the court judgment is in no way inconsistent with any judgment or order previously passed by the Saudi courts.

5. That the judgment does not provide for anything which constitutes a breach of Saudi public order or ethics.

Article 12

The provisions of the preceding Article shall be applicable to the awards issued by arbitrators in any foreign country.

Article 13

Official instruments enforced in any foreign country may be ordered to be enforced in Saudi Arabia on the same conditions as are laid down in the law of that country for enforcing official instruments executed in Saudi Arabia, on the basis of equal treatment.

Article 14

Judgments, court orders, awards of arbitrators and authenticated instruments issued in a foreign country shall be submitted to the judge of the execution court responsible for the enforcement of foreign judgments to verify that they meet the conditions of execution and stamp them with the seal of execution.

Article 15

1) If the debtor admits the right in an ordinary paper, the execution judge may document his declaration and the said paper is deemed an execution document.

2) If the debtor denies all or some of the right, the execution judge may order the debtor to sign a declaration on the reason of objection with the consequence the penalty provided for in this law. The paper is considered an execution document unless objected to. The creditor may file his claim before the court having jurisdiction.

Chapter Three – Disclosure of Property

Article 16

The execution judge may order disclosure of the debtor's property as sufficient to repay the execution document and may also order disclosure and distress after informing the debtor of the execution order. Nevertheless, if it appears to the execution judge that the debtor procrastinates based on his credit record or proofs, he may order disclosure and distress of the debtor's property before informing him of the execution order.

Article 17

All pertinent authorities or those supervising registration of property, the debtor's debtor, the debtor's accountant and his staff shall disclose the assets of the debtor upon the order of the execution judge within a period not exceeding ten days from the date of informing these parties.

Article 18

Property registration authorities or those supervising or managing them shall, as the case may be, shall carry out the following:

1. Create special departments to handle various orders of the execution court,
2. Prepare databases of the property ownership, be they real estate, financial, commercial, intellectual or any other property.
3. Agree to maintain the confidentiality of data and information which the staff have reviewed in connection with their work and shall not disclose for any reason whatsoever.
4. Develop a technological mechanism to ensure prevention of access to data except by permission.
5. Notwithstanding the provisions of the laws, these departments shall inform owners of property with the disclosed data after a period specified by the executive regulations.

Article 19

Disclosure of property shall be exchanged with other states upon the order of the execution judge on the basis of equal treatment. This disclosure shall exclude the things provided for in the laws, the resolutions of the Council of Ministers and those affecting the national security of the Kingdom.

Chapter Four – Property Subject to Execution

Article 20

All debtor's property is deemed as surety for his debts. Seizing of the debtor's property entails that no action he may take on his seized property shall not have any effect.

Article 21

No seizing or execution may be made against the following:

1. Property owned by the state,
2. The house of the debtor in which he dwells with his legally sponsored dependants, if it is appropriate and on condition that the house has not been given as a security to the creditor.
3. The means of transportation used by the debtor and his legal dependants. The execution judge determines how appropriate such means is unless such means is given as a security to the creditor.
4. Salaries and wages except the following:

a. One half the total salary or wage shall be allocated to meeting the maintenance debt;

b. One third the total wage or salary shall be allocated to meeting the other debts.

Where there is lapping, one half of the total salary or wage shall be allocated to meeting the obligations of maintenance debt and third the other half to other debts.

In case of multiple debts, the third of the half shall be divided among creditors in the manner prescribed by the Sharee'ah and the law.

5. The tools needed by the debtor to practise his profession or craft by himself.

6. Personal requirements of the debtor; the judge shall determine their appropriateness.

Article 22

1) The distrainee, whatever distrainment procedures are, may deposit an amount of money equal to the debt in the court's account dedicated for the repayment of the debt. The said deposit shall result in removing distress from the distrained property and transferring it to the deposited amount.

2) No seizing may be placed on the debtor's property except as equal to the amount of the claimed debt unless the distrained property is divisible.

3) The execution judge shall allocate the executable property to realize quick repayment.

Part Two Precautionary Attachment

Article 23

The authority having the jurisdiction under the law to consider the dispute has the authority to place precautionary attachment in accordance with the provisions of the summary court.

Article 24

The creditor may request placing the precautionary attachment on movables subject to debt if the debtor has no fixed residence place in the Kingdom or if the creditor fears, for acceptable reasons, disappearance or trafficking of the debtor's property.

Article 25

The lessor may request placing precautionary attachment on movables or fruits in the leased property as a security for the payment of the accrued rent.

Article 26

The one who claims ownership of the moveable property may request placement of precautionary attachment with the one it is in his custody whenever there is clear evidence supporting his claim.

Article 27

The creditor of a debt fixed at the time of repayment, even if he has no executable judgment, may request placement of precautionary attachment on the debts the debtor has with others, even if they are deferred or conditional and on moveable property or estates in the hands of others. The person in whose custody the distrained property is shall within ten days from notification of the distrainment disclose the debts, estates and property he has in his liability. He shall, within ten days from the date of notification of the judgment on the validity of distrainment, deposit in the court's account the debts he disclosed or the part of it sufficient to repay the debt.

Article 28

The precautionary attachment may not be placed in the previous instances except for the repayment of a visibly existing and on the spot right.

Article 29

The precautionary attachment may not be placed in the cases provided for in the preceding articles except upon an order by the court or the authority having jurisdiction to consider the dispute under whose jurisdiction the place of the residence of person whose property is distrained. The court or the authority having jurisdiction, prior to issuing its order, may conduct necessary investigation if the documents supporting the distress request are not sufficient.

Article 30

If the claim of right is filed before the court or the authority having jurisdiction, the said court or authority shall have the authority to issue the order of placing precautionary attachment.

Article 31

The distrainee and the person the property distrained with shall be given notice of the order of attachment concerned within maximum 10 days from the date of placing it; otherwise the attachment shall be deemed null and void. The creditor shall within the above referenced 10 days period submit before the court or the concerned authority the claim of the right and valid attachment; otherwise, the attachment shall be deemed null and void.

Article 32

The distrainer shall submit to the court or the authority having jurisdiction an authenticated written declaration from a financially capable guarantor or a guarantee of all the rights of the distrainee and the harm that he may incur if it appears that the distrainer has no right to make such a request.

Article 33

The precautionary attachment placed on movables and property of the debtor with others shall be governed by the procedures related to the execution attachment except as related to sale.

Part Three: Execution Procedures

Chapter One – Execution Attachment

Article 34

1) Execution is carried out upon a request submitted by the requestor of execution to the execution judge on the form specified by the executive regulations.

2) a) The execution judge shall check that the execution form is present in the execution document as stated under paragraphs 1, 2 and 3 of article 9 hereof.

b) With the exception of the provisions of 2.a., the execution judge shall check that the execution documents under paragraphs 4. 5. 6, 7 and 8 of article 9 meet the legal conditions and stamps them with a seal containing the phrase "a document for execution" coupled with the name and signature of the execution judge and the court.

3) The execution judge shall immediately issue an order of execution to the debtor accompanied by a copy of the execution document stamped as a true copy with the court's seal. The debtor shall be notified in accordance with the provisions of notifications specified by the executive regulations. If it is not possible to notify the debtor within twenty days from the date of issue of the execution order, the execution judge shall immediately issue the notification in the widest published newspapers in the area of the court head office and the announcement expenses shall be received from the debtor at the time of the repayment of the right.

4) Coordination shall be carried out between the Ministry of Justice and concerned authorities with regard to the disclosure of the addresses of the persons who do not have known residence places.

Article 35

1) The execution attachment is placed on movables by moving to the place of the property by the execution officer or by issuing a written order to the authority having jurisdiction to register it, as the case may be, and the execution officer shall prepare the minutes of attachment upon the order of the judge and initial the property register with the contents of the minutes.

2) If the placement of attachment could not be completed within one day, it may be completed on the next days, even if they were official holidays.

3) The property may not be moved from the place where it is distrained except upon an order from the execution judge.

Article 36

1) The execution judge shall delegate with the execution officer an approved assessor or more specialized in the assessment of the property under execution in order to assess its value and document such assessment in the attachment minutes under his signature. With regard to the little property as specified in the executive regulations, the execution

judge shall assign the execution officer to assess unless the creditor and debtor agree to their value.

2) If the assessment of the moveable property requires entering the real estate, the assessor and the execution officer may enter it in the presence of police. The execution judge may order the use of force if the debtor refuses the execution or if he is absent.

Article 37

The execution officer shall deposit cash, jewellery, precious metals, antiquities and other precious items shall be deposited in the court's account or safe, as the case may be.

Article 38

If necessary, the execution officer shall secure the distrained property and place locks and the court's seal and document the same in the minutes.

Article 39

Fruits and crops shall be distrained before they are ripe and the execution officer shall fix a board at the entrance of the farm on which he shall fix the distrainment minutes to be sold when they are ripe.

Article 40

The attachment minutes shall be prepared in accordance with the provisions of the executive regulations. The minutes shall include the following information:

1. The identity of the distrainer, the distrainee and the distrained with,
2. The execution document, the execution order number, date and place of issue,
3. The distrained property, its description, amount, weight, type, number and qualities by which its value differ, ownership document and data of registration, as the case may be,
4. Type, number, date of issue and place of issue of the deed of ownership as well as location, borders, lengths and area of the real estate,
5. Value of the distrained property as assessed by the assessor,
6. Place of distrainment,
7. Name of the guard assigned to secure and guard it, and
8. Name of the sale agent as well as time, date and place of sale.

The attachment minutes shall include the signature of the execution officer and the debtor, if present, and the guard as well as any person to whom an action is ascribed in the minutes in accordance with the provisions specified in the executive regulations.

Article 41

The minutes of attachment shall be announced at the location where the execution data are published within five days from the date of distrainment; which announcement is deemed a notification to all those concerned with the distrained property. Nevertheless, the execution officer shall notify the distrainee and all those whom the execution judge find to have a kind right on the distrained property if these have addresses known to the execution judge.

Article 42

The execution judge may ask the distrainee to guard the distrained property under his control provided that he provides a guarantee or a financially capable surety that he will not act on the distrained property in any manner that may harm the creditor. If the distrainee refuses to guard the property or if it is not possible to provide a guarantee or a surety, the judge shall appoint a licensed guard.

Article 43

In all cases, the distrained property shall be delivered to the guard with his signature to the same under the distress minutes. The guard may not use or lend the distrained property or cause to be damaged. The execution judge may permit the guard to manage the distrained property if interest dictates the same. He shall keep the profit distrained with the principal property. If the guard is the owner of the distrained property, the execution judge may permit him to use it.

Article 44

The guard other than the owner of the distrained property may receive an equitable wage for guarding and managing the property to be determined under a decision issued by the execution judge and to be calculated as part of the execution expenses.

Article 45

The execution distress is levied on the real estate under distress minutes. The authority which issued the real estate ownership document shall be provided with a copy of the minutes to enter the same in the document record.

Article 46

If the debtor fails to execute or disclose a property sufficient to repay the debt within five days from the date of notification of the execution order or from the date of publishing in a newspaper, if it is not possible to notify him, he is deemed procrastinating and the execution judge shall immediately order the following:

1. Ban the debtor from travel;
2. Suspend issuing deeds of powers of attorney either directly or indirectly with regard to properties and anything that revert to them;
3. Disclose the existing property of the debtor and future revenues in the amount sufficient to repay the execution document, seize the same and execute on them in accordance with the provisions of the present law;
4. Disclose the licences and logs of the commercial and professional activities of the debtor; and

5. Notify a licensed party to record all credit information on the incident of failure of execution;

In addition to the above, as the case may be, the execution judge may take the following actions:

a. Ban governmental authorities from dealing with the debtor, seize his financial dues with them and notify the execution judge with the same;

b. Ban financial firms from dealing with him in any capacity whatsoever;

c. Order disclosure of the property of the debtor's spouse, children and those proofs indicate that his property has been moved to them or treated him with favouritism. If it is suspected that there is evidence or proofs of concealment of property, the request is referred to the subject judge to decide on; and

d. Imprison the debtor in accordance with the provisions of the present law.

Article 47

The execution judge may question the debtor, his account and staff or those who deal with him suspected to have treated him with favouritism and the debtor's debtor in order to track down his property. He may also assign an expert to track down the debtor's property.

Article 48

The original execution document shall be noted with the actual executed parts and the documents data shall be entered in the execution documents with the court.

Chapter Two – Sale of Distrained Property

Article 49

Only already qualified persons shall enter the auction hall. Persons participating in the auction are qualified under certain arrangements taken by the Ministry of Justice in agreement with the Saudi Arabian Monetary Agency. Financial capability of the participants in the auction and the way of deduction and payment of amounts shall be organized immediately after awarding the auction in accordance with the provisions stated in the executive regulations.

Article 50

1) The auction shall be announced within a period not more than thirty days or less than fifteen days before the day appointed for the auction at the site of the execution statement by posting the announcement on the door of the place where the distrained property exists stating the day, hour and place of sale as well as the type and brief description of the property. The execution judge may order publishing the announcement in one daily newspaper or more and the expenses to be deducted from the proceeds of sale.

2) The auction shall start in the presence of the execution officer. The agent shall declare the opening amount of the auction on the distrained property. No sale may be completed at an amount less than the assessed amount. If no offer is provided by any

purchaser, the execution officer shall appoint another date for the auction within a period not exceeding two days. The distrained property shall be sold at the amount the auction ends with unless than property is a real estate, metals, jewellery or the like, in which case the execution judge shall order re-assessment and opens the auction at the amount of the last assessment and such property is sold at the amount the auction ends with.

The person awarded the auction shall pay the price immediately as specified in the executive regulations.

3) If the person awarded the auction fails to pay the price on the appointed time, a further auction shall be held at its own risk in accordance with the provisions of paragraphs 1 and 2 hereinabove. The defaulting bidder shall be liable for settlement of any deficit in the price of the property and the auction expenses and any extra amount shall be returned to him.

Article 51

It is prohibited to influence the prices of the auction by any arrangement resulting in the same. The execution judge shall request the General Prosecutor to conduct necessary investigation if any connivance is suspected.

Article 52

The execution officer stops the sale of the remaining property of the debtor if the proceeds of the sold property are sufficient to repay the debt for which the distrainment is placed in addition to the expenses or execution of if the distrainee provides the amount payable from him.

Article 53

1) The execution officer shall prepare a statement containing the procedures taken, the name of the person awarded the auction and the price.

2) The execution judge shall issue a decision of awarding the auction to the person to whom it is awarded after collecting the amount for the account of the execution court including a summary of the distrainment and sale statements. The decision shall also include delivery of the sold property to the purchaser. The sale decision shall be considered an execution document.

Article 54

The auction award decision shall purify the real estate from any dues towards the person awarded the auction.

Article 55

Financial securities subject to the law of the capital market shall be sold through a person licensed by the capital market in the field of financial brokerage. An agreement shall be concluded between the Ministry of Justice and capital market authority on establishing necessary measures for the sale of these securities in a manner that realizes fair price and execution guarantees.

Article 56

1) Banking accounts shall be opened in the name of the court where the amounts of execution are deposited and withdrawn. The executive regulations shall determine the provisions of deposit, withdrawal and management of these accounts.

2) Precious metals, jewelry and the like shall be deposited in the safe of the bank with which the accounts of the execution court are opened.

The executive regulations shall regulate the provisions and procedures of facilitating participation of banks in the execution activities after the minister and governor of the Saudi Arabian Monetary Agency agree to the same.

Chapter Three – Distribution of Execution Proceeds

Article 57

The execution proceeds shall be distributed upon an order by the execution judge to the distraining creditors and those considered party to the procedures.

Article 58

If the proceeds of sale are insufficient to repay the rights of all concerned parties (distraining creditors and persons considered party to the procedures) and the said parties agree to an amicable settlement on the distribution of the proceeds, the execution judge shall enter the agreement in a statement to be signed the execution officer, the concerned parties and the judge. The said statement shall have the power of an execution document towards them.

Article 59

If the proceeds of sale are insufficient and if the concerned parties fail to agree to an amicable settlement on the distribution of the proceeds, the execution judge shall enter the objection in a statement signed by the execution judge, the execution officer and the concerned parties. The execution judge shall issue a judgment containing the distribution of the proceeds among creditors in accordance with the Sharee'ah and legal rules.

Chapter Four – Distress on Debtor's Property with Others

Article 60

1) Amounts of money due to the debtor shall be distrained in the financial institution specified by the executive regulations through the supervisory authority in accordance with the following rules:

a) Attachment on the credit current accounts shall be placed by the financial institution by preventing the holder of the account from withdrawing from his credit balance and any further deposits added to it. The financial institution, upon the approval of the execution judge, may deduct debt debit obligations occurring to the account prior to the attachment on the balance.

b) Attachment on investment accounts shall be placed by the financial institution by preventing the holder of the account from withdrawing from the credit cash balance and any deposits added to it. If the credit cash balance is dedicated to pay expenses due from investment centres or operations at the time of maturity or those created before notifying the financial institution of the attachment, these shall not be subject to the attachment procedures until the closure of all these centres.

c) The attachment levied on the term deposits shall be done by preventing the debtor from withdrawing them, continuing development thereof in the legal way if the debtor wishes to do so and informing the execution judge of their nature, dates of maturity and consequences of breaking them.

d) The attachment levied on the assets of trust safes shall be done by the execution officer's moving to the financial institution where the safes are opened and their contents are counted under a statement to be signed by the execution officer, the staff of the financial institution and the debtor, if it is possible to bring him, and the other keys of the safes held by the debtor shall be delivered to the execution court.

e) The attachment shall be levied on insurance compensation by noting the contents of the executive document on the debtor's rights record and any compensation due or will become due to the debtor shall be delivered to the execution court account.

2) The execution judge shall be informed with the result of attachment within three working days from the date of receiving the attachment order.

3) The execution judge shall order the authority supervising the financial institution to transfer to the court's account the credit cash balance due to the debtor stated in items a, b, c, d and e of paragraph 1 of this article in the amount sufficient to repay the debt.

Article 61

1) Shares owned in companies and unlisted shares shall be distrained through the Ministry of Commerce and Industry by noting the distrainment on the ownership record and noting the content of the execution document on the company's record.

2) Financial securities shall be distrained through the Capital Market Authority and the execution judge shall be informed of the result of distrainment within three working days from the date of receiving the distrainment order in accordance with the following rules:

a) Financial securities shall be distrained by preventing the debtor from disposing with them, and

b) Standing centres of financial securities shall be distrained by preventing the debtor from disposing with the amounts due to him after closing them.

Article 62

Commercial papers shall be distrained in accordance with the following rules:

1) If the cheque is under the hand of the beneficiary debtor, the execution officer shall prepare the statement of distrainment and the amount of the cheque or the part available of it shall be collected and deposited in the court's account.

2) The amount of the endorsed cheque shall be distrained after notifying the debtor of the execution order by the withdrawee bank when the person for whom the cheque is endorsed appears to collect the amount of the cheque and deposited in the court's account.

3) If no corresponding amount is available for repayment in place of the cheque subject of distrainment, the execution judge shall authorize the debtor to replace the debtor in claiming the amount of the cheque from the withdrawer or the endorser and depositing the same in the court's account. In case the withdrawer or endorser object to pay, he shall file an objection lawsuit before the court having jurisdiction within ten days from the date of requesting him to pay and notify the execution judge of the procedures of considering the case and the consequences. If the said period elapses without submitting an objection claim, he shall pay the amount of the cheque to the court.

4) Bills of exchange and promissory notes held by the debtor shall be distrained by preparing the statement by the execution officer and depositing the value of the commercial paper in the court's account. If it is deferred, collection shall be deferred to the time of maturity.

5) If the withdrawer or the endorser of the promissory note or bill of exchange objects to the right of the beneficiary debtor, he shall file an objection lawsuit in accordance with the provisions of article 3 of this article.

Article 63

Amounts of money to be due to the debtor in the future shall be distrained under the hand of the steward by paying these amounts. The execution officer, the obliged party and the party entitled to such amounts shall prepare a statement of all amounts and the date of maturity. The said amounts shall be deposited in the court's account, whether they are cash, movables or real estate as per the rules provided for in this law for each type of them.

Article 64

Intellectual property shall be distrained through the authority concerned with the registration of intellectual property by noting the record with the content of the execution document. The execution judge shall be informed of the result of distrainment within three working days from the date of receiving the distrainment order.

Article 65

The creditor may place distrainment under his hand on the amounts due from him to his debtor. Distrainment shall be done by a notification to the debtor containing the data that should be mentioned in the paper of distrainment notification. In the cases of distrainment is levied upon an order from the execution judge, the distrainer shall, within the ten days following notification of distrainment to the debtor, file before the court having jurisdiction a lawsuit for the establishment of the right and validity of distrainment; otherwise, the distrainment shall be considered null and void.

Article 66

If the person distrained with has more than one branch, notification of the distrainment to any branch shall be effective vis-à-vis the distrainee.

Article 67

If the person distrained with disposes with the distrained property contrary to the order of the execution judge, the execution judge shall, upon the request of the distrainer, conduct execution on the property of the person distrained with as equal to the amount of the property.

Part Four

Chapter One – Direct Execution

Article 68

If the subject of execution is an action or inaction and the debtor fails to meet his obligation within five days from the date of requesting him to do so in accordance with the provisions of the present law, the execution judge shall order use of the concerned force (police) to take necessary actions of execution unless it is required to carry out the execution by the debtor himself.

Article 69

If it is not possible to carry out the execution by the use of the concerned force or if execution requires the debtor to carry it himself and fails to do so, the execution judge may issue a judgment of a financial fine not more than ten thousand Saudi Riyals daily to be deposited in the court's account for every day the debtor delays execution. The execution judge has the right to cancel the fine of part of it if the debtor proceeds to execution.

Article 70

If it is not possible to carry out the execution by the use of the concerned force or if a financial fine is imposed against the debtor and he fails to execute within the period specified by the execution judge, he may issue an order to imprison the debtor to force him to execute.

Article 71

Direct execution provisions govern the official representative of the private corporate person or the one causing impediment of execution among the employees of the private corporate person.

Article 72

Evacuation of a property shall be executed by the execution officer moving to the location of the property on the day following the lapse of five days from the date of notification of the execution order. The execution officer shall deliver the real estate to the executor and may use force to enter the property if so required.

If the one in whose custody the property is does not appear or objects to delivering the movables, these movables shall be delivered to the judicial steward and the execution judge shall order selling them in an auction after two months unless the custodian receives them and the amount shall be deposited in the court's account.

If the executor is a creditor of the custodian, the provisions of this law shall be applied against the movables of the debtor custodian.

Chapter Two – Execution on Matters of Personal Status

Article 73

Decisions and judgments issued on matters of personal status shall be executed in the manners prescribed in the present law if this requires attachment on and sale of property. If execution states payment of amounts of money on a regular basis, execution shall be carried out through the arrangement specified by the executive regulations.

Article 74

The judgments on guarding and protecting minors, separation between husbands and wives and similar matters of personal status shall be executed by force even if this leads to seeking the help of the concerned force (police) and entry of houses. The judgment shall be re- executed whenever necessary.

Article 75

A judgment issued against the wife to return to the marital house by force shall not be executed.

Article 76

The execution judge shall determine the way of executing the judgment issued on visiting the minor unless the judgment provides for it. Execution shall be carried out by delivering the minor at a prepared place suitable for this type of execution. The Ministry of Justice shall specify such places in the executive regulations, provided that they are not at police stations and the like.

Part Five

Chapter One – Insolvency

Article 77

If the debtor fails to repay the debt on the pretext of insolvency, the execution judge shall consider the establishment of insolvency after completing all procedures of disclosure of property, questioning and tracking in accordance with the provisions of the present law and after an announcement containing the reasons of application of insolvency to be published in a one daily newspaper or more in the area of the debtor.

Article 78

1) If the debtor claims insolvency but the execution judge finds proofs that he is concealing his property, the execution judge shall, upon a judgment he issues, check his condition by imprisoning him for a period not exceeding five years taking into consideration the amount of the debt. The judgment shall be checked by the court of appeal.

2) The execution judge shall summon the debtor during the period of his imprisonment mentioned under paragraph 1 hereof and question him in order to reveal his condition on intervals not exceeding three months as determined by the executive regulations.

3) The executive regulations shall determine the amount of the property of the debtor as per the type of debts and conditions of debtors in coordination with the Ministry of Interior and Minister of Finance.

Article 79

If the debt arises from an accidental criminal incident and the debtor claims insolvency, the execution judge shall establish his insolvency after hearing his evidence. If he has no evidence, the judge shall order him to take the oath confirming insolvency and establish his insolvency.

Article 80

If the debtor claims insolvency and the execution judge finds out that the said insolvency claim is a treacherous one or if the debtor fails to repay the debt as a result of transgression of negligence on his part, the judge shall document the said incident and complete execution procedures by ordering detainment of the accused and referring the accusation file within a period not exceeding seven days to the General Prosecutor to file the lawsuit. Concerned parties may submit a report to the General Prosecutor requesting filing the lawsuit. The subject judge shall consider the case and if the debtor is convicted, the penalty provided for herein shall be applied against him.

Article 81

1) The execution judge shall issue his order to authorities in charge of assets provided for in this law to seize the property that the insolvent debtor may receive in the future.

2) The judge shall notify a licensed firm to register the credit information of the insolvency incident.

3) The creditor may submit the execution document itself in the future to the execution judge if the any property appears for insolvent debtor.

Article 82

In declaring his bankruptcy, the merchant shall be subject to the rules of bankruptcy prescribed by the law.

Chapter Two – Execution Imprisonment

Article 83

Pursuant to the provisions of the present law, the execution judge shall issue a judgment on imprisoning the debtor if it is proved that he refuses to execute. The said imprisonment shall continue until the time of execution.

Article 84

No execution imprisonment may be applied against the debtor in the following cases:

1. If the debtor has apparent property sufficient to repay the right due from him which can distrained and execution levied on it;
2. If the debtor submits a bank guarantee, a financially capable surety or kind guarantee equal to the amount of the debt;
3. If he proves to be insolvent in accordance with the provisions of this law;
4. If it is one of the assets of the creditor unless the debt is a prescribed legal support money;
5. If it is proved by a certificate from the concerned medical board that he has an illness with which he cannot withstand imprisonment; or
6. If the debtor is a pregnant woman or if she has a child not more than 2 years old.

Article 86

The provisions of execution imprisonment shall apply to the legal representative of the private corporate person or any of his employees causing hampering execution.

Chapter Three – Penalties

Article 87

Criminal courts shall have the jurisdiction to consider imposing the penalties provided for in this law and forwarding the same to the General Prosecutor upon a referral issued by the execution judge or upon a notification from the harmed person.

Article 88

1) A penalty of imprisonment for a period not exceeding seven years shall be applied against any debtor who commits any of the following crimes:

a) Refusing to execute the final judgment issued against him or proofing to have concealed, trafficked or refused to disclose his property;

b) Deliberately impeding execution by filing a claim with the intention of impeding execution;

c) Resisting execution by threatening or attacking himself or through others an employee or a licensee carrying out execution or purports any of the above against the executor or any other illegal act intended to resist execution; or

d) Lying in his declarations before the court or procedures or producing untrue and incorrect data and information.

2) The penalty provided for under paragraph 1 hereof shall be applied against any person who help the debtor or assist him in any of the crime provided for in the paragraphs 1. a, b, c and d hereof.

Article 89

The public servant and the like shall be penalized by imprisonment for a period not more than seven years if he impedes or hinders execution. This shall be considered as a dishonesty crime.

Article 90

A penalty of imprisonment for a period not exceeding fifteen years shall be applied against every debtor proves to have become a debtor as a result of a fraud act or have wasted his property if this property is plenty even if he is proved insolvent in both cases. These acts are major crimes that cause detainment.

Article 91

A penalty of imprisonment for a period not exceeding three years shall be applied against:

1. Any person familiar with data related to the assets of the debtor if he leaks such data and the same penalty shall be applied against any person whom gets access to such data without a judicial order;
2. The judicial receiver or steward if either one fails to carry out his duties by way of negligence, aggression, evading to deliver or receive the property; and
3. The assessor, sale agent and their employees or a participant in the auction if any of them deliberately influences the price or misleads others about the fairness of prices.

Article 92

A penalty of imprisonment for not more than three months shall be applied against any parent or others who refuse to execute a judgment issued on guardianship, custody or visit or who resist or impede execution.

General Provisions

Article 93

An agency having the authority of execution shall be created within the Ministry of Justice to be concerned with administrative and financial affairs and undertakes the following:

1. Licensing providers of execution services including:
    a. Judicial paper reporter,
    b. Judicial sale agent,
    c. Judicial receiver,
    d. Judicial steward,
    e. Specialized companies which undertake supervision of the process of receiving moveable property by the lessor in accordance with specific rules laid down by the Ministry of Justice in collaboration with the Ministry of Interior, and

f. Providers of execution services from the private sector following the approval of the Council of Ministers to assign this service to this sector.

The executive regulations shall determine the rules of licensing and qualification including the required financial guarantee, rules of procedures and supervision thereof along with the policies of Appendix C determining of prices that they may receive and the fines that may be imposed against them.

2. Using one company or more to carry all or some execution activities under the supervision of the execution court.
3. Preparing bylaws for the training of staff in the field of execution.
4. Publishing execution data statements.
5. Exchanging disclosure of assets with other countries.

Article 94

The implementation of the present law shall not be in prejudice with the treaties and conventions that the Kingdom has entered with countries and international bodies and organizations.

Article 95

Any person harmed by the procrastination of execution procedures may file a claim against the person responsible for the same before the execution judge requesting compensation for the harm he may have incurred as a result.

Article 96

This law shall supersede articles from 96 thru 232 of the Law of Procedure before Sharee'ah Courts issued by Royal Decree No. M/21 dated 20.5.1421 AH and paragraph g of article 13 of the Law of the Board of Grievances No. M/78 dated 19.9.1428 AH and all other contradicting provisions.

Article 97

The Minister shall issue the executive regulations of the present law within one hundred and eighty days from the date of promulgation of this law, which shall be applied after this law comes into effect.

Article 98

This law shall come into effect after one hundred and eighty days from the date of publishing in the official gazette.

Appendix D

UNCITRAL Model Law on International Commcerial Arbitration

(As adopted by the United Nations Commission on International Trade Law on 21 June 1985, and as amended by the United Nations Commission on International Trade Law on 7 July 2006)

CHAPTER I. GENERAL PROVISIONS

Article 1. Scope of Application

(1) This Law applies to international commercial arbitration, subject to any agreement in force between this State and any other State or States.

(2) The provisions of this Law, except articles 8, 9, 17 H, 17 I, 17 J, 35and 36, apply only if the place of arbitration is in the territory of this State.

(3) An arbitration is international if:

(a) the parties to an arbitration agreement have, at the time of the conclusion of that agreement, their places of business in different States; or

(b) one of the following places is situated outside the State in which the parties have their places of business:

   (i) the place of arbitration if determined in, or pursuant to, the arbitration agreement;

   (ii) any place where a substantial part of the obligations of the commercial relationship is to be performed or the place with which the subject-matter of the dispute is most closely connected; or

(c) the parties have expressly agreed that the subject matter of the arbitration agreement relates to more than one country.

(4) For the purposes of paragraph (3) of this article:

(a) if a party has more than one place of business, the place of business is that which has the closest relationship to the arbitration agreement;

(b) if a party does not have a place of business, reference is to be made to his habitual residence.

(5) This Law shall not affect any other law of this State by virtue of which certain disputes may not be submitted to arbitration or may be submitted to arbitration only according to provisions other than those of this Law.

Article 2. Definitions and Rules of Interpretation

For the purposes of this Law:

(a) "arbitration" means any arbitration whether or not administered by a permanent arbitral institution;

(b) "arbitral tribunal" means a sole arbitrator or a panel of arbitrators;

(c) "court" means a body or organ of the judicial system of a State;

(d) where a provision of this Law, except article 28, leaves the parties free to determine a certain issue, such freedom includes the right of the parties to authorize a third party, including an institution, to make that determination;

(e) where a provision of this Law refers to the fact that the parties have agreed or that they may agree or in any other way refers to an agreement of the parties, such agreement includes any arbitration rules referred to in that agreement;

(f) where a provision of this Law, other than in articles 25(a) and 32(2) (a), refers to a claim, it also applies to a counter-claim, and where it refers to a defence, it also applies to a defence to such counter-claim.

Article 2 A. International Origin and General Principles

(1) In the interpretation of this Law, regard is to be had to its international origin and to the need to promote uniformity in its application and the observance of good faith.

(2) Questions concerning matters governed by this Law which are not expressly settled in it are to be settled in conformity with the general principles on which this Law is based.

Article 3. Receipt of Written Communications

(1) Unless otherwise agreed by the parties:

(a) any written communication is deemed to have been received if it is delivered to the addressee personally or if it is delivered at his place of business, habitual residence or mailing address; if none of these can be found after making a reasonable inquiry, a written communication is deemed to have been received if it is sent to the addressee's last-known place of business, habitual residence or mailing address by registered letter or any other means which provides a record of the attempt to deliver it;

(b) the communication is deemed to have been received on the day it is so delivered.

(2) The provisions of this article do not apply to communications in court proceedings.

Article 4. Waiver of Right to Object

A party who knows that any provision of this Law from which the parties may derogate or any requirement under the arbitration agreement has not been complied with and yet proceeds with the arbitration without stating his objection to such non-compliance without undue delay or, if a time-limit is provided therefore, within such period of time, shall be deemed to have waived his right to object.

Article 5. Extent of Court Intervention

In matters governed by this Law, no court shall intervene except where so provided in this Law.

Article 6. Court or Other Authority for Certain Functions of Arbitration Assistance and Supervision

The functions referred to in articles 11(3), 11(4), 13(3), 14, 16(3) and 34(2) shall be performed by ... [Each State enacting this model law specifies the court, courts or, where referred to therein, other authority competent to perform these functions.]

CHAPTER II. ARBITRATION AGREEMENT

Option I

Article 7. Definition and Form of Arbitration Agreement

(1) "Arbitration agreement" is an agreement by the parties to submit to arbitration all or certain disputes which have arisen or which may arise between them in respect of a defined legal relationship, whether contractual or not. An arbitration agreement may be in the form of an arbitration clause in a contract or in the form of a separate agreement.

(2) The arbitration agreement shall be in writing.

(3) An arbitration agreement is in writing if its content is recorded in any form, whether or not the arbitration agreement or contract has been concluded orally, by conduct, or by other means.

(4) The requirement that an arbitration agreement be in writing is met by an electronic communication if the information contained therein is accessible so as to be useable for subsequent reference; "electronic communication" means any communication that the parties make by means of data messages; "data message" means information generated, sent, received or stored by electronic, magnetic, optical or similar means, including, but not limited to, electronic data interchange (EDI), electronic mail, telegram, telex or telecopy.

(5) Furthermore, an arbitration agreement is in writing if it is contained in an exchange of statements of claim and defence in which the existence of an agreement is alleged by one party and not denied by the other.

(6) The reference in a contract to any document containing an arbitration clause constitutes an arbitration agreement in writing, provided that the reference is such as to make that clause part of the contract.

Option II

Article 7. Definition of Arbitration Agreement

"Arbitration agreement" is an agreement by the parties to submit to arbitration all or certain disputes which have arisen or which may arise between them in respect of a defined legal relationship, whether contractual or not.

Article 8. Arbitration Agreement and Substantive Claim Before Court

(1) A court before which an action is brought in a matter which is the subject of an arbitration agreement shall, if a party so requests not later than when submitting his first statement on the substance of the dispute, refer the parties to arbitration unless it finds that the agreement is null and void, inoperative or incapable of being performed.

(2) Where an action referred to in paragraph (1) of this article has been brought, arbitral proceedings may nevertheless be commenced or continued, and an award may be made, while the issue is pending before the court.

Article 9. Arbitration Agreement and Interim Measures by Court

It is not incompatible with an arbitration agreement for a party to request, before or during arbitral proceedings, from a court an interim measure of protection and for a court to grant such measure.

CHAPTER III. COMPOSITION OF ARBITRAL TRIBUNAL

Article 10. Number of Arbitrators

(1) The parties are free to determine the number of arbitrators.

(2) Failing such determination, the number of arbitrators shall be three.

Article 11. Appointment of Arbitrators

(1) No person shall be precluded by reason of his nationality from acting as an arbitrator, unless otherwise agreed by the parties.

(2) The parties are free to agree on a procedure of appointing the arbitrator or arbitrators, subject to the provisions of paragraphs (4) and (5) of this article.

(3) Failing such agreement,

(a) in an arbitration with three arbitrators, each party shall appoint one arbitrator, and the two arbitrators thus appointed shall appoint the third arbitrator; if a party fails to appoint the arbitrator within thirty days of receipt of a request to do so from the other party, or if the two arbitrators fail to agree on the third arbitrator within thirty days of their appointment, the appointment shall be made, upon request of a party, by the court or other authority specified in article 6;

(b) in an arbitration with a sole arbitrator, if the parties are unable to agree on the arbitrator, he shall be appointed, upon request of a party, by the court or other authority specified in article 6.

(4) Where, under an appointment procedure agreed upon by the parties,

(a) a party fails to act as required under such procedure, or

(b) the parties, or two arbitrators, are unable to reach an agreement expected of them under such procedure, or

(c) a third party, including an institution, fails to perform any function entrusted to it under such procedure, any party may request the court or other authority specified in article 6 to take the necessary measure, unless the agreement on the appointment procedure provides other means for securing the appointment.

(5) A decision on a matter entrusted by paragraph (3) or (4) of this article to the court or other authority specified in article 6 shall be subject to no appeal. The court or other authority, in appointing an arbitrator, shall have due regard to any qualifications required of the arbitrator by the agreement of the parties and to such considerations as are likely to secure the appointment of an independent and impartial arbitrator and, in the case of a sole or third arbitrator, shall take into account as well the advisability of appointing an arbitrator of a nationality other than those of the parties.

Article 12. Grounds for Challenge

(1) When a person is approached in connection with his possible appointment as an arbitrator, he shall disclose any circumstances likely to give rise to justifiable doubts as to his impartiality or independence. An arbitrator, from the time of his appointment and throughout the arbitral proceedings, shall without delay disclose any such circumstances to the parties unless they have already been informed of them by him.

(2) An arbitrator may be challenged only if circumstances exist that give rise to justifiable doubts as to his impartiality or independence, or if he does not possess qualifications agreed to by the parties. A party may challenge an arbitrator appointed by him, or in whose appointment he has participated, only for reasons of which he becomes aware after the appointment has been made.

Article 13. Challenge Procedure

(1) The parties are free to agree on a procedure for challenging an arbitrator, subject to the provisions of paragraph (3) of this article.

(2) Failing such agreement, a party who intends to challenge an arbitrator shall, within fifteen days after becoming aware of the constitution of the arbitral tribunal or after becoming aware of any circumstance referred to in article 12(2), send a written statement of the reasons for the challenge to the arbitral tribunal. Unless the challenged arbitrator withdraws from his office or the other party agrees to the challenge, the arbitral tribunal shall decide on the challenge.

(3) If a challenge under any procedure agreed upon by the parties or under the procedure of paragraph (2) of this article is not successful, the challenging party may request, within thirty days after having received notice of the decision rejecting the challenge, the court or other authority specified in article 6 to decide on the challenge, which decision shall be subject to no appeal; while such a request is pending, the arbitral tribunal, including the challenged arbitrator, may continue the arbitral proceedings and make an award.

Article 14. Failure or Impossibility to Act

(1) If an arbitrator becomes de jure or de facto unable to perform his functions or for other reasons fails to act without undue delay, his mandate terminates if he withdraws from his office or if the parties agree on the termination. Otherwise, if a controversy remains concerning any of these grounds, any party may request the court or other authority specified in article 6 to decide on the termination of the mandate, which decision shall be subject to no appeal.

(2) If, under this article or article 13(2), an arbitrator withdraws from his office or a party agrees to the termination of the mandate of an arbitrator, this does not imply acceptance of the validity of any ground referred to in this article or article 12(2).

Article 15. Appointment of Substitute Arbitrator

Where the mandate of an arbitrator terminates under article 13 or 14 or because of his withdrawal from office for any other reason or because of the revocation of his mandate by agreement of the parties or in any other case of termination of his mandate, a substitute arbitrator shall be appointed according to the rules that were applicable to the appointment of the arbitrator being replaced.

CHAPTER IV. JURISDICTION OF ARBITRAL TRIBUNAL

Article 16. Competence of Arbitral Tribunal to Rule on its Jurisdiction

(1) The arbitral tribunal may rule on its own jurisdiction, including any objections with respect to the existence or validity of the arbitration agreement. For that purpose, an arbitration clause which forms part of a contract shall be treated as an agreement independent of the other terms of the contract. A decision by the arbitral tribunal that the contract is null and void shall not entail ipso jure the invalidity of the arbitration clause.

(2) A plea that the arbitral tribunal does not have jurisdiction shall be raised not later than the submission of the statement of defence. A party is not precluded from raising such a plea by the fact that he has appointed, or participated in the appointment of, an arbitrator. A plea that the arbitral tribunal is exceeding the scope of its authority shall be raised as soon as the matter alleged to be beyond the scope of its authority is raised during the arbitral proceedings. The arbitral tribunal may, in either case, admit a later plea if it considers the delay justified.

(3) The arbitral tribunal may rule on a plea referred to in paragraph (2) of this article either as a preliminary question or in an award on the merits. If the arbitral tribunal rules as a preliminary question that it has jurisdiction, any party may request, within thirty days after having received notice of that ruling, the court specified in article 6 to decide the matter, which decision shall be subject to no appeal; while such a request is pending, the arbitral tribunal may continue the arbitral proceedings and make an award.

CHAPTER IV A. INTERIM MEASURES AND PRELIMINARY ORDERS

Section 1. Interim Measures

Article 17. Power of Arbitral Tribunal to Order Interim Measures

(1) Unless otherwise agreed by the parties, the arbitral tribunal may, at the request of a party, grant interim measures.

(2) An interim measure is any temporary measure, whether in the form of an award or in another form, by which, at any time prior to the issuance of the award by which the dispute is finally decided, the arbitral tribunal orders a party to:

(a) Maintain or restore the status quo pending determination of the dispute;

(b) Take action that would prevent, or refrain from taking action that is likely to cause, current or imminent harm or prejudice to the arbitral process itself;

(c) Provide a means of preserving assets out of which a subsequent award may be satisfied; or

(d) Preserve evidence that may be relevant and material to the resolution of the dispute.

Article 17 A. Conditions for Granting Interim Measures

(1) The party requesting an interim measure under article 17(2)(a), (b) and (c) shall satisfy the arbitral tribunal that:

(a) Harm not adequately reparable by an award of damages is likely to result if the measure is not ordered, and such harm substantially outweighs the harm that is likely to result to the party against whom the measure is directed if the measure is granted; and

(b) There is a reasonable possibility that the requesting party will succeed on the merits of the claim. The determination on this possibility shall not affect the discretion of the arbitral tribunal in making any subsequent determination.

(2) With regard to a request for an interim measure under article 17(2)(d), the requirements in paragraphs (1)(a) and (b) of this article shall apply only to the extent the arbitral tribunal considers appropriate.

Section 2. Preliminary Orders

Article 17 B. Applications for Preliminary Orders and Conditions for Granting Preliminary Orders

(1) Unless otherwise agreed by the parties, a party may, without notice to any other party, make a request for an interim measure together with an application for a preliminary order directing a party not to frustrate the purpose of the interim measure requested.

(2) The arbitral tribunal may grant a preliminary order provided it considers that prior disclosure of the request for the interim measure to the party against whom it is directed risks frustrating the purpose of the measure.

(3) The conditions defined under article 17A apply to any preliminary order, provided that the harm to be assessed under article 17A(1)(a), is the harm likely to result from the order being granted or not.

Article 17 C. Specific Regime for Preliminary Orders

(1) Immediately after the arbitral tribunal has made a determination in respect of an application for a preliminary order, the arbitral tribunal shall give notice to all parties of the request for the interim measure, the application for the preliminary order, the preliminary order, if any, and all other communications, including by indicating the content of any oral communication, between any party and the arbitral tribunal in relation thereto.

(2) At the same time, the arbitral tribunal shall give an opportunity to any party against whom a preliminary order is directed to present its case at the earliest practicable time.

(3) The arbitral tribunal shall decide promptly on any objection to the preliminary order.

(4) A preliminary order shall expire after twenty days from the date on which it was issued by the arbitral tribunal. However, the arbitral tribunal may issue an interim measure adopting or modifying the preliminary order, after the party against whom the preliminary order is directed has been given notice and an opportunity to present its case.

(5) A preliminary order shall be binding on the parties but shall not be subject to enforcement by a court. Such a preliminary order does not constitute an award.

Section 3. Provisions Applicable to Interim Measures and Preliminary Orders

Article 17 D. Modification, Suspension, Termination

The arbitral tribunal may modify, suspend or terminate an interim measure or a preliminary order it has granted, upon application of any party or, in exceptional circumstances and upon prior notice to the parties, on the arbitral tribunal's own initiative.

Article 17 E. Provision of Security

(1) The arbitral tribunal may require the party requesting an interim measure to provide appropriate security in connection with the measure.

(2) The arbitral tribunal shall require the party applying for a preliminary order to provide security in connection with the order unless the arbitral tribunal considers it inappropriate or unnecessary to do so.

Article 17 F. Disclosure

(1) The arbitral tribunal may require any party promptly to disclose any material change in the circumstances on the basis of which the measure was requested or granted.

(2) The party applying for a preliminary order shall disclose to the arbitral tribunal all circumstances that are likely to be relevant to the arbitral tribunal's determination whether to grant or maintain the order, and such obligation shall continue until the party against whom the order has been requested has had an opportunity to present its case. Thereafter, paragraph (1) of this article shall apply.

Article 17 G. Costs and Damages

The party requesting an interim measure or applying for a preliminary order shall be liable for any costs and damages caused by the measure or the order to any party if the arbitral tribunal later determines that, in the circumstances, the measure or the order should not have been granted. The arbitral tribunal may award such costs and damages at any point during the proceedings.

Section 4. Recognition and Enforcement of Interim Measures

Article 17 H. Recognition and Enforcement

(1) An interim measure issued by an arbitral tribunal shall be recognized as binding and, unless otherwise provided by the arbitral tribunal, enforced upon application to the competent court, irrespective of the country in which it was issued, subject to the provisions of article 17 I.

(2) The party who is seeking or has obtained recognition or enforcement of an interim measure shall promptly inform the court of any termination, suspension or modification of that interim measure.

(3) The court of the State where recognition or enforcement is sought may, if it considers it proper, order the requesting party to provide appropriate security if the arbitral tribunal has not already made a determination with respect to security or where such a decision is necessary to protect the rights of third parties.

Article 17 I. Grounds for Refusing Recognition or Enforcement

(1) Recognition or enforcement of an interim measure may be refused only:

(a) At the request of the party against whom it is invoked if the court is satisfied that:

- (i) Such refusal is warranted on the grounds set forth in article 36(1)(a)(i), (ii), (iii) or (iv); or
- (ii) The arbitral tribunal's decision with respect to the provision of security in connection with the interim measure issued by the arbitral tribunal has not been complied with; or
- (iii) The interim measure has been terminated or suspended by the arbitral tribunal or, where so empowered, by the court of the State in which the arbitration takes place or under the law of which that interim measure was granted; or

(b) If the court finds that:

- (i) The interim measure is incompatible with the powers conferred upon the court unless the court decides to reformulate the interim measure to the extent necessary to adapt it to its own powers and procedures for the purposes of enforcing that interim measure and without modifying its substance; or
- (ii) Any of the grounds set forth in article 36(1)(b)(i) or (ii), apply to the recognition and enforcement of the interim measure.

(2) Any determination made by the court on any ground in paragraph (1) of this article shall be effective only for the purposes of the application to recognize and enforce the interim measure. The court where recognition or enforcement is sought shall not, in making that determination, undertake a review of the substance of the interim measure.

Section 5. Court-Ordered Interim Measures

Article 17 J. Court-Ordered Interim Measures

A court shall have the same power of issuing an interim measure in relation to arbitration proceedings, irrespective of whether their place is in the territory of this State, as it has in relation to proceedings in courts. The court shall exercise such power in accordance with its own procedures in consideration of the specific features of international arbitration.

CHAPTER V. CONDUCT OF ARBITRAL PROCEEDINGS

Article 18. Equal Treatment of Parties

The parties shall be treated with equality and each party shall be given a full opportunity of presenting his case.

Article 19. Determination of Rules of Procedure

(1) Subject to the provisions of this Law, the parties are free to agree on the procedure to be followed by the arbitral tribunal in conducting the proceedings.

(2) Failing such agreement, the arbitral tribunal may, subject to the provisions of this Law, conduct the arbitration in such manner as it considers appropriate. The power conferred upon the arbitral tribunal includes the power to determine the admissibility, relevance, materiality and weight of any evidence.

Article 20. Place of Arbitration

(1) The parties are free to agree on the place of arbitration. Failing such agreement, the place of arbitration shall be determined by the arbitral tribunal having regard to the circumstances of the case, including the convenience of the parties.

(2) Notwithstanding the provisions of paragraph (1) of this article, the arbitral tribunal may, unless otherwise agreed by the parties, meet at any place it considers appropriate for consultation among its members, for hearing witnesses, experts or the parties, or for inspection of goods, other property or documents.

Article 21. Commencement of Arbitral Proceedings

Unless otherwise agreed by the parties, the arbitral proceedings in respect of a particular dispute commence on the date on which a request for that dispute to be referred to arbitration is received by the respondent.

Article 22. Language

(1) The parties are free to agree on the language or languages to be used in the arbitral proceedings. Failing such agreement, the arbitral tribunal shall determine the language or languages to be used in the proceedings. This agreement or determination, unless otherwise specified therein, shall apply to any written statement by a party, any hearing and any award, decision or other communication by the arbitral tribunal.

(2) The arbitral tribunal may order that any documentary evidence shall be accompanied by a translation into the language or languages agreed upon by the parties or determined by the arbitral tribunal.

Article 23. Statements of Claim and Defence

(1) Within the period of time agreed by the parties or determined by the arbitral tribunal, the claimant shall state the facts supporting his claim, the points at issue and the relief or remedy sought, and the respondent shall state his defence in respect of these particulars, unless the parties have otherwise agreed as to the required elements of such statements. The parties may submit with their statements all documents they consider to be relevant or may add a reference to the documents or other evidence they will submit.

(2) Unless otherwise agreed by the parties, either party may amend or supplement his claim or defence during the course of the arbitral proceedings, unless the arbitral tribunal considers it inappropriate to allow such amendment having regard to the delay in making it.

Article 24. Hearings and Written Proceedings

(1) Subject to any contrary agreement by the parties, the arbitral tribunal shall decide whether to hold oral hearings for the presentation of evidence or for oral argument, or whether the proceedings shall be conducted on the basis of documents and other materials. However, unless the parties have agreed that no hearings shall be held, the arbitral tribunal shall hold such hearings at an appropriate stage of the proceedings, if so requested by a party.

(2) The parties shall be given sufficient advance notice of any hearing and of any meeting of the arbitral tribunal for the purposes of inspection of goods, other property or documents.

(3) All statements, documents or other information supplied to the arbitral tribunal by one party shall be communicated to the other party. Also any expert report or evidentiary document on which the arbitral tribunal may rely in making its decision shall be communicated to the parties.

Article 25. Default of a Party

Unless otherwise agreed by the parties, if, without showing sufficient cause,

(a) the claimant fails to communicate his statement of claim in accordance with article 23(1), the arbitral tribunal shall terminate the proceedings;

(b) the respondent fails to communicate his statement of defence in accordance with article 23(1), the arbitral tribunal shall continue the proceedings without treating such failure in itself as an admission of the claimant's allegations;

(c) any party fails to appear at a hearing or to produce documentary evidence, the arbitral tribunal may continue the proceedings and make the award on the evidence before it.

Article 26. Expert Appointed by Arbitral Tribunal

(1) Unless otherwise agreed by the parties, the arbitral tribunal

(a) may appoint one or more experts to report to it on specific issues to be determined by the arbitral tribunal;

(b) may require a party to give the expert any relevant information or to produce, or to provide access to, any relevant documents, goods or other property for his inspection.

(2) Unless otherwise agreed by the parties, if a party so requests or if the arbitral tribunal considers it necessary, the expert shall, after delivery of his written or oral report, participate in a hearing where the parties have the opportunity to put questions to him and to present expert witnesses in order to testify on the points at issue.

Article 27. Court Assistance in Taking Evidence

The arbitral tribunal or a party with the approval of the arbitral tribunal may request from a competent court of this State assistance in taking evidence. The court may execute the request within its competence and according to its rules on taking evidence.

CHAPTER VI. MAKING OF AWARD ANDTERMINATION OF PROCEEDINGS

Article 28. Rules Applicable to Substance of Dispute

(1) The arbitral tribunal shall decide the dispute in accordance with such rules of law as are chosen by the parties as applicable to the substance of the dispute. Any designation of the law or legal system of a given State shall be construed, unless otherwise expressed, as directly referring to the substantive law of that State and not to its conflict of laws rules.

(2) Failing any designation by the parties, the arbitral tribunal shall apply the law determined by the conflict of laws rules which it considers applicable.

(3) The arbitral tribunal shall decide ex aequo et bono or as amiable compositeur only if the parties have expressly authorized it to do so.

(4) In all cases, the arbitral tribunal shall decide in accordance with the terms of the contract and shall take into account the usages of the trade applicable to the transaction.

Article 29. Decision-Making by Panel of Arbitrators

In arbitral proceedings with more than one arbitrator, any decision of the arbitral tribunal shall be made, unless otherwise agreed by the parties, by a majority of all its members. However, questions of procedure may be decided by a presiding arbitrator, if so authorized by the parties or all members of the arbitral tribunal.

Article 30. Settlement

(1) If, during arbitral proceedings, the parties settle the dispute, the arbitral tribunal shall terminate the proceedings and, if requested by the parties and not objected to by the arbitral tribunal, record the settlement in the form of an arbitral award on agreed terms.

(2) An award on agreed terms shall be made in accordance with the provisions of article 31 and shall state that it is an award. Such an award has the same status and effect as any other award on the merits of the case.

Article 31. Form and Contents of Award

(1) The award shall be made in writing and shall be signed by the arbitrator or arbitrators. In arbitral proceedings with more than one arbitrator, the signatures of the majority of all members of the arbitral tribunal shall suffice, provided that the reason for any omitted signature is stated.

(2) The award shall state the reasons upon which it is based, unless the parties have agreed that no reasons are to be given or the award is an award on agreed terms under article 30.

(3) The award shall state its date and the place of arbitration as determined in accordance with article 20(1). The award shall be deemed to have been made at that place.

(4) After the award is made, a copy signed by the arbitrators in accordance with paragraph (1) of this article shall be delivered to each party.

Article 32. Termination of Proceedings

(1) The arbitral proceedings are terminated by the final award or by an order of the arbitral tribunal in accordance with paragraph (2) of this article.

(2) The arbitral tribunal shall issue an order for the termination of the arbitral proceedings when:

(a) the claimant withdraws his claim, unless the respondent objects thereto and the arbitral tribunal recognizes a legitimate interest on his part in obtaining a final settlement of the dispute;

(b) the parties agree on the termination of the proceedings;

(c) the arbitral tribunal finds that the continuation of the proceedings has for any other reason become unnecessary or impossible.

(3) The mandate of the arbitral tribunal terminates with the termination of the arbitral proceedings, subject to the provisions of articles 33 and 34(4).

Article 33. Correction and Interpretation of Award; Additional Award

(1) Within thirty days of receipt of the award, unless another period of time has been agreed upon by the parties:

(a) a party, with notice to the other party, may request the arbitral tribunal to correct in the award any errors in computation, any clerical or typographical errors or any errors of similar nature;

(b) if so agreed by the parties, a party, with notice to the other party, may request the arbitral tribunal to give an interpretation of a specific point or part of the award. If the arbitral tribunal considers the request to be justified, it shall make the correction or give the interpretation within thirty days of receipt of the request. The interpretation shall form part of the award.

(2) The arbitral tribunal may correct any error of the type referred to in paragraph (1)(a) of this article on its own initiative within thirty days of the date of the award.

(3) Unless otherwise agreed by the parties, a party, with notice to the other party, may request, within thirty days of receipt of the award, the arbitral tribunal to make an additional award as to claims presented in the arbitral proceedings but omitted from the award. If the arbitral tribunal considers the request to be justified, it shall make the additional award within sixty days.

(4) The arbitral tribunal may extend, if necessary, the period of time within which it shall make a correction, interpretation or an additional award under paragraph (1) or (3) of this article.

(5) The provisions of article 31 shall apply to a correction or interpretation of the award or to an additional award.

CHAPTER VII. RECOURSE AGAINST AWARD

Article 34. Application for Setting Aside as Exclusive Recourse Against Arbitral Award

(1) Recourse to a court against an arbitral award may be made only by an application for setting aside in accordance with paragraphs (2) and (3) of this article.

(2) An arbitral award may be set aside by the court specified in article 6 only if:

(a) the party making the application furnishes proof that:

- (i) a party to the arbitration agreement referred to in article 7 was under some incapacity; or the said agreement is not valid under the law to which the parties have subjected it or, failing any indication thereon, under the law of this State; or
- (ii) the party making the application was not given proper notice of the appointment of an arbitrator or of the arbitral proceedings or was otherwise unable to present his case; or
- (iii) the award deals with a dispute not contemplated by or not falling within the terms of the submission to arbitration, or contains decisions on matters beyond the scope of the submission to arbitration, provided that, if the decisions on matters submitted to arbitration can be separated from those not so submitted, only that part of the award which contains decisions on matters not submitted to arbitration may be set aside; or
- (iv) the composition of the arbitral tribunal or the arbitral procedure was not in accordance with the agreement of the parties, unless such agreement was in conflict with a provision of this Law from which the parties cannot derogate, or, failing such agreement, was not in accordance with this Law; or

(b) the court finds that:

(i) the subject-matter of the dispute is not capable of settlement by arbitration under the law of this State; or

(ii) the award is in conflict with the public policy of this State.

(3) An application for setting aside may not be made after three months have elapsed from the date on which the party making that application had received the award or, if a request had been made under article 33, from the date on which that request had been disposed of by the arbitral tribunal.

(4) The court, when asked to set aside an award, may, where appropriate and so requested by a party, suspend the setting aside proceedings for a period of time determined by it in order to give the arbitral tribunal an opportunity to resume the arbitral proceedings or to take such other action as in the arbitral tribunal's opinion will eliminate the grounds for setting aside.

CHAPTER VIII. RECOGNITION AND ENFORCEMENT OF AWARDS

Article 35. Recognition and Enforcement

(1) An arbitral award, irrespective of the country in which it was made, shall be recognized as binding and, upon application in writing to the competent court, shall be enforced subject to the provisions of this article and of article 36.

(2) The party relying on an award or applying for its enforcement shall supply the original award or a copy thereof. If the award is not made in an official language of this State, the court may request the party to supply a translation thereof into such language.

Article 36. Grounds for Refusing Recognition or Enforcement

(1) Recognition or enforcement of an arbitral award, irrespective of the country in which it was made, may be refused only:

(a) at the request of the party against whom it is invoked, if that party furnishes to the competent court where recognition or enforcement is sought proof that:

(i) a party to the arbitration agreement referred to in article 7 was under some incapacity; or the said agreement is not valid under the law to which the parties have subjected it or, failing any indication thereon, under the law of the country where the award was made; or

(ii) the party against whom the award is invoked was not given proper notice of the appointment of an arbitrator or of the arbitral proceedings or was otherwise unable to present his case; or

(iii) the award deals with a dispute not contemplated by or not falling within the terms of the submission to arbitration, or it contains decisions on matters beyond the scope of the submission to arbitration, provided that, if the decisions on matters submitted to arbitration can be separated from those not so submitted, that part of the award which contains decisions on matters submitted to arbitration may be recognized and enforced; or

(iv) the composition of the arbitral tribunal or the arbitral procedure was not in accordance with the agreement of the parties or, failing such agreement, was not in accordance with the law of the country where the arbitration took place; or

(v) the award has not yet become binding on the parties or has been set aside or suspended by a court of the country in which, or under the law of which, that award was made; or

(b) if the court finds that:

(i) the subject-matter of the dispute is not capable of settlement by arbitration under the law of this State; or

(ii) the recognition or enforcement of the award would be contrary to the public policy of this State.

(2) If an application for setting aside or suspension of an award has been made to a court referred to in paragraph (1)(a)(v) of this article, the court where recognition or enforcement is sought may, if it considers it proper, adjourn its decision and may also, on the application of the party claiming recognition or enforcement of the award, order the other party to provide appropriate security.

Appendix E

New York Convention

United Nations Convention on the Recognition and Enforcement of Foreign Arbitral Awards (New York, 10 June 1958)

Article I

1) This Convention shall apply to the recognition and enforcement of arbitral awards made in the territory of a State other than the State where the recognition and enforcement of such awards are sought, and arising out of differences between persons, whether physical or legal. It shall also apply to arbitral awards not considered as domestic awards in the State where their recognition and enforcement are sought.

2) The term "arbitral awards" shall include not only awards made by arbitrators appointed for each case but also those made by permanent arbitral bodies to which the parties have submitted.

3) When signing, ratifying or acceding to this Convention, or notifying extension under article X hereof, any State may on the basis of reciprocity declare that it will apply the Convention to the recognition and enforcement of awards made only in the territory of another Contracting State. It may also declare that it will apply the Convention only to differences arising out of legal relationships, whether contractual or not, which are considered as commercial under the national law of the State making such declaration.

Article II

1) Each Contracting State shall recognize an agreement in writing under which the parties undertake to submit to arbitration all or any differences which have arisen or which may arise between them in respect of a defined legal relationship, whether contractual or not, concerning a subject matter capable of settlement by arbitration.

2) The term "agreement in writing" shall include an arbitral clause in a contract or an arbitration agreement, signed by the parties or contained in an exchange of letters or telegrams.

3) The court of a Contracting State, when seized of an action in a matter in respect of which the parties have made an agreement within the meaning of this article, shall, at the request of one of the parties, refer the parties to arbitration, unless it finds that the said agreement is null and void, inoperative or incapable of being performed.

Article III

Each Contracting State shall recognize arbitral awards as binding and enforce them in accordance with the rules of procedure of the territory where the award is relied upon, under the conditions laid down in the following articles. There shall not be imposed substantially more onerous conditions or higher fees or charges on the recognition or enforcement of arbitral awards to which this Convention applies than are imposed on the recognition or enforcement of domestic arbitral awards.

Article IV

1) To obtain the recognition and enforcement mentioned in the preceding article, the party applying for recognition and enforcement shall, at the time of the application, supply:

(a) The duly authenticated original award or a duly certified copy thereof;

(b) The original agreement referred to in article II or a duly certified copy thereof.

2) If the said award or agreement is not made in an official language of the country in which the award is relied upon, the party applying for recognition and enforcement of the award shall produce a translation of these documents into such language. The translation shall be certified by an official or sworn translator or by a diplomatic or consular agent.

Article V

1) Recognition and enforcement of the award may be refused, at the request of the party against whom it is invoked, only if that party furnishes to the competent authority where the recognition and enforcement is sought, proof that:

(a) The parties to the agreement referred to in article II were, under the law applicable to them, under some incapacity, or the said agreement is not valid under the law to which the parties have subjected it or, failing any indication thereon, under the law of the country where the award was made; or

(b) The party against whom the award is invoked was not given proper notice of the appointment of the arbitrator or of the arbitration proceedings or was otherwise unable to present his case; or

(c) The award deals with a difference not contemplated by or not falling within the terms of the submission to arbitration, or it contains decisions on matters beyond the scope of the submission to arbitration, provided that, if the decisions on matters submitted to arbitration can be separated from those not so submitted, that part of the award which contains decisions on matters submitted to arbitration may be recognized and enforced; or

(d) The composition of the arbitral authority or the arbitral procedure was not in accordance with the agreement of the parties, or, failing such agreement, was not in accordance with the law of the country where the arbitration took place; or

(e) The award has not yet become binding on the parties, or has been set aside or suspended by a competent authority of the country in which, or under the law of which, that award was made.

2) Recognition and enforcement of an arbitral award may also be refused if the competent authority in the country where recognition and enforcement is sought finds that:

(a) The subject matter of the difference is not capable of settlement by arbitration under the law of that country; or

(b) The recognition or enforcement of the award would be contrary to the public policy of that country.

Article VI

If an application for the setting aside or suspension of the award has been made to a competent authority referred to in article V (1) (e), the authority before which the award is sought to be relied upon may, if it considers it proper, adjourn the decision on the enforcement of the award and may also, on the application of the party claiming enforcement of the award, order the other party to give suitable security.

Article VII

1) The provisions of the present Convention shall not affect the validity of multilateral or bilateral agreements concerning the recognition and enforcement of arbitral awards entered into by the Contracting States nor deprive any interested party of any right he may have to avail himself of an arbitral award in the manner and to the extent allowed by the law or the treaties of the country where such award is sought to be relied upon.

2) The Geneva Protocol on Arbitration Clauses of 1923 and the Geneva Convention on the Execution of Foreign Arbitral Awards of 1927 shall cease to have effect between Contracting States on their becoming bound and to the extent that they become bound, by this Convention.

Article VIII

1) This Convention shall be open until 31 December 1958 for signature on behalf of any Member of the United Nations and also on behalf of any other State which is or hereafter becomes a member of any specialized agency of the United Nations, or which is or hereafter becomes a party to the Statute of the International Court of Justice, or any other State to which an invitation has been addressed by the General Assembly of the United Nations.

2) This Convention shall be ratified and the instrument of ratification shall be deposited with the Secretary-General of the United Nations.

Article IX

1) This Convention shall be open for accession to all States referred to in article VIII.

2) Accession shall be effected by the deposit of an instrument of accession with the Secretary-General of the United Nations.

Article X

1) Any State may, at the time of signature, ratification or accession, declare that this Convention shall extend to all or any of the territories for the international relations of which it is responsible. Such a declaration shall take effect when the Convention enters into force for the State concerned.

2) At any time thereafter any such extension shall be made by notification addressed to the Secretary-General of the United Nations and shall take effect as from the ninetieth day after the day of receipt by the Secretary-General of the United Nations of this notification, or as from the date of entry into force of the Convention for the State concerned, whichever is the later.

3) With respect to those territories to which this Convention is not extended at the time of signature, ratification or accession, each State concerned shall consider the possibility of taking the necessary steps in order to extend the application of this Convention to such territories, subject, where necessary for constitutional reasons, to the consent of the Governments of such territories.

Article XI

In the case of a federal or non-unitary State, the following provisions shall apply:

(a) With respect to those articles of this Convention that come within the legislative jurisdiction of the federal authority, the obligations of the federal Government shall to this extent be the same as those of Contracting States which are not federal States;

(b) With respect to those articles of this Convention that come within the legislative jurisdiction of constituent states or provinces which are not, under the constitutional system of the federation, bound to take legislative action, the federal Government shall bring such articles with a favorable recommendation to the notice of the appropriate authorities of constituent states or provinces at the earliest possible moment;

(c) A federal State Party to this Convention shall, at the request of any other Contracting State transmitted through the Secretary-General of the United Nations, supply a statement of the law and practice of the federation and its constituent units in regard to any particular provision of this Convention, showing the extent to which effect has been given to that provision by legislative or other action.

Article XII

1) This Convention shall come into force on the ninetieth day following the date of deposit of the third instrument of ratification or accession.

2) For each State ratifying or acceding to this Convention after the deposit of the third instrument of ratification or accession, this Convention shall enter into force on the ninetieth day after deposit by such State of its instrument of ratification or accession.

Article XIII

1) Any Contracting State may denounce this Convention by a written notification to the Secretary-General of the United Nations. Denunciation shall take effect one year after the date of receipt of the notification by the Secretary-General.

2) Any State which has made a declaration or notification under article X may, at any time thereafter, by notification to the Secretary-General of the United Nations, declare that this Convention shall cease to extend to the territory concerned one year after the date of the receipt of the notification by the Secretary-General.

3) This Convention shall continue to be applicable to arbitral awards in respect of which recognition and enforcement proceedings have been instituted before the denunciation takes effect.

Article XIV

A Contracting State shall not be entitled to avail itself of the present Convention against other Contracting States except to the extent that it is itself bound to apply the Convention.

Article XV

The Secretary-General of the United Nations shall notify the States contemplated in article VIII of the following:

(a) Signatures and ratifications in accordance with article VIII;

(b) Accessions in accordance with article IX;

(c) Declarations and notifications under articles I, X and XI;

(d) The date upon which this Convention enters into force in accordance with article XII;

(e) Denunciations and notifications in accordance with article XIII.

Article XVI

1) This Convention, of which the Chinese, English, French, Russian and Spanish texts shall be equally authentic, shall be deposited in the archives of the United Nations.

2) The Secretary-General of the United Nations shall transmit a certified copy of this Convention to the States contemplated in article VIII.

Appendix F

Bibliography

1) Laws and International Agreements and Conventions

Arbitration Law, Saudi Arabia, Apr. 24, 1983, Royal Decree No. M/46 (1983).

Charter of the Saudi Arabian Monetary Agency, Dec. 15, 1957, Royal Decree No. 23 (1957).

Code of Law Practice, Saudi Arabia, Oct. 15, 2001, Royal Decree No. M/38 (2001).

Cooperative Insurance Companies Control Law, Saudi Arabia, Jul. 31, 2003, Royal Decree No. M/32 (2003).

Egypt Law No. 27/1994 Promulgating the Law Concerning Arbitration in Civil and Commercial Matters (1994).

English Arbitration Act (1996).

IBA Guidelines on Conflicts of Interest in International Arbitration (2014).

IBA Rules of Ethics for International Arbitrators (1987).

IBA Rules on the Taking of Evidence in International Arbitration (2010).

ICC Rules of Arbitration (2012).

ICDR Arbitration Rules (2014).

Implementation Mechanism of the Law of Procedure before Sharia'h Courts, Saudi Arabia, Mar. 20, 2014, Order No. 39933 (2014).

Implementing Regulations of the Arbitration Law, Saudi Arabia, May 27, 1985, Royal Decree No. 7/2021/M (1985).

Law of Arbitration, Saudi Arabia, Apr. 16, 2012, Royal Decree No. M/34 (2012).

Law of Judiciary, Saudi Arabia, Oct. 01, 2007, promulgated by Royal Decree No. M/78 (2007).

Law of Procedures before the Shari'a Courts, Saudi Arabia, Nov. 25, 2013, Royal Decree No. M/1 (2013).

Law of the Board of Grievances, Saudi Arabia, Oct. 01, 2007, Royal Decree No. M/78 (2007).

LCIA Arbitration Rules (2014).

New York Convention (1958).

Ordinance Concerning the Prosecution of Ministers, Saudi Arabia (1961).

Shura Council Law, Saudi Arabia, Mar. 01, 1992, Royal Decree No. A/91 (1992).

The Basic Law of Government, Saudi Arabia, Mar. 01, 1992, Royal Order No. A/91 (1992).

The Saudi Electronic Transaction Law No. M/18 (2007).

The Saudi Anti Online Crime Law No. M/17 (2007).

The Saudi Child Protection Law, Saudi Arabia, Nov. 25, 2014, Royal Decree No. M/14 (2014).

The Commercial Court Law, Saudi Arabia, Jun. 01, 1931, Royal Decree No. 32 (1931).

The Saudi Companies Law, Nov. 10, 2015, Royal Decree No. M/3 (2015).

The Law of the Council of Ministers, Saudi Arabia, Aug. 20, 1993, Royal Order No. A/13 (1993).

The Saudi Enforcement Law, Jul. 03, 2012, Royal Decree No. M/53 (2012).

The Saudi Labor Law, Nov. 15, 1969, Royal Decree No. M/21 (1969).

The Saudi Labour Law, Sep. 27, 2005, Royal Decree No. M/51 (2005).

The Saudi labor law as amended by a Royal Decree No. M/46 of 05/06/1436 H, 2015

UNCITRAL Arbitration Rules (2010).

UNCITRAL Conciliation Rules (1980).

UNCITRAL Model Law on International Commercial Arbitration (2006).

UNIDROIT Principles of International Commercial Contracts (2010).

Uniform Arbitration Act (RUAA) (2000).

2) Cases

Case No. ق/3/637 (http://www.bog.gov.sa/ScientificContent/JudicialBlogs/Pages/default.aspx) (The Saudi Court of Grievances 2009).

Case No.ق /1/3375 (http://www.bog.gov.sa/ScientificContent/JudicialBlogs/Pages/default.aspx) (The Saudi Court of Grievances 1424H).

Case No.ق/1/2496 (http://www.bog.gov.sa/ScientificContent/JudicialBlogs/Pages/default.aspx) (The Saudi Court of Grievances 1425H).

Case number of appeal 363/2 /س 1434H, available at: https://www.bog.gov.sa/ScientificContent/JudicialBlogs/1434/Pages/default.aspx

Case Number of appeal 2309/2 /س of 1433H, available at: https://www.bog.gov.sa/ScientificContent/JudicialBlogs/1434/Pages/default.aspx

Case Number. of appeal judgment 319/1 of 1434 H, available at: https://www.bog.gov.sa/ScientificContent/JudicialBlogs/1434/Pages/default.aspx

Case Number of appeal judgment 319/1 of 1434 H, available at: https://www.bog.gov.sa/ScientificContent/JudicialBlogs/1434/Pages/default.aspx

Case number of appeal 1207 /ق of 1434 H, available at: https://www.bog.gov.sa/ScientificContent/JudicialBlogs/1434/Pages/default.aspx

Chromalloy Aeroservices and the Arab Republic of Egypt, 939 F. Supp. 907 (D.D.C. 1996).

Iran Aircraft Industries v. Avco Corporation, 980 F.2d 141, (2d Cir. 1992).

Mitsubishi Motors Corp. v. Soler Chrysler-Plymouth, Inc., 473 U.S. 614 (1985).

National Group for Commun. and Computers Ltd. v. Lucent Technologies Intern. Inc, 331 F.Supp.2d 290 (Dist. Court, D. New Jersey 2004).

Parsons & Wh. Ov. Co., Inc. v. Societe G. De L. Du P. (R.), 508 F.2d 969 (2d Cir. 1974).

Petroleum Development (Tmcial Cod) LTD v. The Shiekh of Abu Dhabi, 1 INT'L & COMP. L.Q. 247 (1952)

Ruler of Qatar v. International Marine Oil Company Limited, 20 I.L.R. 534 (1953).

Saudi Arabia v. The Arabian American Oil Co, 27 ILR 117 (1963).

Saudi Basic Industries v. Mobil Yanbu Pet, 866 A.2d 1, A.2d 1 (Del. 2005).

Shamil Bank of Bahrain EC v. Beximco Pharmaceuticals Ltd, [2004] EWCA (Civ) 19 (W.L.R. 2004).

3) Books and Independent Publications

Abdulaziz Alfrayan, Applying the Arbitration National and International Rules in Saudi Arabia (Jun. 27, 2006) (unpublished Master's thesis [in Arabic], Naif Arab University for Security Sciences) (https://international-arbitration-attorney.com/wp-content/uploads/arbitrationlaw193arbitration.pdf).

ABDULLAH IBN QUDAMAH, AL MUGHNI VOL. 10 (Cairo Library 1968).

ABDULLAH IBN QUDAMAH, AL MUGHNI VOL. 4 (Cairo Library 1968).

ABDULLAH IBN QUDAMAH, AL MUGHNI VOL. 7 (Cairo Library 1968).

ABDULWAHAB KHELAF, EULIM 'USUL ALFAQQIH (8th ed. Dar Al Qalam).

ABDULLAH BIN YUSUF AL JUDAI, TAHRIR ALOOM ALHADITH (1st ed. Lebanon AlRayan 2003).

ABDULRAHMAN YAHYA BAAMIR, SHARI'A LAW IN COMMERCIAL AND BANKING ARBITRATION: LAW AND PRACTICE IN SAUDI ARABIA (Ashgate Publishing Ltd 2013).

ALI IBN AHMAD IBN HAZM, AL-IHKAM FI USUL AL-AHKAM (Dar al-Afaq al-Gadida 1983).

ABU ZAKARIA MUHIY AD-DIN YAHYA IBN SHARAF AL-NAWAWI, AL MINHAJ SHARH SAHIH MUSLIM (2nd ed. Dar Ihya al-Turath al-Arabi 1392H).

AHMED A. BIN BAZ, POLITICAL AND CONSTITUTIONAL LAW OF SAUDI ARABIA (Dar Alkharji 2000).

ALBERT HOURANI, A HISTORY OF THE ARAB PEOPLES: UPDATED EDITION (Faber & Faber 2013).

ALBERT J. VAN DEN BERG, THE NEW YORK CONVENTION OF 1958: AN OVERVIEW (2013) (http://www.arbitration-icca.org/media/4/69405158666624/media012125884227980new_york_convention_of_1958_overview.pdf).

AMERICAN ARBITRATION ASSOCIATION, AAA HANDBOOK ON INTERNATIONAL ARBITRATION AND ADR (Juris Publishing, Inc. 2010).

AMERICAN ARBITRATION ASSOCIATION, AAA/ICDR HANDBOOK ON INTERNATIONAL ARBITRATION AND ADR (JurisNet, LLC 2006).

ASSOCIATION FOR INTERNATIONAL ARBITRATION, INTERIM MEASURES IN INTERNATIONAL COMMERCIAL ARBITRATION (Maklu Publishers 2007).

AUDAH BIN HASSAN, 500 HADITHS MEMMA TRAGAA AANHA AL ALBANI (Dar Alnafais 2003).

AUGUST REINISCH, THE PROLIFERATION OF INTERNATIONAL DISPUTE SETTLEMENT MECHANISMS: THE THREAT OF FRAGMENTATION VS. THE PROMISE OF A MORE EFFECTIVE SYSTEM? SOME REFLECTIONS FROM THE PERSPECTIVE OF INVESTMENT ARBITRATION (Martinus Nijhoff Publishers 2008).

BERNARD G. WEISS, THE SPIRIT OF ISLAMIC LAW, VOL. 5 (University of Georgia Press 1998).

BRIAN KETTELL, INTRODUCTION TO ISLAMIC BANKING AND FINANCE, VOL. 1 (John Wiley & Sons 2011).

CHRISTOPHER M. BLANCHARD, SAUDI ARABIA: BACKGROUND AND US RELATIONS (Diane Publishing 2010).

E. ALLAN FARNSWORTH ET AL., CONTRACTS, CASES & MATERIALS (7th ed. Foundation Press 2008).

E. ALLAN FARNSWORTH, CONTRACTS (4th ed. Aspen Publishers 2004).

FABIO BORTOLOTTI, DRAFTING AND NEGOTIATING INTERNATIONAL COMMERCIAL CONTRACTS: A PRACTICAL GUIDE (International Chamber of Commerce 2013).

FEISAL ABDUL RAUF, MOVING THE MOUNTAIN: A NEW VISION OF ISLAM IN AMERICA (Free Press 2012).

FRANCIS E. PETERS, THE HAJJ: THE MUSLIM PILGRIMAGE TO MECCA AND THE HOLY PLACES (Princeton University Press 1994).

FRANK E. VOGEL, ISLAMIC LAW AND THE LEGAL SYSTEM OF SAUDÍ: STUDIES OF SAUDI ARABIA (Brill 2000).

HOSSEIN ESMAEILI ANN BLACK, NADIRSYAH HOSEN, MODERN PERSPECTIVES ON ISLAMIC LAW (Edward Elgar Publishing Ltd 2013).

IBP USA, SAUDI ARABIA COMPANY LAWS AND REGULATIONS HANDBOOK (International Business Publications 2008).

IBRAHIM BIN MOSA BIN MUHAMMAD AL-SHATIBI, AL-MUWAFAQAT, VOL. 1 (1st ed. Dar Ibn Affan 1997).

IBRAHIM BIN MOSA BIN MUHAMMAD AL-SHATIBI, AL-MUWAFAQAT, VOL. 5 (1st ed. Dar Ibn Affan 1997).

JALAL ALDEEN AL-SUYUTI, MUFTAH AL JANNAH FEE EHTEJAJ BE AL SUNNAH (3rd ed. Islamic University Publisher 1989).

JAMAL J. NASIR, THE ISLAMIC LAW OF PERSONAL STATUS (Brill Archive 1990).

JAMES R. SILKENAT ET AL., THE ABA GUIDE TO INTERNATIONAL BUSINESS NEGOTIATIONS: A COMPARISON OF CROSS-CULTURAL ISSUES AND SUCCESSFUL APPROACHES (American Bar Association 2009).

JAN MICHIEL OTTO, SHARIA INCORPORATED: A COMPARATIVE OVERVIEW OF THE LEGAL SYSTEMS OF TWELVE MUSLIM COUNTRIES IN PAST AND PRESENT (Leiden University Press 2010).

JASON FRY ET AL., THE SECRETARIAT'S GUIDE TO ICC ARBITRATION: A PRACTICAL COMMENTARY ON THE 2012 ICC RULES OF ARBITRATION FROM THE SECRETARIAT OF THE ICC INTERNATIONAL COURT OF ARBITRATION (ICC Publishing 2012).

JASSER AUDA, MAQASID AL-SHARIAH AS PHILOSOPHY OF ISLAMIC LAW (The International Institute of Islamic Thought 2008).

JEAN-FRANÇOIS POUDRET & SÉBASTIEN BESSON, COMPARATIVE LAW OF INTERNATIONAL ARBITRATION (Sweet & Maxwell 2007).

JOHN S. MURRAY ET AL., ARBITRATION (Foundation Press 1996).

JOHN W. HEAD, GLOBAL BUSINESS LAW (3rd ed. Carolina Academic Press 2012).

KATHERINE VAN WEZEL STONE, ARBITRATION LAW (Foundation Press 2003).

KENNETH W. DAM, THE LAW-GROWTH NEXUS: THE RULE OF LAW AND ECONOMIC DEVELOPMENT (Brookings Institution Press 2007).

Khalid Al-dakheel, Arbitration in Saudi Law According to Islamic Jurisprudence (Jun. 06, 2004). (unpublished Master's thesis [in Arabic], Naif Arab University for Security Sciences) (http://www.nauss.edu.sa/Ar/DigitalLibrary/ScientificTheses/Documents/Master_1424-1425_CJ_18.pdf).

LAMEEN ALNAJI, OLD AND NEW IN SHAFI'I JURISPRUDENCE (1st ed. Dar Ibn Affan 2007).

MADAWI AL-RASHEED, A HISTORY OF SAUDI ARABIA (Cambridge University Press 2010).

MARGARET L. MOSES, THE PRINCIPLES AND PRACTICE OF INTERNATIONAL COMMERCIAL ARBITRATION (Cambridge University Press 2012).

MICHAEL MUMISA, ISLAMIC LAW THEORY & INTERPRETATION (Amana Publications 2002).

MOHAMED MATTAR ET AL., MIXED LEGAL SYSTEMS, EAST AND WEST (Ashgate Publishing Ltd 2015).

MOHAMMAD HASHIM KAMALI, PRINCIPLES OF ISLAMIC JURISPRUDENCE (The Islamic Texts Society 1991).

MOHAMMED BIN AHMED ABU ZAHRA, ZAHRAT AL TAFSEER, VOL. 1 (Dar Al fikr alarabi 1987).

MOHAMMED BIN AHMED ABU ZAHRA, ZAHRAT AL TAFSEER, VOL. 2 (Dar Al fikr alarabi 1987).

MOHAMMED ISMAIL AL-BUKHARI, SAHIH AL-BUKHARI (1st ed. Dar Tawq Al najah, 1422H).

MOHAMMED OBAIDULLAH, ISLAMIC FINANCIAL SERVICES (Scientific Publishing Centre, King Abdulaziz University 2005).

MUHAMMAD 'AHMAD ALKHATIB, MAGHNI ALMUHTAJ 'IILAA MAERIFAT MAEANI 'ALFAZ ALMUNHAJ (1st ed. Dar Alkutub Aleilmia 1994).

MUHAMMAD AYUB, UNDERSTANDING ISLAMIC FINANCE (John Wiley & Sons 2009).

MUHAMMAD RASHID RIDA, INTERPRETATION OF AL-MANAR (Egyptian General Authority of Book 1990).

MUSLIM IBN AL-HAJJAJ, SAHIH MUSLIM (Dar Ihya al-Turath al-Arabi 1392H).

MUSTAFA SIBAI, THE SUNNAH AND ITS POSITION IN THE ISLAMIC LEGISLATION (Islamic Office 1982).

NADIA E. NEDZEL, LEGAL REASONING RESEARCH, AND WRITING FOR INTERNATIONAL GRADUATE STUDENTS (Wolters Kluwer Law & Business 2012).

NOEL JAMES COULSON, A HISTORY OF ISLAMIC LAW (AldineTransaction 2011).

RAJ BHALA, UNDERSTANDING ISLAMIC LAW (LexisNexis 2011).

Rayan Alkhalawi, Legal Education Reform in Saudi Arabia: A Case Study of Taibah University (May 22, 2015) (unpublished Master's thesis, Indiana University Maurer School of Law) (http://www.repository.law.indiana.edu/etd/15/).

RICHARD CLARK, THE DISPUTE RESOLUTION REVIEW (Law Business Research 2013).

ROBERT GLEAVE, ISLAM AND LITERALISM (Edinburgh University Press Ltd. 2012).

SAFIUR RAHMAN MUBARAKPURI, AR-RAHEEQ AL-MAKHTUM (1st ed. Dar Al Fikr 1996).

SAHIHAB ALDDIN 'AHMAD 'IIDRIS ALQURAAFI, ALDHDHAKHIRA, VOL. 10 (1st ed. Aar Algharb Al'iislami 1994).

STIG STENSLIE, REGIME STABILITY IN SAUDI ARABIA: THE CHALLENGE OF SUCCESSION (Routledge 2012).

WAYNE H. BOWEN, THE HISTORY OF SAUDI ARABIA (2nd ed. ABC-CLIO 2014).

WILLIAM W. PARK, ARBITRATION OF INTERNATIONAL BUSINESS DISPUTES: STUDIES IN LAW AND PRACTICE (Oxford University Press 2012).

WORLD BANK'S DOING BUSINESS, DOING BUSINESS RANK (World Bank Group 2014, 2015).

Television Interview Hewar Almajd with Sheikh Ibrahim Hugail, Chairman of the Saudi Board of Grievances and the Judicial Council, by Fahad Alsunaidy (Al Majd TV Ed., Dec. 12, 2010).

4) Articles and Contributions (Chapters) to Edited Works

A. A. Miftah, Refusal on Qiyas and Implications for Development Contemporary Islamic Law (Study on the Ibn Hazm Critics to Qiyas), 8(4) INT'L. J. INNOVATION & APPLIED STUD. 1545-1553, 2014.

Abdul Rahim Abdul Wahab et al., Islamic Takaful: Business Models, Shariah Concerns, and Proposed Solutions, 49(3) THUNDERBIRD INTERNATIONAL BUS. REV. 371-396, 2007.

Abdulrahman Mamdoh Saleem, A Critical Study on How the Saudi Arbitration Code Could Be Improved and on Overcoming the Issues of Enforcing Foreign Awards in the

Country as a Signatory State to the New York Convention, 2012 (https://ssrn.com/abstract=2315728).

Ahmed A. Al-Ghadyan, Insurance: The Islamic Perspective and Its Development in Saudi Arabia, 14(4) ARAB L. Q. 332-338, 1999.

Anna Rogowska, English Law in Saudi Arabia, 27(3) ARAB L. Q. 271-279, 2013.

Arthur J. Gemmell, Commercial Arbitration in the Islamic Middle East, 5(1) SANTA CLARA J. INT'L L. 2006 (https://ssrn.com/abstract=2639355).

Aseel Al-Ramahi, Sulh: A Crucial Part of Islamic Arbitration, 2008 (https://ssrn.com/abstract=1153659).

Ata Ur Rehman et al., The Concept of Independence of Judiciary in Islam, 4(2) INT'L J. BUS. SOC. SCI. 2013.

Al-riyadh, Scholars and Elders: Women Engage in 'Shura' Model Reflects the Right to Consultation and Practical Application of Islam., AL-RIYADH NEWSPAPER, Issue No. 16291, January 30, 2013 at http://www.alriyadh.com/806045.

Amani Hamdan, Women and Education in Saudi Arabia: Challenges and Achievements, 6(1) INT'L. EDUC. J. 42-64, 2005.

Barbara L. Seniawski, Riba Today: Social Equity, the Economy, and Doing Business Under Islamic Law, 39 COLUM. J. TRANSNAT'L L. 701 (2000).

Bernard Weiss, Interpretation in Islamic Law: The Theory of Ijtih?d, AM. J. COMP. L. 199-212, 1978.

Caroline E. Foster, Burden of Proof in International Courts and Tribunals, 29 AUST. YBIL 27, 2010.

Cindy Silverstein, Iran Aircraft Industries v. AVCO Corporation: Was a Violation of Due Process Due, 20 BROOK. J. INT'L L. 443 (1993).

Charles O. Verrill Jr, Discovery From Non-Parties (Third-Party Discovery) in International Arbitration, 76 ARB. 113-124, 2010.

Charles P. Trumbull, Islamic Arbitration: A New Path for Interpreting Islamic Legal Contracts, 59 VAND. L. REV. 609, 2006.

David J. Karl, Islamic Law in Saudi Arabia: What Foreign Attorney's Should Know, 25 GEO. WASH. J. INT'L L. & ECON. 131, 1991.

Eleanor Abdella Doumato, Education in Saudi Arabia: Gender, Jobs, and the Price of Religion, 239-258, in WOMEN AND GLOBALIZATION IN THE ARAB MIDDLE EAST (Eleanor Abdella Doumato & Marsha Pripstein Posusney, Lynne Rienner Publishers, 2003).

Elizabeth Peiffer, The Death Penalty in Traditional Islamic Law and as Interpreted in Saudi Arabia and Nigeria, 11(3) WM. & MARY J. WOMEN & L. 507-39 (2004).

Emmanuel Gaillard & Yas Banifatemi, Negative Effect of Competence-Competence: The Rule of Priority in Favour of the Arbitrators, Vol. 257, in ENFORCEMENT OF ARBITRATION AGREEMENTS AND INTERNATIONAL ARBITRAL AWARDS: THE NEW YORK CONVENTION IN PRACTICE (Cameron May, 2008).

Emmanuel Gaillard, Reflections on the Use of Anti-Suit Injunctions in International Arbitration, 235-266, in PERVASIVE PROBLEMS IN INTERNATIONAL ARBITRATION (Kluwer, 2006).

Faisal Kutty, The Shari'a Factor in International Commercial Arbitration, 28 LOY L.A. INT'L & COMP. L. REV. 565, 2006.

Faris Nesheiwat & Ali Al-Khasawneh, The 2012 Saudi Arbitration Law: A Comparative Examination of the Law and Its Effect on Arbitration in Saudi Arabia, 13 SANTA CLARA J. INT'L L. 443, 2015.

F. M. Goadby, The Moslem Law of Civil Delict as Illustrated by the Mejelle, 21(1) J. COMP. LEGIS. & INT'L L. 62-74, 1939.

Frank Emmert, Stare Decisis: A Universally Misunderstood Idea, 6(2) LEGISPRUDENCE 207-27 (2012)

George Sayen, Arbitration, Conciliation, and the Islamic Legal Tradition in Saudi Arabia, 24 U. PA. J. INT'L ECON. L. 905, 2003.

Gregoire Marchac, Interim Measures in International Commercial Arbitration Under the ICC, AAA, LCIA and UNCITRAL Rules, 10 AM. REV. INT'L ARB. 123-559 (1999).

Harvey Sicherman, King Fahd's Saudi Arabia, 55(3) ORBIS 481-488, 2011.

Hossein Esmaeili, On a Slow Boat towards the Rule of Law: The Nature of Law in the Saudi Arabia Legal System, 26 ARIZ. J. INT'L & COMP. L. 1, 2009.

Ilhyung Lee, Practice and Predicament: The Nationality of the International Arbitrator, 31 FORDHAM INT'L L. J. 603, 2007.

Ilhyung Lee, Introducing International Commercial Arbitration and Its Lawlessness, by Way of the Dissenting Opinion, 4(1) CONTEMP. ASIA ARBITR. J. 19-35 (2011).

Irene Welser & Christian Klausegger, Fast Track Arbitration: Just fast or something different?, 259(260) AUSTRIAN ARB. Y.B. 267-269, 2009.

James E. Meason & Alison G. Smith, Non-lawyers in International Commercial Arbitration: Gathering Splinters on the Bench, 12 NW. J. INT'L L. & BUS. 24, 1991.

James R. Murray, Role of Analogy in Legal Reasoning, The, 29 UCLA L. REV., 833 (1981).

Jan Paulsson, Delocalisation of International Commercial Arbitration: When and Why It Matters, 32(01) INT'L & COMP. LAW QTRLY, 53-61 (1983).

Jean-Benoit Zegers, Foreign Investment Protection in Saudi Arabia, 9(1) Y.B. ISLAMIC MIDDLE E. L. 65-87 (2002).

John R. Bowen, How could English courts recognize Shariah, 7 U. ST. THOMAS LJ, 411 (2009).

Julio C. Colon, Choice of law and Islamic finance, 46(2) TEX. INT'L LJ (2010).

Joseph L. Brand, Aspects of Saudi Arabian Law and Practice, 9 BC INT'L & COMP. L. REV., 1 (1986).

Kristin T. Roy, New York Convention and Saudi Arabia: Can a Country Use the Public Policy Defense to Refuse Enforcement of Non-Domestic Arbitral Awards, The, 18 FORDHAM INT'L LJ, 920 (1994).

Lee Anna Tucker, Interim Measures under Revised UNCITRAL Arbitration Rules: Comparison to Model Law Reflects Both Greater Flexibility and Remaining Uncertainty, 1 INT'L COM. ARB. BRIEF, 15 (2011).

Leon Trakman, The impartiality and independence of arbitrators reconsidered, 10 INT'L ARB. L. REV., 999 (2007).

Maren Hanson, The Influence of French Law on the Legal Development of Saudi Arabia, ARAB LAW QUARTERLY, 272-291 (1987).

Mark C. Modak-Truran, Reenchanting the Law: The Religious Dimension of Judicial Decision Making, 53 CATH. U. L. REV. 709, 2004.

Martin Platte, An Arbitrator's Duty to Render Enforceable Awards, 20(3) J. INT'L ARB. 307-313, 2003.

Martina Polasek, SGS Société Générale de Surveillance SA v. Islamic Republic of Pakistan (ICSID Case No. ARB/01/13) Introductory Note, 18(1) ICSID REV. 290-2 (2003).

Md Shahadat Hossain, Arbitration in Islamic Law for the Treatment of Civil and Criminal Cases: An Analytical Overview, 2013 (https://www.mysciencework.com/publication/show/d2d495211d38f5bbdb93968b77e27fad).

Mirèze Philippe, Are Specific Fast-Track Arbitration Rules Necessary? 253-284, in PERMANENT COURT OF ARBITRATION/PEACE PALACE PAPERS, THE (HRSG.), ARBITRATION IN AIR, SPACE AND TELECOMMUNICATIONS LAW (Den Haag 2002).

Moore Jr, Richter H. Moore Jr, Courts, Law, Justice, and Criminal Trials in Saudi Arabia. 11(1-2) INT'L. J. COMP. APPL. CRIM. JUSTICE 61-7 (1987).

Myres S. McDougal et al., Freedom from Discrimination in Choice of Language and International Human Rights, 1 S. ILL. U. L. J. 151 (1976).

Najmaldeen K. Kareem Zanki, Codification of Islamic Law Premises of History and Debates of Contemporary Muslim Scholars, 4(9) INT'L. J. HUM. SOC. SCI. 127-37 (2014).

Nancy B. Turck, Arbitration in Saudi Arabia, 6(3) ARBITR. INT'L. 281-91 (1990).

Nancy B. Turck, Dispute Resolution in Saudi Arabia, 22(2) INT'L. LAWYER 415-43 (1988).

Natalija Kaminskiene, Application of Interim Measures in International Arbitration: The Lithuanian Approach, 1(119) JURISPRUDENCIJA (2010).

Nsisong Anthony Udoh & Kudirat Bimbo Sanni, Supplanting the Venom of Litigation with Alternative Dispute Resolution: The Role of Counsellors and Guidance Professionals, 43(5) BR. J. GUID. COUNS. 518-29 (2015).

Othman Talbi, Tort Reform in Saudi Arabia: Obstacles and Solutions, (2015).

Patrick S. Ottinger, Principles of Contractual Interpretation, 60(3) LA. L. REV. (1999).

PM Unveils Plans for New Islamic Index on London Stock Exchange (Gov.uk, Press release, 29 October 2013).

R. Mithani, Saudi Arabia: The Emerging Arbitration Landscape, Jan-Mar CORP. DISPUT. MAG. 2-5 (2014).

Radwa S. Elsaman, Factors to Be Considered Before Arbitrating in the Arab Middle East: Examples of Religious and Legislative Constraints, 1(2) INT'L. COM. ARB. BRIEF 8-14 (2011).

Rashed Aba-Namay, The Recent Constitutional Reforms in Saudi Arabia, 42(2) INT'L. COMP. L. Q. 295-331 (1993).

Ray Y. Chan, Enforceability of Annulled Foreign Arbitral Awards in the United States: A Critique of Chromalloy, 17 B. U. INT'L L. J. 141 (1999).

Sa'id Adekunle Mikail & Mahamad Arifin, Application of Doctrine of Judicial Precedent in Shariah Courts, 2 MALAYS. COURT PRACT. BULL. (2013).

Saud Al-Ammari & A. Timothy Martin, Arbitration in the Kingdom of Saudi Arabia, 30(2) ARBITR. INT'L. 387-408 (2014).

Susan D. Franck, The Liability of International Arbitrators: A Comparative Analysis and Proposal for Qualified Immunity, 20(1) N. Y. L. SCH. J. INT'L & COMP. L. (2000).

T. Jeremy Gunn, The Complexity of Religion and the Definition of Religion in International Law, 16 HARV. HUM. RTS. J. 189-215 (2003).

Thomas D. Halket, The Use of Technology in Arbitration: Ensuring the Future Is Available to Both Parties, 81 JOHN'S L. REV. 269-306 (2007).

Thomas H. Webster, Obtaining Evidence from Third Parties in International Arbitration, 17(2) ARBITR. INT'L. 143-62 (2001).

William W. Park, Judicial Supervision of Transnational Commercial Arbitration: The English Arbitration Act of 1979, 21(1) HARV. INT'L. L. J. 87 (1980).

William Wang, International Arbitration: The Need for Uniform Interim Measures of Relief, 28(3) BROOK. J. INT'L L. 1059-99 (2002).

Ya'akov Meron, The Mejelle Tested by Its Application, 5(2) ISR. L. REV. 203-15 (1970).

Zaid Ahmad Ansari, Analysis of the Impact of Reforms on Insurance Industry of Saudi Arabia, 1(8) INTERDISCIP. J. RES. BUS. 28 (2011).

5) Websites

The International Institute for the Unification of Private Law (UNIDROIT) website at: http://www.unidroit.org/about-unidroit/overview

Saudi Shura council website available at http://www.shura.gov.sa

The Saudi Department of Zakat and Income website available at https://dzit.gov.sa/.

Available at http://www.alarabiya.net/articles/2013/01/11/259877.html.

Information about Mecca city available at see http://www.encyclopedia.com/topic/Mecca.aspx.

Information about Kaaba which is a cuboid building at the center of a sacred mosque in Mecca city in the Kingdom of Saudi Arabia available at: http://www.olemiss.edu/orgs/muslims/Al-Kaabah.html.

Saudi Ministry of Commerce and Industry website at: http://mci.gov.sa/Laws-Regulations/SystemsAndRegulations

The history of administrative judicial in Saudi Arabia available at its website at www.bog.gov.sa/AboutUs/Pages/Engender.aspx.

Ministry of Justice website at: https://www.moj.gov.sa/ar.

The history of The Committee for the Settlement of Banking Disputes is available at Saudi Arabian Monetary Agency website: http://www.sama.gov.sa/en-us/about/pages/samahistory.aspx.

Al Imam Muhammad Ibn Saud Islamic University website at https://admission.imamu.edu.sa/programs/ProgramsLinks.

Institute of Public Administration website available at http://www.ipa.edu.sa/Arabic/About/summary/Pages/default.aspx.

Judicial institutional Academy website available at https://sij.imamu.edu.sa/Pages/default.aspx.

Saudi Bureau of experts of the council of ministers website at: https://www.boe.gov.sa/ViewSystemDetails.aspx?lang=ar&SystemID=122&VersionID=152#M17986.

The Kingdom started publishing the previous decisions by different volumes, and they are available on the website of The Board of Grievances available at the Board of Grievances website at: http://www.bog.gov.sa/ScientificContent/JudicialBlogs/Pages/default.aspx.

The New York Convention website http://www.uncitral.org/uncitral/en/uncitral_texts/arbitration/NYConvention.html.

a service to research about accredited arbitrators available at the Ministry of Justice website at: https://www.moj.gov.sa/ar/eServices/Pages/Muhamah.aspx.

the case No 114/2/S in 2007 is available at Diwan Almazalim website at http://www.bog.gov.sa/ScientificContent/JudicialBlogs/Blog1428/Documents/.

"term of reference" ICC website for more information at http://www.iccwbo.org/about-icc/organization/dispute-resolution-services/icc-international-court-of-arbitration/.

The American Arbitration Association website at: https://www.adr.org/aaa/faces/s/about

The London Court of International Arbitration website at: http://www.lcia.org/LCIA/introduction.aspx.

the Cairo Regional Center for International Commercial Arbitration website at: http://crcica.org.eg/.

The Bahrain Chamber for Dispute Resolution (BCDR-AAA) website at: http://www.bcdr-aaa.org/en/about-us/.

GCC Commercial Arbitration Centre website at: http://www.gcccac.org/en/about-centre.

Dubai International Arbitration Centre (DIAC), website at http://www.diac.ae/idias/services/diac/.

The DIFC- LCIA Center website at http://www.difc-lcia.org/Default.aspx.

Council of Saudi Chambers website at http://www.csc.org.sa/Arabic/News/Pages/2014085ff.aspx.

The NAFTA Secretariat website at: see https://www.nafta-sec-alena.org/Home/Alternative-Dispute-Resolution/Selecting-an-Arbitration-Institution.

The UNCITRAL provides a useful checklist, which is entitled "UNCITRAL Notes on Organizing Arbitral Proceedings. This checklist is available at UNCITRAL website at: https://www.uncitral.org/pdf/english/texts/arbitration/arb-notes/arb-notes-e.pdf.

The Committee that established the IBA Rules on the Taking of Evidence in International Arbitration. All of the information about this committee is available in its website at: http://www.ibanet.org/LPD/Dispute_Resolution_Section/Arbitration/Default.aspx.

List of contracting states at New York Arbitration Convention at http://www.newyorkconvention.org/list+of+contracting+states.

The United Arab Bank website at: http://www.uab.ae/islamic-banking/tawarruq.

Bank Muaamalat of Malaysia website at: http://www.muamalat.com.my/business-banking/corporate-banking/financing/tawarruq.html.

For more information about Murabaha in Islamic banks, see the bank website at: http://www.dib.ae/corporate-banking/products-and-services/murabaha.

For more information about the history of insurance in Saudi Arabia and its framework, see Saudi Arabian Monetary Agency website at http://www.sama.gov.sa/en-US/Insurance/Pages/AboutISD.aspx.

The Consumer Due Process Protocol and the Consumer Arbitration Rules of the American Arbitration Association (AAA) available at its website at: https://www.adr.org/aaa/faces/aoe/gc/consumer/registrywelcome?.

Also published by the Council on International Law and Politics

International Business and Trade Law:

Talia Einhorn & Frank Emmert: International Business Transactions – Documents, 2nd rev. ed., Chicago 2013, ISBN 978-09858156-2-2

Joseph E. Miller: Changing Our Approach to Changing the World – Encouraging and Enhancing American Engagement in International Philanthropy Through Tax Law Reform, Chicago 2013, ISBN 978-09858156-3-9

Frank Emmert (ed.): Corporate Social Responsibility in Comparative Perspective, Chicago 2014, ISBN 978-09858156-4-6

Frank Emmert (ed.): World Trade and Investment Law – Documents, Indianapolis 2018, ISBN 978-0-9858156-7-7

Csongor István Nagy (ed.), Investment Arbitration and National Interest, Indianapolis 2018, ISBN 978-0-9858156-8-4 (forthcoming)

Islamic Law Library:

Ahmed M. El Demery: The Arab Charter of Human Rights – A Voice for Sharia in the Modern World, with a Foreword by Prof. M. Cherif Bassiouni, Chicago 2015, ISBN 978-0985815653

Ahmed A. Altawyan: International Commercial Arbitration in Saudi Arabia, Indianapolis 2018, ISBN 978-0-9858156-9-1

Rakan F. Alharbi: The Development of Saudi Women's Rights – Theory, Practice, Challenges, and Solutions – a Critical and Analytical Study of the Impact of Cultural Norms on the Recognition of Women's Rights of Employment and Freedom of Movement, Indianapolis 2018 (forthcoming)

Mohammad M. Bayoumi Ibrahim: Women's Rights Under International, American, Islamic and Egyptian Law: An Irresolvable Conflict?, Indianapolis 2019 (forthcoming)

All publications of the Council on International Law and Politics are available on Amazon and from leading booksellers.

www.ingramcontent.com/pod-product-compliance
Lightning Source LLC
LaVergne TN
LVHW080023210926
848481LV00011B/3092